SET ON A

SET ON A HILL

A Strategic View over Scottish History

ROBIN BELL

BIRLINN

First published in 2012 by
Birlinn Limited
West Newington House
10 Newington Road
Edinburgh
EH9 1QS

www.birlinn.co.uk

ISBN: 978 1 84158 994 7

British Library Cataloguing-in-Publication Data
A catalogue record for this book is available from the British Library

Dr John Reid, who grew up in Auchterarder after the Second
World War, made a generous financial donation towards the production costs of this book, enabling the history of his native
town to take its place in a global context. The Auchterarder
Common Good Fund also made a financial contribution, while
the Auchterarder and District Local History Association gave
great encouragement to the author.

Endpapers show a detail of Map 18 from John Thomson's *Atlas
of Scotland* (1820).

Typeset by Brinnoven, Livingston
Printed and bound by MPG Books Ltd, Bodmin

He either fears his fate too much
Or his deserts are small
That puts it not unto the touch
To win or lose it all.

James Graham, 1st Marquis of Montrose. *To His Mistress*

We need new versions of history to allow for our current prejudices.
Bill Watterston, *Homicidal Psycho Jungle Cat (Calvin and Hobbes)*

What is past is prologue.
National Archives of the USA *Motto*

Contents

Each chapter is designed to be as self-contained as possible. You may wish to think of *Set on a Hill* as a collection of 43 booklets rather than one long book.

Introduction
Choosing a Viewpoint

*A good history book should contain enough abrasive
material to scour away old layers of tacky cultural polish*

Set on a Hill abolishes the false distinction between local, national and international
history. Most accounts are written from the perspective of capital cities and
public institutions. *Set on a Hill* is different. It lets us see the global picture, and
recurring patterns across the centuries, by looking from one strategic ridge that
has consistently witnessed major events. These range from the construction of
the Northern Frontier of the Roman Empire in 79 AD to the Gleneagles G8 in
2005 when the leaders of the industrialised world first acknowledged the need to
tackle climate change and world poverty.

This strategic ridge rises from Strathearn, where the Scottish Highlands and
Lowlands meet. It is the heartland of the Pictish kingdom that grew to become
the first united Scotland. In the Middle Ages, the Royal Burgh and Castle of
Auchterarder saw the English King Edward I house his troops before seizing
Scotland's Stone of Destiny from nearby Scone. A few years later, the area saw
Scotland collapse into anarchy after Robert Bruce died. The intervening Battle
of Bannockburn was not the decisive victory that later propagandists claimed.

During the Reformation, the Peace of Auchterarder was the first treaty
between Scottish Protestants and Catholics. In the eighteenth century, Jacobites
burned the Royal Burgh and neighbouring villages as they retreated after the
Battle of Sheriffmuir. Not surprisingly, the rebuilt community later congratulated
the Duke of Cumberland for defeating the Jacobites at Culloden.

Across the centuries, politicians and armies have learned that you cannot hold
Scotland for long without holding this ridge. It has seen times of extreme poverty,
but today the world's super-rich build homes on its green slopes. Queen Elizabeth
II is descended from Strathearn families on both her father and mother's sides.
Prince William, Britain's future king, was created Earl of Strathearn in 2011.

The area has constantly reinvented itself. It has been home to canny farmers
and radical weavers with a sound grasp of global economics. Last century, it
staged the first golf tournament between Britain and the USA. Decades later,
Commonwealth heads of government met here to outlaw racism in international
sport. Justice and fair play are the keys to the area's reputation.

1

The Evolving Landscape
and the First Settlers

In which we meet fierce animals and ingenious immigrants,
and learn what the names Strathearn, Auchterarder and Gleneagles mean

The most dramatic route to Strathearn also happens to be the best way to see the landscape division between the Lowlands and the Highlands of Scotland. You travel north from Edinburgh across the River Forth to Dunfermline, then take the A823 to Glendevon.

The road then winds up through the old volcanic Ochils and emerges, looking down into Gleneagles and Strathallan and across the old red sandstone of Strathearn towards the slate and granite peaks of the Grampians. The strategic ridge with the ancient Royal Burgh of Auchterarder links the Highlands and Lowlands, both in landscape and culture.

This is the geographic centre of Scotland. You can also approach it along routes taken by the earliest settlers, eastwards from the Clyde Valley or westwards from the Forth and Tay estuaries. Today the A9, Scotland's main tourist route, runs through Strathearn.

Strathearn was formed by millions of years of volcanic activity, raising and folding the earth's crust, with ice ages creeping eastwards, eroding the mountains and pushing heaps of moraine to form lower foothills and ridges above the silty river-beds of the Earn and Ruthven Water. The mountains were once as high as today's Alps, which are younger and much less eroded.

In the last Ice Age, from about 24,000 BC to 14,000 BC, Britain was part of the European land mass. As ice melted, hunters, from what are now Germany and the Netherlands, followed mammoths, reindeer and elk westwards and built settlements. Sea levels rose. Britain became an island. The earliest evidence of human activity in Scotland is from about 14,000 BC near Biggar in Lanarkshire.

Sometimes a place name tells you just what the land is like. For example a 'kame' is made up of terraces of debris, sorted by water flowing between a shrinking glacier and the valley side, and a 'knowe' is a promontory on a hillside. This exactly defines the location of the farm named Kaimknowe where Gleneagles meets Glendevon.

River estuaries grew broader and deeper. Most of the landscape was boggy and flooded by snowmelt in winter. Long before there were solid roads, the best way to transport goods was by river. Logboats found at Carpow, near Abernethy, and at other nearby locations, show that the Earn–Tay river junction was actively used around 1000 BC and probably much earlier.

At that time, elk, red deer, horses, aurochs (wild oxen), boar, hares and beavers lived on the meadowland or on hazel and birch-forested slopes. Their main predators were lynx, wolves, foxes, brown bears and humans.

The earliest nomadic hunter-gatherers lived in timber-framed, brushwood- or skin-covered houses, some like Native American tepees. They made tools and weapons from stone, wood, antler and bone. In winter, they wore animal skins. Their diet included, in season, fish, oysters, berries, nuts, edible roots, eggs and crawling insects.

Prehistoric Auchterarder was settled both from the west and the east. From the Mediterranean, up the western seaboard of Europe, came small, dark-haired people who planted barley and wheat. From the east came descendants of nomadic Asian shepherds, taller and fairer, who crossed the plains of Europe, arrived in Southern Britain, then migrated north.

The oldest known evidence of local human activity consists of Neolithic standing stones, parts of stone circles, or henges, probably built to replace earlier timber structures. They were smaller versions of Stonehenge and used for religious or official activities. Two of these sites lie near present-day road junctions; one where Easthill Road meets Tullibardine Road, west of Auchterarder. The other is at Peterhead Farm, near where the A823 crosses over the busy A9. Archaeologists date these standing stones somewhere between 3000 and 2000 BC.

Archaeologists excavated other henge sites, at Belhie, north of Aberuthven, and North Mains at Strathallan. These sites were first developed four or five thousand years ago and re-used for thousands of years. At North Mains, archaeologists in 1970 found traces of thirty-one Bronze Age cremations. They also found thirteen long graves, probably early Christian burials, showing the site evolved culturally. In one stone cist (coffin) lay the body of a young woman with a pot of ale flavoured with meadowsweet, a talisman to accompany her into the next world. A necklace of jet was found in another grave.

Most of the earliest sites are visible only as cropmarks, which show up best in dry summers. Other Neolithic burial sites have been discovered at Thorn, between the A9 and the railway south of Abbey Road, and at Westerton Farm, south of Aberuthven, where in 1936 archaeologists found a polished stone ritual axe, made of porcellanite produced in the Tievebulliagh or Rathlin area of Northern Ireland.

Each generation of visitors and settlers brings new technology. Today, golfers from all over the world swing high-tech clubs on the Gleneagles courses, close to Bronze Age hut circle settlements whose inhabitants made metal tools two thousand years ago. The early settlers knew enough mechanics to transport and lever huge standing stones into place. They hunted wild animals without guns, and grew crops without artificial fertilisers. They were vulnerable to bad harvests and disease, but knew how to use plants for healing. They had a practical grasp of astronomy and cyclical change. They made pottery and jewellery. In our twenty-first century global economy, the inhabitants of the Auchterarder area are far less self-sufficient than those of three thousand years ago.

Skills are gained and lost, depending on their relevance. Even when the author of this book was growing up in the nineteen-forties, most adult men were able to use a scythe, and many were able to catch a trout by guddling it with their fingers. These skills have currently been replaced by those required to start a power mower or heat an instant meal in a microwave oven. The earliest farmers cleared land to make it arable. In the late twentieth century, farmers, profiting from European Community agricultural policy, could earn money by letting land revert to nature in 'Set-Aside'.

The dominant early settlers spoke a Celtic language. Their place names describe the landscape. The Ochil hills come from *uchel* the Celtic word for 'high'. The most prominent peak is Craigrossie, from *craig* or 'crag' and *rosach* or 'wooded hill'. Glendevon comes from *Glen Dubh abhainn* or 'glen of the black river'.

The ancient village of Aberuthven was named because it lay where the River Ruthven met the River Earn. The confluence of the rivers has moved north since the village was first named. Strathearn means 'valley of the Earn'.

The origin of the name Earn is less certain. It may be many thousands of years old, coming from the Gaelic *ár* meaning 'slaughter'. Strathearn, as a strategically important corridor for invasions, certainly saw many battles. The name could, more peaceably, come from *ar*, meaning 'ploughing', showing the area's reputation for good arable land. It may, of course, carry both meanings, reflecting pragmatic farmers' taste for grim puns. The name Strathearn may be no older than the sixth century and be *Strath Erin* or 'Land of the Irish', after the area was extensively settled by Irish Christian missionaries whose little churches and groups of monks' huts transformed the landscape. Gleneagles comes from *Glen eaglais*, meaning 'glen of the church', not 'glen of the eagles'.

The name Auchterarder is pre-Christian. The word has three elements. Auchter (*air uachdair*) means 'on top of'. Ard (*aird*) means 'high'. Der (*dwr*) means 'water'. Auchterarder therefore means both 'a well-irrigated superior community' and 'that place up on the boggy ridge'. Take your pick.

By 500 BC, central Scotland had evolved into a complex political structure. There were many kingdoms and subkingdoms, shifting as often as today's local and national government restructuring. Protection money was levied or forcibly extracted from individuals to pay for the activities of rulers and their officials.

By this time, much of the forest had been cleared. The economy was based on stock rearing on grassland, with barley fields, vegetable patches and orchards. Wild Highland cattle had been tamed and bred, not just for their milk and meat. Their red hair was used for plaiting into ropes, strengthening plaster and caulking boats.

On the slopes of the Ochils, many hillforts appeared, notably at Ben Effray, Rossie Law, Ogle Hill and Castle Craig. Another fort, beside the slip road to today's A9, commanded the entrance to Gleneagles. These were defensive sites, designed to deal with local conflicts, not massive foreign military invasion.

2

The Romans.
The Flavian Occupation

In which local farmers and tradesmen see a large money supply marching towards them

The Roman Empire was Europe's first unifying government. Beginning in the eighth century BC, it radiated outwards from central Italy, absorbing small kingdoms and rival empires. By the first century BC it extended eastwards beyond Greece into Asia and ruled the Mediterranean shores of the Near East and North Africa. It controlled mainland Europe as far north as the rivers Rhine and Danube.

In 55 BC, Julius Caesar crossed the English Channel to invade the island the Romans called Brittania, but abandoned the project in order to concentrate his personal authority in Rome. In AD 43 the Emperor Claudius established a military colony in the south of England. Most of the southern half of Britain was then rapidly brought into the administrative and trading framework of the Roman Empire.

In AD 77, Emperor Vespasian, founder of the Flavian Dynasty, selected a soldier-politician, Agricola, as governor of Britain. Agricola crushed a revolt in North Wales, and then led his legions north.

In AD 79, Agricola's army of some 18,000 men arrived in Scotland. They marched up the long valley corridor from the River Forth, through Strathallan, into Strathearn.

There had never been a defined northern boundary to the Roman Empire. Agricola set about creating one, by building a line of forts diagonally across Scotland. Today's archaeologists keep finding more of them, in a line from Barochan near the Clyde up to Stracathro near Brechin. At the centre of this frontier is the heavily fortified Gask Ridge with its huge fort at Ardoch, west of Auchterarder.

Local people knew about the Romans long before they arrived here. Traders would report luxurious villas, heated baths and fancy food available down south, plus a bureaucratic government machine backed by harsh enforcement.

Our only written source comes from Tacitus who, as Agricola's son-in-law, argues a Roman case. Their troops moved swiftly and efficiently. At Ardoch, they set up camp and surrounded it with defensive ditches within days. Their surveyors assessed the terrain and located watchtowers and smaller forts on the Gask Ridge.

In the pastures by the Earn and Ruthven and in their own hill forts on the north-facing slopes of the Ochils, local people looked at the invaders with glowering resentment or grudging admiration. Decisions had to be made. Should there be armed resistance, or should profits be made from supplying the usual necessaries for the appetites of a superpower army?

Tacitus tells us there were skirmishes, but archaeologists have not found evidence of a major battle anywhere near the Gask Ridge. Before the Romans, there was chaotic local clan warfare, now there was efficient Roman peace.

The farmers and traders of the Auchterarder area chose peace instead of war. The Romans then built their frontier along the Gask Ridge, enclosing the agricultural community within their protection. That is why there is no typical 'glen-blocker' Roman fort to guard the pass through Gleneagles to Roman-occupied Fife. There is, however, overlooking the glen at Loaninghead, a substantial pre-Roman site.

Tacitus tells us the Romans slaughtered an alliance of warlike northern clan chiefs at the Battle of Mons Graupius in AD 84.

Where is Mons Graupius? Some historians argue that Graupius means Grampian and believe the battle site to be in Aberdeenshire. Others say the Latin *Mons* (mountain) is combined with a Latinised form of the Celtic word *crub* (crouch) and that the true site is Duncrub (crouching hill), five miles east of Auchterarder. Certainly, the description fits the nearby Craigrossie. Also 'Dorsum Crup' is mentioned in the Pictish Chronicle and the local topography matches Tacitus's account.

Farmers, craftsmen and traders in the Auchterarder area may well have welcomed the Roman victory at Mons Graupius, just as, centuries later, Auchterarder Presbytery welcomed the Hanoverian victory at Culloden in 1746 and the slaughter of the Jacobites who had previously looted and burned the burgh and surrounding villages.

It was in the interests of the Romans and the local stock-rearing farmers to maintain a good supply of food from year to year. Fighting wrecks agriculture. Peace usually encourages it. The Roman Empire liked to keep its administrative costs down by doing deals with local leaders, letting them have considerable autonomy, provided they kept the peace and collected taxes. It was called the Pax Romana (Roman peace).

In 1784, during the digging of the foundations of the old Parish Church, off Auchterarder High Street behind today's Aytoun Hall, a coin was found, dating from the time of the Emperor Vespasian.

Sometimes what archaeologists do not find reveals as much as what they dig up. For example, there is an absence of wood ash from the fortlets on the Gask Ridge. Did the soldiers really have no heating in winter? A more likely explanation is that local men cut wood, traded it to the Romans and, with each new delivery, took away the old ash which was a valuable fertiliser, particularly good for apple trees, a fruit which the Romans loved.

At Cuiltburn, near the large fort of Strageath where the River Earn is easily forded north of Auchterarder, archaeologists in 2001 discovered a substantial non-military site dating from the Flavian occupation. It may have belonged to a senior Roman official or, more likely, is the residence of a local leader who co-operated with the Romans and adopted their building technology and imported luxuries. Not far from Strageath is Caerlaverock. 'Laverock' is the Scots word for a lark. Lark pie was a favourite Roman delicacy.

The Flavian occupation of this area lasted from AD 79 until about AD 87, when all the troops were redeployed to help combat military threats to the Roman Empire around the Danube and the Near East. There is archaeological evidence to show they left in a hurry, not knowing when or if they would return. They were gone a long time.

3

The Romans. The Antonine and Severan Occupations

In which an empire learns that you can't be everywhere at the same time and creates the world's most famous martyr

In AD 142, fifty-five years after their withdrawal, the Romans returned to Scotland. Emperor Antoninus ordered a wall to be built from the Forth to the Clyde. Some forts further north on the old Gask Ridge frontier, including Ardoch, were brought back into use. This occupation lasted about twenty years.

Many of the Roman troops occupying Strathearn were no more Italian than the Auchterarder locals. They came from across the Empire, from fearsome eastern Scythian archers to career officers from Spain. An inscription found at Ardoch commemorates Ammonius, a centurion of the First Cohort of Spanish Auxiliaries. It is unclear how many attempts the Romans made to conquer parts of Scotland. They repeatedly established themselves here, only to withdraw to deal with emergencies elsewhere in the Empire.

Emperor Commodus (AD 180–92) probably brought troops here. In the nineteen-fifties, near Aberuthven, two coins were found, one showing the Emperor Commodus, the other showing his mother, Faustina, wife of Emperor Marcus Aurelius.

There is more archaeological evidence for the period after AD 208, when Emperor Septimius Severus led a full-scale invasion. Severus reinstated the main Gask Ridge forts and built a huge new one at Carpow, where the Earn joins the Tay. Strathearn already had a well-established water-transport route. Severus improved the road building necessary for a long-term trade infrastructure.

Severus died in 211, only three years later. His sons Caracalla (emperor 211–17) and Geta (rival emperor in 211) made treaties with local leaders then returned to Rome.

Around 306, Constantius Chlorus, the father of Emperor Constantine the Great, returned to Scotland. Archaeologists have established that his troops reoccupied the fort at Carpow. It is likely that he followed the pattern set by previous Roman generals and advanced to Gask and the Auchterarder area.

Roundhouses, built by local people during the Roman occupation, are domestic and agricultural, without defences, suggesting that canny co-existence was a way of life. Most professional soldiers departed with their legions, but it would be unusual if some of an army's cooks, tradesmen and camp-followers did not form local liaisons and stay, keeping up army contacts for business reasons.

It would be wrong to think that troop withdrawal meant the end of Roman influence in Strathearn. The Empire's northern frontier was now Hadrian's Wall, between Carlisle and Newcastle. Roads were poor and bridges were few but coastal trade routes were viable, even if pirates and local politics presented problems. Pictish tribes made several profitable peace treaties with Rome, whose occupation of southern Britain lasted until AD 410.

During the three centuries of intermittent Roman occupation, the local inhabitants of the Auchterarder area worshipped the visible forces of the natural world, like the sun, water and storms. Far away in a remote south-eastern corner of the Empire, an event occurred which was later to alter dramatically the way people saw the natural and supernatural worlds.

In 33 AD in Jerusalem, the Roman provincial governor Pontius Pilate allowed the execution of an inspirational Jewish preacher, Jesus Christ. The repercussions changed the course of global history.

In his lifetime, Jesus was regarded as a new prophet, demanding respect for God and for human rights. After Jesus was crucified, his followers elevated his martyred status, claiming he was the Son of God. At a time when official corruption and political sleaze were rife in the Roman Empire, Jesus was hailed as a beacon of integrity.

Early Christianity was pacifist, relying on Jesus' guiding principle 'Do unto others as you would have them do unto you'. From the first to the third centuries, the more the Empire persecuted Christians, the more their religion seemed an attractive alternative to the multiple gods of Roman state religion, especially when emperors such as Nero declared themselves to be gods.

As with all religions, stories of miraculous divine intervention became attached to the central moral code of Christian faith. In October 312, after having a vision of the cross on which Jesus was executed, the Emperor Constantine I the Great defeated his rival Maxentius at the Battle of Milvian Bridge near Rome. Constantine made Christianity the official religion of the Roman Empire. He adopted the cross as his battle sign with the motto *In hoc signo vinces* (With this sign you will conquer). Militant Christianity was born.

To consolidate his power in the east, Constantine renamed the ancient city of Byzantium, calling it Constantinople, and made it the eastern capital of the Roman Empire. Constantinople's importance grew as the authority of the Rome-based Western Empire declined. The Western Empire shrank until 476 when Romulus Augustulus, the last Emperor of Rome, died. In the east, the Roman Empire survived for another thousand years till Constantinople was captured and renamed Istanbul by the Muslims in 1453.

We do not know exactly when Christian beliefs first appeared in Strathearn. The earliest record comes from the Roman historian, Tertullian, writing around the time of the Severan invasion in 208. He said that Christianity had already reached the northern frontier of the Roman Empire in Britannia. It is still here.

4

Picts, Scots, Britons and the New Europeans

In which waves of immigrants cross Europe, Christians argue about the number of gods, the Scottish clans appear and nationalist leaders keep forgetting that attacking England leads to disaster

The Roman Empire, like all empires, broke up unevenly. Its eastern frontier was over-run by waves of invaders. The Huns, originally from Mongolia, swept into central Europe in the fourth century and consolidated their presence in the fifth century under their leader Attila. The Visigoths, or Western Goths, headed south and, led by Alaric, captured Rome in 410. The Vandals followed into Italy, Spain and North Africa.

Roman emperors did political deals with all these invaders, ceding more and more power to successful immigrant leaders. Throughout Europe, local independence movements further severed old Roman multinational administrative and trade links.

This period used to be called 'The Dark Ages', reflecting a Roman point of view. The word 'vandal' is still a synonym for 'mindless destroyer'. The old guard in collapsing empires always claims that its opponents are cultural vandals. The truth is more complex. The new eastern immigrants brought their own arts and technologies, but they also rapidly absorbed and developed the ways of the Christian Roman Empire.

By the fourth century, the Roman Church had moved away from the original Judeo-Christian concept of a single all-powerful God. Instead, it worshiped 'The Trinity', made up of God, Jesus Christ and the Holy Ghost, a mysterious spirit. The invaders from the east generally adopted Christianity, but preferred one god to three. Supporters of a single Christian God were called Arians, after Bishop Arius. Supporters of the Trinity were called Athanasians, after Bishop Athanasius.

In 325 Constantine called rival churchmen to meet at the Council of Nicea in Asia Minor to settle disputes. The more politically powerful Roman Church had its doctrine of the Trinity declared the only acceptable Christian doctrine. The Arians did not give up. Ulfilas, an Arian bishop, who died in 381, devised a new Gothic alphabet for his translation of the Bible, which was enormously influential.

Do these points of religion matter in the big picture of global history? Yes. The Athanasian Roman Church, headed by Popes (from the Latin word papa or 'father'), stuck to the concept of the Trinity, identifying its own bureaucratic authority with the Holy Ghost. Arian Christianity focuses on a more direct relationship between man and God, regarding the Roman priestly hierarchy as redundant middlemen. From this doctrinal division grew centuries of Christian civil war that engulfed global politics.

From the perspective of some communities, like Auchterarder, on the fringe of the Roman Empire, these fourth-century religious divisions had little impact for two hundred years, then became engrained in Scottish culture. New generations of Christians took sides, either for Rome or for protesting alternatives. Today's sectarian chanting at Rangers and Celtic football matches has its origin in the Arian versus Athanasian dispute. That is why Rangers fans are nicknamed 'Huns'. 'Visigoths' would be equally appropriate, but sectarian abuse rarely stretches to three syllables.

When an empire withdraws its armies, local power struggles follow. In the Roman period, the Auchterarder area had been on a wild frontier, like modern-day Afghanistan or the Balkans, but at least there was a rich protector. After the Romans left, the inhabitants of the Auchterarder area tried to maintain arable and stock-rearing farming, in a volatile political climate. Local kingships rose and fell, as waves of immigrants, opportunists and refugees, appeared with their own skills and traditions.

Hill forts and roundhouses continued, modified, rebuilt and relocated, just as today's housing evolves. Some were linked to souterrains, underground barns for storing produce at a constant temperature. Old structures were recycled. One of the standing stones at Peterhead Farm, dating from 3000–2000 BC, had Pictish symbols, a goose and a rectangle, carved on to it around AD 500.

The Picts were descended from the first settlers who came to Scotland around 14,000 BC. In Roman times, the two Pictish main tribes were the Caledones, whose lands ran north to Inverness, and the Maeatae or Verturiones, who extended into Angus. In the third century, another Pictish tribe, the Dicalydones, drove a wedge between them. These are early Scottish clans, allying and dividing with each generation of leaders.

The Romans called these tribes 'Picti' (painted people) because of their tattoos, body painting and bright formal clothes. Today, if you watch international games at Hampden Park or Murrayfield, you still see Scottish faces painted blue. The Picts had a reputation for being home-loving and welcoming, but fierce when provoked, a pattern repeated in Auchterarder across the centuries.

Huns, Visigoths and Vandals swept into Western Europe in the fourth century. Mass immigration to Scotland followed, as a ripple effect of population movement. In the late fifth century came the Dál Riata, Scots from northeast Ireland. They settled first in Strathclyde, then moved towards Strathearn. For the first time, there were significant numbers of Scots in Scotland.

The Dál Riata spoke an old form of Gaelic, today called Q Celtic. The Picts spoke another Celtic language, today called P Celtic, rather like old Welsh. The two could communicate rather like today's local shopkeepers with American tourists.

From Wales came the Britons, who spread through the Forth and Clyde valleys towards the Ochils. The Votadini, a British tribe, evolved into the powerful and sophisticated Goddodin. In the sixth century, their ruler Mynyddawg assembled his allies and led them south on a mounted assault on the Northumbrian Angles. The men from Scotland were slaughtered at Catterick in Yorkshire.

Generations of Scottish leaders failed to learn the lesson of Catterick. It has repeatedly been possible to persuade some Scots to attack the powerful southern neighbour. In 937, Constantine II invaded western England and was heavily defeated at Brunanburh. In 1138, David I led an army south. It was decimated at the Battle of the Standard. In 1513, James IV made the same mistake at Flodden. Bonnie Prince Charlie's foray into England led to retreat and defeat at Culloden in 1746. The cocky Scottish banks' wild charge into English and foreign money markets ended in humiliating capture in 2008. Scottish invasions of England are good for inspiring gloomy songs, but not much else.

5

The Coming of Christianity to Scotland

In which we meet Irish saints, the Loch Ness monster and arguments about haircuts

Christianity thrived in some parts of Roman Britain and, according to the Roman historian Tertullian in 208, is likely to have been practised by some soldiers in Strathearn. We do not know for certain if Christianity continued locally after the Romans left in the early fourth century, but there is no reason to think it died out.

Truth and legend are hard to separate in early oral accounts of any religion. The earliest substantial historical source for Christianity in Britain comes from the Venerable Bede, a Northumbrian monk who compiled his great *Ecclesiastical History* in the early eighth century, basing it on earlier sources, now long lost.

Bede says that St Ninian, a Briton who established a church, Candida Casa (The White House) at Whithorn in Galloway in 397, went on to convert the Southern Picts to Christianity. Strathearn lies in the southern territories of the Picts. St Ninian's was the first large-scale conversion in the area. Despite his efforts, most Picts remained pagans.

Around 432, Patrick, probably the son of a Roman Imperial civil servant from southwest Scotland, established a successful Christian mission to Ireland, developing a network of monasteries and evangelists. He called the Picts *'gens extera ignorans Deum'* (a foreign race which does not know God). Writing in 540, the monk Gildas was even more scathing, referring to 'foul hordes of Scots and Picts, like dark throngs of worms who wriggle out of narrow fissures in the rocks when the sun is high and the weather grows warm.'

In the late fifth century, some Dál Riata, Scots from Ireland, began to settle in what is now Scotland. In 563, Columba, descended from Irish warlords, landed on Iona and founded an abbey, which became the driving force in bringing Christianity to the Picts. According to his biographer Adamnan, writing a century later, Columba achieved a political coup when he converted their King Bruide, and further enhanced his reputation by winning an encounter with the Loch Ness monster, the first 'historical' mention of Scotland's most elusive creature.

The Picts, like other Celtic peoples, worshipped spirits in the natural world, the sun, trees and rivers. As they did worldwide, Christian missionaries adapted local totems to fit their new religion. Sacred springs were rededicated as holy wells. The Celtic salmon, symbol of wisdom, became the Christian fish (from the Latin *icthus*, whose first two letters connote Iesus Christus) still used on badges today. The Celtic sacred rowan tree became a Christian protection against witches. In the Auchterarder area today there are woodcutters who will not cut down a rowan.

Christianity brought its own international literacy, new architecture and decorated stone crosses. Early clergy lived in clusters of wooden or stone huts. They fed themselves by farming.

There were many early Christian buildings in Strathearn. St Mackessog's, at Powhillock on the northern edge of Auchterarder, was created for Kessog, a contemporary of Columba. It was built, like many religious settlements, on good agricultural land beside a stream, which was given the name Kirkton Burn.

The 'mac' in Mackessog is the Gaelic *maol* meaning 'shaven-headed', indicating a monk, not the usual 'mac', meaning 'son of'. St Kessog and St Mackessog are the same person. In the Christian calendar, the Feast of St Kessog is on 10 March.

There has been no archaeological investigation to confirm it, but a secular community probably preceded the church or developed soon after. Successive buildings formed a parish church until 1660. St Mackessog's Well remains to the east of the ruined church, but is almost invisible now. Until it became Hunter Street in the mid-nineteenth century, the road from the High Street to the church was known as Powhillock Road and marked the eastern edge of the town.

St Kessog was reputed to heal the sick with an infusion of *lus* (the Gaelic word for herbs, including St Kessog's favourite yellow iris), which gave its name to another of his religious foundations on the west shore of Loch Lomond. In Auchterarder, St Kessog's name was revived in 1896 for the handsome Scottish Episcopalian Church just north of the High Street.

In Aberuthven, beside the modern cemetery, stand the ruins of St Cathan's, a mediaeval chapel, built to replace a sixth-century establishment. Cathan's nephew, Blane, founded Dunblane Cathedral fourteen miles away.

The mediaeval churches dedicated to St Serf in Dunning, and St Bean in Kinkell, probably stand on the sites of much earlier Christian foundations. In Gleneagles, St Mungo's Well was reputed to have miraculous healing powers from very early times, though it may have gained its name as late as the twelfth century when the Haldane family built a chapel further north in the glen, dedicating it to St Mungo.

As with all great religions, the original generous guiding principles of Christianity became entangled with the trivial preferences of bureaucrats and fanatics. In 325, at the Council of Nicea in Asia Minor, the Christian Church had recognised the split between its powerful Roman clergy, who believed in a triple God, and more fragmented elements of the Church who believed in a single one. In Scotland, the Celtic clergy fell out with their powerful Northumbrian counterparts over the date of Easter and the correct form of tonsure (haircut).

These disputes blocked a unified structure for Christianity in Britain until a broad assembly of churchmen at the Synod of Whitby in 664 agreed standard, mainly Roman, practices, creating bishops to head dioceses (districts) and administer local parishes. Auchterarder lay in the Diocese of Dunblane. Monasteries remained separate. This structure remained for nine hundred years, till it fragmented again in the Reformation.

From the sixth century, churches in Strathearn had links with the Christian Church throughout Europe and, through the Abbey of Kilrymont in St Andrews, as far as Byzantium in today's Turkey. There were opportunities for clergy to study in France and Italy. Monasteries became centres of scholarship. Early bishops and abbots gained their authority by converting local people. Later ones enhanced it by engaging in national and international politics. Elsewhere in Britain, chroniclers, such as Bede, wrote histories that glorified their religion.

As always, it was fashionable for some local people to name their children after foreign celebrities. By the ninth century, the senior Pictish royal family was led by King Constantine, named after the Roman emperor, Constantine the Great, who converted to Christianity. Constantine the Great had a local connection. His father, Constantius Chlorus, led a Roman occupation of Scotland in the fourth century.

It is likely that the name Strathearn came to have connotations of 'Erin' after the unusually extensive sixth-century Irish Christian church settlements in the area. It may be that the river had an older name, now forgotten. It is equally likely that the name Strathearn was already established when the Christians arrived and derives from the old Gaelic *ár*, meaning 'slaughter', or *ar*, meaning 'ploughing'.

6

Fortriu, Islam and the Vikings

In which a new religious power appears in Europe, the first united Scotland emerges and people are glad the River Earn is shallow in summer

In the sixth and seventh centuries, Europe consisted of many small states. Sometimes one grew by devouring another, but there was no central European authority to replace the disintegrating Roman Empire.

In the seventh century, a new political force appeared to the east of Europe: Islam. The name in Arabic means 'surrender to God's will'. Its founder, the prophet Mohammed, died in 632. Like the Jews and early Christians, he believed in a single, all-powerful God.

As with most religious movements, Mohammed's adherents believed their way of worshipping God was superior to any other. It was a short psychological step, politically convenient to some leaders of Christianity and Islam, to claim that the two religions worshipped different Gods. In Scotland, the word 'Mahoun', a corruption of 'Mohammed' became a synonym for 'The Devil'.

Christianity had evolved from its early pacifist roots, when the Roman Emperor Constantine the Great adopted the cross as his battle insignia in 312. Christianity's main fighting force then disintegrated with the Roman Empire.

Islam was militant and military from the start. Its Muslim armies conquered the Near East, seizing the key Christian city of Jerusalem, where Mohammed's successor Abd-al-Malik built a great mosque, the Dome of the Rock in 693. Muslim forces swept across North Africa and occupied Spain. By the beginning of the eighth century, the Islamic Empire was poised to invade Europe from both south-east and south-west.

In 717 and 718, its armies besieged Constantinople, the capital of the eastern Christian Roman Empire, but failed to capture the city. In 732 Islamic troops swept north from Spain, but were crushed at the Battle of Poitiers in what is now mid-western France. The victor of Poitiers was the Frankish King Charles Martel. Like Constantine the Great, he harnessed Christianity to war.

Centuries before, the Celts had migrated to occupy most of the western seaboard of Europe. Christianity began in the Middle East and also advanced up the western seaboard of Europe into Scotland. Islam had similar geographic origins to Christianity, but its northwestern advance was stopped short by Charles Martel. He confined European Muslim political power to the Iberian Peninsula.

All wars are marketed as ideological conflicts. It is easier to rally your troops if they can be made to think their fundamental beliefs are different from those of their leader's political enemies. Muslims looked and sounded different from Christians. In the twenty-first century, extremists on both sides still find the differences easy to exploit.

Islam had no active impact on the Auchterarder area until the Crusades, beginning in the late eleventh century, when Scottish nobles joined in Middle Eastern campaigns.

In these centuries when the kingdoms of mainland Europe were preoccupied with potential invaders from the east, what new political authorities appeared in the old Province of Brittania, abandoned by the Romans in 410? Not surprisingly, like the rest of Europe, it fragmented into a muddle of civil wars.

In the sixth century, Scotland was divided into many kingdoms. After defeating the Goddodin at Catterick, the Northumbrian Angles dominated the Lothians. The west was colonised by the Dál Riata from Ireland, under King Aedan, while the Picts controlled the north. Auchterarder lay at the frontier of all three power-blocs. Christianity became the dominant religion. Wars were now fought, not only between Christian and pagan kings, but also between Christian and Christian.

In the seventh century, two Pictish brothers, Owain and Bruide, won battles that changed the course of Scottish history. At Strathcarron in 642 Owain defeated King Domhnall Breac of Dál Riata. At Dunnichen (Nechtansmere), near Forfar, in 685, Bruide crushed King Egfrith's Northumbrians.

It was now theoretically possible for a united Pictish kingdom to rule most of what we think of as Scotland, including the Orkneys, which Bruide had subdued in 682. The Picts, however, were not a unified imperial power like the Roman Empire. Instead, they were a federation of kingdoms, some subordinate to others, with conflicting external alliances, rather like today's European Community.

Bruide became the dominant figure in this evolving Pictish structure. He belonged to the Maeatae or Verturiones tribe, whose Latin name survives as Fortriu, also called Fortrenn (now Strathearn), his power base at the south edge of the Pictish heartlands.

Fortriu was strategically strong. At its western end lay the great hill fort of Dundurn (from the Celtic *dun* meaning a fort, and *dubron*, meaning 'by the water'), near St Fillans, at the east end of Loch Earn. Dundurn fought off the Dál Riata with a siege-defence in 683.

To the east of Dundurn lies Comrie, whose name in Irish Gaelic is formed from *comrach* (a confluence of waters), while in Pictish it is *cwm rhiedd* (valley of the kings), or perhaps *cymreig* (Welsh town, after Briton settlers arriving along Loch Earn). Forteviot, in mid-Strathearn, served as administrative capital.

Abernethy, near the junction of the Earn and the Tay, was Fortriu's dominant religious centre. Not far away, on Moncreiffe Hill, another hill fort dominated the eastern river approach to the kingdom. Fortriu had a fleet that patrolled the Tay estuary and traded along the east coast of Scotland. Smaller boats worked the River Earn, providing transport to the Auchterarder area and beyond, with a vital link to Dundurn, on Loch Earn, at the other end of the kingdom.

The Auchterarder area lay in the heart of Fortriu, with good deer-hunting ground, farmland and a tradition of stock rearing. It also had an established transport system by water and Roman road, linking it to ports on the Rivers Tay and Forth with cultural and trade sea routes to Europe.

The area's concentration of religious houses indicated a higher than usual level of education, adding to a reputation for metal craftsmanship from its smithies. Even today, Aberuthven is known locally as Smiddy Haugh, though the last smithy closed in the mid twentieth century.

The Pictish kingdom, based on Fortriu, was at its height in the mid eighth century under Oengus MacFergus. He ruled all land north of the Forth and allied with the Angles in the Lothians. After Oengus died in 761, the Dál Riata again fought the Picts, each trying to consolidate and extend their kingdoms.

The Dalriadic King Aed won a battle in Fortriu in 768 and introduced 'The Laws of Aed', Scottish customs and organisational structures, to the area. The Picts fought back. From 789 to 820, their King Constantine dominated both Pictland and Dál Riata, despite frequent uprisings. Frustratingly for those who would like a clearer, more reliable account of this period, contemporary sources are few and contradictory.

In the ninth century at Dupplin, six miles west of Auchterarder, a 2.6-metre-tall red sandstone cross was placed on a hillside facing the Pictish capital of Forteviot. It has carvings, showing a king, probably Constantine, on horseback, and a host of soldiers. The cross was a highly visible symbol of authority to anyone travelling along the River Earn, the main thoroughfare through Fortriu. The cross was moved in 2002 to a sheltered location in St Serf's church in Dunning.

Meantime, a new figure was creating the first great European empire since the fall of Rome. Charlemagne, King of the Franks from 768 to 814, built on the victories of his grandfather, Charles Martel. He consolidated his power over the many sub-kingdoms in what we today call France, the Netherlands and the western part of Germany. He then conquered much of eastern Europe and Italy.

Charlemagne held the Muslim Empire at bay in Spain and southeastern Europe. On Christmas Day 800, Charlemagne was crowned Holy Roman Emperor by Pope Leo III. The coronation was held in Rome, and symbolised the unity of Christendom against its rivals.

This Christian unity was maintained by force. Charlemagne, although he never found time to learn to read and write, astutely invested in scholarship, arts and architecture, to create an image of a powerful, desirable Christian culture. Paris and Aachen flourished as centres of learning, attracting scholars from all over the Christian world, including Britain. In Fortriu he was seen as a great defender of the faith.

Patterns of history show that mainland European empires usually try to invade the largest offshore island, Britain. What stopped Charlemagne from following in the footsteps of the Romans and sending armies to occupy England and Scotland?

He refrained because he knew the problems of undertaking wars on too many fronts. Instead, he formed an alliance with Offa, King of Mercia in central England. He later allied with Egbert, Saxon King of Wessex, who had previously been in Charlemagne's service and became king of most of England. These alliances helped protect Charlemagne in his battles with powerful new invaders from the north, the Vikings, who sent their longships raiding down the coastlines of northwest Europe.

Danish Vikings swept south to occupy the eastern seaboard of England. Norwegian Vikings swept south to occupy the Orkneys, Caithness, the Western Isles and Galloway, the Dál Riata heartland. An Irish chronicler records that in 839 an army of Dublin-based Vikings defeated the men of Fortriu. It is likely that the battle took place near Abernethy, where men of Fortriu intercepted Viking longships on the River Tay.

To combat this menace, Picts and Scots set aside their differences in 840, uniting under King Kenneth MacAlpine, who had a Dál Riata father and a Pictish mother. He is the first king of a united Scotland. He based himself in Fortriu, with his palace at Forteviot, a short boat journey along the River Earn from the agricultural heartland around Auchterarder. King Kenneth MacAlpine maintained some degree of peace. After he died in 858, his brother Donald I sustained peace for four more years. When he died in 862, Scotland split again. Kenneth's sons Constantine and Aed formed rival dynasties.

Constantine I never achieved peace for long. In 864, and again in 866, Vikings plundered eastern Fortriu, and took hostages, demanding tribute money as ransom. Constantine died in battle against Danish Vikings in 877. The site of the battle is uncertain, but it was probably near Forgandenny, dangerously close to Forteviot, Fortriu's administrative capital. His brother Aed succeeded him as king. The following year, another dynastic rival, King Giric MacDonald, killed King Aed in Strathallan then tried to stave off Viking invasions in western Scotland. Giric, aided by his cousin Eochaid, ruled Fortriu in the late ninth century. Giric died at Dundurn, near St Fillans, in 889. Constantine I's son, King Donald II, continued the fight against the Vikings from 889 to 900. He died in battle.

In mainland Europe, Charlemagne's empire, divided between his three sons after he died in 814, evolved into the warring nations of France, Germany and Italy. The Vikings established themselves in Normandy (Land of the Norsemen).

In the south of the British mainland, King Alfred, of the Saxon House of Wessex, reached a peace settlement with the Vikings in 878. After he died in 899, his son, Edward the Elder, consolidated the new kingdom of England. The Anglo-Saxon Chronicle says that, the by time Edward died in 924, 'The King of the Scots and all the people of the Scots . . . and the King of the Strathclyde Welsh chose him as their lord.'

It was Aed's son, King Constantine II, who acknowledged the English King Edward the Elder as his overlord. It was more a recognition of the military might of the House of Wessex than a constitutional arrangement between England and Scotland. Constantine II, who ruled from 900 to 943, was always under threat from rival Pictish factions. He maintained his power by doing deals with the Vikings and the kings of Strathclyde. Then, as now, political deals were often preceded by armed conflict.

Viking longships raided the Scottish coast and navigable rivers in summer, then went back to their Irish bases for the winter. In 903, Irish-based Vikings sailed up the Tay and ravaged Dunkeld. They invaded the Forth as far as Stirling. Luckily for Auchterarder, though the River Earn led to the heartland of Fortriu, it was not deep enough for Viking sea-going vessels. Nor did the Vikings have any taste for route marches across boggy terrain at either the east or west ends of Fortriu.

The Vikings did not always win their battles. In 918, the men of Fortriu defeated a Viking army at the eastern end of the kingdom, and then executed many prisoners, perhaps in revenge for previous Viking summary executions. In 937, Constantine II made the classic royal error of invading England. His armies were slaughtered at Brunanburh, probably near the Mersey, by Edward the Elder's son, King Athelstan. Constantine II was forced to acknowledge Athelstan as his overlord.

Northern Britain fragmented again. Constantine retired from active kingship in 943 and became a monk in St Andrews, where he died in 952. His cousin Malcolm I succeeded him and fought rival kings to the north and south until he was killed in the Mearns in 954. Constantine II's son, King Indulf, seized Edinburgh from the Northumbrians. In 962, Indulf died fighting the Vikings.

In 965, at the Battle of Duncrub, near Dunning, five miles east of Auchterarder, King Duff (Dubh), of the Constantine MacAlpine dynasty, defeated Colin, leader of the rival Aed MacAlpine Pictish royal line. Powerful national leaders, like the Mormaer (steward) of Atholl and Duncan, Abbot of Dunkeld, were killed in the battle. Duff's victory was not enough for him to create a unified Scotland again. He lasted only one more year. Colin succeeded him as king till 971, when Duff's brother Kenneth II brought more stable rule.

Kenneth II, who reigned from 971 to 995, maintained good relations with the English King Edgar. In 973, Edgar gave Kenneth a palace beside the Thames in London for his use when visiting the English capital. To this day, it is called Scotland Yard. In 980, Kenneth II intercepted Danish Vikings, who had sailed up the Tay aiming for the rich Abbey of Dunkeld, and defeated the invaders at the Battle of Luncarty. Kenneth II was murdered in 995, probably by his successor Constantine II, son of Colin.

The House of Wessex produced astute kings of England until 975 when Ethelred, called 'The Unready' (badly advised), came to the throne. Viking attacks grew. In 1009, Sweyn Forkbeard, King of Denmark, invaded England and forced Ethelred into exile. When Sweyn died in 1014, his son Cnut made England his own. He defeated Ethelred's son, Edmund Ironside, at the battle of Assandun in 1016, married Ethelred's widow, Emma of Normandy, became a Christian, and was crowned King of England in London in 1017. Cnut cleverly allied with Godwine, Earl of Wessex, who commanded authority among the Saxons.

In Scotland, internecine warfare had continued till 1005, when King Malcolm II, son of the murdered Kenneth II, destroyed a rival alliance of kings at the Battle of Monzievaird near Comrie. Malcolm II then seized control of the Kingdom of Lothian and in 1018 defeated King Cnut's ally, Earl Uhtred at the Battle of Carham near the Tweed. In 1031, near the end of a long war-scarred reign, Malcolm II made a peace treaty with Cnut who had invaded northwards as far as the Tay to subdue his powerful neighbour.

The history of ninth- and tenth-century Scotland, between the reigns of Kenneth MacAlpine and Malcolm II, is brutal and confusing, with little reliable documentary evidence. In England, the Saxon House of Wessex did not suffer dynastic infighting to quite the same extent. Paradoxically, England fell to the Danes. Scotland did not.

As the new king of England, did Cnut automatically take over the House of Wessex English kings' status as overlords of Scotland? No. It was not that simple. Cnut was preoccupied with establishing his rule in England. His priority was to establish harmony between Anglo-Saxons and Danes. Celtic Britain lay on the fringes of his effective control.

In Wales, where kings had paid taxes to the House of Wessex, there were nationalist uprisings. In Scotland, King Malcolm II, like his predecessors, was mainly concerned with wiping out opposition from rival factions within his own royal family. Malcolm II, Cnut and Llewellyn consolidated the Scottish, English and Welsh frontiers much as we know them today. The borderlands remained debatable.

The eighth-century Muslim advance northward through Europe had been halted seven hundred miles from Auchterarder. The tenth-century Viking advance southward came within twelve miles of the town. By the time Cnut swept towards the Tay in 1031, the Viking pirates had become landowners and Kings of England.

No tangible evidence of the Vikings has yet been found in Auchterarder itself. There are no obvious Viking place-names near Auchterarder but Norse words like *byre* (enclosure for farm animals) came into use alongside the Gaelic *fank* (sheep-pen). The Viking name Hrolf or Rollo survives locally to this day as the family name of the Barons of Dunning, though they are descended from much later Normans from France who came north after William the Conqueror seized England in 1066. The Rollo motto 'La Fortune Passe Partout' (Good luck goes everywhere) must be one of the most cheerfully optimistic in all heraldry.

There was reputed to be a longship burial site at Tornavie on the slopes of the Ochils, near Craigrossie, but this is due to a mistranslation. Tornavie is not 'Thor's ship', an unlikely combination of Norse and Latin words. Instead, Tornavie (a contraction of Tor Nemeton) is Celtic for 'hill of the sacred grove'. Just over the Ochil ridge lies Tormaukin, 'hill of the hare', sacred to the Celts.

In the Auchterarder area, it was advantageous to use the Gaelic of the new King Malcolm II and his churchmen, who dominated written communication. Pictish words fell out of use, just as the globalised English of today's Internet accelerates the demise of written Scots vocabulary, though our spoken language remains rich in Scots.

The Picts did not leave Fortriu when it became Strathearn. In Aberuthven lies the burial vault of the MacDuff-Duncans, who claimed descent from King Dubh and lived here till the twentieth century. There are Auchterarder families today whose landholdings go back to the Middle Ages. A few are descended from Normans who came in the eleventh century. The rest have Pictish blood in their veins.

7

The Normans

*In which we meet Macbeth, King Great-head
and his saintly wife, and William the Conqueror*

'Viking' in Old English means 'pirate'. The settlers from Norway and Denmark preferred to call themselves Norsemen. Opposite the south coast of England lay Normandy, land of the Norsemen, whose rulers were descended from Rollo who became Duke of Normandy in 932 as the European empire founded by Charlemagne finally disintegrated. Normandy was in theory a sub-kingdom of France. In practice, French kings had no real control and depended on alliances.

Rollo's successors' nicknames give some idea of their warlike nature: William Longsword, Richard the Fearless and Robert the Devil, whose son William the Conqueror became Duke of Normandy in 1035. In the same year, the English King Cnut died. Malcolm II of Scotland had died the year before. Neither throne was secure. Cnut was succeeded by his son Harold I. Malcolm II was succeeded by his grandson Duncan I.

In 1040 Duncan led an army to suppress Macbeth, the Mormaer (steward) of Moray, who had developed a power base in the lands of the northern Picts. Duncan was killed in battle. Macbeth became King of Scotland. Macbeth's reputation has never recovered from Shakespeare's play, although he probably was no more bloodthirsty and scheming than previous kings. The Lady Macbeth of Shakespeare's play was Queen Gruoch, niece of King Malcolm II and cousin of the murdered King Duncan's mother Bethoc.

Duncan's son, Malcolm III Canmore (from the Gaelic *Can Mor*, meaning great or large head), married Ingebiorg, widow of the Viking warlord Thorfinn the Mighty, Earl of Orkney. Backed by his Viking allies, Malcolm III revenged his father's death by killing Macbeth at the Battle of Lumphanan, between the River Don and the River Dee, in 1058. Queen Gruoch had a son, Lulach, by a previous marriage. Malcolm III trapped and killed him to eliminate a potential dynastic rival.

Meantime, in England, the Danish dynasty did not last long. Harold I died in 1040. His brother Harthacanute succeeded him but died two years later. The Saxon dynasty returned to the throne in King Edward the Confessor, younger son of Ethelred the Unready and brother of Edmund Ironside, whom Cnut had deposed. By now, Cnut's Saxon ally Earl Godwine had become the most powerful man in England. Godwine's daughter Eadgyth married King Edward the Confessor then, when Edward died in 1066, Godwine's own son became King Harold II of England.

Harold was not the only candidate for the English throne. Edmund Ironside's grandson, Edgar Atheling, had a better claim by royal descent. Then, from across the Channel, Duke William of Normandy claimed that Edward the Confessor had promised the crown of England to him. William also claimed to be King Harold II's overlord because Harold, as a young man, had served in William's army in Brittany.

The confusion was resolved by force. William invaded England. His army routed the Saxons and killed King Harold at the Battle of Hastings in 1066.

William I the Conqueror imposed his authority on Britain with an efficiency not seen since the Roman Empire had withdrawn six hundred years before. He legitimised his military conquest with a coronation ceremony at Westminster Abbey. He granted a charter to London, enhancing its mercantile and capital city status and reduced the power of the great Saxon and Danish earldoms.

William I restructured land ownership by introducing the feudal system, by which the king owned all the land. The nobility held their estates as tenants of the king, paying him both money and military service. Lesser barons were tenants of the great dukes and earls, in a pyramid hierarchy reaching all the way down to the serfs who had duties of service but minimal rights.

To enforce his authority, William I brought loyal Norman allies and granted them estates in England, encouraging them to build strong castles. He also reformed the Church, bringing Lanfranc from Normandy to be Archbishop of Canterbury, initiating a programme of magnificent cathedral building.

In 1085, William I commissioned the Domesday Book, documenting land tenure throughout England. It was completed in a year, giving the king for the very first time a clear picture of what he might be able to levy in taxes and military service. Within a short twenty-year period, England was no longer focussed on relations with Northern Vikings but with mainland Europe.

William the Conqueror's victory in 1066 at Hastings on the south coast of England had a dramatic impact on Auchterarder, high on a strategic ridge in far-off Scotland. The Scottish King Malcolm III had made a useful Viking alliance by marrying Ingebiorg, widow of Thorfinn the Mighty. When she died, Malcolm in 1070 made a new dynastic alliance. It would have been politically astute to marry a Norman princess. Malcolm did the opposite. He married the saintly Margaret of the House of Wessex, great-niece of Edward the Confessor, the last undisputed Saxon King of England.

Like many European princesses, Margaret was well travelled and well educated. She had spent some time in Hungary, a nation with new-found Christian zeal. Christianity had blossomed in central Europe in the tenth century, much influenced by Wenceslas, Duke of Bohemia 930–935, the 'Good King Wenceslas' of Christmas carol fame.

Margaret was the sister of Edgar Atheling, who had a more direct inheritance claim to the English crown than William I the Conqueror. Margaret lingered in

England after William invaded but, in 1069, she fled by ship along with others of the Saxon royal family, accompanied by a retinue including Maurice, founder of the great Perthshire family of Drummond. When Margaret's ship was driven ashore on the Forth at Queensferry, named after her, King Malcolm brought her to his palace at Dunfermline.

To romantic historians, Saint Margaret is the bringer of civilised European ways and pious Christianity. To William the Conqueror, this Scots-Saxon dynastic marriage threatened his northern frontier. To Auchterarder, it brought a new era.

Unlike the Irish-based Norwegian Vikings who had harried Fortriu (Strathearn) for centuries but never stayed for long, William the Conqueror came from Danish Viking stock who had a tradition of settling on conquered land. He and Malcolm III fell out over Northumbria.

William saw Northumbria as part of England. Malcolm III saw Northumbria as an old separate kingdom that he might add to the other old kingdoms, Lothian and Strathclyde, which had come under the control of Fortriu as an expanding Scotland. Malcolm III led forays into Northumbria. William retaliated in 1071 by sending a fighting force up the eastern seaboard to subdue his troublesome neighbour.

William's ships sailed up the Forth and Tay. His armies swept into Fortriu. He forced Malcolm to swear an oath of allegiance and sign a peace treaty at Abernethy. Duncan, Malcolm's son by his first wife Ingebiorg, was taken to England as a hostage. It was a practice that English kings were to repeat over the centuries when they defeated the Scots. Malcolm broke the Abernethy peace treaty repeatedly until he was killed in 1093 at Alnwick, yet another Scottish leader who came to grief by invading England.

Like his Pictish predecessors, Malcolm liked hunting game in Fortriu. His hunting grounds along the Earn east of Aberuthven included Dalreoch (field of the king).

To defend against future Norman attacks, Malcolm built Auchterarder Castle on the north side of the town, overlooking Strathearn with its river access. The castle may sit on top of earlier fortifications, possibly dating back to pre-Roman times.

Malcolm's successors developed Auchterarder Castle with a moat surrounding the massive central keep. The castle survived until the late eighteenth century when a farmer demolished it to use its stone for farm buildings, recycling a few architectural fragments into a little square structure. Parts of the castle's west and south outer fortifications remain, still visible as earth mounds. In 1984, an ancient sixty-foot-deep stone-lined well shaft was discovered in the castle courtyard. It provided an all-year-round water supply, something the later High Street wells never achieved.

The landscape of Fortriu was marked with towers, of which the round tower at Abernethy survives, along with towers at Dunning and Muthill. The Abernethy round tower is characteristic of Irish Celtic towers and, with one other in Brechin, is unique in Scotland. Dunning and Muthill have square Norman towers. We do not know much about Norman structures in Auchterarder itself. Astonishingly for a royal castle, there has never been an archaeological investigation.

Today, there are plans for a massive housing development on the northern edge of Auchterarder close to the castle and to the early Christian St Mackessog's Church. Worryingly, when Perth & Kinross Council refurbished the Aytoun Hall bewteen 2009 and 2011, its archaeological advisers said there was no need to conduct a survey of that site, although they knew it had been an important market, military and church location since the Middle Ages and that Roman artefacts had been found there during an earlier phase of construction.

Much archaeological evidence has vanished in the tons of rubble removed from the Aytoun Hall. Unless the Council chooses better archaeological advice, more important historical sites may be destroyed without a survey.

William I the Conqueror died in 1087. He left Normandy to his eldest son Robert, and England to his second son, who became King William II Rufus. This tidy division was complicated in 1096 when Robert mortgaged Normandy to William II to raise funds to go on the First Crusade to recover for Christianity the city of Jerusalem, which had been captured in 1076 by Islamic Turks.

After Malcolm III Canmore died in battle in 1093, his brother Donald III became king for four years, a reign interrupted for a few months by Duncan II, son of Malcolm III and Ingebiorg. Duncan II was killed by his uncle's allies. A monarch's eldest son did not automatically inherit the throne. Royal succession depended on power struggles at court.

Most of Malcolm III's children by Margaret fared better. Their sons became Kings of Scotland: Edgar 1097–1107, Alexander I 1107–24 and David I 1124–53. Their younger daughter Mary married Eustace, the powerful Count of Boulogne. Their older daughter Matilda married William the Conqueror's third son who became King Henry I of England in 1100 and ruled for thirty-five years.

As today, heads of state exchanged gifts as tokens of friendship. Celtic monarchs often displayed exotic international taste. In 1105, King Edgar gave an elephant 'of marvellous bigness' to Murdoch O'Brian, High King of Ireland.

Elephants retain their symbolic significance among European monarchs today. The very first foreign honour to be bestowed upon our present Queen Elizabeth II, when she was still Princess Elizabeth in 1947, was the Order of the Elephant of Denmark.

In the eleventh century, with Norman battlefields now extending as far as the Middle East, the dynastic alliance between the royal houses of Scotland and England was intended to help keep the peace in Britain. Under the influence of Queen Margaret and the Norman families at the Scottish court, Scotland adopted increasingly European ways. The lands of the Pictish and Scots tribes evolved into earldoms (from the Norse word *jarl* or lord).

Fortriu became the Earldom of Strathearn. The first Earl whose name appears on written records is Malise who, with other earls, signed the foundation charter of Scone as a witness in 1128. Ten years later he fought alongside King David I at the disastrous Battle of the Standard near Northallerton in Yorkshire, close to Catterick where the Goddodin had made the same invasive mistake six hundred years before.

8

The Rise of Royal Burghs

*In which we meet charter-granting kings,
too many Matildas and very slow officials*

Ten years before he came to the throne in Scotland in 1124, the future King David I married Maud, daughter of Waltheof, Earl of Northumbria and Judith, niece of William I the Conqueror. Through his new wife, David acquired the Honour of Huntingdon with lands in the East Midlands. His position was ambivalent. As an English earl, David owed homage to the English king. As King of Scotland, David tried to take possession of his father-in-law's estates in the north of England.

While Henry I was King of England, with his Scottish wife Matilda, there was peace between the two countries. Henry was more concerned with suppressing revolts in Normandy and controlling the English barons. To do so, he imprisoned for twenty-eight years in Cardiff Castle his elder brother Robert, who had mortgaged Normandy to England to finance the First Crusade to Jerusalem, but then returned to Europe.

When Henry I died in 1135, England slid into civil war. Henry had no surviving son to inherit the throne, so the crown passed to his nephew Stephen, who was married to another Matilda. Her parents were Count Eustace of Boulogne and Mary, daughter of King Malcolm III of Scotland.

Henry I, however, did have a daughter, confusingly also called Matilda. Known as 'The Empress', she was first married to the Holy Roman Emperor Henry V, then to the Norman Geoffrey Plantagenet, Count of Anjou. Could a woman inherit the throne of England? The country divided into rival factions. Stephen's power lay mainly in London and the east. Matilda's power lay in Bristol and the west. Baronial families were divided. Castle building ran amok.

King David I of Scotland took advantage of a weakened England. In 1136, he seized Cumberland. In 1138, he tried to take Northumberland. He was defeated at the Battle of the Standard, so called because the banners of St Cuthbert of Durham, St Wilfred of Ripon, St Peter of York and St John of Beverley were mounted on a wagon at the head of the English army.

King David promised to keep the peace and handed over to King Stephen five noble hostages, including a son of Malise, 1st Earl of Strathearn. By 1141, David

I made war in England again. On behalf of the Empress Matilda, he besieged the old Saxon capital Winchester, but was forced to flee. He was rescued by David Olifard, or Oliphant, who was granted lands in Strathearn.

In 1149, the Empress Matilda's son Henry came to Carlisle, where David I felt secure enough to issue coins as King of Cumbria. As heir to his mother's claim to the English throne, Henry needed to be knighted by a reigning monarch. King Stephen was not about to legitimise his rival. David I of Scotland knighted Henry instead, extracting a promise that, if Henry became King of England, David could have Northumberland. David died in 1153, succeeded by his son Malcolm IV. Stephen died in 1154, succeeded by Henry who, as King Henry II of England, not only failed to hand over Northumberland but reclaimed Cumbria as well.

How were these wars financed? The old tribal warlord way of fighting had been replaced by the more formal feudal system, though old ways persisted, particularly in the north and west of Scotland. The feudal system provided knights for an army, but more money was needed. In England, Henry I granted charters to towns to increase stability and raise revenue. David I did the same in Scotland by creating royal burghs.

Royal burghs had both benefits and liabilities. They enjoyed the king's protection and had monopolies on trade with foreign countries. They could hold markets and fairs with exclusive rights. Their prestige attracted new business and investment. On the other hand, they owed extra taxes.

Strathearn was now a complex mixture of old Pictish clan ways and new Norman feudalism. The most important local figure for running mediaeval royal burghs was the sheriff. He not only administered justice, he was responsible for raising troops and levying revenue for the king. These taxes could be assessed in cash or in kind, for example in precise quantities of wheat, barley or cattle.

As today, local government was in constant flux. The king might bypass his sheriff and deal direct with the bailies appointed by the town. Merchants, trading in several sheriffdoms, might try to negotiate a special deal with the king's chamberlain. Officials were created whose public worth was not always obvious.

In the heart of the old Kingdom of Fortriu, there arose the Royal Burgh of Auchterarder beside the castle that had grown from David I's father's hunting lodge. No other community in Fortriu, now called Strathearn, was granted royal burgh status.

In the huge county of Perthshire, there are only two royal burghs, Auchterarder and Perth. We do not know which is senior. Neither founding royal charter has survived.

It seems likely that both royal burghs received their charters from King David I who created many royal burghs. The earliest clear reference to Auchterarder as a royal burgh is in 1226, when King Alexander II granted a tenth of the income from his lands in Auchterarder to the Abbey of Inchaffray to be collected by 'our balies of Auchterarder'.

The oldest surviving charter to carry the seal of the Royal Burgh of Auchterarder shows William, son of Malise, granting to the Abbey of Inchaffray some lands on today's Abbey Road, which he had bought from John, son of

Baltin. This charter dates from around 1370. It is witnessed by Walter of Moravia (Murray), Lord of Tullibardine, who did not acquire that estate until 1362.

There were three main reasons for Auchterarder being chosen as a royal burgh. It lay in a strategically important location. It was rich in agriculture and hunting grounds. It had a stone-built castle on a site favoured by King Malcolm III Canmore. Perth's wooden castle, beside the flat North Inch, was swept away in 1210 when the River Tay flooded, leaving Auchterarder with the only royal burgh castle in Perthshire.

The need for flood defences in Perth was obvious. After nearly eight hundred years of meetings between officials, Perth finally built appropriate flood defences at the end of the twentieth century. Soon after, in 2010, Perth celebrated 'Perth 800', which was misleadingly interpreted as celebrating the founding of the royal burgh. In fact, the Perth charter of 1210 granted to the existing royal burgh the right to increase taxes after the floods earlier that year. For 'Perth 800', Perth & Kinross Council organised events and parades. Most participants did not realise they were cheerfully commemorating tax increases.

In the Middle Ages, many royal burghs had harbours and grew rapidly through trade. Auchterarder had no harbour and was served by roads that lacked bridges. The town stayed small. From The King's Household Accounts in the late twelfth century, it seems that Auchterarder was the only royal burgh in Scotland where the burgh land and the local lord's land were farmed together and paid joint taxes.

9

The Power of the Mediaeval Church

In which we see symbols evolve into bureaucracy, meet rich investors in the afterlife and encounter an unfortunate pilgrim

When politicians go to war, their claim that God is on their side grows louder. In the early twenty-first century, both the Christian American President George Bush and the Islamic internationalist leader Osama Bin Laden assured their opposing forces in the war in Afghanistan that they had divine backing. King Oengus MacFergus said the same thing in the mid eighth century as he brutally extended the power of Fortriu over northern Pictish kingdoms and controlled the Tay transport waterway.

Ownership of religious symbols plays a crucial role in political authority. The word 'crucial' itself comes from the Latin *crux*, meaning 'a cross', the Christian symbol. Oengus exploited divisions between the Angles by forming an alliance with the Lothian Angles on the one hand and becoming a patron of the great Northumbrian Abbey of Lindisfarne on the other.

In a spectacular piece of religious one-upmanship, Oengus acquired around 740 relics of St Andrew, who was the elder brother of St Peter, 'the rock' on which the Christian Church and the Papacy were founded. The official legend, in a direct parallel with Constantine the Great's vision before the Battle of Milvian Bridge in 332, is that Oengus had a vision before going into battle. In Oengus's case, his vision was of St Andrew, whose corpse was conveniently being conveyed from Constantinople to Brittany and thence to Scotland by a monk called Regulus. In fact, Oengus probably bought the St Andrew relics from Bishop Acca, who was expelled from Hexham near Durham in 732.

Oengus installed the relics in the Culdee Abbey of Kinrymont on the promontory of what became the town of St Andrews, south of the Tay estuary. Kinrymont was closely linked to Oengus's capital Forteviot in Fortriu.

About 820, King Constantine I is reputed to have brought relics of St Columba to the Abbey of Dunkeld on the Tay. Abernethy, the traditional religious capital of Fortriu, now had a symbol-rich rival downriver at St Andrews and upriver at Dunkeld. From the King's point of view, each great abbey or cathedral brought prestige and authority.

Symbolic sites of civil authority also became more diverse. King Kenneth MacAlpine, who ruled from 840 to 858, made Scone on the opposite bank of the Tay from Perth, with its 'Stone of Destiny', the coronation site of Scottish kings. In 906, King Constantine II had held a council there, intended to make a distinction between the rights of the Church and of the state, something that has never been resolved for long.

The Viking raids of the ninth and tenth centuries hit the mediaeval Church hard, Abbeys like Dunkeld on the Tay and Lindisfarne on the Northumberland coast were ripe for plunder. The MacAlpine dynasty's capital Forteviot was relatively safe inland on the shallow River Earn.

Transport for commerce, government and war was mainly by water. Roads were few. Bridges were fewer. By the eleventh century, as their authority expanded, Scottish kings moved their power base south from the Rivers Earn and Tay to the River Forth. Malcolm III's palace at Dunfermline was thus linked to Edinburgh, the capital of the old Kingdom of Lothian, and to Stirling at the eastern end of the old Dál Riata territories. Whenever he wished to return to Fortriu, the king had three choices. He could sail up the Forth to Stirling. He could sail from Dunfermline round the Fife coast and up the Tay or ride the shorter twenty-mile overland route to his castle in Auchterarder.

The role of the Church grew as the saintly Queen Margaret helped transform it, encouraging new European ways. With the help of Lanfranc, Archbishop of Canterbury, she brought Benedictine monks to Dunfermline, where she built a church close to King Malcolm III's palace, looking down on the River Forth.

In the twelfth century, the power of the Church increased dramatically. David I, before he became King of Scotland in 1124, spent time at the English King Henry I's court and admired the piety, scholarship and discipline of Norman clergy. King David I granted lands to the great religious orders and used the expertise of well-educated clerics. The words *cleric* and *clerk* have the same Norman origin. They administered the King's records and, with their international links, advised on politics and trade.

The European Church, with the Pope at its head, had developed two administrative structures for its own government. One was a hierarchy of bishops and archbishops, adapted from the model of Roman provincial governors, with a cathedral as the local head church ruling smaller parish churches. The other was a system, based on communities of monks living in abbeys, governed by the order of its particular European mother house. As in any huge imperial bureaucracy, these administrative structures frequently overlapped, conflicted and merged.

What was the main difference between monks and friars? As a very broad generalisation, monks were the successors to the communities of hermits of the early Christian Church who shut themselves off from the world in a life of religious devotion. Friars also lived collectively but went out to preach. Local practice varied greatly.

In the parts of Scotland around Strathearn, which had evolved from the old Kingdom of Fortriu, several great religious orders received lands. They built churches, buildings to house the clerics, and other structures appropriate to their particular business, ranging from hospitals to farm steadings.

St Benedict, who lived from 480 to 547 and founded the monastery of Monte Cassino in Italy, wrote *The Rule of St Benedict*, which became a popular handbook on how to run a monastery. In 1128, King David I granted lands for a Benedictine abbey in Dunfermline. Abbeys often gained rights to lands some distance away. For example, Dunfermline Abbey had the right to revenues from St John's Kirk in Perth.

The Cistercians were formed in 1098 at Citeaux in Normandy as an austere version of the Benedictines. St Bernard of Clairvaux, an eloquent preacher and prolific writer, fired enthusiasm for the Second Crusade against Islam in 1146. The Cistercians built a fine abbey at Coupar Angus, north of Perth in 1161. At Culross, over the Ochil pass from Auchterarder, they built another abbey in 1217. Near to where the rivers Tay and Earn meet, they built a nunnery at Elcho in 1241.

The Augustinians were named after St Augustine from Hippo in North Africa, who lived from 354 to 430. He was a passionate advocate of the doctrine of the Trinity and strong centralised Papal authority. The Augustinians received lands in Scone in 1120, beside Loch Tay 1122–24, St Andrews 1140 and Abernethy 1272–73. An 1149 charter shows Cambuskenneth Abbey in Stirling ruling a church in Gleneagles. Most importantly for the Auchterarder area, Augustinians took over the Abbey of Inchaffrey, near Madderty, in 1198.

St Dominic, who lived from 1170 to 1221, was born in Spain and inspired the Albigensian Crusade, so called because it was a Papal attack on the Cathars, based at Albi in south-western France, in a revival of the old 'Trinity versus Unity' conflict from the early days of the Church. Dominican friars were known as 'Black Friars' because of the colour of their robes. In 1231 they created Blackfriars Monastery in Perth. In 1233, they revived Dunblane Cathedral when Friar Clement was made Bishop of Dunblane Diocese.

The Carmelites were founded in the twelfth century and named after Our Lady of Mount Carmel in Palestine. They dressed in white and founded Whitefriars Monastery in Perth in 1262.

Monastic foundations continued through the Middle Ages. Greyfriars in Perth was founded as late as 1492, the year Columbus arrived in America, though their monastic order was founded in Italy in the early thirteenth century by St Francis of Assisi.

Kings were not the only men to endow great religious houses. Gilbert, 3rd Earl of Strathearn from 1171 to 1220, married the Anglo-French Maud d'Aubigny. Like today's major landowners, he had estates not only in Scotland but also in England. Earl Gilbert changed the ways of the local church.

Although Queen Margaret introduced European sophistication in 1070, the Celtic Culdees (from *Céle De*, vassals of God), a strict sect of celibate monks, remained the dominant force in Scottish religious communities until the Norman clerical invasion, invited by David I. Their name survives in Strathearn at Culdees, near Muthill.

Earl Gilbert preferred the more outgoing, worldly Augustinian canons. In 1198, he reformed the existing Culdee community at Inchaffray, near Madderty, by bringing Augustinians from Scone. It was a shrewd political move, linking

Inchaffray to the great Augustinian Holyrood Abbey down the royal mile from Edinburgh Castle.

Inchaffray, in Gaelic, means 'isle of the mass'. Gilbert funded the new establishment with one tenth of his entire rent income, making it rich and powerful. When funding priorities change, somebody else suffers. The bishopric of Dunblane, also under Earl Gilbert's patronage, was run down by his successors, and its cathedral church left with barely the means to hold a service, until the Dominicans revived its fortunes in 1233.

Why did rich men invest in monasteries? Monks would pray daily for the souls of their benefactors. It was generally believed that God would pay more attention to repeated requests from monks, so men like Gilbert stood a better chance of going to heaven.

The Abbey of Inchaffray was built on the classic Norman model, with a church attached to an open cloister and domestic buildings. Its ruins still survive. Gilbert brought the old Celtic churches of St Cathan in Aberuthven and St Mackessog in Auchterarder under Inchaffray's control, and gave the monks privileges including 'liberty for fishing and fowling through all his lands, waters and lakes; also he grants, from his woods, timber for their buildings and other uses; and pannage (pig-grazing) and bark and fuel.' These rights were granted on what had been the royal hunting grounds of Fortriu.

Gilbert's charter spells Aberuthven *Abbeyruthven*, blurring name origins. There had indeed been a religious establishment on the same raised site since the sixth century, but the Gaelic name, with *aber* meaning confluence of the Ruthven and the Earn, is probably older than the foundation of a local abbey.

The new monks continued the church's local farming tradition and international links. Their Norman influence brought improved agricultural and architectural technology, and an expanded menu for those who could afford it. The Abbey of Inchaffray and the Royal Burgh generally worked well together.

Auchterarder looked north to Inchaffray for its monastic authority. The little church in Gleneagles looked west to Cambuskenneth Abbey, near Stirling. The name *Gleneagles* is unlikely to have anything to do with birds. It is probably the Gaelic *Glen eaglais* (Glen of the church), referring to the sixth-century St Mungo, after whom a chapel was named. With much reconstruction through the centuries, the chapel remains in the glen today.

Another great abbey, Arbroath, gained St Cathan's in Aberuthven later in the Middle Ages. Inchaffray, however, backed by the Earls of Strathearn, remained the dominant religious authority in the area throughout the Middle Ages.

When Henry II succeeded to the English throne in 1154, he set about introducing fiscal and military controls to prevent another civil war. He also tried to curb the increasing power of the Church. He fell out with the Archbishop of Canterbury Thomas Becket, who had served him as chancellor. Henry insisted that bishops were barons whose appointment required his approval. Becket insisted that bishops were responsible only to the Pope. In 1170 Henry had Becket murdered in Canterbury.

Like his Norman predecessors, Henry II had ambitions on the mainland of Europe. He was Duke of Normandy and ruled Anjou, Maine and Touraine.

In 1152, he had married Eleanor, divorced wife of the French King Louis VII. Through her, he acquired Aquitaine and lands stretching south through France as far as the Pyrenees. Throughout his reign he was embroiled in wars, first with Louis VII, then with his son Philip Augustus.

Malcolm IV became King of Scotland in 1153, the year before Henry II succeeded to the English throne. Malcolm kept up his grandfather David I's pattern of granting charters to promote trade and develop royal burghs. Malcolm not only surrendered his claim to Northumberland and Cumbria, but fought in Henry's army when the English king tried to capture Toulouse in the south of France.

When Malcolm returned to Scotland in 1160, he found a divided country. He was besieged in Perth by rebel nobles including Ferteth, Earl of Strathearn. Galloway was a law unto itself, controlled by the warlord Earl Gilbert. In Argyll, Somerled, Lord of the Isles, established a semi-independent kingdom until Malcolm killed him in battle in 1164. The following year Malcolm IV died. He was succeeded by his brother, William I the Lion, who was crowned at Scone in the presence of seven great earls, including Ferteth, 2nd Earl of Strathearn.

At first William the Lion supported the English King Henry II, joining his campaign in Normandy in 1166. Sensing that Henry's European empire was overextending his military capability, William saw an opportunity to take Northumberland and Cumbria. In 1173, he invaded. The English retaliated by invading Lothian and burning Berwick. William was captured at Alnwick when his horse slipped from under him. He was taken to Normandy where he was required to sign a treaty at Falaise, assigning castles, including Edinburgh and Stirling, to Henry II, before the English king let him go. William also acknowledged Henry as his overlord.

In 1186 Henry II arranged for William the Lion to marry Ermengarde de Beaumont, from a minor Norman family with no powerful dynastic links. As part of the deal, Henry handed over Edinburgh Castle as Ermengarde's dowry.

Like Henry II, William the Lion sought to control the appointment of bishops and had a long dispute with the Pope over who should be Bishop of St Andrews. Religious affairs took a dramatic turn when the Muslim leader Saladin captured the Christian holy city of Jerusalem in 1187. Henry II was too stretched militarily in France to undertake a crusade. The following year, his own sons, Richard and John united with the French King Philip Augustus against their father. Henry died in 1189 at Chinon.

Richard I inherited the English crown. He needed money for a new war against Saladin. Richard accepted William the Lion's offer of 10,000 Scots merks to buy back the other Scottish castles ceded by the Treaty of Falaise. He continued to regard the Scottish King as his feudal vassal. Richard set off for Jerusalem on the Third Crusade in 1190 and earned the nickname Lionheart. He was rarely in England and died, fighting against the French whom he had once supported, at Chalus in 1199.

While Richard was fighting in the Middle East and Normandy, he left his brother John to rule England. In reaction to John's despotism, the feudal structure began to break down. After John inherited the throne of England, he was forced to cede Normandy to Philip Augustus. Soon only Aquitaine remained of England's European empire. John rounded on Scotland. King William the Lion fought back but John bullied him into accepting the Treaty of Norham in 1209 by which William had to pay John the huge sum of 15,000 Scots merks to ensure the English King's 'good will'. A council was called at Perth in 1210 to discuss payment, but the delegates had to retreat to Stirling when Perth Castle was washed away in a flood.

By the time William the Lion died in Stirling in 1214, he had reigned for fifty-nine years, longer than any monarch of Scotland before or since, with the exception of Queen Victoria (1837–1901) and our present Queen Elizabeth II who came to the throne in 1952 and celebrates her diamond jubilee in 2012.

In William the Lion's time, Strathearn remained a strategic location. The King's brother David held the huge Honour of Huntingdon in the English Midlands. With William's help, Earl David saw one of his knights, Nigel de Lovetoft, given lands near the old Roman camp at Strageath by the Earn, changing his name to Nigel de Dalpatrick after his new estate.

William the Lion's three daughters all married great English barons. Margaret married Hubert de Burgh, Justiciar of England; Isabel married Roger Bigod, Earl of Norfolk; his third daughter, also called Margaret, married Gilbert, Earl Marshall. William the Lion's heir, Alexander, married King John's daughter Joanna. Political intrigue and mercenary demands surrounded all three marriages, but William achieved dynastic links for the next generation that had been denied to him in his own marriage.

Soon after Alexander II became King of Scotland, he saw a powerful alliance of English barons and bishops curtail King John's powers in the Magna Carta of 1215. Alexander knew that a similar alliance in Scotland could limit his own authority.

King John died in 1216, succeeded by his young son Henry III. The new kings of Scotland and England were brothers-in-law. There was a tangle of old charters and disputes relating to their respective rights. In 1237, Pope Gregory IX was asked to help resolve matters. His legate Otto brokered a deal where Alexander gave up most of his claims to Northumberland and Cumbria in exchange for money.

Queen Joanna did not produce an heir for the Scottish throne. She died in 1238 on a pilgrimage to the shrine of St Thomas Becket at Canterbury. The following year Alexander II married a French noble's daughter, Marie de Coucy, who brought no great dynastic links but did bear him a son and heir, the future Alexander III, in 1241.

Henry III feared a Scottish–French military alliance might outflank England, a fear repeated for the next six hundred years, always more fantasy than reality. Alexander II died in 1249, after a reign troubled by baronial uprisings, leaving to his son Alexander III a Scotland whose boundaries are similar to those today. In 1251, to reinforce the dynastic links between Scotland and England, Alexander III married Margaret, daughter of Henry III. The Scots King and his bride were both ten years old. The New queen arrived in the knowledge that a previous Queen Margaret of Scotland, Malcolm Canmore's second wife, had recently been made a saint.

The power of the Church, like that of the barons, remained a potent force that could enhance or destroy. The king needed the Church to give the monarchy its sacred status and to protect his soul. He used his lands to pay for these privileges. In 1226, King Alexander II granted ten per cent of the income from the Barony of Auchterarder to the Abbey of Inchaffray, relying on his local bailies to collect and distribute the taxes.

The Church was the great international organisation of the Middle Ages. Many nobles and senior clergy, especially scholars, travelled overseas. Local tradesmen also made long journeys, not just for business. Pilgrimages to Jerusalem were popular. In 1201, William of Perth, a baker, set off for the Holy Land. He got as far as Rochester in Kent, where he was murdered. He was buried in Rochester Cathedral. His tomb gained a reputation for miraculous healing and itself became a pilgrim venue, as a well-worn flight of steps attests today. St William of Perth was canonised in 1256.

David Murray, Earl of Atholl, was a successful crusader but, in 1269, he complained to King Alexander III that, while he was absent abroad, another landowner had invaded Atholl and begun building a castle at Blair. This was John Comyn (or Cumming) of Badenoch, whose family was to play an important role in Scotland's ruinous wars of independence.

10

The First British United Kingdom

In which a little girl's death leads to William Wallace and other tribal
warlords wrecking the Scottish economy in the name of independence

In England the power of the nobles and burghs resulted in the Magna Carta of
1215, limiting the king and establishing greater rights for a parliament consisting
of the great powers in the land. At first the English Parliament met as one assembly.
It did not divide into two Houses, the Lords and the Commons, until 1341.

The first evidence of a Scottish Parliament dates from 1235. Nobles, churchmen
and burghers all met in the same House. Scotland never developed separate
Houses for Lords and Commons. By the end of the thirteenth century, the royal
burghs, including Auchterarder, had the right to send commissioners to the
Scottish Parliament.

Henry III had come to the throne of England as a nine-year-old boy in 1216.
First William the Marshal, then Hubert de Burgh acted as his regent. Hubert,
who was married to Margaret, daughter of the Scottish King William the Lion,
managed to restrain the power of the Church and the barons until Henry III
dismissed him in 1232. From then on, Henry III not only failed to regain the
Norman Empire that his father John had lost, but surrendered more power to the
Church and saw England collapse again into civil war.

Simon de Montfort led a faction of barons, which was successful for a while
until Henry III's son and heir Lord Edward defeated and killed Simon de Montfort
at the Battle of Evesham in 1265. By the time he succeeded to the throne in 1272,
Edward I had a formidable reputation as a soldier and leader.

Edward I was determined to crush any opposition within the British Isles.
In Wales, Llewellyn ap Gruffyd had renounced his homage to the English king
and tried to make Wales an independent kingdom. Edward I repeatedly invaded
Wales until Llewellyn ap Gruffyd was killed in 1282. Edward then made a show
of creating his own son, the future Edward II, Prince of Wales at Carnavon
Castle in 1284. Ever since, the heir to the British throne has been given the title
'Prince of Wales'.

Alexander III inherited the throne of Scotland in 1249 at the age of eight.
Two years later, he married Henry III's daughter Margaret, a dynastic marriage
that brought peace to Scotland in their lifetimes. Alexander III grew up to be
an astute king. In 1263, after an indecisive Battle at Largs against the forces of

King Haakon IV of Norway, a treaty was signed at Perth in 1266, by which the Isle of Man and the Western Isles were handed over to Scotland in exchange for payment. The great age of the Vikings was over.

Alexander III made peace with John Comyn of Badenoch, who controlled the central Highlands. He also divided the troublesome region of Galloway between two rival families, the Bruces and the Balliols.

Peace brought prosperity to Scotland in the mid thirteenth century. Towns grew and trade flourished. The Auchterarder area, long famous for its hunting grounds and stock rearing, thrived. Crops grew on the arable land of the Royal Burgh and fields locally belonging to Inchaffray Abbey. The peasantry were poor and had few rights, but they lived free from the destruction and looting of war.

Robert 4th Earl of Strathearn from 1220–1240 continued his father Gilbert's support of Inchaffray and was a leading figure at the court of Alexander II, witnessing a treaty in 1237 at York between Alexander II and Henry III.

Malise 5th Earl of Strathearn from 1240 to 1271 acquired estates in Angus and Northumberland and was one of Alexander III's regents. When Malise attended Alexander III's coronation at Scone in 1249, he could not know he was witnessing the last coronation in Scotland on the Stone of Destiny. Malise's son, the 6th Earl of Strathearn, also called Malise, was one of the guarantors of the alliance between Scotland and Norway in 1281, sealed by the marriage of Alexander III's daughter Margaret to King Eric II of Norway.

The process of uniting kingdoms in the British Isles had continued since Roman times. During the thirteenth century, Scottish and English landed interests were intertwined. Nine out of the thirteen Scottish earldoms, including Strathearn, owned English land, while seven out of twenty-two English earldoms had Scottish property. Scottish nobles and kings swore fealty (loyalty and obedience) to kings of England for any lands they owned south of the border.

Scottish kings' repeated invasions of Northumbria led to a further degree of submission to England. According to the *Anglo Saxon Chronicle*, King Alfred's son Edward the Elder, by the time he died in 924, was recognised as the overlord of the King of Scots. King Constantine II recognised King Athelstan as his overlord after the Battle of Brunanburh in 937. William the Conqueror forced King Malcolm III to swear allegiance to him at Abernethy in 1071. This was a well-established pattern by 1255, when Henry III of England, 'by the advice of our magnates', including Malise, 5th Earl of Strathearn, wrote to 'our beloved and faithful son' Alexander III, telling him how to govern Scotland.

In 1286, Alexander III was killed in a riding accident at Kinghorn in Fife. In 1173, his grandfather William the Lion had been captured by the English at Alnwick when he fell from his horse. For Alexander III and for the peace of Scotland, his fall was fatal. Alexander had no surviving children. His heir was his three-year-old granddaughter Margaret, the 'Maid of Norway'. She was engaged to Edward, Prince of Wales. Before the dynastic alliance with England could be sealed, Margaret died on board ship on her way to take up the Scottish throne. There was now no clear successor to the Scottish crown.

Thirteen different claimants appeared, among them two deadly rivals from the southwest of Scotland, Robert Bruce and John Balliol, both descended from

David, Earl of Huntingdon, the younger brother of King William the Lion and of Malcolm IV.

'The Guardians', a consortium of Scottish nobles and churchmen, dithered over the various claimants' rights. Edward I of England intervened, claiming the right to select a new Scottish king. Edward could have claimed the Scottish throne himself, as a descendent of Malcolm III Canmore's daughter Matilda, who married Henry I of England.

Instead, Edward preferred to be the feudal overlord of the Scottish king. In 1292, in the presence of Malise, 6th Earl of Strathearn and other Scottish, English and Irish dignitaries, Edward I chose John Balliol.

Earl Malise described himself as a farmer in the royal burgh of Auchterarder when he rendered his accounts to the Scottish exchequer in 1290. More importantly, Strathearn had a feudal link to Huntingdon.

Edward I was both a shrewd constitutional monarch and the inheritor of the Norman warrior spirit. He waged war in Gascony against the French King Philip IV and fought to retain Aquitaine. In 1295, King John Balliol made the mistake of signing a treaty with France, betrothing his son Edward to Philip IV's niece Joanna. To avoid being outflanked by a Franco-Scottish alliance, Edward I summoned 'The Great and Model Parliament', rallying, not only the barons and bishops, but the counties, cities, boroughs and lower clergy to support his cause. The following year, Edward I set out to subdue Scotland. He led an army north. He won a battle at Dunbar in 1296, and marched into Strathearn.

Backed by Malise, Edward quartered his troops at Auchterarder Castle. He then advanced to Scone to remove the Stone of Destiny, on which generations of Pictish and Scottish kings had been crowned. He placed it under the coronation chair in Westminster Abbey to mark his authority over Scotland. It remained till St Andrew's Day 1996, when a Conservative government, desperate for Scottish votes, placed it symbolically in Edinburgh Castle, only to lose the next election.

Scotland disintegrated into civil war. Edward imprisoned John Balliol in England, then sent him to Normandy, far from Scotland. Scottish tribal warlords seized their opportunities, especially William Wallace, from southwest Scotland, an area occupied by Welsh speakers in the early Middle Ages. The name Wallace means 'Welsh', just as Inglis means 'English'. While Edward I fought the French in Flanders, Wallace rallied an anti-English campaign. He defeated an army led by the Earl of Surrey at the Battle of Stirling Bridge in 1297.

Edward responded by personally leading an army into central Scotland and routing Wallace's forces at the Battle of Falkirk in 1298. Sir John Graham whose family owned Kincardine Castle, on the south side of Auchterarder, was killed in the battle. He had been one of Wallace's key allies and, like his great seventeenth-century kinsman James Graham, 1st Marquis of Montrose, a man famous for personal integrity and a brilliant military strategist.

The 1995 Hollywood film *Braveheart*, with its comic-book xenophobia, exploits Wallace to reinforce the myth of a crude north–south division of Britain. It was never that simple. *Braveheart* does, however, manipulate symbols to great emotional effect and has become a useful political invocation of national pride.

John Balliol's kingship had collapsed in 1296, but the title to the Scottish throne was no clearer. The Bruces, hoping to secure the crown, at first fought for Edward I against the Balliol faction. The Bruces, however, thought they could rally public opinion by asserting the idea of an independent Scotland. Edward I did not. He saw the Scottish kingship as his to grant as feudal superior.

Civil war destabilised the agricultural economy of the Auchterarder area. In 1303 Edward I regained Gascony. He could now concentrate on Scotland. His army took Stirling in 1304. Wallace was captured and taken to London for execution in 1305.

In February 1306, Robert Bruce, grandson of the Bruce who had claimed the crown in 1286, killed John 'The Red' Comyn, Lord of Badenoch, one of King John Balliol's leading supporters. Robert Bruce had himself crowned King of Scotland at Scone in April 1306, despite the fact that the Stone of Destiny was far away in Westminster Abbey. Within the year, Robert Bruce was defeated at the Battle of Methven, west of Perth, by a mainly English army led by Aylmer de Valence. Bruce fled and hid in his home territory in southwest Scotland. Edward I still regarded his prisoner John Balliol as king of Scotland.

Political boundaries kept shifting. So did opportunists. In 1304 Sir Malcolm Innerpeffray was Sheriff of Auchterarder. He was also Sheriff of Clackmannan, creating a political entity that joined both sides of the Ochils. This geographical oddity was not repeated until the twenty-first century when a Labour government changed constituency boundaries, joining Strathearn to Clackmannan to create a winnable seat in Westminster. Sir Malcolm Innerpeffray, though he owed his appointments to Edward I, switched sides and supported Robert Bruce.

In Auchterarder, the question in the fourteenth century, as in the twenty-first, was which political faction offered the best prospects for peace and prosperity? Malise 7th Earl of Strathearn vacillated between supporting Balliol, Bruce or Edward I. The English eventually tried him for treason in Westminster. He was acquitted, returned to Scotland and is buried in Inchaffray.

Edward I died in 1307. The new English King Edward II was weak and had military distractions in France. Robert Bruce reasserted his kingship and became more able to impose his authority. When David of Strathbogie, 11th Earl of Atholl, refused to support him, Bruce seized the Atholl estates for the Scottish crown. Bruce fought a war of attrition. Slowly he subdued the areas where John Balliol had most support, the central Highlands dominated by the Comyns, Argyll and Balliol's own homeland of Galloway. In 1313, John Balliol died, leaving Robert Bruce as the only King of Scotland. The same year, Sir William Mountfichet or Montifex, Governor of Dundee and loyal to King Edward II, was forced to surrender the city to Edward Bruce, brother of King Robert.

As it had been to centuries of invading armies before, the corridor through Strathearn was a key to controlling Scotland. King Robert gathered his forces at Stirling. On 24 June 1314, Maurice, Abbot of Inchaffray, backed him, saying mass for his troops before King Robert faced Edward II's army, which consisted of both English and Scots, at the Battle of Bannockburn. King Robert won and gave Maurice the Bishopric of Dunblane. Robert tried to build on his victory. His brother Edward became High King of Ireland in 1316, but was killed at the Battle of Dundalk in 1318.

Scotland's stability after Bannockburn was short-lived. In 1318 Pope John XXII excommunicated King Robert, citing his persistent attacks on what the Church saw as lawful English overlordship. In 1320 the Scottish Parliament sent a letter, The Declaration of Arbroath, to the Pope, claiming that Scotland had always been an independent nation and giving a long, mainly mythical, list of ancient kings.

Without the blessing of the Church, Bruce's kingship lacked a crucial symbol of authority. The Pope wrote back, exhorting the Scots and English to make peace. It was a pious hope. Even in the twenty-first century, Scottish nationalists drag up the Declaration of Arbroath as an anti-English totem whenever something goes wrong in Scotland. Bruce was a charismatic leader and kept the English at bay during his reign, but his diplomatic legacy was a failure. His expensive wars left Scotland in poverty and insecurity.

Sir William Montifex switched to supporting King Robert Bruce and was appointed Justiciar of Scotland. In 1328 he was given the Barony of Auchterarder, which had belonged to the Scottish crown since the time of Malcolm III Canmore. As a balance to Montifex's new power as baron, Bruce reserved for the town itself the liberties of the Royal Burgh of Auchterarder 'as they were in the days of King Alexander III'.

As baron of Auchterarder, Sir William Montifex had to provide half the services of a knight for Bruce's army. Since Bruce was constantly fighting the English at home and away in Scotland, England and Ireland, it was just as well for Sir William's purse that Bruce died in 1329.

When Bruce died, his five-year-old son David II succeeded him. The old rivalries for the Scottish throne broke out again. In 1332, John Balliol's son Edward won the Battle of Dupplin, near the old Pictish capital of Forteviot, defeating the armies of David II's regent Donald, Earl of Mar, which had been camped at Auchterarder.

Edward Balliol was crowned King of Scotland in Scone, without the Stone of Destiny. Once again, there were two simultaneous kings of Scotland. Auchterarder, set on a strategic ridge between the Bruce-dominated south and Edward Balliol's stronghold of Perth, was again caught up in civil war.

It was not the last time that Auchterarder was to suffer from civil war and Earls of Mar. Four centuries later, another Earl of Mar, known as 'Bobbing John' for his creepy sycophancy and attempts at opportunism, was responsible for the greatest disaster in Auchterarder's history. He gave the order to burn the town on 17 January 1716, while his Jacobite army lingered in Strathearn after retreating from the Battle of Sheriffmuir two months earlier.

Practical questions about a British United Kingdom were never so much about the constitutional niceties of Scots swearing allegiance, as about England's protecting itself from cross-channel invasion. In the eighteenth, just as in the fourteenth century, whenever unstable Scottish leaders intrigued with France, a violent English reaction was guaranteed.

11

The Great Mediaeval Families of Central Scotland

*In which we meet the ferocious armoured ancestors
of today's amiable tweed-jacketed lairds*

Edward II's reign brought violent instability to England. His gay favourite Piers Gaveston rose to power then fell foul of the king's cousin Thomas Earl of Lancaster, who had him executed. The Battle of Bannockburn in 1314 was a humiliation for England and Lancaster was suspected of dealing with the Scots. Lancaster himself was executed as the king's party, led by the Despenser family from South Wales, regained power. Queen Isabella left Edward II and fled to France with her lover, Roger Mortimer, and her son, the future Edward III.

In 1326, as Edward II's rule became more cruel, greedy and arbitrary, Isabella and Mortimer returned to England. The leading Despensers were murdered. Edward II was imprisoned and then disappeared, probably murdered in Berkley Castle in 1327.

Edward III came to the throne of an England that was divided. It was soon in danger of losing its remaining possessions in Europe, when King Philip VI of France, first of the Valois dynasty, came to the throne in 1328. The two monarchs fought for the control of Flanders, whose cloth industry had brought riches to the English wool trade.

After the Battle of Dupplin in 1332, King Edward Balliol retained precarious power in the Auchterarder area. Balliol tried to seize the lands of Malise 8th Earl of Strathearn. He awarded them to John de Warenne, Earl of Surrey, successor to the Earl of Surrey whom Wallace had defeated at Stirling Bridge in 1297. Now there were two rival Kings of Scotland and two rival Earls of Strathearn.

Malise, descended from Pictish warlords, did not give up easily. The Earl of Surrey was never able to take possession of Strathearn, even when Edward Balliol's rival for the Scottish crown, Robert Bruce's son, David II, retreated to Normandy in 1334. The French King Philip VI helped David establish a Scots Court in exile at Château Gaillard.

In 1335, Edward III and Edward Balliol occupied Perth with a huge army. Edward Balliol remained in Scotland, while Edward III headed south. The same year, plague ravaged Perth and its surroundings. The economy of Auchterarder struggled to survive amid war and disease. Crops were destroyed and people starved. The chronicler Andrew Wyntoun says there were episodes of cannibalism around Perth.

In 1337, the Hundred Years War broke out between England and France. David II's government in exile arranged for French pirates to blockade the River Tay in 1338, cutting off Edward Balliol's garrison in Perth from supplies by sea. The impoverished agricultural heartland of Auchterarder could provide nothing for Edward Balliol and, in any case, it was now controlled by Robert the Steward, David II's nephew.

Robert besieged Perth and destroyed its walls but within a year a Scottish parliament met there. The Hundred Years War and the Scottish civil war dragged on.

In 1340, Edward III won the naval Battle of Sluys, mainly because of the skill of his English archers who were becoming a potent military force. In 1346, at the Battle of Crecy, English archers again won the day, decimating the charges of heavily armoured French cavalry.

In 1340, King David II fought in Flanders alongside the French King Philip VI. The following year David II returned to Scotland. He was yet another Scottish king who thought a distracted England might make an easy target. In 1346, he invaded but was defeated at the Battle of Neville's Cross, near Durham. Maurice Moray, 9th Earl of Strathearn, was killed. His friend, John Graham, Earl of Menteith, was captured and taken to London, where he was hung, drawn and quartered.

David II was captured too. For eleven years, he remained Edward III's prisoner and swore loyalty to the English king. The accounts of the Great Chamberlain for 1366 show that The Burgh of Auchterarder still owed thirty-one shillings as a contribution to the King's ransom. It appears to have taken eight more years for Auchterarder to pay up.

Since Maurice Murray (or Moray) left no heir, the Earldom of Strathearn was given to David II's nephew, Robert the Steward, who ran the captive king's affairs in Scotland. Robert was the son of Robert Bruce's daughter Marjory and Walter the Steward, an able ally who had fought alongside Bruce at Bannockburn in 1314.

In 1348, an epidemic of bubonic plague, The Black Death, swept through England, killing so many people that there was an immediate shortage of agricultural labourers and soldiers. The epidemic was much less widespread once it reached Scotland. In characteristic xenophobic fashion, Scots referred to the plague as 'the foul death of the English'.

While David II's power increased, Scotland's other king, Edward Balliol, ran out of power and money. He retired in 1356 with a pay-off from the English King Edward III. In the same year, Edward III's son, also called Edward, but better known as 'The Black Prince' because of the colour of his armour, won a decisive victory over the French at the Battle of Poitiers. The new French King John and his son Philip, later known as Philip the Bold of Burgundy, were captured.

By the Peace of Bretigny in 1360, Edward was acknowledged as the overlord of Calais, Ponthieu and Guines in Northern France and of Guienne, Gascony,

Poitou and Santonge in the South. His son, the Black Prince, was Duke of Aquitaine. In exchange, Edward III gave up claims to other parts of France north of the Loire and returned King John in exchange for a ransom.

King David II of Scotland died in 1371. Robert the Steward, Earl of Strathearn, succeeded him in 1371 as King Robert II, first of the charismatic, unstable Stewart dynasty. In an echo of Pictish Fortriu, the Earl of Strathearn was now king of Scotland. In 2011, Queen Elizabeth II made her elder grandson Prince William Earl of Strathearn. In due course, he is expected to become king, not only of Scotland, but of the United Kingdom of Scotland, England, Ireland and Wales, unless the two-thousand-year-long trend of British unification is reversed.

Auchterarder entered a phase of comparative peace. Local people adapted their skills to suit market demand. Since the Iron Age, Auchterarder had been a centre for metal craftwork. In the Middle Ages, chain mail, strong, flexible and made by mailers, gave an advantage to fighting men. The Auchterarder Mailer family remains today, owning modern skilled trade businesses.

The Auchterarder area's main industry was agriculture, particularly cattle farming and associated trades. Cowhides were valuable raw material for footwear, saddles and leather jerkins that could deflect the thrust of a blade. Calfskins were used for delicate products, especially vellum on which both Church and state depended for writing documents. It would be another hundred years before paper, a Chinese invention, became readily available in Scotland.

The Auchterarder shoe-making industry lasted until the twentieth century, notably in the hands of the Mallis family, an echo of the Malise earls of Strathearn. Wool was also an important local product, exported to Bruges in Flanders. The fertile Auchterarder area was good for production, but lacking in efficient transport to the nearest port, Perth. There was no nearby bridge over the River Earn. Pack horses had to plod the long Pictish route via Dunning and Forteviot to Bridge of Earn. The alternative was to use expensive water transport down the Earn, which could be shallow and marshy in summer and a raging torrent in winter.

Throughout the Middle Ages, the most prominent buildings in the Royal Burgh of Auchterarder were the castle, set on the northwest side of the ridge, and St Mackessog's Church, down by the Kirkton. The commercial centre was near where the Aytoun Hall stands today. Older townspeople still call it 'The Cross', though there has been no standing cross or crossroads here for a hundred and forty years. In the Middle Ages, there was an open square with Chapel Wynd running alongside the market place and a small chapel. Merchants' houses with storerooms grew up beside the market place. Tenants of the barons and the Abbey of Inchaffray lived in small houses with long rigs of land, running back from the High Street. There was a Tollbooth and a tron for weighing goods.

In the Middle Ages, much of the land in Strathearn was owned by a few great families who still have a presence in the twenty-first century. After Malise, 8th and last Pictish Earl of Strathearn, died in 1333, the title passed to the Murrays, then the Stewarts, then the Grahams, families with many branches who waxed and waned over the centuries, according to the political shrewdness of each generation.

Depending on the wording of each Act of Parliament creating a title, some hereditary peerages can be held only by males, a nonsense which still persists. The Earldom of Strathearn, however, could be held by a woman. When King Robert II's son, David, 11th Earl of Strathearn died in 1389, his daughter Euphemia became Countess Palatine of Strathearn in her own right.

Countess Euphemia was named after her grandmother, Robert II's queen. She married her cousin Sir Patrick Graham who succeeded as 12th Earl when she died in 1406. In 1413, their son Malise became 13th Earl of Strathearn when Patrick was killed by his brother-in-law Sir John Drummond.

Grahams, Drummonds and Murrays intermarried and fought throughout the Middle Ages, forming complex land-owning dynasties.

The Murrays are descended from Pictish warlords who ruled as The Mormaers (Stewards) of Moray in Northern Scotland, most famous of whom was Macbeth, King of Scotland from 1040 to 1058. Confusingly, in the Middle Ages, they were known as 'de Moravia', not because they came from Slovakia, but because 'de Moravia' is a clumsy legal Latin way of saying 'of Moray'. In the mid twelfth century, Kind David I granted lands in West Lothian to Freskin de Moravia. The Murrays' land-holdings in southern Scotland were enlarged by his grandson, William, from whom the Murrays of Tullibardine are descended.

The Murrays founded the powerful House of Atholl. In 1284, Sir William Murray became the first Laird of Tullibardine. In the Middle Ages, these lands in fertile Strathearn complemented the Murrays' chief Highland powerbase in the north of Perthshire. Andrew Murray of Tullibardine granted an annuity to Inchaffray Abbey and supported King Edward Balliol. David II's allies captured him in Perth in 1332 and executed him for treason. Today, the heir to the Dukedom of Atholl carries the title Marquess of Tullibardine. In 1446, Sir David Murray built Tullibardine Chapel, which remains the best-preserved mediaeval building in the area.

The Drummond family was founded by Maurice, grandson of Andrew, King of Hungary. In 1069, Maurice accompanied Margaret, future wife of Malcolm III Canmore, to Scotland. Malcolm granted him lands in Stirlingshire and Dumbarton. In 1315, after the Drummonds had supported King Robert Bruce at Bannockburn, Sir Malcolm Drummond was granted lands in Perthshire, including the present Drummond Estate near Muthill.

Robert Bruce's son, King David II took Margaret Drummond as his mistress. Her married name was Lady Margaret Logie. The King was married to Princess Joan of England. When their respective spouses died, King David II made Margaret his queen 'by force of love which conquers everything' as the *Scalachronica* puts it, only to divorce her in 1369 when she failed to produce an heir.

In a foreshadowing of the English King Henry VIII's divorce two hundred years later, which led to the Reformation of the Church in Britain, Queen Margaret persuaded Pope Gregory XI to threaten to place Scotland under an interdict. David II died in 1371 before the threat could be carried out.

The Grahams are probably descended from Normans who arrived in England with King William I the Conqueror in 1066 and sought their fortunes further north. William de Graham witnessed the foundation charter of Holyrood Abbey in Edinburgh in 1128. His elder son, Peter, acquired lands in the Borders. His younger son, Alan, was grandfather of Sir David Graham, who built Kincardine Castle about 1250, after receiving its lands as a dowry on marrying Amabil, daughter of Malise 5th Earl of Strathearn.

Sir John Graham became one of William Wallace's closest allies. He was killed at the Battle of Falkirk in 1298 and buried with the inscription *Mente Manuque Potens, Conditus Hic Gramus* (Here lies Graham, powerful in mind and hand).

Wars divide families. Another Graham, Sir David, backed John Balliol, King Edward I's choice for king of Scotland. In 1299 at Selkirk, a fight broke out after Sir David asked to take over William Wallace's lands, because Wallace's troops were rampaging out of control of The Guardians, appointed to run the kingdom. David Graham and Wallace's brother, Malcolm, attacked one another with knives. John 'The Red' Comyn grabbed Robert Bruce by the throat until other nobles broke up the fight.

Over the Ochils, above Dollar (from *douleur* or gloom) sat Castle Campbell, built in the fifteenth century by the Grahams' deadliest enemies. The Campbells (from *Caim Beul* or 'crooked mouth') came from Argyll before the Norman Conquest.

The Campbells were noted for their stealthy attacks. On one occasion, they tried to raid the Kincardine Estate just as the Grahams were sitting down to dinner in the Castle. The skirmish gave rise to the local saying 'Ye'll get Grahams' grace', as a warning of disruption to a meal. The saying fell into disuse in the late twentieth century, becoming irrelevant when most families ceased dining together and adopted fragmentary eating patterns.

The Grahams, Murrays and Drummonds were all to have ambivalent relationships with the Stewart monarchy, sometimes as ardent supporters, sometimes as angry opponents.

These four great families were neatly summed up in a later prayer:

From the pride of the Grahams,
The guile/greed of the Campbells,
The ire of the Drummonds,
And the wind of the Murrays,
Great God deliver us.

Other distinguished families of Norman origin have remained in the Auchterarder area. To the east of Auchterarder, Richard Rollo was granted land in the old Pictish Thanage of Dunning in the twelfth century by King David I. The Rollos received a charter for Duncrub in 1380 which they kept until the 1950s. They still retain the nearby Pitcairns.

The Oliphants owned land near the Earn, granted to them after David Olifard or Oliphant helped King David I escape from the Battle of Winchester in 1141. Sir William Oliphant of Gask became governor of Stirling Castle, which he defended in 1304 for three months against the armies of Edward I. He then switched sides and defended Perth on behalf of Edward II in 1313.

At about the same time, Sir Roger de Hauden (Haldane) founded the Gleneagles

Estate. Gleneagles Castle was built shortly afterwards. Its ruins remain today. By the fifteenth century a Haldane, Sir John, had risen to become Lord Justice-General of Scotland.

In Pictish times, the Auchterarder area had many hill forts, consisting of wooden structures and defensive earthworks. The Norman era brought stone strongholds, dominating the landscape: Malcom III's Auchterarder Castle was followed by the Grahams' Kincardine Castle, the Murrays' Tullibardine Castle and the Haldanes' Gleneagles Castle. To the northwest lay the great Drummond Castle, to the southwest Ogilvie Castle near Blackford, another Graham site, and later to the south through Gleneagles and Glendevon, the gloomy Castle Campbell. All these families developed new properties in the area over the following centuries.

Local farmers had their territorial ambitions too. A royal charter of 1362 settled a wrangle over land between William Fenton and Alexander Chisholm, names that still recur in the Auchterarder area. By the time of the Battle of Bannockburn in 1314, much of today's social structure of Strathearn was already in place.

12

The Death of Chivalry

*In which we see romantic notions on horseback, reality
on foot and a local girl become Queen of Scotland*

Ever since 1070, when King Malcolm III married Queen Margaret, the Scottish court followed the cultural fashions of Europe, particularly of France. The blustering nationalism of the 1320 Declaration of Arbroath was about political self-determination, not cultural identity.

All political systems need an ethical code to give them moral authority. For the feudal system in Europe in the Middle Ages, that code was chivalry. It emphasised honour, comradeship, respect for one's leader and duty to fight. The *Chanson de Roland*, written in France about 1100, romanticised Charlemagne's imperial battles. In the later twelfth century, Chrétien de Troyes wove legends round the semi-mythical King Arthur and the Holy Grail. The code and the legends resonate today in Christian versus Islamic warfare, the global best-selling novel *The Da Vinci Code* by Dan Brown, and the ways of the Mafia.

In fourteenth-century Scotland, the paradoxes of chivalry made it possible to admire the English King Edward III and his sons Edward the Black Prince and John of Gaunt as the embodiments of warrior chivalry, but to conspire and fight against them. In 1365 Jean Froissart, the great French chronicler was welcomed at the Scottish court where King David II had imported yet more European ways after his exile at Château Gaillard and captivity in England.

Inevitably, Scotland produced its own chivalric warrior legend. John Barbour, Archdeacon of Aberdeen, wrote *The Bruce* around 1375, early in the reign of King Robert II. It glorified the deeds of his ancestor namesake King Robert I.

The Hundred Years War began to go badly for England. In 1372 the English fleet was defeated at La Rochelle and lost control of the English Channel. Edward the Black Prince died in 1376. His father Edward III died in 1377. The Black Prince's ten-year-old son became King Richard II, despite opposition from his uncle John of Gaunt who wanted the throne for himself.

John of Gaunt remained a powerful political force until the Peasants' Revolt exploded in England in 1381. There had been an ever-increasing divide between rich and poor. Resentment grew against exploitative clergy, greedy businessmen and oppressive landlords. In 1380 a poll tax was imposed 'on every lay person in the realm except beggars'. To charge rich and poor exactly the same amount

of tax usually provokes revolt. Six hundred years later, British Prime Minister
Margaret Thatcher began to fall from power when she imposed a poll tax.

In 1381 the poll tax provoked violent demonstrations, led to a much stronger
House of Commons and caused John of Gaunt to flee when a mob torched his
Savoy Palace in London. He escaped to Edinburgh and took refuge in Holyrood
until the Peasants' Revolt was over.

Robert II was fifty-five, an old man by the standards of the day, when he
succeeded his uncle David II in 1371. King Robert II promptly passed his Earldom
of Strathearn to his son, David. It was a shrewd move that helped secure stability
in mid Scotland. By 1377 the neighbouring Earldoms of Menteith, Atholl and
Fife were all controlled by the royal family.

Robert II was the son of Robert the Bruce's daughter Marjory who had
married a senior official, Walter, the sixth hereditary Steward of Scotland.
Robert II took his father's title as the royal family name, spelled it Stewart and
founded a dynasty.

There was social mobility in Robert II's reign, especially when money and
title were attracted to one another. John Mercer, a rich merchant burgess of
Perth, married a Murray of Tullibardine and rose to become Chamberlain of
Scotland. In 1376 John Mercer was shipwrecked on the Northumberland coast.
He was captured and held to ransom in Scarborough Castle, provoking a naval
raid by his son Andrew and retaliation by a London merchant named Philpott,
who captured Andrew Mercer's fleet.

The 1380s saw a series of battles between Scottish and English armies in the
debatable lands of the Borders. In 1384, John of Gaunt besieged Edinburgh but,
chivalrously recalling how he had been given refuge there only three years before,
he did not sack the town but merely held it to ransom. In 1385 a bungled Franco-
Scottish joint military enterprise led to the looting of the rich Border Abbeys
Melrose, Dryborough and Newbattle. St Giles in Edinburgh was also burned.

While war raged in southern Scotland, the Auchterarder area enjoyed relative
peace. Robert II died in 1390, succeeded by his son Robert III whose Queen
Annabella was closely linked to the Barony of Auchterarder. The crown owned
the Castle and Barony of Auchterarder until in 1328 King Robert Bruce granted
them to Sir William de Montfichet or Montifex, Justiciar of Scotland. In 1360,
Sir William Montifex's eldest daughter, Maria, married Sir John Drummond,
7th Thane of Lennox, who was given the Barony of Auchterarder, Cargill and
Kincardine in Menteith as his dowry.

Separate from the Barony of Auchterarder was the Common Muir, extending
west from the town to today's junction with the A9 and north to include the
White Muir towards Blackford. Because of Auchterarder's Royal Burgh status,
all this land was for the use of the townspeople as pasture for animals, peat
cutting and recreation.

Local townspeople have tried to guard their rights to the Common Muir
ever since. Neighbouring landowners have tried to grab the land. In the early
nineteenth century, the lairds of Strathallan, Kincardine Castle and Abercairney
combined to appropriate the Western Commonty where the privately owned
Gleneagles Hotel and golf courses stand today. The Eastern Commonty was

successfully saved for the town. Today's Auchterarder's Common Good Fund derives much of its income from the town's own Golf Course, built on the Eastern Common Muir. In Maria Montifex's day, archery and football were more likely recreations.

Annabella, eldest daughter of Maria Montifex and Sir John Drummond, married King Robert III. They were crowned King and Queen of Scotland at Scone in 1390. Our present Queen Elizabeth II is descended, on her father's side, from Maria Montifex of Auchterarder Castle.

Queen Elizabeth II is also descended from a local family on her mother's side. John Lyon of Forteviot married Joanna, daughter of King Robert II, in 1376. John Lyon became Chamberlain of Scotland and Thane of Glamis. Six centuries later in 1923, his descendant Elizabeth Bowes Lyon of Glamis married the future King George VI. Their first child, born 1926, became today's Queen of the Commonwealth of Nations.

Neither Richard II of England nor Robert III of Scotland had the warrior audacity of their namesake predecessors Richard I the Lionheart and Robert Bruce. Richard II had a volatile political relationship with his uncle John of Gaunt, founder of the House of Lancaster, whose symbol is a red rose. Richard also sought to weaken Parliament by delegating its powers to a small council of cronies. Naturally, a rival faction grew.

When John of Gaunt died in 1399, his son deposed Richard II and had himself crowned King Henry IV. The new king's cousin Roger Mortimer had as good a claim, if not better, to the throne. Roger Mortimer's heirs founded the House of York, whose symbol is a white rose. The Lancaster versus York conflict evolved into the Wars of the Roses. Even today the fierce rivalry, when the Yorkshire versus Lancashire county cricket teams meet, is called 'The Roses Match'.

Richard II died in captivity in Yorkshire in 1399. His body was taken to London and displayed. In 1400 Henry IV invaded southern Scotland but 'out of respect for Queen Annabella' did not lay it waste, according to the chronicler Walter Bower. For many years, Richard was rumoured to be alive and living in Scotland, plotting a fight-back in alliance with the Scots and French. As late as 1417, the Duke of Albany said he was funding 'King Richard of England', a claim angrily refuted by Henry IV.

In Scotland, Robert III tried to buy off baronial revolts by offering retaining fees, a sort of heritable pension. The result was to drain the Treasury without ensuring loyalty. Robert III's brother Alexander Earl of Buchan, known as The Wolf of Badenoch, ran his part of Scotland as he pleased. Donald, Lord of the Isles, also operated largely beyond the control of King or Parliament.

Queen Annabella was widely admired for her cultivated tastes. She brought an inheritance of love of poetry, music and dancing to the Stewart dynasty. She died in 1401, mourned as the wise wife of a weak king.

In 1406, her six-year-old son, the future King James I, was on his way to France when he was captured by English pirates and handed over to the English King Henry IV. King Robert died less than a month later. James I was a prisoner of the English monarchy for eighteen years, seven years longer than his predecessor, King David II. King John Balliol was a prisoner for seventeen years.

While James I was kept in England, his uncle Robert, Duke of Albany, acted as regent. War between English and Scots broke out again in the Borders, complicated by the powerful Earl of Northumberland's revolt against Henry IV. In Wales, Owen Glendower led a nationalist rebellion and called himself the Prince of Wales, a title reserved for the heir to the English throne.

Henry IV responded by crushing the Earl of Northumberland in 1408 at Bramham Moor. He sent his son, the future Henry V, whom he regarded as the real Prince of Wales, to seize Welsh castles and force Owen Glendower to flee.

Fortunately for Henry IV's stretched resources, France was in no position to pursue a unified attack on England in the Hundred Years War. The French King Charles VI had become mentally ill. Warring factions, the Orleanists and the Burgundians, sought control of his realm.

The word 'chivalry' comes from the French *cheval*, meaning 'a horse'. The knight on horseback was the epitome of mediaeval warfare, run by kings and nobles for their own benefit. Although cavalry regiments remained until the twentieth century, the fifteenth century saw a potent new type of soldier emerge: foot soldiers armed with powerful longbows. In Scotland, the heroic notion of the king on horseback endured until the eighteenth century when the disastrous Bonnie Prince Charlie, called 'The Young Chevalier', by his romantic supporters, ended the tradition.

Henry IV died in 1413. His son Henry V tried to reclaim the European Empire that had been long lost to England. He went even further and claimed the French crown. In 1415, his well trained archers routed a huge French army at Agincourt. By 1420, he had conquered Normandy and allied with the Burgundians. He concluded the Treaty of Troyes by which he was to act as regent for the remaining lifetime of the mad King Charles VI and then to succeed him as King of France.

Henry married a French princess, Catharine de Valois. In 1421 a son and heir was born, also called Henry. The political divisions of France meant that Henry V always knew he would have to rely on military might to enforce the terms of the Treaty of Troyes.

European religious politics were divided as well. In 1377, the Church split in The Great Schism. For the next forty years, rival Church grandees set themselves up in Rome, Avignon in the south of France, and elsewhere, claiming to be the true Pope and inheritor of the keys of St Peter.

In Scotland, there was a muddle over which Pope to support. As the Declaration of Arbroath in 1320 had shown, Scottish kings and institutions begged Papal endorsement for their constitutional legitimacy. By the time Scotland's first university was founded in the historic religious town of St Andrews, the schism had not been resolved. A group of masters, mainly graduates of the University of Paris, established a school in St Andrews in 1410. It was chartered as a university in 1413 by Pedro de Luna, Pope Benedict XIII, who lived in Peñiscola Castle in Aragon on the Iberian peninsula, ignored by most of the Christian world.

A Council of churchmen was called at Constance in Switzerland in 1414 to try to heal the Great Schism. Like many a pan-European bureaucratic institution, it took a long time to arrive at a conclusion. In 1417, the Council of Constance elected a new Pope Martin V, acceptable to all of Europe, except for Armagnac, Peñiscola and Scotland.

The Duke of Albany defended Benedict XIII, employing Franciscan scholar Robert Harding to argue his case at a Scottish Parliament in Perth. Harding used an elaborate metaphor in which the Church was a huge fallen elephant that required the little elephant of the Scottish Church to help it to its feet. The influential Parisian-educated masters of St Andrews were unimpressed. They turned and bit the hand that had fed them their charter. Albany accepted the inevitable and sent a delegation to acknowledge Pope Martin V. Albany died in 1320, aged over eighty, a remarkable political survivor.

Meantime, the Scots King James I's captivity in England was not too onerous. Aeneas Sylvius, who became Pope Pius II, described him as 'thick-set and oppressed by much fat'. He wrote erudite poetry, *The Kingis Quair* (The King's Book). On St George's Day, 23 April, 1421, Henry V knighted James I and awarded him the prestigious Order of the Garter.

Had Henry V become universally recognised as King of France, a Franco-Scottish relationship would have been no threat to England. It was not to be. When Henry V contracted dysentery and died in 1422, James I accompanied his funeral procession between the cathedrals of Rouen and Westminster.

Henry VI was only one year old when he inherited the English throne in 1422. The mad King Charles VI of France died in the same year, leaving a nineteen-year-old son, the Dauphin Charles. Which boy would be crowned King of France? Henry VI's uncle John, Duke of Bedford, acted as his regent in France, but English resources were stretched on too many frontiers. To raise funds, the captive James I was restored to Scotland in 1424 in exchange for a huge ransom plus 27 noble hostages. It did not bring Anglo-Scottish peace. Scots knights went to France to fight against the English.

In 1429, there arose a tide of French nationalism, driven by a seventeen-year-old girl, Joan of Arc, who claimed divine inspiration, with visions of St Michael and other angels. She led a charge of French knights to relieve the besieged city of Orleans, then accompanied the Dauphin to Reims, where he was crowned King Charles VII. Soon after, Joan of Arc was captured by England's Burgundian allies. She was handed over to the English authorities in Rouen and burned as a heretic. Ever since, she has been the warrior-martyr symbol of France.

James I had married Joan of Beaufort, granddaughter of John of Gaunt by his mistress Catharine Swynford. The Beauforts had become powerful political figures, sensitive about their illegitimacy. Marriage to a king was a political coup. Henry Beaufort, Bishop of Winchester, led a peace party in England, but the Hundred Years War dragged on. After Bedford died in 1435, his younger brother Humphrey, Duke of Gloucester and the Governor of Normandy, Richard, Duke of York, battled on, despite losing the support of Burgundy. The English King Henry VI's claim to the French throne looked less and less enforceable.

In 1436, King James I's daughter Margaret, aged eleven, married Louis, the thirteen-year-old Dauphin of France and future King Louis XI. This new Franco-Scottish dynastic marriage provoked more fighting on the Scottish–English border. Margaret, like her father and grandmother Annabella, loved music and wrote poetry. She was obsessed with being slim and elegant. She died in 1445 without bearing Louis an heir.

One of the noble hostages, traded to the English in 1424 in exchange for releasing King James I, was Malise Graham, 13th Earl of Strathearn. James then changed the rules. He appointed his own uncle Walter Stewart, brother of David the 11th Earl, to be 14th Earl of Strathearn in 1427 and gave Malise a reduced Earldom of Menteith instead.

The Grahams were furious. Malise's uncle, Sir Robert Graham, denounced James I in parliament for his cynical abuse of the Scottish people, physically attacked him, then fled to 'the wild countries of the Scots'. The King expected the new Earl Walter to support him. Instead, Earl Walter sided with the Grahams against the king. In 1437, with other aggrieved nobles, Robert Graham intercepted James who was celebrating an extended 'solemn feast of Christmas' with cronies in the Dominican Friary of Perth. The fat king hid in a sewer. He was caught and killed. Earl Walter and Sir Robert Graham were soon captured, tortured and executed. The deprived Earl Malise lived until 1492.

King James I had been fond of Perth. He held many parliaments there, and founded a Carthusian monastery, the last great Scottish monastery of the Middle Ages. He also petitioned the Pope to grant a charter, transferring Scotland's university to Perth, away from the doctrinally fractious St Andrews. Nothing happened. Today St Andrews has a thriving university. Perth has never had enough political influence to acquire a university of its own.

In the years before his death, James I's Parliament, including commissioners from Auchterarder, introduced a host of new laws. They ranged from the environmental – rooks' nests and wolves should be destroyed and fish nets should have a mesh of at least three inches in fresh water – to the sartorial – in royal burghs, only aldermen, bailies and councillors were allowed to wear furs. Parliament also banned football, but encouraged archery with a programme of setting up archery butts near parish kirks. Burgesses were made responsible for providing inns and for creating fire-brigades. Brothels, considered particularly combustible, had to be located only at the town edge.

Amid the wheeling-dealing of powerful landed families, Auchterarder remained one of Scotland's smallest royal burghs. It had little political power in its own right, largely because it lacked a port and the foreign trade revenues which the crown valued. Auchterarder Castle was expensive to maintain. Nobody took responsibility for modernising it.

In contrast, the astute Bishop Michael Ochiltree of Dunblane had a bridge built about 1430 to allow pack horses to cross the River Knaik near the old Roman Camp at Ardoch. He built another bridge across the Machany Water near Muthill, also to provide better transport links across his diocese. It is still called Bishop's Bridge. Around Auchterarder, most roads remained poor until the nineteenth century.

In the later Middle Ages, as now, some local people moved to bigger towns to find better jobs. In 1373, Thomas of Strathearn became Master of the Royal Mint in Perth. Exchequer Rolls of the period show that the King earned six times more from coinage made at the Perth Mint than from his Edinburgh Mint.

13

The End of the Middle Ages

*In which kings die violent deaths but Strathearn
is the comparatively peaceful eye of the storm*

The Hundred Years War entered its final phase in 1445, when King Henry VI of England married Margaret of Anjou, hoping to secure Normandy and Guienne, but give up Anjou and Maine. It was not to be. Richard, Duke of York, and Humphrey, Duke of Gloucester, lacked the resources to fight against a resurgent France. Humphrey saw his wife Eleanor condemned for witchcraft in an eerie counterpart to the condemnation of Joan of Arc.

In an age when religious authority was powerful but divided, the burning of heretics and witches made a public show of whichever power prevailed locally. In Perth in 1405, John Resby, an English preacher, was burned for expressing his anti-papal opinions.

Gloucester died in Calais in 1447 in suspicious circumstances. The English peace party, led by Henry VI's Queen Margaret of Anjou, the Beauforts and John de la Pole, Duke of Suffolk, was suspected of arranging his murder. By 1453, all that remained of England's European empire was the port of Calais.

Margaret was seen as responsible for stirring up the French and Scots against England. Her heraldic badge, the swan, suited her well: elegant, greedy and violent. Her husband, King Henry VI, was pious and weak. England divided under two more heraldic badges, Henry's red rose of Lancaster and the white rose of Richard, Duke of York. Richard returned to England, resentful that his campaigns in France had failed because of lack of support from the Lancastrian faction that controlled Parliament. The Wars of the Roses were soon to break out.

After James I of Scotland was murdered in Perth in 1437, Scotland also teetered on the brink of civil war. The six-year-old James II was crowned at Holyrood in Edinburgh, where the royal party felt more secure than at the traditional coronation site of Scone, close to where the old king had been killed.

An epidemic of plague in 1438 was followed by widespread famine. It was a repeat of the suffering a hundred years before. Wherever there is new poverty, someone acquires new riches. The Church fragmented in a new schism, exploited by James I's nephew James Kennedy, who accumulated huge wealth by becoming the Bishop of Dunkeld, the Abbot of Scone and the Bishop of St Andrews. He did not even have to be present to perform duties in Scone, holding the abbacy and its revenues as a commendator.

Bishop Kennedy was the son of James I's sister, Princess Mary Stewart and James Kennedy of Dunure in southwest Scotland. As the grandson of Queen Annabella, Kennedy understood the strategic importance of Strathearn. Princess Mary Stewart had four husbands, two with strong Strathearn connections. Her first husband was George Douglas, the powerful Earl of Angus. Her second was Bishop James Kennedy. Her third husband was Sir William Graham of Kincardine, from whom Auchterarder's most famous son, the sixteenth-century James Graham, Marquis of Montrose is descended. Her fourth was Sir William Edmonstone of Culloden.

In 1444 Bishop Kennedy and Margaret Beaufort, the Queen Mother, tried to wrest control of the royal burghs away from the collectors appointed by the King's Council. The same year, the young King James II, with his allies the Douglases and the Livingstons, took part in the siege of Methven Castle, twelve miles east of Auchterarder. The King's supporters then rampaged across Fife, looting communities where Kennedy had support. When the Queen Mother died in 1445, Kennedy lost his most important ally.

In 1449 James II married Mary of Guelders, a choice approved by both Charles VII of France and Philip the Good, Duke of Burgundy. As part of the marriage contract, James II promised to provide his new wife with a huge income of £5000 Scots per year. To achieve this, James II granted her the Earldoms of Atholl and Strathearn, which had been confiscated after Walter Stewart 14th Earl of Strathearn, also Earl of Atholl, had been executed in 1437 for his part in the murder of the King's father, James I. The crown of Scotland was once again bonded to the lands of the old Kingdom of Fortriu out of which it had arisen.

In Scotland, factions grouped and regrouped. New families gained national influence. A family's fortunes are only as good as the current generation's ability to manipulate the powers that be. The Livingstons, Crichtons and Kennedys came from the landed gentry, not the old nobility. Bishop Kennedy manoeuvred his way back into favour with James II. In 1452, he was even trusted to look after the pregnant Queen Mary at his castle in St Andrews, where she gave birth to a son, the future King James III.

The Campbells held extensive lands in Argyll, but their chief residence, Inveraray Castle, was too far from Scotland's capital city Edinburgh where their political ambitions lay. Colin Campbell became Master of King James II's Household and Justiciar for the South of Scotland. He acquired 'The Lands of Gloom' near Dollar in Clackmannanshire around 1453 when he was created 1st Earl of Argyll. He built a tower house, which he called Castle Campbell. It lies a convenient distance from both Edinburgh and Stirling Castles and a short journey through the Ochil passes to the strategic ridge of Auchterarder and the lands of his rivals the Grahams, Drummonds and Murrays. The Haldanes of Gleneagles, with their own political ambitions, had to use all their diplomatic skills to live peaceably with their warring neighbours.

In the fourteenth and fifteenth centuries, the Douglas family, from southwest Scotland, had risen to prominence at court and on the battlefield. The Douglases had made themselves indispensable to the Stewart dynasty, but had also intrigued with the fiercely independent MacDonald Lords of the Isles and other rivals to Stewart authority. In 1452, James II and his chancellor Sir William Crichton invited William, 8th Earl of Douglas, to dinner at Stirling Castle. The King stabbed Douglas with a knife. Other courtiers finished him off.

No age is free of treachery, but Scotland in the fifteenth century is worse than most. The dead Earl's brother James became 9th Earl of Douglas and tried to form an alliance against King James II. Despite this, the King commissioned him to negotiate on his behalf with the English King Henry VI.

Douglas was instrumental in securing the release of Malise Graham, who had been traded as a hostage for the release of King James I back in 1437 and had then seen the Stewarts help themselves to his Earldom of Strathearn, awarding him a slice of the Earldom of Menteith in exchange. In 1455, the Earl of Douglas fell out with the King again and fled to England. Most of Douglas's allies, including Malise, deserted him and voted in Parliament to condemn him.

James II, like so many Stewarts, was short of money. At first, his allocation to Queen Mary of the revenue from the Earldoms of Strathearn and Atholl raised so little funding that the Queen's Burgundian relatives withheld part of her dowry, complaining that the King was failing to give his Queen the £5,000 Scots annual income he had promised.

James II tried to revise revenue collection by putting it in the hands of royal bailies rather than sheriffs. These bailies could be nobles or gentlemen who collected crown land rents through a network of tacksmen (tenants holding long leases) and sub-tenants. Small royal burghs like Auchterarder produced little. Collection of money due to the treasury had become inefficient and late. As a means of stimulating the rural economy, James II introduced legislation that encouraged arable farming and tree planting.

The University of St Andrews had been doctrinally fractious ever since it was founded in 1413 during the Great Papal Schism. Bishop James Kennedy numbered the Chancellorship of St Andrews University among his many important posts. To balance Kennedy's power, King James II created a second Scottish university. He did not choose Perth, which had come close to gaining a university in the fourteen-thirties. Nor did he choose Edinburgh, although Perth lay close to the old coronation site of Scone and Edinburgh contained the new coronation site of Holyrood. Instead, James II in 1451 successfully petitioned Pope Nicholas V to grant university privileges in the rising commercial city of Glasgow. The King issued a confirming charter in 1453.

In the same year, an event occurred which reshaped Christendom. While James II of Scotland tried to balance rival political and religious interests, England and France also engaged in internal battles. As Western European kingdoms looked inwards, the old active crusading spirit had faded away, leaving only a romantic literary legacy and an Eastern Europe vulnerable to Islamic invasions. In 1453, the Turks captured Constantinople, now called Istanbul. It had been the home of the Eastern Christian Church since 312, when the newly converted Roman Emperor Constantine made it his base.

Islam had gained ground in Europe for over a hundred years, particularly since 1359 when the Ottoman Turkish Sultan Murad I came to power. He and his successor son, Bazajet the Thunderbolt, eroded the old Byzantine Empire. At the Battle of Kosovo in 1389 the Turks shattered a Christian Balkan alliance. A startled Christian Western Europe sent an inadequate army of knights, mainly from France, which was routed at Nicopolis on the Danube in 1396.

Why did it then take until 1453 for the Turks to capture Constantinople? It was not a Christian alliance that held them back, but a new global power, Timur, also known as Tamurlane. From his capital Samarkand in today's Uzbekistan, Timur and his Tatar warriors conquered India, Persia, Syria and Armenia and then turned on the Turks. Bazajet was captured at the Battle of Angora in 1402 and died the following year.

Fortunately for Europe, Timur turned his attentions towards China and died in 1405. The Turkish Empire slid into civil war till Sultan Murad II took control in 1421 and made deals with his Christian neighbouring kings. Murad's son Mohammed II made peace treaties with Hungary, Bosnia and the great mercantile seapower Venice. Mohammed II captured Constantinople in 1453.

In the short term, the capture of Constantinople made little difference to Auchterarder, a far-off royal burgh on a ridge that was strategically important to Scotland but had no significance to the Turkish Empire. Unlike the Roman Empire, the Turks never successfully advanced west beyond Central Europe.

In the longer term, the fall of Constantinople had a much greater local impact. The Turks and Timur's Empire controlled the profitable overland trade route to Asia, which had been used by the West since the Venetian merchant traveller Marco Polo had gone as far as China over a hundred years before. To avoid the Turks and the Tatars, the Kingdoms of Western Europe now had to engage in a new era of maritime exploration to open up new trade routes. In 1492, Christopher Columbus crossed the Atlantic. In 1497, Vasco da Gama sailed round the southern tip of Africa and across the Indian Ocean to Calicut in South India. Their voyages opened up a new political and economic geography that lasted until the twenty-first century.

James II allied with the French King Charles VII and tried to win the support of other major European powers, including Burgundy, Aragon, Castile and Milan. As the Wars of the Roses began to tear England apart, James II first supported the Lancastrian King Henry VI, then switched to support Richard Duke of York. On 10 July 1460, the Yorkists defeated Henry VI's army at Northampton and captured the King. On 4 August, James II's army besieged the English-held Castle of Roxburgh in the Scottish Borders. James was killed when one of his huge guns exploded beside him. He was twenty-nine years old.

Henry VI's Queen Margaret of Anjou roused the Lancastrian cause during her husband's captivity. On 30 December 1460, Richard Duke of York was defeated and killed at Wakefield. His head was displayed in York, decorated with a paper crown. In 1461, his fourteen-year-old son won the Battle of Towton and was crowned King Edward IV of England.

After the death of James II, his eight-year-old son was quickly crowned James III at Kelso a few miles away. The Queen Mother, Mary of Guelders, acted as regent. She became remarkably rich. She was able to draw income from the

Earldom of Strathearn and her others lands largely because James II's policies of agricultural improvement could be implemented in peace.

Auchterarder, as a royal burgh, had the right to trade abroad. Because it lacked a port and good road or river transport to the coast, it could never compete with coastal royal burghs. Between 1450 and 1516, fifty-one new lesser burghs were created. They could only trade within Scotland, but they were serious competition for a small landlocked royal burgh like Auchterarder.

Peace in Auchterarder did not mean peace throughout Scotland. The deposed English Lancastrian King Henry VI and his Queen Margaret fled to Dumfries in 1460. Margaret arranged an alliance with her French Angevin relatives. The Borders and Northumberland dissolved into a violent muddle.

In 1463, Henry VI and Queen Margaret, accompanied by the Scottish King James III and his mother Queen Mary, laid siege to Norham Castle, but retreated when a Yorkist army appeared. Margaret fled to France, leaving Henry in St Andrews, housed by Bishop Kennedy, who became the greatest power in Scotland when the Queen Mother Mary died later in the year.

Kennedy decided that it was better for Scotland to recognise the Yorkist Edward IV, and give up supporting the Lancastrians, rather than depend on a nebulous alliance with the French King Louis XI. Edward IV awarded Bishop Kennedy a handsome pension. St Andrews was no longer a secure refuge for Henry VI. He left and was captured by the Yorkists in Lancashire in 1465.

Kennedy had seen his heartlands, Perthshire and Fife, harried in 1444, when his power had temporarily waned. From then on, he made it his business to keep warfare well away from the profitable agricultural lands, which increased the wealth of his dioceses of St Andrews and Dunkeld and his abbacy of Scone.

Kennedy died in 1465. He was succeeded as Bishop of St Andrews by his nephew Patrick Graham. Since the nineteenth century, students of St Andrews University have staged an annual pageant, the Kate Kennedy procession, to celebrate Kennedy's probably fictional niece. Bishop Kennedy's nephew Patrick Graham was all too real.

Bishop Kennedy was an astute politician who got away with acquiring huge church riches by skilled diplomacy. Bishop Graham was equally greedy but more naive. He had been Bishop of Brechin when his uncle died, but agreed to pay the Pope 3,300 gold florins as a bribe to appoint him to the richer diocese of St Andrews. In 1472, Bishop Graham, without consulting the King, Parliament, or other bishops, persuaded Pope Sixtus IV to elevate St Andrews to a metropolitan see and promote him to becoming Scotland's first archbishop.

The Pope awarded Archbishop Graham superiority over twelve other bishops, including those of Dunblane, Dunkeld, Glasgow and Aberdeen. He also made Graham responsible for collecting one tenth of the incomes of all Scottish clergy, in order to fund a crusade against the Turks and drive them out of Constantinople.

The Scots clergy were furious. So was King James III, who was jealous of Papal interference and rich clergy. The King asserted his authority by seizing for himself all income from Bishop Graham's church lands. Pope Sixtus IV, when Graham failed to pay the fees due for his promotion, excommunicated him in 1478. Graham was imprisoned and died insane in one of his own monasteries, beside Loch Leven. There was no Scottish finance for a Papal crusade to Constantinople. An ineffectual attack on the city was easily repelled.

Since the time of the Vikings, the Orkneys and Shetlands had been a political anomaly, linked by economic reality and religious authority to Scotland, but paying tribute to Scandinavia. In 1469, King James III married Margaret, only daughter of King Christian I of Norway-Denmark. The bridegroom was eighteen. The bride was twelve. The marriage treaty awarded the Orkneys and Shetlands to the Scottish king until Norway-Denmark paid off the Queen's dowry. The dowry remained unpaid. These isles have been part of Scotland ever since.

In England, the Wars of the Roses continued. In 1470, there was a co-ordinated Lancastrian revolt against the Yorkist King Edward IV. The rising was crushed at the Battle of Tewkesbury in 1471. Henry VI's son and heir Edward was killed and the deposed King Henry VI was himself murdered in the Tower of London soon after. His Queen, Margaret of Anjou, died later in France.

In Scotland Robert Lord Boyd, a powerful politician from southwest Scotland, intrigued with the Yorkists when King James III favoured a Lancastrian–Scottish–French alliance. The King punished Boyd by seizing his lands, including Renfrew. Four hundred years later, this was to prove handy for the future King Edward VII, whose extremely active private life led him to sign discreetly into Paris hotels as Baron Renfrew, rather than more recognisably as the Prince of Wales.

Edward IV maintained power, much as his Norman ancestors had done, by building alliances with most of his powerful nobles, including his brother Richard, Duke of Gloucester, the future King Richard III. The English Parliament was weakened. It met only once between 1475 and 1483.

In 1474, Edward IV's daughter Cecily was engaged to James III's son and heir, the future James IV. The proposed Yorkist–Scottish dynastic alliance never happened. By 1480 Scotland and England were again at war. James III's brother Alexander Duke of Albany intrigued with Edward IV. The English King sent Richard, Duke of Gloucester to attack Scotland with a view to installing Albany as 'King Alexander of Scotland'. Gloucester seized Berwick and besieged Edinburgh. In 1482, King James III was imprisoned in Edinburgh Castle.

Auchterarder had remained remote from war. Agriculture thrived but tax collection was inefficient. By 1479, Auchterarder was heavily in arrears for the revenue it owed to the crown. Albany's rise now threatened to plunge Scotland into civil war. Luckily for Strathearn, the balance of power changed when Edward IV died in 1483.

The Duke of Gloucester suddenly had priorities higher than attacking Scotland. He succeeded his brother as King Richard III, after arranging the murder in the Tower of London of his two young nephews, one of whom was briefly recognised as King Edward V. There was a frantic flurry of diplomacy between Scotland and England. King James III was set free. Albany fled to England in 1483 where he died in 1485.

Richard III's reign was short. The Lancastrians had a new leader, Henry Tudor, Duke of Richmond, descended from the marriage between King Henry V's widow Catharine de Valois and a Welsh courtier, Owain Tudor. Henry Tudor's weak claim by birthright was outweighed by his potential as a peacemaker and the barons' distrust of Richard III. At the Battle of Bosworth in 1485, Richard was killed. The Lancastrian Henry Tudor was crowned Henry VII. He promptly married the Yorkist Edward IV's daughter Elizabeth. The two houses were united, thus ending the Wars of the Roses.

The Tudor rose became a symbol of the English crown. The Scottish King James III also chose a prickly plant to represent monarchy. He adopted the thistle, which appears on his coinage. There is some evidence to suggest that he founded the Scottish Order of the Thistle, in imitation of the order founded by the Duke of Bourbon in France in 1370.

King James III, distrustful of his Stewart relatives and of Scotland's old noble families, promoted new men at his court. Among them was Sir John Haldane, whose Gleneagles lands were created into a free barony, adjoining the Royal Burgh of Auchterarder. Sir John rose to be Lord Justice General of Scotland.

King James III's efforts to maintain peace with the new English King Henry VII were not helped by his fractious nobles, particularly in the Borders, where the Bothwells and the Homes were great landowners with political ambitions at court. By 1488 Scotland was lurching towards civil war again. James III fled from Edinburgh Castle and tried to rally support north of the River Forth.

In Strathearn, the Drummonds hesitated over supporting James III, but Lord Ruthven, Sheriff of Strathearn, brought a thousand horsemen and two thousand foot soldiers to attend the King in Perth as a display of royal authority. The King, who had a great fondness of horses, was presented with a magnificently swift grey charger. On 11 June 1488, James III rode into battle at the Sauchie Burn near Stirling, not far from Bannockburn where Robert Bruce had won a symbolic victory in 1314. James III was supported by men from Strathearn, Fife, Angus, Atholl and the North. He faced a rebel army from southern Scotland, led by Alexander 1st Lord Home and other lords.

Ironically, the rebels wanted to replace the King with his own teenage son and heir. They succeeded. The King was murdered after the battle. His son was quickly crowned King James IV. The coronation took place at the old Celtic site of Scone, judged safer than Edinburgh, which had increasingly become Scotland's ceremonial and administrative capital, though the Scottish Parliament continued to meet in other cities, including Perth and Stirling. The new King James IV, although just fifteen years old, was shrewd and quick to restore order to Scotland. He did not exact retribution on his father's supporters but tried to establish a stable political and economic climate.

Sir John Drummond, Chamberlain of Strathearn, was a Scottish ambassador to England in the turbulent year of 1483. He was created 1st Lord Drummond in 1487 and built Drummond Castle near Muthill. Royal charters of 1493 and 1508 extend the lands of the Barony of Auchterarder, which he owned. A charter of 1507 shows William, Earl of Montrose and owner of the neighbouring Kincardine Estate, agreeing to 'make no impediment to the watergang and passage of the Water of Ruthven to Lord Drummond's Mill at Auchterarder'. Grahams and Drummonds could co-operate when it was in their business interests to do so. The old days of mediaeval warlords were drawing to a close in Scotland, though old enmities lay just below the surface, needing little excuse to flare up again.

14

The Start of the Modern World

*In which religion comes second to imperial growth while we
see expansive voyages of exploration and narrow local feuds*

In 1453, the 800-year-long battle between the two militant Middle Eastern religions, Christianity and Islam, took a new turn. The Ottoman Turks captured Constantinople with its well-equipped shipyards and renamed it Istanbul. For the first time, an Islamic state was a major seapower.

Sultan Mohammed II now could not only build galleys to rival the great Venetian and Genoese fleets, he also controlled the gateway to the fertile Black Sea regions and to the valuable silk and spice trades of the East.

Mohammed II was a cultured leader who knew Greek and preserved the ancient buildings of Constantinople and Athens. The fact that he derived his moral authority from an Islamic vengeful God, rather than a Christian one, was less of a problem to Western monarchs than Mohammed's very traditional European imperial ambitions. He even called himself Kaiser-I-Rum (Roman Emperor).

After the fall of Constantinople in 1453, there was no more of a simple Christian versus Muslim conflict than there is in the twenty-first century. Political alliances are much more complex and shifting. The Ottoman Turks were Sunni Moslems whose bitter rivalry with the Persian (Iranian) Shiite Moslems endures today. There was a similar division in Europe, where the two great Christian powers detested one another. France had become a much more cohesive state than in the fractious days of the Hundred Years War. France's main foreign policy was now to contain the rising Hapsburg family who controlled the Holy Roman Empire in Central Europe.

During the next hundred years, Venice allied with the Hapsburgs, who encouraged the Persian Shiites to attack the Sunni Ottomans and distract them from spreading into Eastern Europe. In contrast, France came to support the Ottoman Turks, particularly when the Hapsburg Empire grew to include Spain, after the Spanish princess Joanna married the Hapsburg Archduke Philip and bore a son who became the great Holy Roman Emperor Charles V in 1515.

In the fifteenth century, once the Muslims controlled the eastern Mediterranean and overland trade routes to the profitable spice trades of India and slave trades of Africa, Christian Europe began to look westwards for commercial expansion.

Over a thousand years before, Christian imperial missions had spread northwards up the western seaboards of Europe. Now it was time to look south. Even before the fall of Constantinople, the Portuguese Prince Henry 'The Navigator' financed expeditions along the African coast. Prince Henry was the son of John I of Portugal and Philippa, sister of the English King Henry IV and daughter of the English warrior John of Gaunt, who had been King of Castile. The treaty of Windsor in 1386 between England and Portugal remains in force today, making Portugal England's longest-standing ally.

Prince Henry's successors, Affonso 'The African' and John II profited from the gold mined in West African kingdoms and imported slaves from the Congo and Senegal deltas. In 1486 Bartholomew Diaz sailed round the Cape of Good Hope, charting it as the southernmost tip of Africa.

Portugal's near neighbours, the kingdoms of Aragon and Castile, had long been rivals, much like England and Scotland. In 1469 Ferdinand of Aragon and Isabella of Castile married, creating a powerful new nation, Spain. In 1492 they drove out the Moors from Spain. These black Muslims had, particularly in Cordoba, Seville and Granada, maintained a culture throughout the Middle Ages that advanced scientific progress and, in libraries full of ancient manuscripts, preserved the texts of classical Greek and Latin authors. Now the prevailing cultural force in Spain was dominated by the fervently religious Queen Isabella, known as 'muy catolica', whose brand of militant Christianity produced the fearsome Spanish Inquisition.

Could Spain find an alternative sea route to India and China, avoiding the Portuguese-dominated West African coast? Christopher Columbus, a sea captain from Genoa in Italy, believed it must be possible to reach the Indies by sailing westwards across the uncharted Atlantic Ocean. For fifteen years he tried to persuade the rulers of Portugal, then France, then England, then Spain to finance a voyage of exploration. Finally, Ferdinand and Isabella decided to invest in Columbus and in August 1492 he set off from Spain with three ships.

Columbus landed, not in India or China, but in the Bahamas, then sailed on to Cuba and Haiti before returning to Spain. For the first time, the huge South American continent became known to European states. Portugal immediately contested Spain's right to claim all of South America for itself. In 1493, the formidable Roderigo Borgia, Pope Alexander VI issued a decree defining the rights of Spain and Portugal in the New World.

Portugal also continued its trade routes via Africa. In 1497 Vasco da Gama sailed round the Cape of Good Hope and up the East African coast as far as Mozambique and Mombasa. He then sailed across the Indian Ocean to Calicut, an important port for the pepper trade near the southern tip of India. He returned to Portugal in 1499, proving that the East India trade route was viable.

News of these voyages aroused curiosity in Scotland. James IV and his court had a taste for the exotic. African luxury items had been known in Scotland for centuries, probably since Roman times, when imperial soldiers saw service in widely differing parts of the Empire. By 1105, when the Scottish King Edgar gifted an elephant to Murdoch O'Brian, High King of Ireland, African goods were highly valued.

To sixteenth-century Scotland, Negroes were just another exotic product. Their novelty was more valued than their humanity. In 1508, James IV staged a jousting tournament at Holyrood, favouring a 'black lady' much in the same way that a modern media celebrity might be paraded at a Highland Games. The poet William Dunbar, struck by Negro features, wrote about a 'ladie with the meikle lips'. As the slave trade developed, Negroes became less rare and often less well treated, though within Britain they were generally used as exotic personal servants, rather than exploited as mass labourers.

Scottish scholars had, since the early Middle Ages, learned and taught at universities throughout Europe. St Andrews University had particularly strong links with Paris. The Italian Renaissance of the fourteenth and fifteenth centuries did not produce many spectacular new churches in Scotland in the way that Norman architecture had produced great Scottish cathedrals. There were, however, many fine small-scale private developments. A mile to the north of Auchterarder lies Tullibardine Chapel, built by Sir David Murray in 1446, a handsome building whose fine detail is well maintained by Historic Scotland.

King James IV indulged in secular prestige projects. He admired the windows and turrets of Renaissance French chateaux and Italian palaces. He copied them by creating magnificent great halls in both Edinburgh and Stirling Castles. Stone was carted from quarries on the slopes of the Ochils outside Auchterarder to build Stirling's great hall. James also created, at vast cost, a new royal palace at Holyrood, a mile downhill from the ancient fortress of Edinburgh Castle. It was a flamboyant display of national confidence. The expensive show was repeated five hundred years later across the street, when a new Scottish Parliament building replaced a brewery.

Auchterarder Castle, belonging to the Drummonds, was by now an old-fashioned stronghold, not a smart new structure like Drummond Castle to the north. It was probably never modernised. There has been no investment in archaeology to discover what lies on this strategic historic site. Auchterarder's parish church, St Mackessog's, kept its old Celtic name rather than adopt the newly popular cult of the Virgin Mary, promoted by trinkets and rosaries sold by pedlars. Frustratingly, like Auchterarder Castle, there has been no attempt by archaeologists to discover whether the church adopted new European fashions. Today's dismal ruin, riddled with ivy, is a testament to modern Council and Parliament neglect, rather than historic religious observance.

Formal knowledge was very much in the hands of the Church. The only schools were run by priests. Nobles had their own chaplains, whose duties included teaching the children of their patrons and favoured employees. The only portable written words in the Middle Ages were on manuscripts, mainly religious works laboriously copied by monks. Things changed when Johannes Gutenberg invented the printing press in Strasbourg in 1439. For the first time, multiple copies of a book could be made quickly.

It was not until 1507 that the first printers, Walter Chepman and Andrew Myllar in Edinburgh, were licensed in Scotland. They produced religious books and printed copies of Acts of Parliament that could be distributed throughout the kingdom. The first recorded bookbinder in Perth is Archibald Steedman in

1587, but by then foreign books had been in local private hands for a hundred years. William Caxton, a wealthy English merchant in the wool trade in Flanders, realised the profits that could be made from printing entertaining secular books. He learned the printing trade in Cologne and, with his assistant Wynken de Worde, began printing books in Westminster in 1476. Among his first titles were *The History of Troy, Reynard the Fox* and works by the English poet Geoffrey Chaucer.

Scottish readers lapped up these works, none more so than the poet William Dunbar, whose fondness for the vibrant culture of the English capital is expressed in his poem describing London 'the flower of cities all'. Dunbar and his contemporaries Robert Henryson and Gavin Douglas replaced the old Scottish tradition of long battle sagas by writing quick-witted fables, popular histories and bawdy stories.

Gavin Douglas, a son of the Earl of Angus, was educated at St Andrews University. He combined a lively vocabulary, not disdaining Scots words, with a sophisticated European outlook. His translations of Virgil's *Aeneid* made one of the key works of classical literature available to people who could not read Latin. Douglas became Bishop of Dunkeld but, caught up in the political intrigue of the second decade of the sixteenth century, he left for a more secure life in England.

Renaissance Europe looked east to the classical cultures of Rome and Greece and west to the Americas. Spain and Portugal carved up South America between them. What opportunities were there for northern European nations? The Vikings had sailed from Scandinavia to North America as early as the tenth century, but had not established an empire there.

John Cabot, a Genoese mariner who became a citizen of Venice, tried to find a backer for an exploration of a northerly route across the Atlantic. He found one in the English King Henry VII and set sail from Bristol in 1497. He arrived on Cape Breton Island, then Labrador in Canada. England was slow to exploit the possibilities of North America, perhaps because it appeared to have a lot of cod fish while South America had gold.

Henry VII was more concerned with maintaining a balance of power nearer home. With his own marriage, he united the warring houses of Lancaster and York. England's traditional enemy, France, remained a threat. There was also the perennial possibility of Scotland creating problems in the north.

Perkin Warbeck, a Yorkist pretender to the English throne, hung around the Scottish court. In 1492 Henry VII signed the Treaty of Etaples with the French King Charles VIII, who withdrew his support for Warbeck. In 1496, Henry VII signed the Magnus Intercursus, a commercial treaty, with Count Philip of Flanders, son of the Holy Roman Emperor Maximilian, who also withdrew support for Warbeck. In 1498, Warbeck unwisely left Scotland. Henry VII captured and eventually hanged him.

In little more than a decade after winning the Battle of Bosworth in 1485 and seizing the English crown, Henry VII's diplomacy had achieved a position for England as a balancing power between the might of France and that of the Holy Roman Empire.

What could James IV of Scotland achieve by comparison? When he became

King in 1488, his options for foreign alliances were wide open, but first there were pressing matters at home. In October 1489, an alliance of James III's former supporters, now marginalized from power, occupied Dumbarton, a key strategic site on the River Clyde. The rebel ringleaders were John Stewart, Earl of Lennox, whose custody of Dumbarton Castle had been forfeited, along with Alexander, 4th Lord Forbes and Alexander, 3rd Earl of Huntly from the North of Scotland.

In Strathearn, John 1st Lord Drummond chose to back the new king and rode with him to Aberfoyle. They then routed the rebel forces on Stirling Moss. The Drummonds no longer had the security and prestige at court that they enjoyed when Annabella Drummond was Robert III's Queen. Lord Drummond's military support against the rebels was not enough to win the King's unequivocal favour.

In 1490, a band of Drummonds clashed with their local Strathearn rivals, the Murrays, at Monzievaird, where King Malcolm II in 1005 had defeated a rival alliance of lesser Scottish kings in a crucial battle. The Drummonds chased the Murrays into Monzievaird Church and set fire to it, killing many. James IV had Lord Drummond's heir, the Master of Drummond, executed for his part in the atrocity.

Within six years, Margaret Drummond, sister of the dead Master of Drummond, became the mistress of King James IV, the man who had ordered her brother's execution. Margaret bore the king a son, but dynastic politics prevented another Drummond–Stewart royal marriage. In 1502, the King was betrothed to Margaret Tudor, daughter of the English King Henry VII. Shortly after, Margaret Drummond and her two sisters died suddenly, apparently poisoned. They are buried in the nave of Dunblane Cathedral.

By the time James IV came to the throne, it had become standard practice for Scottish Kings to hold a meeting of Parliament about once a year. For the first few years of his reign, James IV held annual parliaments, then came to rely instead on meetings of his royal council. In the last seventeen years of his long reign, James held only three parliaments. Unlike his father, however, James IV was able to manipulate public opinion successfully.

James IV had political debts to repay and reward the nobles that had backed him against his father James III. To balance the power of the archbishopric of St Andrews, a new archbishopric of Glasgow was created, promoting Bishop Robert Blackadder, one of James IV's most influential supporters. The Hepburns and the Homes, whose earlier generations had battled in the Borders and Northumbria, were rewarded with important posts in Central Scotland. Alexander Home became James IV's Chamberlain. Patrick Hepburn was made keeper of Stirling Castle, then given the title Earl of Bothwell and made Admiral of Scotland.

The marriage between James IV and Margaret Tudor was hailed as 'The marriage of the Thistle and the Rose'. It was intended to bring peace between Scotland and England. It did not. Henry VII died in 1509, succeeded by his son Henry VIII, who had made a name for himself as a glamorous Renaissance prince.

James had seen how much seapower mattered in global terms. When Henry VIII built a huge flagship, the *Mary Rose*, in 1509 James built one half as big again, weighing about 1,000 tons. This monster warship was called the *Michael*.

The ancient Pictish hunting forests of Tullibardine and Strathallan, north of Auchterarder, were felled to provide oak for the ship's hull. The timber was taken south to Newhaven beside the Port of Leith where a huge new shipyard was created for its construction. The *Michael* was good business for the Murrays, who owned the Tullibardine and Strathallan estates.

In 1513, James IV made the classic royal blunder of invading England. He and many of Scotland's nobility were killed at Flodden in Northumberland. The Abbot of Inchaffray was slain alongside his king.

King James IV's flagship the *Michael* never fought for Scotland. It was sold off to the French and eventually scrapped. Nothing survives of it. One tangible reminder remains, a huge pit in the outline of the *Michael* on the Strathallan estate. The expensive building at Holyrood remains, a grandiose reminder of failed militaristic nationalism.

15

The Reformation Begins

In which we see the Western Church hierarchy slide into disrepute,
while kings find it hard to breed heirs but easy to breed dissent

Throughout the Middle Ages, Western European monarchs derived their authority from divine approval, symbolised in Christian ritual coronation ceremonies. The arbiter of divine approval was the Pope, with all the possibilities for political intrigue that his position implied. Like all political institutions, the Papacy went through phases of strong leadership, inertia and division. By the early sixteenth century it had become a byword for greed and corruption.

The Borgia Pope Alexander VI (1492–1503) was a dissolute Renaissance prince with luxurious tastes in art and a ruthless suppressor of those who offended his dynastic ambitions. His successor Julius II (1503–13) was arrogant and warlike. Pope Leo X (1513–21) milked his flock to fund the lavish new St Peter's in Rome in 1517.

New opportunities for riches in the exotic Indies and Americas were paralleled by long-established needs for riches in heaven. People believed that priests could grant forgiveness of sins, and therefore make the difference between a soul's going to heaven or hell. Many priests took advantage of their position by selling indulgences, instant pardons from sin without the sinner having to bother with penance or formal display of guilt.

Across Europe, public anger grew at these abuses. People generally continued to believe in an afterlife and that priests influenced access to it. On the other hand, the institutionalised greed and hypocrisy of the Church led some churchmen to question points of Catholic doctrine in search of a return to the guiding principles of Jesus Christ.

As early as 1405, John Resby, an English preacher, was burned at the stake in Perth for denying the Pope's authority and questioning whether bread and wine in the Catholic mass were really magically transformed into the body and blood of Christ.

The full name of the Western Church, with its headquarters in Rome, was 'The Holy Catholic and Apostolic Church', meaning that it was sanctioned by God, operated universally and was governed by inheritors of Jesus' inner circle of followers. In fact, other branches of the Christian Church had been operating ever since the religion began to organise itself in the first century AD. The Orthodox Church in the East and the Coptic Church in Africa were independent of the Roman Catholic Church.

When a political hierarchy is forced to defend its moral practices, conflict is inevitable but permanent division is not. Desiderius Erasmus, a Dutch scholar, lucidly exposed the immoral practices widespread in the Catholic Church. He wrote with dignity and wit. He neither associated himself with more radical reformers, nor avoided those whose practices he condemned. In 1506 in Padua, he was tutor to the Scots King James IV's illegitimate son Alexander, who became Archbishop of St Andrews. Alexander was the son of Margaret Boyd, the mistress who was replaced in James IV's affections by Margaret Drummond from Strathearn.

In 1517, Martin Luther, a German priest, wrote a series of 95 criticisms against indulgences, denying that priests could forgive sins, and nailed his document to the door of the church in Wittenburg. There followed a flurry of debate, informed by books of all kinds, scholarly, abusive and incendiary. The reformers came to be known as Protestants, because they protested, or advocated, a simpler form of Christian faith, adhering to the word of the Bible, rather than the legislation of the Catholic hierarchy. Luther's teaching spread rapidly across Europe. Scottish merchants in the Netherlands saw pamphlets and brought them back to Scotland.

When King James IV was killed at Flodden in 1413, his son and heir James V was only one year old. The 25-year-old widowed Queen Margaret Tudor, sister of the English King Henry VIII, was pregnant with a son. At birth, he was christened Alexander, Duke of Ross, but died young.

Who would act as regent on behalf of the infant King James V? The choice lay between the dowager Queen Margaret and John, Duke of Albany, son of James III's brother Alexander. Margaret Tudor was naturally pro-English. Albany was pro-French. Predictably, leading Scots nobles preferred the French option. In 1515 Margaret was forced to hand over her infant sons. The three-year-old King James V walked out across the drawbridge of Stirling Castle and put its massive key into Albany's hands.

Queen Margaret married Archibald Douglas 6th Earl of Angus, to whom she bore a daughter, also called Margaret, who grew up to marry Matthew, 4th Earl of Lennox and bore him a son called Henry Darnley in 1546. Queen Margaret's son, King James V was to have only one surviving heir, Mary, Queen of Scots, born in 1542. These cousins, Darnley and Mary, married in 1565 and produced a son who, as King James VI of Scotland and James I of England, united the two warring crowns.

In 1515, all this was in the future. The immediate problem for Scotland was how to stave off a hostile Henry VIII. A hundred years earlier, another Duke of Albany, brother of King Robert III, had been regent for the infant King James I, son of Robert III and Annabella Drummond. The fifteenth-century Duke of Albany was a great schemer and survivor. Would the sixteenth-century Albany be the same? For fifteen years, Albany shuttled back and forth between Scotland and France, plotting military action against the English in the Borders, to the annoyance of Henry VIII who had other things on his mind. He wanted a male heir. His Queen Catharine of Aragon had produced a girl, Mary, in 1516, but no boy.

Henry VIII was a Catholic who detested Luther, regarding him as a populist rebel. In 1521, Henry supported a pamphlet, *Assertio Septem Sacramentorum*, which defended the Roman Catholic liturgy. The delighted Pope gave Henry the title *Fidei Defensor* (Defender of the Faith). The letters F.D. remain on all British coins issued today, a pocket reminder of the links between Church and State.

Henry VIII's relations with the Papacy broke down when he decided he needed a different wife to provide a male heir. He sought a divorce from Catharine on technical grounds, which the new pope, Clement VII, rejected. Henry was furious. He asserted that the King, not the Pope in Rome, had authority over the Church in England and proceeded to divorce Queen Catharine in 1533. He immediately married a new Queen, Anne Boleyn. Since he now controlled Church affairs, Henry took advantage of public hostility towards exploitative churchmen and abolished the rich monasteries, helping himself to their revenues.

When he succeeded to the throne in 1519, the Hapsburg Holy Roman Emperor Charles V saw his resources stretched between Spain, with its possibilities of an Empire in the Americas, and the lands in Germany where he was overlord. Influenced by Luther, many northern German princes became Protestant sympathisers. Charles V, rather than suppress the Lutherans, chose first to deal with his greatest European rival, King Francis I of France. At the Battle of Pavia in Italy in 1525, Charles V's troops crushed the French army and captured Francis I. The French King was freed only after he agreed to abandon all claims in Italy and to hand Flanders, with its profitable wool trade, over to Charles V.

The Battle of Pavia happened on Charles V's twenty-fifth birthday. By coincidence, in 1746 William, Duke of Cumberland celebrated his twenty-fifth birthday before slaughtering Bonnie Prince Charlie's army at Culloden. Both were victories for Germanic efficiency over French bravado. Both had an impact on the future of Scotland.

After the Battle of Pavia, the town of Bruges, the main market for exports from Strathearn, was no longer held by Scotland's French allies. Should Scotland negotiate new deals with France's enemy, Charles V, who controlled Bruges and whose perspective on trading opportunities encompassed different territories? The alternative would be to stay loyal to the French and try to create a trade route to Europe through French ports. This would mean sailing south down the English Channel with increased risk of attack from English ships.

In Scotland, King James V assumed personal rule at the age of fifteen in 1528, emerging from Albany's shadow. The old Scots–French alliance was not as secure as it had been. In 1528 Henry VIII signed a peace treaty with France, which was in disarray after the Battle of Pavia. The treaty was designed to protect English and French commercial interests and to marginalise Scotland. James V's response was to sign a treaty with the victor of Pavia, the Holy Roman Emperor Charles V, ensuring protection of Scottish trade to Flanders. James V had endeared Scotland to Charles in 1538 by the burning in St Andrews of Patrick Hamilton who had preached Lutheran freedoms, anathema to the Holy Roman Empire.

The Drummonds continued their tempestuous relationship with the Stewart monarchy. A royal charter of 1535 refers to lands forfeited by John 1st Lord Drummond 'for the treasonable and violent putting of hands' on Lord Lyon, King of Arms. In the charter, King James V restores these lands to Drummond's great-grandson, David, who then married the King's niece, Margaret and paid him £2,000.

James V of Scotland, son of Henry VIII's sister Margaret Tudor, was second in line to the English throne after Henry VIII's daughter Mary. To continue Tudor and Stewart royal dynasties, it was vital that both James and Mary married soon. Should they marry one another and potentially unite the two thrones? A flurry of diplomacy ensued. The main sticking point was Church wealth. Henry VIII had never abandoned the Catholic faith, though he denied the authority of the Pope. On the other hand, the English crown now had control of English Church finances, something that the devoutly Catholic James V would almost certainly cede back to the Pope if James inherited the English crown. To Henry, it was an unattractive prospect.

On the Scottish side, a range of possible French, Spanish, Danish and other brides was discussed. The pro-French Albany died in 1536. His final act was to negotiate a marriage between James V and Madeleine, daughter of the French King Francis I. They were married at Nôtre Dame in Paris on 1 January 1536. By 7 July, Madeleine had taken ill and died at Holyrood. Within a year, having decided on a French bride, James V chose another to replace the one he had lost. His new Queen Mary, daughter of Claude, Duke of Guise, came from a family with labyrinthine Church and royal connections. They were implacably opposed to the Protestant cause.

Mary of Guise was the 22-year-old widow of Francis, Duke of Longueville, who died in 1537. He left Mary with a baby son who bore his father's Christian name and title. James V, having chosen her as his wife, did not bother to go to Paris for the wedding ceremony. He married her by proxy, with Lord Maxwell acting his role in Nôtre Dame Cathedral on 18 May 1538. James showed more interest when she arrived in Scotland and staged a pageant and second marriage ceremony in St Andrews in mid June.

In England, Henry VIII's preferred option for the succession was to father a son. His new Queen Anne Boleyn bore him a daughter, Elizabeth in 1533, but no son. Henry accused her of adultery and had her executed on May 19 1536. His divorced Queen Catharine of Aragon died the same year, leaving her daughter Mary, who had inherited the devout Spanish Catholicism of her mother.

The day after Anne Boleyn's execution, Henry VIII married Jane Seymour. She bore him a son, Edward, the following year. Jane died soon after the birth. There was now a male heir to the English throne, plus two female heirs: Mary, aged twenty-one and Elizabeth, aged four. James V of Scotland was no longer close to the English succession.

There was a problem for Henry, however. The Pope did not recognise Henry's marriages to Anne Boleyn and to Jane Seymour. Therefore, in the eyes of the Catholic Church, Princess Elizabeth and Prince Edward were illegitimate and had no title to the English crown. Popes Leo X and Clement VII had tried to avoid a complete political break with England. Clement died in 1536. The new Pope Paul III excommunicated Henry in 1538.

Henry VIII was ruthless and an astute diplomat. Until 1530, his chief minister was Cardinal Thomas Wolsey, who copied James IV's practice of holding few parliaments and worked with a small royal council. Wolsey favoured Church reform, but not separation from Rome. He fell from power and died in disgrace when he failed to persuade Pope Clement VII to grant Henry a divorce.

Wolsey's successor, Thomas Cromwell, managed the dissolution of the monasteries and took a much stronger Protestant line. When the rival leaders of Catholic Europe, the Emperor Charles V and the French King Francis I, signed a peace treaty in Nice in 1538, Henry needed European Protestant support to protect England. Cromwell arranged a fourth marriage for the king, this time to Anne of Cleves, whose father the Duke of Cleves was sympathetic to the Protestant cause in Germany. Henry VIII agreed to marry Anne for political reasons and on the strength of Hans Holbein's flattering portrait of her. When he met Anne, Henry disliked her, calling her 'his Flanders mare' for her unhygienic habits and braying laugh, but married her anyway in January 1540.

Cromwell was not forgiven for promoting Anne. Henry had him executed in July 1540 and divorced Anne. He promptly married Catharine Howard, niece of the Catholic Duke of Norfolk. Catharine lasted two years. She failed to produce the male heir that Henry wanted as a spare to Prince Edward and was executed on the same spurious adultery charge as Anne Boleyn. Henry then married his sixth wife, Catharine Parr, widow of Lord Latimer, whose claim to fame is that she outlived Henry.

Before he fell from favour, Thomas Cromwell initiated the Act of Union of England and Wales. From 1536, the two countries shared one Westminster-based government, ending centuries of battles for Welsh independence. Legislation did not suppress local feelings. Occasional rebellions persisted. Ireland was given a different constitutional solution, insofar as it is ever possible to give a constitutional solution to Ireland. In 1541, the many warring kingdoms of Ireland were made into a single kingdom with Henry VIII as monarch. The Irish Parliament remained independent of Westminster.

In Scotland, James V watched his uncle Henry VIII's whirlwind of marriages, constitutional and religious reform, eyeing up the opportunity for promoting his own claim to the English throne. He was well aware that Prince Edward and Princess Elizabeth were illegitimate in the eyes of Catholic Europe, leaving only the unmarried Princess Mary between him and the crown of England.

Like Henry VIII, James V wanted a male heir. In 1540 his Queen Mary of Guise bore him a son, James. The following year, a second son, Arthur was born. Soon after, both infants died. The Queen fell pregnant again. In November 1542, a few weeks before she was due to give birth, James V led an army to attack England. His troops were crushed at Solway Moss in the Borders. Many Scottish nobles were captured. On 8 December the baby was born. It was a girl. Disappointed and defeated, King James V had her christened Mary. He died six days later. The infant Mary, Queen of Scots was a political prize that all the crowned heads of Europe wanted to grasp.

16

The Peace of Auchterarder

*In which we see a rough wooing, competitive sectarian atrocities,
John Knox's Protestants running amok, Mary, Queen of Scots'
Catholic mother fighting back and Auchterarder hosting a peace deal*

Religious reform has political objectives. In England, King Henry VIII wanted an English Church free of the overlordship of Rome, but he remained faithful to the doctrines of the mediaeval Church. His Statute of Six Articles in 1539 reinforced Catholic practices and rejected Lutheran reforms. Under Henry's rule, death by burning at the stake was the penalty for denying transubstantiation, the belief that bread and wine are magically transformed into the flesh and blood of Jesus Christ during the Catholic mass.

In Scotland, the death of King James V in 1542 brought yet another infant to the Scottish throne. The six-day-old Mary, Queen of Scots, was cared for by her mother, the astute Mary of Guise, who had the support of a network of powerful Catholic relations in France and a Scottish Catholic political faction led by the ambitious Cardinal David Beaton and Matthew, Earl of Lennox.

Other Scottish nobles saw an independent Church, on the English model, as the way to achieve control over Church finances and national politics. James 2nd Earl of Arran was appointed Governor of the kingdom, although he was hostile to Rome. The Scottish Parliament recognised Arran as the infant Queen Mary's heir, should she die before bearing a child. Both Arran and Lennox were descended from King James III's sister Mary. Lennox felt he should take precedence over Arran as heir to the throne.

Arran built up a faction of nobles sympathetic to Henry VIII's religious reforms. They included several who had been captured at the Battle of Solway Moss in 1542, but had been freed with a clear political purpose, to arrange a marriage between Henry VIII's heir, the six-year-old Prince Edward, and the baby Mary, Queen of Scots. Arran led a Scottish movement denouncing the Pope but, like Henry VIII, he remained faithful to the Catholic mass.

To many in both Scotland and England the appetite for religious reform ran much deeper than just a change of personnel at the head of the Church. The development of the printing press in the late fifteenth century increased the incentive to learn to read. As with the Internet in the late twentieth century, it was suddenly possible to gain access to material that those in authority did not want the general public to read. Lurid disclosures of Church corruption and abuse were lapped up from books like Simon Fish's *A Supplication for the Beggars* (1529).

From the time of the Celtic missionaries in the sixth century, the Christian Church had been the main source of literacy and scholarship. In the Middle Ages, many of Strathearn's nobility, through international commitments, could understand spoken Gaelic, English, French and Latin. As today, tradesmen also learned as much as they needed to advance their businesses. Legal documents and accounts were handwritten. Before the printing press made multiple copies of books quickly available, there was little to read for pleasure, except for Latin religious manuscripts, transcribed by monks. Only the very rich owned these works of art. Now it was possible to read the translations of the New Testament in English, notably the version by William Tyndale, an Englishman who was captured and executed in Antwerp in 1536, after evading Henry VIII and European Catholics for many years while he worked at making the Bible accessible to ordinary readers.

In 1543 there were violent demonstrations in Perth against the abuses of the Catholic Church. The friaries bore the brunt of the anger. Robert Lamb made a satirical protest by adding devil's horns and a tail to the statue of St Francis outside Greyfriars in Perth. Cardinal Beaton retaliated. He had Lamb and four others hanged and had Lamb's wife drowned.

The Treaty of Greenwich, signed in July 1543, agreed a marriage between the English heir Edward and the Scottish heir Mary. Henry VIII wanted Mary brought up in England. Most Scots nobles disagreed, reluctant to let Mary fall into Henry VIII's hands. Mary of Guise's pro-French faction gained more support. On 11 December 1543, the Scottish Parliament rejected the Treaty of Greenwich. Personal opportunism took precedence over religious belief. The Protestant-leaning Arran switched sides and supported a Scottish–French alliance. Sensing an opportunity to promote himself as Mary's heir, the Catholic Lennox also switched sides and supported Henry VIII.

In May 1544, Edward Seymour, Earl of Hertford and brother of Henry VIII's dead Queen Jane, attacked Edinburgh by land and sea. His forces seized ships in Leith and looted Holyrood Palace. Hertford failed to enter Edinburgh itself. He retreated through the Borders, pillaging farms and churches. This campaign to enforce the Treaty of Greenwich was known, ironically, as 'The Rough Wooing'. In 1545, Hertford raided Scotland again.

Scotland was divided. Many nobles in the Borders and on the east coast as far as Fife and Angus saw Henry VIII as the likely winner in any Scottish–English conflict. They swore an oath of allegiance to him, in the way that many Scottish nobles had sworn an oath of allegiance to King Edward I while the Bruce and Balliol factions were fighting a civil war in Scotland in the early fourteenth century.

In Strathearn, remote from the Borders and east coast, the Drummonds, Murrays and Grahams continued to support Mary of Guise's party, at least nominally, waiting for the political situation to become clearer.

On 29 May 1546, the Scottish Catholics lost their chief religious politician.

Cardinal Beaton was murdered in his own Castle of St Andrews by a band of Fife nobles. It was revenge for the burning of the Protestant preacher George Wishart a few weeks earlier. St Andrews had seen Protestants burned before, Patrick Hamilton in 1528 and Henry Forrest in 1533. Beaton's assassination was a sign that Protestantism was no longer just a populist movement but a force gaining credibility among those who wielded political power.

Henry VIII died in January 1547. His sometime rival and ally Francis I of France died the same year. The Earl of Hertford, uncle of the new ten-year-old King Edward VI, was made Protector of England and promoted to Duke of Somerset. He repealed Henry VIII's Statute of Six Articles, abolished the Catholic mass and, with the assistance of the scholarly Thomas Cranmer, Archbishop of Canterbury, produced the First Book of Common Prayer, promoting a plain form of worship.

In revenge for Cardinal Beaton's murder, Mary of Guise had a French force seize St Andrews Castle in 1547. Several of the senior anti-Beaton faction were shipped to imprisonment in France. Others were forced to serve in the French galleys, among them the preacher John Knox, a fiery Protestant despite, or perhaps because of, studying at the politically conservative St Andrews University.

The Duke of Somerset repeated the invasions of Scotland that he had earlier led when he was Earl of Hertford. He crushed a Scottish army at Pinkie in the Borders on 10 September 1547 and established English garrisons in castles along the east coast of Scotland.

Mary of Guise removed her daughter, the five-year-old Mary, Queen of Scots, from Stirling Castle, which no longer seemed secure from attack by the Duke of Somerset and the growing Scottish Protestant faction. Mary sheltered at Inchmahome Priory on an island in the Lake of Menteith, deep in Graham country. Arran negotiated with the new French King Henri II and achieved not only a stronger French alliance, but also a treaty signed on 7 July 1548 by which Mary, Queen of Scots would go to live in France and be engaged to marry Francis the Dauphin, heir to the French throne. Later that month Mary set sail. She was not to return to Scotland until 1561.

Mary of Guise then set about extending her support among the Scottish nobility, mainly with the help of large sums of French money. Arran was given the Duchy of Châtelherault with a huge income. In 1550 Mary of Guise personally took to France a party of Scottish nobles, many of whom had been pro-English, including the Earls of Huntly and Glencairn, and also key figures from the area southwest of Edinburgh like James Sandilands, Laird of Torphichen and the influential preacher John Spottiswoode, parson of Calder.

Mary of Guise returned to Scotland in 1551, bringing with her Henri D'Oysel who, as leader of the French delegation to Scotland, wielded increasing political power now that so many Scottish nobles had been bought.

In England, as well as Scotland, an infant monarch meant a power vacuum which rival factions fought to fill. The Duke of Somerset was ousted as Protector in 1549, not because he championed religious reform, but because John Dudley, Earl of Warwick seemed a better option as leader to nobles who saw opportunities of enriching themselves at the expense of the Church. Warwick was promoted to Duke of Northumberland and had Somerset executed in 1552.

Northumberland intensified religious reform in England. Archbishop Thomas Cranmer, influenced by the austere doctrines of the French theologian John Calvin, devised a Second Book of Common Prayer, more Protestant than the first. Northumberland seized more Church lands and distributed the income to his supporters.

Northumberland withdrew English garrisons from Scotland, hoping to win the support of Mary of Guise. It was not to be. Mary of Guise was a steadfast Catholic. Northumberland was committed to the Protestant cause. He persuaded the fifteen-year-old unmarried King Edward VI to declare his two sisters, the Princesses Mary and Elizabeth, illegitimate and ineligible to become monarchs. Instead, Edward VI named as his heir Lady Jane Grey, granddaughter of Henry VIII's sister Mary.

Edward VI died in 1553, probably of pneumonia following smallpox. There was a violent reaction against the corruption and greed of pro-Protestant politicians. Edward's elder sister was crowned Queen Mary I. She was a staunch Catholic, committed to the faith of her mother Catharine of Aragon, the first wife that Henry VIII divorced for failing to produce a male heir.

Mary I swiftly had Lady Jane Grey and Northumberland executed. Protestant legislation was reversed. Protestant bishops were burned at the stake, including Thomas Cranmer in 1556. Many Protestants fled abroad.

Mary was determined to secure a Catholic succession to the throne of England. In 1554 she married Philip, Archduke of Burgundy, son and heir to the Hapsburg Emperor, Charles V. The persecution of Protestants was so extreme that Charles V urged Philip and Mary to be more moderate for fear of alienating the majority of the nobles and common people.

Philip stayed in England for only fourteenth months. Charles V had his own problems of succession. In 1555, in poor health, he retired to the monastery of Yuste in Spain. The huge Hapsburg Empire was divided. His brother became Holy Roman Emperor Ferdinand I in religiously fractious eastern Europe. Charles V's son became King Philip II of Spain. Any child of the marriage between Mary I and Philip II would unite the crowns of England and Spain with control of Flanders and colonies in Mexico and Peru.

There was no child. Mary I died of cancer on 17 November 1558. By then the unfortunate political marriage had lost England its last territory in Europe. Philip II had continued his father's wars against the French. He failed. Francis Duke of Guise captured Calais in January 1558, much to the dying Queen Mary I's chagrin.

From 1554, Mary of Guise had been Regent of Scotland. She was more pleased with her French brother Duke Francis's success than regretful that Catholic England had lost its European port. Philip II lived until 1598, always seeking an opportunity to invade the England where he had once been married to the monarch remembered as 'Bloody Mary'.

Mary of Guise was short of finance after spending so much to gain political backing. Some supporters now lent her money. In 1555, the Bishop of Dunblane lent her £4,400, confident that his Strathearn diocese would replenish his coffers.

As Regent, Mary of Guise at first pursued a much more tolerant religious policy in Scotland than Queen Mary I in England, but appointed so many Frenchmen to senior positions at court that many of the old Scottish nobility became resentful. De Roubay effectively supplanted George Gordon 4th Earl of Huntly as Chancellor. The traffic was not all one-way. Many Scots enjoyed privileged positions at the French court.

There was also considerable cultural exchange between France and Scotland. The great French Poet Pierre de Ronsard, a lifelong friend of Mary, Queen of Scots, served two terms as a page at the Scottish court. Sir David Lindsay served in France and returned to write *The Satire of the Three Estates*, laying bare the quirks and foibles of nobles, clergy and common people in a robust Scots tongue. In the Auchterarder area, Lindsay caused amusement with his *History of Squire Meldrum*, a thinly disguised account of a spectacular romantic incident involving Marjorie Lawson Haldane of Gleneagles Castle.

Across Strathearn, the Abbey of Inchaffray was declining in political influence. In the fifteenth century, Abbot George made Lawrence, Lord Oliphant, bailie of monastery lands, effectively handing over control to the local landowner. In the early sixteenth century, Gavin Dunbar, Archbishop of Glasgow, held the Abbacy of Inchaffray as one of many titles. In 1539 Bishop Dunbar granted the income from land near Madderty to another local landowner, Anthony Murray, as a reward for supporting the bishop's legal confirmation.

The last Abbot of Inchaffray was Alexander Gordon, brother of the Earl of Huntly, who failed to be elected Bishop of Glasgow when Bishop Dunbar died. Abbot Alexander held the impressive-sounding but worthless title of Archbishop of Athens. In 1558, he confessed to the General Assembly of the Church that he had failed in his religious duties, had sold off land, and had resigned Inchaffray to James Drummond of Innerpeffray, son of David, Lord Drummond. James Drummond was created Lord Madderty in 1609. By that time, the Abbey had long since been looted and the Catholic priests forced to flee.

Throughout history, the people of Auchterarder have never been collectively over-excited by the finer points of religious or political doctrine. On the other hand, issues of patronage and liberty have created, in the words of nineteenth-century radical weaver poet Thomas Stewart, 'Famed Auchterarder for disputes,/ Men independent, lang lawsuits'.

The Church was central to the affairs of the Royal Burgh. Apart from Inchaffray Abbey lands and the parish church of St Mackessog's, there was also a chapel, down Chapel Wynd off Auchterarder High Street on the site of the later seventeenth-century church tower, which stands beside the cemetery. The first mention of this chapel is 1477, but a church building is likely to have existed on this site throughout the Middle Ages. By the sixteenth century, the chapel-yard was used for holding the Burgh Courts.

On 24 April 1558, Mary, Queen of Scots, now aged fifteen, married Francis, the French Dauphin at Nôtre Dame in Paris. The bride was a cultivated, charismatic European princess. The bridegroom was a timid, sickly fourteen-year-old boy of whom the bride was genuinely fond during the years they grew up together at the French court. The Queen of Scotland was now married to France, just as the Queen of England was married to Spain.

Within a few weeks Mary, Queen of Scots became Queen of France. On 30 June 1558, Francis's father King Henri II, an enthusiastic sportsman, was accidentally killed in a jousting tournament. His blameless opponent was Jacques, Count Montgomery, a Norman Scot and Colonel of the King's Guard. Francis II was crowned King of France on 18 September, his glamorous bride by his side. The new King's mother, the formidable Catharine de Medici, looked on. Fortunately for Mary, Catharine liked her. Mary, for her part, was content and astute enough to leave the complexities and intrigues of French government to her Guise relatives and the Dowager Queen Catharine.

In Scotland, opinion was divided on the dynastic alliance between France and Scotland. In Strathearn, a charter of David Lord Drummond in 1559 refers to Mary and Francis as Queen and King of Scotland. Not everyone saw Francis as King of Scotland, especially the powerful Campbell family, headed by Archibald 4th Earl of Argyll and his son Archibald, Marquis of Lorne. They were Protestant sympathisers, as were Alexander Cunningham, 5th Earl of Glencairn and James Douglas, 4th Earl of Morton. Arran, now Duke of Châtelherault, intrigued with Elizabeth and sided with the Scots Protestant lords.

The rising star of the Scottish Protestant cause was John Knox. He spent two years penal servitude in French galleys for his part in occupying St Andrews Castle after the murder of Cardinal Beaton in 1547. He was freed in February 1549 after an appeal, probably by Archbishop of Canterbury Thomas Cranmer, and spent four years in England, latterly as a chaplain to King Edward VI. When Queen Mary I came to the throne in 1553, Knox fled to Europe and lived in Frankfurt am Main, then Geneva.

In September 1555, John Knox returned to Scotland. He preached sermons, but warily secured himself in Protestant strongholds like Castle Campbell, known as 'Castle Gloom' towering over the Dollar (from the French *douleur* or grief) Glen. From 1556 until early 1559, Knox established himself in Geneva, where he wrote religious tracts heavily influenced by the French theologian John Calvin, who also sheltered in Geneva. Calvin believed in an austere form of worship, rejecting ornate Church decoration and the magic elements of Catholic ritual. He also advocated a democratic form of Church government, by which congregations would elect their own priests. He hoped this would bring an end to corrupt patronage and influence by the wealthy.

In 1558, Knox published *The First Blast Of The Trumpet Against The Monstrous Regiment Of Women*. His targets were the bloodthirsty Queen Mary I of England and the manipulative Mary of Guise, Regent of Scotland but, by implication, their heirs Queen Elizabeth I and Mary, Queen of Scots were caught up in Knox's invective.

In 1558, the Hapsburg Holy Roman Emperor Charles V died. In March 1559, France and Spain signed the Treaty of Cateau–Cambrésis, ending more than half a century of enmity. Charles V's son, Philip II of Spain whose wife, the English 'Bloody Mary', had died the previous year, now married Elizabeth de Valois, eldest daughter of King Henri II of France. The two great European Catholic powers were now friends again.

In Scotland, the Protestant noble faction needed to act fast to prevent Mary of Guise enhancing her power. At a populist level, there were open threats to religious houses. From early 1559, 'Beggars' Summons' appeared, notices telling friars to vacate their rich houses and let them be occupied by the poor and sick, saying that 'Flitting Friday', 12 May, was the date by which they had to go. They were nailed to the doors of Perth friaries, in an echo of Martin Luther's momentous gesture in Wittenburg in 1517.

With the death of Queen Mary I in November 1558 and the accession of her sister Queen Elizabeth I, a moderate Protestant, England no longer posed a threat to the Scottish Protestant cause. John Knox was invited back to Scotland. He arrived on 2 May 1559 at Leith. Mary of Guise, sensing trouble, ordered Protestant preachers to appear at Stirling on 10 May. They knew Stirling was in the hands of Henri D'Oysel and stayed away. Instead, John Knox preached an incendiary sermon in St John's Kirk in Perth.

Freedom of expression is the natural enemy of establishment doctrine. Knox expressed himself freely. He denounced idolatry. His congregation took him at his word and stripped the Kirk of its religious symbols, then stormed outside and looted every friary in the burgh. Within days, Protestant nobles and angry commoners rallied to form an army in Perth. The Earls of Argyll and Glencairn joined the rebels, as did Campbell of Glenorchy. Some churchmen, like Patrick Hepburn, Bishop of Moray, and Alexander Gordon, Bishop of Galloway, backed Knox. Gordon's brother George, 4th Earl of Huntly, wavered, waiting to see which side was most expedient to support, a policy followed by his heirs for generations.

As Knox's armed congregation grew in Perth, Mary of Guise sent an army under Henri D'Oysel to confront the rebels. D'Oysel advanced from Stirling and occupied Auchterarder, feeling that he was in comparatively safe territory among Drummonds, Murrays and Grahams, who were loyal to the crown and had no love for the Campbell rebel leaders.

Instead of engaging in battle, the two sides agreed a truce on 29 May 1559, the Peace of Auchterarder. D'Oysel promised not to install a French garrison in Perth, provided the rebels stopped their looting.

Up to this point, Mary of Guise as Regent had never acknowledged the existence of a concerted, religious political opposition. The Peace of Auchterarder is the first time that the Scottish Crown formally engaged in diplomacy with the Protestants. It is the first official recognition of Protestantism as a political entity in Scotland.

17

A Catholic Queen and Her Protestant Son

In which Mary, Queen of Scots loses three husbands and three kingdoms, and we see a procession of ill-fated Regents

The Peace of Auchterarder on 29 May 1559 was an important step in recognising political reality, but it did not resolve the Scottish Protestant versus Roman Catholic conflict. Even in the twenty-first century, hostilities lie close to the surface in many communities, particularly in the urban west of Scotland.

As a treaty, it bought both sides some time and avoided a pitched battle. Many nobles and common people hesitated over which side to join. Henri D'Oysel wrote on 15 June 1559, 'You cannot tell friend from enemy, and he who is with us in the morning is on the other side after dinner'. The Catholic D'Oysel did not keep his side of the Peace of Auchterarder. He marched into Perth to the sound of military music and remained for a month till he was driven out.

The Protestants observed the Peace in so far as they stopped looting Perth. Instead, they looted Scone Abbey, despite their own leader, John Knox, telling them it was politically stupid to wreck the historic site where Scottish kings had been crowned. The Protestant 'congregation', now out of control, advanced through Strathearn, looting churches in the name of reform, on the way to Stirling, Linlithgow and Edinburgh.

Mary of Guise died in June 1560. As Regent, she had performed an extraordinarily difficult balancing act with great skill and calmness, preferring diplomacy to armed conflict. Her daughter, Mary, Queen of Scots, was now seventeen, renowned in Europe as the brilliant young Queen of France. How would the government of Scotland be managed? Would its new Queen and the French King Francis II divide their time between Scotland and France?

The questioned never had to be answered. On 5 December of the same year, King Francis II died of an ear infection, an illness that today would be quickly cleared up by antibiotics. There was no place in France for a teenage ex-queen. On 14 August 1561, Mary set sail from Calais. She arrived five days later in Leith to take up her birthright as Queen of Scots.

Mary had grown up in Fontainebleau, at the most culturally sophisticated court in Europe. She imported to Scotland as much of that culture as she could. Grahams, Drummonds, Murrays and others from the noble families of Strathearn attended her court in Edinburgh, where music, painting and poetry thrived. Auchterarder's land-owners and tenant farmers thrived, as long as they could play the ever-shifting game of religious politics.

As early as 1545, Pope Paul III tried to strengthen the Roman Catholic Church by creating The Council of Trent. Until it was dissolved in 1563, this assembly of bishops tried to eliminate corrupt practices that Luther and other Protestant reformers had denounced. The Catholic Church emerged with a clearer code of dogma and a reinforced authority for the Pope over his believers.

Protestantism had gained credibility and political force because of its well-educated, charismatic preachers, like John Calvin and John Knox. The Catholic Church tried to do the same, creating a Counter Reformation. The Society of Jesus, or Jesuits, founded in 1534, were disciplined, military-style evangelists. Some of its leaders, like Ignatius de Loyola and Francis Xavier, were Spaniards who had grown up seeing the effectiveness of the ruthless Spanish Inquisition, promoted by the 'muy catolica' (very Catholic) Queen Isabella of Castile. The Jesuits preached and taught in Europe, but also grasped opportunities newly opened up by global exploration to the Americas and Far East. Xavier successfully preached in India, Malaya and Japan.

Elizabeth I, when she succeeded her Catholic sister, 'Bloody Mary', as Queen of England in 1558, restored moderate Protestantism. She became Supreme Governor of the Church in England. She did not at first persecute those who preferred the Roman form of church service, but she was acutely aware that the Pope did not recognise her as the legitimate Queen of England. In Catholic eyes, Mary, Queen of Scots had the best claim to the English throne through her grandmother, Margaret Tudor. With the help of her able Secretary William Cecil, Lord Burghley, and his intelligence network, Elizabeth was always one step ahead of Catholic plots against her. When the Treaty of Cateau–Cambrésis in 1559 ended the wars between France and Spain, the great political divide in Europe was no longer between warring Catholic states, but between a Catholic alliance and a Protestant one.

When Mary, Queen of Scots returned from France to become Queen of Scotland in 1561, she was a Catholic landing on an island increasingly dominated by Protestants. The first time she attended mass after her return, only one noble was present, William Graham, 2nd Earl of Montrose. She felt safe in Graham country, remembering how she was sheltered at Inchmahome Priory on the Lake of Menteith when she was a little girl. Mary spent time with the Earl of Montrose in 1562 at his home, Kincardine Castle, just south of Auchterarder. Other Scots nobles jockeyed for power in a court as full of violent intrigue as any of its contemporary Italian Renaissance principalities.

Mary's own poetry and embroidery show a fascination for symbols. James III had already adopted the French thistle on his coinage. Mary reinforced the thistle as the symbol of Scotland by using it on her Great Seal for all official documents. She also granted the thistle, the emblem of the Guises of Lorraine, her mother's arch-Catholic family, as a heraldic device to James Sandilands of

Calder in West Lothian in 1564, when he became Lord Torphichen. His old title, Lord St John, had ceased that year with the abolition in Scotland of the International Order of the Knights of St John. James Sandilands was a shrewd diplomat. He accompanied Mary of Guise to France in 1550, but also welcomed John Knox to Calder House in 1555. The thistle lost its Catholic association soon after. By 1641, the Protestant Covenanter general Alexander Leslie accepted the thistle on his coat of arms when he became Earl of Leven.

Mary needed a husband to provide an heir to the throne. Various dynastic alliances were considered. Instead, she fell in love with her Stewart cousin, Henry Lord Darnley. They married on 29 June 1565. She was twenty-two. He was eighteen. It seemed an opportune marriage. Both bride and groom were grandchildren of Henry VIII's sister Margaret, wife of King James IV. Darnley, like Mary, loved sport and dancing. They had much in common. On 19 June 1566, Mary gave birth to a son, James. Scotland had an heir. Since Queen Elizabeth I was unmarried, James was heir to the throne of England as well.

By the time James was born, his parents had fallen out of love. Mary had a powerful sense of duty to her native land and tried to play a central role in its government. Darnley had little interest in affairs of state. His drinking, sexual liaisons and sneering arrogance made him a political liability. On 10 February 1567, an explosion destroyed the Edinburgh house where Darnley was staying. He was found strangled in the garden. Who killed him? The main suspect was James Hepburn, Earl of Bothwell, Mary's close adviser and friend. He was charged with murder but acquitted when he appeared for trial in Edinburgh accompanied by a small army. He made it plain to John Manderstoun, canon of Dunbar, that 'there shall not fail to be noses and lugges (ears) cut and far greater displeasures' if Bothwell did not get what he wanted.

Bothwell was powerful and ruthless. Mary, widowed for the second time, began to see him as the strong consort she needed to govern Scotland and protect her infant son. He saw Mary as a means of becoming King of Scotland. Protestants and Catholics combined to make the marriage possible. On 3 May 1567 the Protestant Commissary Court granted Bothwell a divorce from his wife, Jean. On 7 May, the Catholic Archbishop Hamilton pronounced an annulment of Bothwell's current marriage. On 15 May, Mary and Bothwell were married by a Protestant minister in the great hall at Holyrood Palace.

Mary was on the edge of mental collapse. The day after her marriage, Sir James Melville heard her ask for a knife to kill herself. When her equerry Arthur Erskine tried to calm her, she said she would drown herself instead. An alliance of Scots nobles moved rapidly to prevent Bothwell exerting more power. This meant removing the Queen.

On 15 June 1567, at Carberry Hill in East Lothian, Bothwell and Mary led an army to meet the massed forces assembled by nobles, including Morton, Home, Atholl, Mar, Glencairn, Lindsay, Ruthven and Kirkcaldy of Grange. As with the confrontation at Auchterarder eight years before, there was no battle.

The difference between the Peace of Auchterarder in 1559 and the parley at Carberry Hill in 1567 was that Auchterarder saw a truce between evenly balanced opponents, whereas Carberry Hill saw the collapse of Mary, Queen of Scots' rule. Bothwell was given a safe conduct and fled to Norway where he fell into the hands of a relative of his former mistress Anna Throndsen. This was Erik Rosencrantz, one of the few real-life characters in Shakespeare's play *Hamlet*. Bothwell was placed in solitary confinement and died insane in 1578.

Mary was taken to Edinburgh where, the day after Carberry Hill, she was seen leaning from a window, half-naked and dishevelled, screaming she had been betrayed. She was moved to Loch Leven Castle, where she was forced to sign papers abdicating the throne and creating her one-year-old son King James VI of Scotland. Her claim to the English throne was in tatters. By the age of twenty-four, Mary, Queen of Scots had lost three husbands and three kingdoms.

Mary was never to see her son again. The infant King James VI was placed in the protection of her half-brother, James Stewart, Earl of Moray, illegitimate son of King James V. Moray was a pragmatic politician and moderate Protestant, who had taken refuge on the continent as Bothwell rose to power. Now he returned as Regent of Scotland. To him, security for Scotland meant forming a defensive alliance with Protestant England. Negotiations were compromised on 25 March 1568 when Mary, Queen of Scots escaped from Loch Leven Castle, rallied a small army, which Moray and Morton defeated at Langside on 13 May. She then fled to England, and took shelter in Carlisle Castle where, as she wrote to the Earl of Cassilis, she was 'right well and honourably treated'.

What was Queen Elizabeth I to do with her unwanted guest? It was not the first time that a Scottish monarch had been a prisoner in England. David II and James I had spent long periods of captivity, and had served the English crown. Mary, Queen of Scots' case was different. Catholics saw Mary as the legitimate Queen of England. Elizabeth did not want to provoke a rebellion or Catholic invasion by executing or harming her rival. Instead, Mary was moved from one English castle to another, usually in reasonable comfort with a retinue of servants, a prisoner increasingly devoted to philosophical reflection.

Mary's writings show that she remained a devout Catholic but had no taste for religious persecution. She wrote poetry in French, the language in which she could best express the subtlety of her thoughts. In one poem *Méditation sur l'inconstance et vanité du monde*, she tries to reconcile the conflicting Protestant and Catholic doctrines of salvation. Catholics believed in salvation by good works (Heaven is the reward for observing the law of God during your lifetime on Earth). Protestants believed in predestination (Before you are born, God has already decided whether he wants you in heaven).

The imprisoned Mary, Queen of Scots increasingly focussed on heaven. Her followers had more earthly matters in mind. Most leading Scots nobles were by now Protestant, but there remained a pro-French faction led by Arran, an expedient Catholic and now Duke of Châtelherault, and his Hamilton family friends. John Knox continued to preach hatred of Catholicism. The tricky Earl of Argyll, the unreliable Marquis of Huntly and the even more unreliable William Maitland of Lethington intrigued with both sides. The Earl of Moray was murdered, shot in Linlithgow by Hamilton of Bothwellhaugh on 23 January 1569. He was replaced as Regent by Matthew Stewart, 4th Earl of Lennox, father of Mary's murdered husband Henry, Lord Darnley.

Elizabeth I had backed Lennox, hoping to gain from his hatred of the Catholic Hamiltons. Lennox did not last long as Regent. He was killed on 3 Sept 1571 in Stirling when a fight broke out, following a raid by Kirkcaldy of Grange who controlled Edinburgh Castle. John Erskine, 1st Earl of Mar, became Regent. He died in October 1572.

Scottish politics became so unstable that there was no durable party with which foreign nations could engage with any confidence. Political pamphlets urged various forms of extremism. Edinburgh was unsafe. Even John Knox withdrew to St Andrews. On 24 November 1572, John Knox died. The same day, James Douglas, 4th Earl of Morton, became Regent. He set about milking crown revenues for his own benefit and that of his many relatives. On 23 February 1573, Châtelherault and other Catholic nobles signed the Pacification of Perth, belatedly acknowledging Mary's abdication.

Morton was ruthless and lasted longer than his predecessors. Arran died in 1575. Morton had Kirkcaldy of Grange executed. Maitland of Lethington died mysteriously. Morton fell from power when the teenage King James VI became extremely fond of a Catholic man twenty years older than himself, Esmé Stewart, nephew of Matthew, 4th Earl of Lennox.

James VI had previously been influenced by his tutor, George Buchanan, a brilliant scholar and unscrupulous flatterer, who praised Mary, Queen of Scots as her courtier, then wrote vicious, Protestant extremist tracts against her when she was deposed. Esmé Stewart was made 1st Duke of Lennox. He accused Morton of complicity in the murder of Henry Darnley. Morton was executed in June 1581 on the Maiden, a guillotine that he himself had introduced to Scotland. The last of James VI's ill-fated Regents was dead. Buchanan died in 1582.

James VI was by now fifteen years old and began to rule in his own right with Esmé, 1st Duke of Lennox as his trusted adviser. In 1582, William Ruthven, 1st Earl of Gowrie, seized the King with the support of leading Protestant nobles. Esmé Stewart fled. The Ruthven administration only lasted a year. In 1583, James VI escaped its clutches, backed by moderate reformers, including the Earls of Montrose and Argyll who temporarily put aside their traditional Graham versus Campbell dislike. Gowrie was executed the following year.

James Stewart, Earl of Arran who, confusingly, had been given the title in 1581 when the Hamiltons were out of favour, led the new government. Although Arran was John Knox's brother-in-law, he avoided religious extremes. He ended up pleasing neither side and fled from Scotland in 1585.

Scotland's economy depended largely on the land. Agriculture needs stability to flourish. Small towns, no matter how strategically important, decline without intelligent investment. In the Auchterarder area, the bluster and intrigue of Edinburgh politics and the sectarian violence in the port of Perth were ruinous to trade. The once royal castle of Auchterarder never received the Renaissance upgrading afforded to Edinburgh and Stirling Castles, nor did the Drummonds make it a fashionable small palace, as the Crichtons did with their castle in the Borders. The Royal Burgh of Auchterarder was surrounded by Drummonds, Murrays and Grahams, but their homes lay outside. Religious reform did not feed the cattle nor make the crops grow better.

18

Inquisitions and Visitations

In which we see fabulous riches abroad and leaking roofs at home

During the mid sixteenth century, amid the chaos of many regencies and political lurching between Catholicism and Protestantism, the Scottish economy had suffered. In Europe, Scotland's traditional outlets, Bruges, Antwerp and Middleburg, were in the hands of an increasingly oppressive Spanish government. King Philip II, far away in Madrid, ruled the Netherlands through governors, first the ineffectual Margaret, Duchess of Parma, then the brutal Fernando, Duke of Alva backed by the Spanish Inquisition and a large army.

The Council of State, made up of nobles from the seventeen principalities of the Netherlands, was marginalized. The Protestant printing industry was driven underground. It became hard to smuggle reforming tracts to Scotland. Taxes were levied to make the Dutch pay for the troops that occupied their country. In 1568, Prince William I of Orange, a moderate Catholic who turned Protestant, led a revolt. He was called 'William the Silent' because of his tacit diplomacy.

Alva crushed the rebel army, but William the Silent survived and continued his opposition. He won the support of Protestants who increasingly dominated the textile and brewing industries that suffered under heavy Spanish taxation.

The battle of the faiths was wider and more complex than a Catholic versus Protestant conflict. The Spanish Inquisition tried to exterminate Islam in Spain, where Black African and Arab Moriscos had worked as traders, manufacturers and scholars for centuries. In 1526, their Moorish names, clothing and the Arabic language were banned. In 1566, a new Inquisitor General, Espinosa, promoted even more severe edicts, including destruction of the Moorish baths, which were popular cultural centres. A Morisco revolt flared up. It was crushed by Philip II's half brother, Don John of Austria, an illegitimate son of the Emperor Charles V.

Philip II feared the international power of Islam, particularly the Ottoman Turkish Empire. In the Eastern Mediterranean, the Turks, Venice and Genoa fought for control of trade, making and breaking alliances with France, Spain and the Hapsburg Empire. The Turks captured the Island of Rhodes in 1530, ousting the Knights Hospitallers of St John, a fabulously wealthy Crusading Order.

In 1565 a Turkish fleet besieged the island of Malta where the Knights of St John now lived. From June to September, the Knights held out until they were relieved by a Christian force drawn from across Europe, led by Don Garcia de

Toledo. The wealthy, secretive Knights of St John Hospitallers had links all across the Christian world. In Scotland, they established the Preceptory of Torphichen in West Lothian as early as the twelfth century.

The Christian Western Mediterranean remained vulnerable to Islamic Turkish fleets until August 1571 when Don John of Austria rallied a huge Armada and attacked the Turkish navy at Lepanto in their own home waters. Don John's heavy cannon sank around eighty Turkish ships. Over a hundred Turkish galleys were captured. It was a rout that reduced the Turks to a minor sea power.

In 1573, Philip II replaced the Duke of Alva with a more diplomatic Governor of the Netherlands, Don Luis de Requesens, but when he died in 1576, Spanish troops ran amok in Antwerp, murdering and looting. Philip then appointed Don John of Austria. Illegitimacy was no bar to high office. The Emperor Charles V's bastard, Don John, was appointed Governor of the Netherlands, just as King James V's bastard, the Earl of Moray, had been Regent of Scotland.

As with Scottish Regents, Governors of the Netherlands did not last long. Unlike Scotland, they did not die violently. Philip II replaced Don John with Alexander, Duke of Parma, a capable soldier, not a dashing admiral like Don John. In 1579, by the Union of Utrecht, William the Silent organised the northern provinces into a league, the United Provinces. This divided the Netherlands into a mainly Protestant north and a mainly Catholic south, similar to the states of Holland and Belgium today. The Duke of Parma combined diplomacy and force in his attempt to control both.

On 10 July 1584, William the Silent was assassinated. He had successfully kept the cause of Dutch independence alive and, by shrewd diplomacy, encouraged a new rift between France and Spain. His son, Maurice of Nassau, succeeded him and kept up pressure on the Spanish occupying forces. Elizabeth of England sent her close friend Robert Dudley, Earl of Leicester with an army to support the Protestant Dutch. Leicester's bungling intrigues alienated him from all sides. In 1587 he retreated to England and died of a fever soon after.

From 1568, Mary, Queen of Scots had been a prisoner in England, following in the footsteps of King David II and King James I centuries before. Unlike them, she was never allowed to visit the English court nor serve the English monarch. Elizabeth I and Mary, Queen of Scots never met, though they wrote to one another. Elizabeth was aware that Mary was seen by Catholics as the rightful Queen of England, especially after Pope Pius V excommunicated Elizabeth in 1570 and issued a Papal bull declaring her deposed from the throne of England.

Elizabeth I reacted by imposing penal statutes against Catholics. In 1571, Elizabeth's secret service, led by Sir Francis Walsingham, was alerted to Catholic plots. Walsingham's attitude to Mary, Queen of Scots was uncompromising. He wrote that Mary was a member of the House of Guise 'a race that is both enemy to God and the common quiet of Europe'. In 1571, an Italian financier, Roberto Ridolfi, contrived a plan to assassinate Elizabeth and have Mary, Queen of Scots married to the leading Catholic peer, the Duke of Norfolk. The plot was uncovered and, on the basis of evidence, some of which may have been faked by Walsingham, the Duke of Norfolk was executed.

Mary, Queen of Scots was moved from castle to castle in the north of England.

Her jailer was the Earl of Shrewsbury, a kindly hard-working man with a powerful sense of duty to Elizabeth I. He had made an unfortunate marriage to Bess of Hardwicke, a grasping, spiteful woman whose selfishness, ill-temper, greed and treachery became a torment to her husband. Life in their household was tense and unpleasant.

Shrewsbury enjoyed Mary's company, though he complained about the cost of keeping her. Mary's retinue during most of her imprisonment was between thirty and forty servants and officials. When Elizabeth first gave Mary to Shrewsbury to guard in 1569, he was allowed £52 each week to maintain her household. In 1575, this was cut to £30 per week. Shrewsbury complained, but the notoriously stingy Elizabeth told him to bear the extra cost himself, implying that he would fall from her favour if he did not.

Bess of Hardwicke sought to ingratiate herself with Mary. The two women spent hours making embroideries, many of which survive today. Mary loved word-games. Her embroideries are full of them, including *En mon fin est mon commencement* (In my end is my beginning). She made enigmatic anagrams of her name, Marie Stuart, like *Sa vertue m'attire* (I am drawn to his/her virtue).

Locked in prison, it was hard for her to have a picture of the political realities outside. In 1581, she learned that the Regent Morton had been executed for his part in the murder of Mary's husband Darnley fourteen years before. Mary stood accused of the same crime, though she had never been allowed to see the evidence compiled and manufactured against her. She had not seen her son, King James VI, since he was snatched from her as a one-year-old baby in 1567 and indoctrinated by the devious Protestant extremist George Buchanan. James's polite, businesslike letters to her gave no hint of his feelings.

Mary, Queen of Scots still saw herself as the leader of the Catholic cause in the British Isles. In 1583, Francis Throgmorton, an Englishman with Jesuit links, plotted with Spanish and French Catholics to assassinate Elizabeth I and make Mary, Queen of England. Walsingham caught him, uncovering correspondence implicating Mary. Throgmorton was executed. Elizabeth I expelled the Jesuits from England, but continued to think Mary was less of a threat as a live prisoner than as a dead martyr.

Elizabeth's Secretary of State, William Cecil, Lord Burghley, wanted Mary disposed of once and for all. In 1586, Sir Anthony Babington, a former page to the Earl of Shrewsbury, tried to organise another plot to assassinate Elizabeth and place Mary on the English throne. He wrote to Mary. Mary replied, unaware that Walsingham was monitoring their correspondence. On 15 October, English parliamentary commissioners found Mary guilty of conspiracy against Elizabeth. The only possible penalty was death.

Elizabeth was reluctant to sign the death warrant, aware that to authorise the execution of a monarch could set a dangerous precedent for herself. Months passed. Elizabeth, nagged by Burghley and Walsingham, finally signed the death warrant. Mary was executed in Fotheringhay Castle in Northamptonshire on 7 February 1587.

Catholic Europe sought revenge for Mary's execution. In May 1588, a huge Spanish Armada set sail from Portugal. The intention was to transport the Duke of Parma's troops for an invasion of England. Bad weather and superior English seamanship broke up the Spanish fleet. The leading English captains, Francis Drake, John Hawkins and Martin Frobisher, were men with great international experience. Drake had already sailed round the world (1577–80) and plundered Spanish ships in South America.

The English fleet attacked the Spanish Armada in the English Channel and chased it in late summer and autumn of 1588 as far north as the River Forth estuary. The Spaniards continued their escape round the north of Scotland and down the west coast, devastated by storms. Only fifty-three of the original one hundred and thirty-two ships survived to return to Spain.

Elizabeth I was now secure on her throne. She never married. Her nearest kinsman and heir was the Scottish King James VI. Elizabeth and her shrewd advisers Cecil and Walsingham were satisfied that James shared their beliefs in a religious 'via media' (middle way) and in marginalizing all extremists. They were under no illusions that it would be easy to suppress extremists in Scotland.

Quite apart from the Spanish Armada, Scotland's eastern coastal waters had long been dangerous for merchant vessels. Dutch and English pirates threatened shipping in the English Channel. The French fleet patrolled the east coast of Scotland and sometimes held the Port of Leith. The Port of Perth, the main trade outlet for Strathearn's agricultural produce, was now a hotbed of Protestant revolution, inspired by John Knox. Auchterarder's export of animal hides dwindled away. The local economy slid into decline. By the late sixteenth century, it had become a subsistence economy and a home for petty criminals.

In 1570 and 1581, The Royal Burgh of Auchterarder no longer felt able to send Commissioners to Parliament which lamented that, 'Ochterardair was very puir and meikle infested with gipsies and sorners (vagrants who demanded free lodging).' Parliament then passed an act 'Ratification of the Fair of Auchterarder' to stimulate business, designating 25 November as the date for an annual fair. This event, changed to 6 December by the reformed calendar, continued until the twentieth century and became the local date for settling annual accounts. A second Auchterarder Annual Town Fair date was later set for 29 June.

With the decline of the Abbey of Inchaffray, the parishes of Auchterarder and Aberuthven came under the control of the Bishop of Dunblane. Andrew Graham, first Protestant Bishop of Dunblane, secured his bishopric in 1575 with the help of his kinsman, John Graham, 3rd Earl of Montrose, who later became High Treasurer, Chancellor and Viceroy of Scotland. As thanks for his job, Bishop Graham feued the lands and rents of his entire diocese to the Earl. Catholic financial abuse was replaced by an equally brazen Protestant variant.

The Reformation restructured church government in Scotland. Rule by bishops was replaced by new, theoretically democratic, collectives, called presbyteries. The Stewart monarchy, however, preferred bishops as a means of enforcing royal authority. The freedom to make local religious decisions became a frequent battleground in Auchterarder for three hundred years.

After 1560, St Mackessog's was converted to a Protestant parish church, with a reader David Murye. In 1568 John Hamyll became the first Protestant minister of the parish, arriving from neighbouring Dunning.

The importance of Auchterarder in the late sixteenth century was shown in 1591 when the fifteen parishes of Strathearn formed a presbytery and named it Auchterarder Presbytery, an administrative body that has lasted to this day.

By that time, the Protestant Church in the Dunblane Diocese had the power to exclude Catholics from posts such as local government officials or schoolmasters. Commissioners were appointed to examine each parish. People could be prosecuted for celebrating Catholic mass, or a holy day, or going on a pilgrimage. Paranoia grew. Lighting a bonfire could be taken as evidence of witchcraft.

On 14 October 1586, the Commissioners spent the morning in Aberuthven. In front of Kirk elders Watson, Spence, Smith, Robson, Murray and others, they noted the parish had only a reader (lay preacher) and lacked a minister of its own, but the Rev. John Hamyll came to preach occasionally. Their hunt for adulterers revealed only James Mackie, a smith, whose affair with Janet Cortie they knew about already.

The Commissioners tried to get Aberuthven to denounce the Rev. John Hamyll, who had been suspended by Perth Synod but, as the official record grudgingly shows, 'the people present spoke nothing of him but good'. Nor did local people seem much concerned about James and Janet. On the other hand, four different people claimed the right to income from the Parish Kirk's glebe (church land). The Commissioners went away, unable to sort this out.

Before they went, they inspected the old parish Kirk, whose ruins still stand at the west end of the village. They told the Earl of Montrose's tacksman, as patron of the local Kirk, to fix a hole in its thatched roof. He said he would. The Commissioners noted that they had found no witches or papists in Aberuthven that morning and moved on to Auchterarder for the afternoon.

In front of elders Drummond, Cairney, Watt, Brough, Arthur, William Graham, burgess John Graham and deacons Drummond and Patterson, the Commissioners noted that Rev. John Hamyll was also part-time in Auchterarder. They found two cases of adultery. Robert Clark had moved in with his brother's wife, Christiane, some fourteen years before. The Commissioners noted they were 'obstinate'. Adam Sharp's servant Annie Cairnie had borne him two children. What Sharp's wife, Agnes Kirk, thought about it is not recorded.

The Commissioners' report for Auchterarder does not mention the chapel that had stood down Chapel Wynd since the Middle Ages, nor its little parish school. They may have fallen into disuse by 1586. Instead, the Commissioners concentrated on the Kirk, St Mackessog's, whose ruins lie beyond the end of today's Hunter Street (then called Powhillock Road). It was in poor condition even in 1586. It had been stripped of ornaments, probably by Knox's rampaging 'congregation' in 1559, and its thatched roof was leaking badly. James Drummond of Kirkhill and others agreed to form a committee to sort it out.

The Reader, David Murye, complained that he had not received his salary for two years. The Commissioners said they hoped to do something about it. Finally, the Commissioners found no witches or papists in Auchterarder and went away. The Church of Scotland still conducts parish visitations, ever concerned with finance and order, though not at present with witches.

19

The Union of the Crowns
and the Burning of Witches

*In which we see a King with two hats, the publication of the
world's biggest best-seller, and herbal healers burned as witches*

While Elizabeth I of England and James VI of Scotland pursued a 'middle way' of religious tolerance to promote political unity and marginalize extremists, France was torn apart.

Mary, Queen of Scots' first husband, King Francis II of France, died in 1560. His brother Charles IX succeeded him. The Protestant cause in France was led by the Huguenots, whose name comes from the Swiss French *Eyguenets*, a confederation of Calvinists who opposed the Duke of Savoy. The Huguenot Gaspard de Coligny rose to become an admiral and close adviser of King Charles IX, much to the anger of the King's Catholic mother, Catharine de Medici. With all the deceit and brutality of her Italian Renaissance relatives, Catharine encouraged the Catholic Guises to attack the Huguenots.

An unknown assassin shot and wounded Coligny in 1572, shortly after the wedding of the Huguenot leader Henri de Navarre to Margaret de Valois, for which all France's leading Huguenots had assembled in Paris. Two days later, on St Bartholomew's Day, 24 August, the Guises and other Catholic nobles sent armed gangs to massacre the Huguenots.

The Catholics murdered Coligny. His mutilated body was hung up for display, much as the Protestants had dangled Cardinal Beaton's defiled corpse from a window in St Andrews Castle in 1546. Hundreds of Huguenots were massacred. Henri of Navarre was captured and chose to accept the Catholic mass rather than face death.

In 1574 Charles IX died. He was succeeded by his brother Henri III, whose retinue of effete homosexuals earned him the nickname 'Prince of Sodom'. His mother Catharine de Medici desperately clung to power, conceding more freedom to the Huguenots. Their leader Henri de Navarre, married to the King's sister, was now heir to the French throne.

In the years 1587 to 1589, the Roman Catholic cause in north-west Europe suffered a series of damaging blows. The Spanish Armada was defeated. Mary, Queen of Scots was executed. Her influential cousins, Henri, Duke of Guise and his Cardinal brother Louis were both murdered in France. Catharine de Medici did not live long enough to see her last son Henri III stabbed to death by a Dominican friar Jacques Clément who believed he acted as the agent of God.

Henri de Navarre inherited the throne of France. He was an astute general and decisively defeated a Catholic army at the Battle of Ivry in 1590. He had once converted to Catholicism under pain of death, after the St Bartholomew Day's Massacre, but had reverted to Protestantism. On 15 July 1593, he converted to Catholicism again in order to have a coronation approved by the Pope. In 1598, he issued the Edict of Nantes, which granted freedom of worship to the Huguenots. Did this end the wars of religion in Europe? No. The worst was yet to come.

The old generation of warring sixteenth-century monarchs was almost gone. Philip II of Spain died in 1598. His successor, Philip III, fought a long war of attrition in the Netherlands against Maurice of Nassau, son of William the Silent and leader of the Protestant United Provinces. Maurice gained ground when Spanish armies were diverted to help the Catholic cause in France. Despite the Triple Alliance of the United Provinces, England and France in 1598, Maurice was not able to establish a stable trading economy for the Dutch ports.

Across the North Sea, Elizabeth I of England was old and unmarried. She had secured a Protestant succession by executing the Catholic Mary, Queen of Scots and establishing good relations with Mary's Protestant son, James VI of Scotland, who was the most direct legitimate descendant and heir of his great-great grandfather, King Henry VII.

Just as Henry VII began a new royal dynasty in England, the Tudors, so James VI of Scotland brought the Stuart dynasty to the English throne when Elizabeth I died on 24 March 1603. As long before as 1071, the Scottish King Malcolm III Canmore, with his Castle in Auchterarder, had sworn fealty to King William I the Conqueror of England, but it had taken over five hundred more years for the Scottish and English crowns to be united in one person.

Union of the crowns did not bring peace. Even in the twenty-first century, public opinion is split. Some today cite the 1320 Declaration of Arbroath, a letter from Scottish barons to the Pope after the Battle of Bannockburn, and make a case for Scottish independence from England. Other Scots regard England, particularly London, as an opportunity to acquire top political and financial jobs in the British Isles. King James VI and most of his nobles took the latter view and headed south with his court soon after he inherited the English throne in 1603.

By 1603, James VI and I was a married man with children. In his teenage years, James had had a preference for male rather than female company. It was the King's duty to father an heir and a wife had to be found for him. In 1590 his choice was made. Anne, younger daughter of King Frederick II of Denmark, had much to commend her politically. She was a Protestant. Her father's kingdom had strong trading links with Protestant states in northern Europe. From the twenty-four-year-old James VI's point of view, she was a sixteen-year-old willowy blonde with a friendly disposition. They were married on November 23 1590 in Oslo, which was under Danish rule.

James VI did not return to Scotland until May 1 1591. He made the most of his stay in Denmark. He found his young wife delightful and wrote poems in her praise. He also enjoyed erudite debates with Danish theologians and spent time with the astronomer Tycho Brahe, who produced detailed calculations showing that the Earth was a ball revolving round the Sun. To Catholics, this finding was heretical. The Spanish Inquisition continued to argue that the Earth was flat and the fixed centre of God's universe.

James VI had an inquiring mind and a passion for writing. In 1590, he produced *Basilikon Doron*, in which he argued that the King had a divine right to have final say in matters of State and Church. He offended the ultra-Protestant theologian Andrew Melville, who favoured rule by Parliament and the General Assembly of the Church of Scotland. Melville was Principal of Glasgow University, then advanced to Principal of St Mary's College of St Andrews University, which had long been a hotbed of vindictive controversy.

Aberdeen University's Principal Hector Boece had written *Histories of the Scots from the Origins of the Race* in 1527, a piece of nationalist special pleading that formed the model for James VI's tutor George Buchanan's *History of Scotland*, a multi-volume Puritan rant which he completed shortly before he died in 1582. Buchanan had been made Principal of St Leonard's College at St Andrews University in 1566, a post requiring the approval of Mary, Queen of Scots to whom he had devoted Latin flattery. When she fell from power the following year, Buchanan wrote *Ane Detection of the Doings of Mary Quene*, a vicious amalgam of fact and fiction designed to harm her and further his own political career. Both he and Melville became Moderators of the General Assembly of the Church of Scotland.

James VI, once in the security of England, banned his old tutor's *History of Scotland* as a seditious tract. James himself was never short of opinions on all matters. In 1604, he wrote *A Counterblaste to Tobacco*, deriding doctors' and retailers' claims for its therapeutic value. He wrote *The Perfyte Poet*, defining what is worthwhile in poetry.

His greatest literary achievement was to commission a new translation of the Bible that would be accurate and thorough. The Pope insisted on a Latin Bible only, keeping the scriptures in the grasp of priests. This seemed a nonsense to the scholarly James VI, who favoured mass education. The Geneva Bible, with its Calvinist prejudices, was equally unacceptable to him. In 1604, the year after he became King of England, James appointed the English scholar Lancelot Andrewes to direct a team of translators at Westminster. John Harding at Oxford and Edward Lively at Cambridge led more translators. The best Hebrew and Greek original texts were consulted.

In 1611, the Authorised Version, also known as the King James Bible, was printed. It remains the best-selling book ever published. Its dignity and clarity made it ideal for reading out loud in Church or for study at home. It is contemporary with the late plays of Shakespeare and shares their vigour of language. Because of its wide distribution, the King James Bible standardised spelling and grammar in the English language as never before.

James VI's sensitivity to language made him use the French form of his surname, Stuart, rather than the Scottish form, Stewart, which betrayed his family origins as fourteenth-century stewards, servants of the crown, rather than kings themselves. The French Stuart also, in print at least, avoided the obvious pun on 'stews', the seventeenth-century term for brothels.

James VI and I was more comfortable in England than he had ever been in Scotland, where murder was never far away. In 1600 at Gowrie House in Perth, there had been a more violent repeat of the 1582 Ruthven Raid. James came close to being stabbed. His attendants killed his Presbyterian attackers, John Ruthven, 3rd Earl of Gowrie and his brother, Alexander Gowrie, Master of Ruthven. In London, assassins never came within touching distance, although, on 5 November 1605 a Catholic plot, led by Robert Catesby and Guy Fawkes, to blow up the Houses of Parliament was narrowly foiled. To this day, bonfires are lit all over Britain and firework displays light up the sky on 5 November to celebrate the foiling of the Gunpowder Plot. Until the end of the twentieth century, 'Guys' were burned in effigy on Bonfire Night. Today even Catholic-led Councils put on a show, though its historical symbolism is left unspoken.

James soon discovered that his Queen Anne of Denmark made an excellent teenage girl, fond of dancing and fun, but a dull, shallow adult. She had no taste for his intellectual pursuits, nor for the business of government. The couple did their dynastic duty. On 15 February 1594, a male heir was born at Stirling Castle and named Henry Frederick after his two grandfathers, Henry Lord Darnley and Frederick II of Denmark. To England, the name Henry also conjured up the might of the Tudor Kings Henry VII and Henry VIII. Queen Anne bore two daughters, Elizabeth, who grew up to marry the German Protestant leader Frederick, Elector of the Palatine, and Margaret, who died in infancy.

In 1600 at Dunfermline, a second son, Charles, was born. It was just as well that there was an heir and a spare. Prince Henry died of typhus on November 6 1612. His mother, Queen Anne, and King James VI drifted apart. They kept separate households in London. The King bore her no ill will and wrote a gentle elegy when she died on 2 March 1619.

England was developing global trading links that left Scotland behind. Ambitious Scots needed to associate themselves with successful English-based enterprise. Helpfully, a panel of English judges ruled that all Scots born after the Union of the Crowns in 1603 had the same rights in England as James's English-born subjects.

English mariners had explored routes that led to the formation of profitable companies. In 1553 Richard Chancellor sailed north-east, hoping to find an Arctic passage to India and the Spice Islands. Instead, he arrived in the Russian port of Archangel. The Emperor Ivan the Terrible was impressed. The Muscovy Company was soon created. New possibilities of Baltic trade opened up.

There was no viable northern route to the Indian Ocean but the southern route round Africa provided great opportunities. The East India Company, founded in 1600, was granted a monopoly of trade east of the Cape of Good Hope. In 1612 the East India Company defeated their Portuguese trading rivals at the sea battle of Swally Roads, north of today's Mumbai. With the permission of the Great Mogul of India, the company built a factory at Surat and expanded its influence rapidly.

In the West Indies, Sir John Hawkins tried but failed to compete in the slave trade dominated by Spain. There were other opportunities in the Americas. In 1579, during his voyage round the world, Sir Francis Drake took theoretical but not yet practical possession of British Columbia for Queen Elizabeth I. In 1583, Sir Humphrey Gilbert did the same in Newfoundland on the opposite coast of Canada. In 1584, Sir Walter Raleigh tried to found a settlement in Virginia, which he named after Elizabeth I, the Virgin Queen.

After King James VI of Scotland became James I of England, exploration turned into colonisation. Barbados was captured in 1605. In 1606, James granted charters to the London Company, which founded Jamestown, the first durable colony on the North American mainland. The Native American Princess Pocahontas rescued from death the colony's leader Captain John Smith. Their story quickly became the stuff of romantic legend. In 1606, James also granted a charter to the Plymouth Company, which tried unsuccessfully to found a colony in chilly Maine.

The Plymouth Company's most lasting exploit was to license a group of extreme Protestants, uncomfortable with King James' 'middle way' of religion, to sail west in 1620 in search of a new home. They founded New Plymouth, north of today's Boston. These Pilgrim Fathers, led by William Bradford, developed a stern Puritan regime that gave its character to New England.

James VI's instinct for religious tolerance extended to his own Queen Anne of Denmark, who came to prefer the Catholic mass but owed no allegiance to the Pope in Rome. James, who was obsessed by orderly structures, believed that Christianity in Britain would be better governed by a hierarchy of bishops, on the Church of England model, rather than by an egalitarian General Assembly of representatives from presbyteries like the Church of Scotland. Royally appointed bishops in Scotland sat in an uncomfortable relationship with the presbyteries.

In 1607, a move to unite the English and Scottish Parliaments broke down because too many private interests would have been swept away by a unified system. Officials and lesser politicians never vote for a reduction in public jobs with personal incentives. It took another hundred years for the British government to offer a level of bribes high enough to achieve the Union of the Parliaments in 1707. It then took almost three hundred years more for another British government to offer sufficient political bribes to break up the Union of Parliaments again in 1999.

In Ireland, most of the population remained Catholic. As in the Scottish Highlands, much of the poor peasantry remained loyal to the clan system. From 1606, King James encouraged Lowland Protestant Scots to colonise Ireland. Some Catholic Irish peers, like the Earls of Tyrconnel and Tyrone, fled to Europe. The Protestant 'Plantation of Ulster' created sectarian hostilities that remain to this day.

King James VI and I sought a balance of dynastic alliances. Across the English Channel, the moderate King Henri IV was murdered in 1610. His successor Louis XIII brought a more relentlessly Catholic regime to power. To outflank France, James VI and I arranged the marriage of his daughter Elizabeth in 1613 to the powerful German Protestant leader Frederick, Elector of the Rhine Palatinate. Given the influence of Spain in the Netherlands, James believed that a Spanish dynastic alliance would be helpful to trade. He tried to persuade his heir Prince Henry to agree to marry a Spanish princess if a suitable one could be found. Henry refused to marry a Catholic, but, when Henry died of typhus in 1612, his brother Charles had no such religious objections.

Objections to a Catholic royal marriage were voiced in the Parliaments. In 1623, Prince Charles, heir to the united crowns of Scotland and England, went to Spain under the name John Smith in a secret mission to meet the Spanish Infanta with a view to marrying her. Negotiations broke down when King Philip IV of Spain refused to give back the Rhine Palatinate, which the Hapsburgs had captured from Charles's brother-in-law Frederick in 1620. Instead, a bride was sought from Spain's old enemy, France. In June 1625, Charles married the Catholic Henrietta Maria, youngest daughter of the murdered King Henri IV. King James VI and I, remembered as 'the wisest fool in Christendom', did not live to see the wedding. He died on March 27 1625, leaving the Protestant succession precariously balanced.

Elizabeth I's and James VI's 'middle way' of religious tolerance did not last long. The scholarship that went into the Authorised Version of the Bible did not eliminate violent superstition.

Seventeenth-century Scotland was a mixture of sophisticated verbiage and backward agriculture. It was the stuff of humour. Auchterarder was well known to King James VI, even though its Royal Castle had long since fallen into ruins, and the High Street of Auchterarder was notorious for its 'cundies', evil-smelling open drains. Householders laid planks across from their front doors to reach the street. Once, at James's court in Edinburgh a visiting English courtier boasted to the king about splendid English fortified towns, each with a drawbridge. George Buchanan squashed the English boast by snapping back, 'In Scotland there is a town with a hundred drawbridges: Auchterarder,' omitting to say what these drawbridges were.

In Perth, the bridge situation was no laughing matter. As long before as 1210, Perth Castle was swept away when the River Tay flooded after a snowy winter. After four hundred years of officials discussing the problem, no flood defences had been built. In 1621, Perth Bridge was swept away in another Tay flood, cutting the city off from the ancient Scottish coronation site of Scone and the road to Dundee on the opposite bank of the river. Officials met for a further 150 years before the bridge was replaced. It took 200 years more before Perth built flood defences, just in time for the New Millennium.

Auchterarder's drawbridges offered no protection against Puritans. Witch-hunts in the area were at their busiest in the seventeenth century. The word 'witch' comes from the old English *wicce* and means 'a person with alternative wisdom and powers'. The newly established hard-line Puritan Protestants tolerated no alternatives. Anyone with knowledge of medicinal plants was regarded with deep suspicion.

Alexander Drummond, 'The Warlock of the Kirktoun of Auchterarder', was accused by the Kirk Session of Perth of 'unlawful arts, charms and abuses of the people', having healed both people and farm animals with herbal infusions. He was executed in 1629.

It is ironic that the sixth-century St Kessog, whose church stands at the Kirkton, was also a healer who used herbs. St Kessog was revered as a saint. After over a thousand years of 'progress', Alexander Drummond was executed for doing the same thing.

Jean Bendie lived on a croft near Blackford. In 1660, she was charged on two accounts of witchcraft. First, she was accused of brewing love-philtres, magic potions to make unwary innocents fall in love. Jean told the court she only made tansy tea, a refreshing drink, which she sold for a farthing a cup. Secondly, she was accused of curing a child of 'scab' (impetigo) by 'wiles, charms and divers mixtures'. She said that her shepherd father had taught her how to brew certain herbs and mix them into an ointment with goosefat to treat sheep, cattle and pigs suffering from scab. The sick child's mother had asked for some ointment to see if it worked on human skin. It did. Jean Bendie denied uttering any incantations. She was burned as a witch. She was remembered by a thorn tree by the Blackford roadside, Jean Bendie's tree, which survived until the 1930s.

Usually, witches had no monument, but on the road from Aberuthven to Dunning there stands a cairn with the inscription 'Maggie Wall burnt here 1657 as a witch'. Her crime was to make a herbal mash for cows to restore their milk-producing ability.

In 1643, John Brough was condemned to be strangled and burned for digging up three corpses in Glendevon Cemetery and placing the decaying flesh in some farmers' byres to destroy their cattle. He was also convicted of selling what would today be called herbal remedies and for using an 'enchanted stone the size of a dove's egg' for healing. Just before she was executed, another witch, Katharine Mitchell, said she had seen John Brough with the Devil at Rumbling Bridge.

John Brough had learned his trade from Neane Nikclerith, the daughter of Strathearn's most famous witch, Nike Neiving (also known as Kate McNiven) from Monzie. In 1563 she was convicted of theft of cutlery and changing herself into a bee. As she burned to death, she cursed the Campbells of Monzie Castle, who condemned her. She then bit a blue moonstone off her necklet and spat it out to Graham of Inchbrakie, who had treated her well, prophesying that, as long as it was kept by his family, their line would never lack a male heir. Monzie Castle burned down. The male heir of the Grahams of Inchbrakie owns the jewel today.

20

The Thirty Years War

In which empires are made and broken while Scots wield swords and prayer books

King Henri IV of France founded the royal house of Bourbon, succeeding two centuries of Valois kings. Like Elizabeth I and James I of England, Henri IV stabilised his country by a combination of religious moderation and efficient tax collection. Unlike Elizabeth and James, Henri budgeted well, ably assisted by his Huguenot minister Henri Béthune, Duke of Sully.

A Catholic fanatic stabbed Henri IV to death in a Paris street in 1610. His son, Louis XIII, was only ten years old. The Queen Mother Regent, Marie de Medici, Henri IV's second wife, squandered much of Sully's economic work. She promoted a young courtier, Armand du Plessis, who became Cardinal Richelieu, the most powerful politician in Europe. Louis XIII recognised Richelieu's ruthless genius for foreign affairs, making and breaking alliances with Protestants and Catholics whenever expedient.

In 1618, Europe became entangled in a complex war that was to last thirty years. On 22 May 1618, Count Henri Matthias von Thurn, with some Protestant friends, threw the Holy Roman Imperial Regents, Jaroslav Martinitz and William Slavata, out of a window in the Hradschin Palace in Prague. The city was the capital of Bohemia, ruled by the Archduke Ferdinand, heir to the Hapsburg Emperor Matthias. The 'defenestration of Prague' sparked an open revolt. Frederick V, Elector of the Rhine Palatinate, claimed the throne of Bohemia. Frederick was well known to the Scottish and English courts as the husband of King James VI and I's daughter Elizabeth.

When Matthias died in 1619, the new Emperor Ferdinand II led a coalition of southern German Catholic states to reclaim Bohemia and crush the Protestants in Central Europe. On 8 November 1620, at the Battle of the White Hill near Prague, a Catholic army led by Prince Maximilian of Bavaria defeated the Elector Frederick's Protestants. The Emperor Ferdinand then granted the Rhine Palatinate to Maximilian. Frederick and Elizabeth fled, sold the crown jewels and settled in the Protestant United Provinces of the Netherlands.

King Christian IV of Denmark, brother of King James VI and I's Queen Anne, tried to revive concerted Protestant military operations in Europe, but made no headway. For ten years, the Holy Roman Imperial generals Albert von

Wallenstein and Jan Tserklaes, Count of Tilly, made gains for the Catholic cause. Wallenstein drove north towards the Baltic, threatening the profitable northern European trade routes. King Gustavus Adolphus of Sweden rallied a Protestant resurgence.

The Thirty Years War was not a straightforward Catholic against Protestant conflict. The old rivalry between French kings and Hapsburg Holy Roman emperors overrode religious principles. Internal revolt was another matter. The French Cardinal Richelieu crushed a Huguenot armed uprising at La Rochelle in 1626, but then allowed them to practise their Protestant faith and profited from their commercial enterprises. Richelieu also negotiated with Christian IV of Denmark. Queen Marie de Medici grew to resent her protégé and plotted against him. She failed. In 1631 Richelieu persuaded King Louis XIII to exile his own mother. Richelieu also succeeded in reducing the power of the French Parlements and of the provinces of Burgundy, Dauphiné and Provence, which had been semi-autonomous. By advancing the glory of his king and country, Richelieu's own power grew.

Glory costs money. Richelieu drained the French economy in a series of wars. He expanded the army and built a formidable navy with new shipyards at La Rochelle, Brest and Brouage. His primary objective was to reduce the power of Spain, which had already lost its grip on the northern United Provinces of the Netherlands.

Richelieu's leading diplomat was a Capuchin monk, François le Clerc de Tremblay, known as Père Joseph or l'Eminence grise (the grey Eminence). Richelieu backed the Protestant Swedish King Gustavus Adolphus's invasion of Germany. When Gustavus Adolphus was killed at the Battle of Lutzen in 1632, the new Queen Christina and her shrewd chancellor Axel Oxenstierna kept accepting French money to keep a Swedish army in the war. Many Scottish soldiers, such as Alexander Leslie and James, 3rd Marquis of Hamilton, served in the Swedish army, especially after 1636 when France declared war on Spain. Scots merchants settled in Sweden. John Maclean of Duart established a successful business in Gothenburg under the name Hans Maclier.

Richelieu died in 1642 after a long illness. Louis XIII died the following year. Richelieu's successor, Cardinal Jules Mazarin, followed his predecessor's policy of centralising everything on the autocratic authority of the king. The new monarch Louis XIV thrived on splendour and became known as Le Roi Soleil (The Sun King). Mazarin controlled the Royal Council with the help of Nicholas Fouquet, who became hugely rich by skimming off money from the nation's taxes.

The Thirty Years War left Europe's economy in tatters. Trade and agriculture were precarious. The domestic predators, who profit from war, rose and fell with each phase. On 24 October 1648, the major participants signed the Peace of Westphalia, halting the European conflict. Scotland and England saw no peace.

When King James VI and I moved his court to London in 1603, someone had to be left in charge of Scotland. The King chose John Graham, 3rd Earl of Montrose, as Viceroy of Scotland. He had already been Lord Treasurer and Lord Chancellor. He was well connected locally as well as nationally. He married his second cousin Jean, daughter of David, 1st Lord Drummond. Their son, John, 4th Earl of Montrose, was a Royal Commissioner to the General Assembly of the Church of Scotland and became President of the Scottish Privy Council in 1625.

In the same year, the 4th Earl's kinsman and near neighbour, Sir William Graham of Braco, became one of the first Barons of Nova Scotia. This was an attempt to found and fund a Scottish colony in North America. It failed as all attempts at a Scottish empire have failed. Individually, Scots thrive on international business. Collectively, Scottish governments have always bungled imperial projects.

The 4th Earl of Montrose died in 1626, one of the first in Scotland to ruin his health with tobacco, newly imported from the American colonies. He was buried in the family vault in Aberuthven cemetery. His funeral feast at Kincardine Castle lasted eight weeks. Huge quantities of venison, wildfowl and other game from the Graham estates were consumed along with sides of beef and lamb, washed down with gallons of ale and fine wines.

The lavish Graham hospitality showed what could be produced in an Auchterarder economy that had profited from the last two peaceful decades of James VI's long reign. Farming was still primitive. Manure was scarce and used only in fields close to tenants' houses where oats and barley were grown. Wheat, potatoes and turnips were exotic foreign produce.

Auchterarder's commonty, extending from the Townhead to the White Muir, west of the Muirton, was essential grazing land. Cattle were fattened on summer pastures. Most were slaughtered in autumn to save the expense of winter feeding when the few milk cows grew thinner. The market in the centre of the Royal Burgh was the focus of local trade and gossip, imported by travellers and merchants who brought cloth and other products from overseas. There was plentiful fish, especially trout, in the Ruthven Water that flowed through Graham lands. James VI's encyclopaedic knowledge produced legislation of all kinds. Today's environmental protection against pollution in rivers is based on laws introduced in James VI's reign.

The Grahams had been engaged in the question of independence since the late thirteenth century, when Sir John Graham was William Wallace's most trusted ally. His nephew, Sir David Graham, signed the Declaration of Arbroath. Two great houses were united when John, 4th Earl of Montrose, married Margaret Ruthven. She was the sister of John, 3rd Earl of Gowrie, who had been killed in 1600 in front of King James VI in Gowrie House in Perth in mysterious circumstances.

When the 4th Earl's son James was born in 1612, it was rumoured that witches examined him and foretold, 'This boy will trouble all Scotland.' They were right. When the fourteen-year-old James Graham became 5th Earl of Montrose in 1626, Scottish independence was again a major issue.

Even in the twenty-first century, there is still no way of shortening the name King James VI of Scotland and I of England without offending some political faction. The process of smaller kingdoms uniting to form bigger ones had been a persistent trend over the fifteen hundred years since the Romans first named the isles Britannia. The creation of a single United Kingdom of the British Isles had an inevitability about it, paralleled by the unification of other European nations over the next three centuries.

Inevitability is not necessarily popular, particularly when accompanied by big, remote bureaucracy. In the seventeenth century, as today, there were many in the British Isles who preferred regional independence with all its possibilities for individual profits and the enforcement of narrow beliefs.

Kings have always claimed to have God on their side. The only debate is about what God has appointed them to do. Early in his reign, King James VI and I had asserted the divine right of kings to rule Church and state. By 1618, he tried to force an Episcopal liturgy on Scotland by the Five Articles of Perth, but he was astute enough to compromise when divine right and political reality came into conflict. When James died in 1625, his son King Charles I had no talent for compromise. He had inherited his mother Anne of Denmark's vanity plus the Stewart kings' general preference for courtly flattery over wise counsel.

Charles I also inherited a nation in debt. He proceeded to spend heavily, supporting the Protestant cause in Europe, where his uncle Christian IV of Denmark and sister Elizabeth in the Rhine Palatinate needed funds to fight against the Hapsburgs. As an enemy of the Catholic Holy Roman Empire, however, he was automatically an ally of Catholic France, enhanced by the fact that he had a French wife, Henrietta Maria.

The English Parliament, dominated by articulate Protestants like John Pym and John Hampden, was in no mood to support expensive foreign wars. Charles had a preference for more Catholic-leaning advisers, like his chief minister William Laud, Archbishop of Canterbury, or pragmatic advocates of the divine right of kings, like Thomas Wentworth, Earl of Strafford. As Lord Deputy of Ireland from 1632, Strafford was hated for ruthlessly enforcing English rule. When Parliament refused to approve his taxation plans in 1629, King Charles I dissolved it. He did not call another Parliament till 1640.

In Scotland, James VI tried to avoid political confrontation. His son Charles I did not, introducing new taxes and bringing back bishops to give him control over the Church. To Scottish Presbyterians, bishops smelled of Popery. To the nobility and to traders, the level of taxes was intolerable. To the king, his divine right was absolute. Others thought differently.

One who questioned the extent of royal prerogative was James Graham, 5th Earl of Montrose. As a young man he had made a grand tour of Europe in the midst of the Thirty Years War. He studied military tactics at Angers in France, where the vast castle showed state-of-the-art fortification. He learned the same campaign strategies and tactics that the Swedish King Gustavus Adolphus used successfully.

On Montrose's return to Britain in 1636, he was presented at King Charles I's London court. Montrose's sponsor was James, 3rd Marquis and later Ist Duke of Hamilton, who had served in Gustavus Adolphus's army, though with no distinction. Hamilton, jealous of the articulate, good-looking young Montrose, confined his sponsorship to formalities. The King barely spoke to Montrose, who returned to Scotland distrustful of Hamilton but still loyal to the king.

Charles was provocative in person and in politics. Things came to a head in

1637 when he tried to impose a new Prayer Book on the Scottish Church without consulting the Scottish Parliament or Presbyterian leaders. They condemned the Prayer Book and its architect William Laud, Archbishop of Canterbury, whom they believed had no place in Scottish religion. Public demonstrations broke out, especially in Edinburgh where the Prayer Book was hurled at the preacher in the High Kirk of St Giles.

Alexander Henderson, a statesmanlike minister from Fife, joined with a fanatical Presbyterian lawyer, Archibald Johnston of Wariston, to draft The National Covenant. This document promised allegiance to the King, but protested against his financial and religious policies and constant over-ruling of the Scottish Parliament. Montrose and other Scottish nobles signed the National Covenant on 28 February 1638 and became known as Covenanters.

Charles sent the Marquis of Hamilton as commissioner to deal with the Covenanters. Hamilton sensed the possibility of armed rebellion and persuaded Charles to withdraw the Prayer Book as a conciliatory gesture. This was not enough for the Covenanters.

In November 1638, Montrose was the Presbytery of Auchterarder's representative elder at the Glasgow General Assembly, which deposed the bishops and denied Charles's right to be Head of the Church of Scotland.

Charles could not tolerate such open flouting of his authority. On 27 March 1639 he left London with an army to teach the Covenanters a lesson. Hamilton was sent with a fleet to Aberdeen. Thomas Wentworth, soon to be Earl of Strafford, was asked to rally an army in Ireland, sail up the River Clyde, and invade Dumbarton.

The Covenanters were ready. Montrose led an army north and captured Aberdeen on 19 June. Hamilton's fleet could only sit ineffectually offshore. At the same time, Alexander Leslie, an able soldier who had served under Gustavus Adolphus in his German campaigns, led an army to confront King Charles at Duns. There was no battle. The two sides agreed a peace treaty at nearby Berwick on 18 June 1639. A chastened Charles agreed to come to Scotland peacefully in the autumn to attend Parliament and the General Assembly.

Charles did not keep his word. On 20 August 1640, Montrose led an army across the Tweed and occupied Newcastle, cutting off the coal supply to London. By the Treaty of Ripon in October 1640, a chilly Westminster government gave the Scottish Parliament the right to approve royal appointments and regulate much of its own affairs.

21

James Graham,
1st Marquis of Montrose

*In which we find that passionate moderation is the hardest of all political positions
and observe Scotland's great cavalier poet and military strategist in action*

For Montrose, it was enough that King Charles I gave new powers to the Scottish
Parliament. Not so for another Covenanter, Archibald Campbell, 8th Earl of
Argyll, who sought to make himself master of a Presbyterian Scotland. Montrose
wanted to replace the King's policies. Argyll wanted to replace the King.

Montrose was a brilliant soldier with a lifelong appetite for reading. He and
his sisters moved in the highest level of Scottish intellectual society, with all its
opportunities for friendships, jealousy and scandal. His eldest sister Lilias married
Sir John Colquhoun of Luss, an urbane scholar who had travelled widely in
Europe. Montrose's second sister Margaret married Archibald Napier, son of the
great Scottish mathematician and inventor of logarithms, John Napier. Lilias's
marriage collapsed when her husband ran off with her younger sister Katherine,
amid rumours of drugged love philtres and necromancy. Archie Napier, like
Montrose an articulate political moderate, remained his friend for life.

The leading contemporary poet, William Drummond of Hawthornden, held
Montrose in the highest regard and wrote 'The Golden Age is returned' when
Montrose gave him protection to publish previously suppressed work. Montrose
was an able writer himself. He wrote a long poem *To His Mistress*, which, in the
ingenious metaphysical style of the day, works on two levels, both as a declaration
of love to a lady and an affirmation of loyalty to Scotland, but with a warning
that they should not meddle with evil influences.

Montrose's third sister, Dorothy, had married the boy next door, James Rollo,
whose Dunning estates adjoined those of Kincardine Castle. In 1632, Montrose
wrote, asking Rollo and the Graham lairds of Orchill and Balgowan to reassure
John Drummond, 2nd Earl of Perth, that there would never be any dispute over
the Ruthven Water flow from Montrose's Kincardine Estate to the Drummond
Mill at Auchterarder, 'because of the many ties between our families'.

The Earl of Perth, a Privy Councillor to both James VI and Charles I, was
much concerned with improving his estates. He remodelled Drummond Castle
and from 1630 to 1636 created the magnificent Renaissance gardens which

remain today. He employed John Mylne, the King's Master Mason, to design a splendid obelisk sundial at the heart of the formal gardens.

It was not unusual for a Graham to agree with a Drummond. Agreeing with a Campbell was a different matter. Montrose's sister Dorothy died in 1638. James Rollo then married Argyll's half-sister, Lady Mary Campbell. The next-door neighbour was now brother-in-law to Montrose's worst enemy.

The characteristic pride of the Grahams versus the greed of the Campbells was never more explicit than in Montrose and Argyll. Argyll rose to become leader of the Puritan Presbyterian-dominated Scottish Parliament, whose political demands became increasingly anti-monarchist. In contrast, Montrose and twenty other Scottish peers signed the 'Cumbernauld Bond' in 1640, swearing continued allegiance to both King Charles I and the National Covenant, but opposed to the 'particular and indirect practicing of the few'. Parliament imprisoned him for five months for failing to renounce the King. Argyll's Puritans ransacked Kincardine Castle in 1641, hoping to find incriminating evidence. They merely found some old love letters from his days at St Andrews University.

In England, King Charles I was losing control. On 3 November 1640, he summoned Parliament to resolve disputes. The results were not what he had expected. Parliament impeached the Earl of Strafford, accusing him of high treason for deploying an army in Ireland. Archbishop Laud was also impeached. Strafford was executed in 1641. Laud followed him to the scaffold in 1645.

Charles I had been crowned King of England in 1625. On 14 August 1641, he finally came to Edinburgh to be crowned King of Scotland. Parliament tried to humiliate him. James 3rd Marquis of Hamilton, accompanying the King but minding his own back as ever, belatedly signed the National Covenant. There were rumours of assassination plots against the King and against Argyll. King Charles managed to negotiate Montrose's release from prison. He also promoted Argyll from an Earl to a Marquis.

The King left Scotland in November 1641 to deal with other matters. Ireland had just exploded into civil war. Without the iron-willed Strafford to restrain them, Irish Catholics massacred many English and Scots Presbyterians who had been granted land on favourable terms since the early seventeenth century in the 'Plantation of Ulster'. The conflict, with alternate phases of violence and mutual dislike occasionally tempered by tolerance, continues today.

Charles made the mistake of trying to impeach five leading Puritan members of Parliament, including John Pym. They sheltered in the city of London, where Puritan Roundheads, so called because they favoured the short-cropped haircuts of apprentices, outnumbered Royalist Cavaliers, who gained their name from the French *chevalier* (a noble on horseback).

Parliament then demanded 'Nineteen Propositions' including control of religious affairs, and appointments of Privy Councillors and government ministers. Charles, unwilling to have his royal prerogative emasculated, raised an army at Nottingham on 22 August 1642. Parliament appointed Robert Devereux, Earl of Essex, to command an army to confront the King. On 27 August, King Charles wrote to Montrose at his Auchterarder home, 'You are one whom I have found most faithful and in whom I repose greatest trust.'

Charles advanced on London, but was held at Edgehill on 23 October. Neither army was well organised. Charles's nephew, Prince Rupert of the Rhine Palatinate, was a dashing cavalry leader but no strategist. The Earl of Essex was strong in infantry recruited as local militias but came to be known as 'the elephantine general' for his slowness. Most of 1643 was an uncomfortable stalemate.

Montrose remained a passionate moderate, the most difficult of all political positions. In June 1643, a delegation of Covenanters, aware of Montrose's successful military record, offered to make him Lieutenant General of the Puritan army in Scotland. Montrose, loyal to the King and distrustful of Argyll, refused. The Covenanters then asked him to sign The Solemn League and Covenant, which was a declaration of intent for the Scottish and English Puritan Parliamentary forces to unite in the name of 'the true Protestant religion' against King Charles. It was a step towards a religious fundamentalist republic. Montrose would have nothing to do with it.

From that point onwards, the term 'Covenanter' meant those who pursued the political agenda of The Solemn League and Covenant. Montrose remained a Presbyterian, loyal to The National Covenant and to the King. Argyll's violent fundamentalists, who had shifted their own overt stance, accused Montrose of switching sides by not shifting with them.

On 1 February 1644, Montrose accepted King Charles's commission to be his Lieutenant in Scotland. On 6 May, Montrose was promoted from an Earl to a Marquis. He set about raising an army. Most of his troops were agricultural workers from the straths and glens who came with their Royalist lairds. They were supplemented by a gathering of mainly Irish Catholic MacDonalds, traditional enemies of the Campbells, led by the great warrior Alasdair MacColla, known as Colkitto.

Montrose's campaign was swift, brilliantly executed and devastating. On 1 September 1644, he won a battle at Tippermuir, today's Tibbermore, between Auchterarder and Perth, then swept north, scoring victories at Aberdeen and Fyvie. That winter, he led his troops into Argyll's homeland and crushed his army at Inverlochy, near today's Fort William, on 2 February 1645, before winning battles at Dundee, Auldearn near Inverness and Alford in Aberdeenshire.

Montrose then swept south across Fife. As he advanced along the south side of the Ochils, his troops sacked the Campbell lands around Dollar in revenge for Argyll's ransacking Kincardine Castle four years earlier. A band of Macleans, who served in Montrose's army, tried but failed to capture Castle Campbell itself. Montrose pressed on to Kilsyth, beyond Stirling, where he scored another resounding victory.

A new professionalism entered the Civil War. On the Puritan side, Sir Thomas Fairfax from Yorkshire and Oliver Cromwell from East Anglia raised companies that were well drilled and mobile. In July 1644 they defeated Prince Rupert at the Battle of Marston Moor in Yorkshire. They developed the New Model Army, and routed the Royalists at Naseby in June 1645.

By the summer of 1645, Montrose's volunteer armies were exhausted after campaigns and depleted when many men simply went home at harvest time. On 13 September at Philiphaugh in the Borders, his remaining men were defeated by a new Puritan army, made up of professional soldiers, led by David Leslie, no relation to Alexander Leslie, but a skilled general with similar military experience under Gustavus Adolphus.

Then, as now, Scottish leaders emerged from predictable backgrounds. Montrose, Argyll and David Leslie had all won the silver arrow prize for archery as students at St Andrews University. Montrose is also Auchterarder's first recorded golfer. He played a game at St Andrews the day before his marriage to Magdalene Carnegie in 1629. It is said that the Battle of Waterloo in 1815 was won on the playing fields of Eton. In the same way, the golf courses of Scotland are training grounds for the battlefields of business and politics.

Montrose, left with only a tiny army after the Battle of Philiphaugh, tried to rally support for the Royalist cause. In the north, the Marquis of Huntly prevaricated. In southern and central Scotland, the Puritan fundamentalists were dominant.

In England, Prince Rupert's wild cavalier charges failed to win battles. He surrendered the key Royalist towns of Bristol and Oxford. King Charles went on the run. Queen Henrietta Maria escaped to her native France and set up a British court in exile. Rupert also went to France, but returned as admiral of an English fleet. He had no more success as a sailor than as a soldier. The Puritan admiral Robert Blake attacked and destroyed most of his ships. The republican Oliver Cromwell became increasingly powerful.

In Strathearn, some of Montrose's own kinsmen decided it was too dangerous to continue supporting him. Sir John Graham of Braco and another John Graham, 3rd Laird of Orchill, testified against him to the fearsome Presbyterian Committee of Estates. Patrick Graham, known as 'Black Pate' the redoubtable Laird of Inchbrakie, stayed loyal but there was now no chance of Montrose's mustering an army to repeat his victorious campaign of only two years before.

On 2 March 1646, the Puritan General John Middleton besieged Kincardine Castle, then pounded it to ruins with artillery brought up from Stirling. Archie Napier, George Drummond of Balloch and the Laird of MacNab escaped. Some of the Castle's small garrison were sent as prisoners to the Tolbooth in Edinburgh. Others were summarily executed. The siege trenches dug by Middleton's troops are still visible today.

Montrose's wife, Magdalene, died in November. Montrose kept up a rearguard action in Speyside. In the summer of 1646, King Charles made the mistake of entering the camp of the Puritan Scottish army that had advanced as far as Newark in Nottinghamshire. He had hoped to negotiate. Instead, William Kerr, 3rd Earl of Lothian, took him prisoner. The King wrote to Montrose, telling him to disband his army.

On 22 July 1646 Montrose negotiated with Middleton, near Rattray in east Perthshire. Montrose agreed to disband, taking time to achieve a pardon for his men, though not for himself.

From September 1646 to 1650, Montrose lived in exile in war-torn Europe, trying to raise funds for King Charles I. At Henrietta Maria's court in exile in Paris, housed in the Louvre Palace, Henry Lord Jermyn had control of the royal purse. While he and his cronies chattered and danced, no funds could be found to help Montrose raise an army. Montrose then approached the French government. Unknown to Montrose, France was negotiating with Cromwell's parliamentarians. The French refused to provide Montrose with money to help King Charles. Instead, aware of Montrose's military prowess, Louis XIV's chief minister Cardinal Mazarin offered him the high office of Marechal de France with a huge salary. Montrose declined.

On 30 January 1647, Charles's Scottish captors handed him over to the English Puritan Parliament in exchange for a down payment of £200,000 with another £200,000 promised.

Frustrated by intrigue in Paris, Montrose sought support for Charles from France's enemies, the Hapsburgs. He went to Vienna then to Prague, where the Emperor Frederick III made him a Marshal of the Holy Roman Empire with the authority to raise troops in Flanders. He arrived in Brussels just after Frederick's brother Archduke Leopold had suffered a heavy defeat at Lens on 20 August 1648 and was in no position to offer any aid.

On 30 January 1649, King Charles I was executed in London. Oliver Cromwell signed his death warrant. The Marquis of Hamilton was executed in March. England became a Commonwealth without a king. Montrose heard the news of King Charles's execution when he was at the Hague where the King's heir, the future Charles II, had set up his own court in exile, far away from the bickering shambles of his mother Henrietta Maria's court in exile in Paris.

On hearing of Charles's execution, Montrose wrote a poem ending with, 'I'll sing they obsequies with trumpet sounds / And write thy epitaph in blood and wounds'. It was no idle boast. He had scored victories for the crown before and had every intention of doing it again.

At The Hague, Montrose made a friend in Charles I's sister Elizabeth, whose husband Frederick, Elector of the Rhine Palatinate, had died in 1632. Known as 'The Winter Queen', she had a good ear for court intrigue and gave Montrose encouragement and timely warnings. Her son Prince Rupert had a reputation as a glorious cavalier or a foolhardy loser, depending on whom you asked. Her younger daughter Sophie married Ernst Augustus, Elector of Hanover. In 1714 Sophie's son succeeded to the thrones of England and Scotland as King George I.

One of the intriguing 'what ifs' of history surrounds Princess Louise, the Winter Queen's older daughter. She was a shy girl who, like Montrose, despised courtly superficialty. Louise was devoted to painting and was a pupil of Gerard Van Honthorst. Montrose sat for the famous portrait, which he then gave to Louise's mother. Sophie's memoirs suggest that Montrose and Louise were in love. If they had married, their heirs and not Sophie's would have become British monarchs. It was not to be. Montrose decided that his duty lay in raising an army for the new King Charles II. Louise became a nun and lived till 1709.

Argyll realised too late that a powerful Cromwell was more of a threat to his own ambitions to rule Scotland than a weak Stewart monarchy ever was. The Scottish Parliament sent commissioners to The Hague, dressed in mourning for the King whom they had handed over to the English Puritans. They asked the uncrowned King Charles II to make Presbyterianism the established Church in Scotland, England and Ireland and agree to sign any legislation that Parliaments might make in future. They also demanded that he sack Montrose.

Instead, on 21 May 1649, Charles II made Montrose Viceroy of Scotland, Captain General of the Armed Forces and Admiral of the Scottish Seas. It was a grand title, but there were no resources to support it, other than whatever could be raised by Montrose's charisma and personal reputation.

Montrose went to Copenhagen and secured £10,000 from King Frederick IV's brother in law Korfits Ulfeldt. Montrose raised a further £25,000 in Sweden through John Maclean of Duart who had changed his name to Hans Maclier and become a wealthy merchant in Gothenburg. In March 1650 Montrose arrived in Orkney with about five hundred men and rallied another thousand there. He marched south towards Inverness, uncertain who was an enemy or a friend to the new King.

On 27 April, Montrose's small army reached Carbisdale, near Bonar Bridge on the Dornoch Firth. He was ambushed by Archibald Strachan, a fanatical Puritan. Montrose's Orcadians fled from Strachan's cavalry charge. Montrose's German and Danish mercenaries retreated, then were hunted down and killed. Montrose escaped, wounded, and took shelter with Neil MacLeod of Assynt at Ardvreck Castle.

To the eternal shame of the MacLeods, Neil MacLeod handed Montrose over to the Puritans to receive a reward of £20,000 plus a bonus of £5,000 worth of meal. Montrose was taken to Edinburgh. He was allowed to stop at Kinnaird Castle in Angus where his father-in-law, the Earl of Southesk, was caring for Montrose's two youngest children, Robert and Jean. His other son, James, heir to the Montrose title, was in exile with other Scots in Flanders.

King Charles II was no help. On hearing that Montrose had been captured, he wrote to the Scottish Parliament saying he was 'heartily sorry' about the invasion. Many ordinary Scots felt differently. When the Puritan Covenanters paraded the captive Montrose on a cart up Edinburgh High Street, they encouraged the crowd to jeer. Instead, Montrose's quiet dignity commanded complete silence. Argyll did not dare give his articulate enemy a trial. The Puritan extremist lawyer Archibald Johnston of Wariston read out his death sentence. On 21 May 1650, he was publicly executed on a scaffold outside the Edinburgh Tolbooth. His last words were, 'May God have mercy on this afflicted kingdom.'

Montrose remained loyal to the House of Stewart, despite its arrogance and dithering, believing that the alternatives were worse. He lost his own life but was instrumental in winning his generation's battle against violent intolerance.

Perhaps Montrose's best memorial is one of his verses, still quoted to encourage people to do the right thing:

He either fears his fate too much
Or his deserts are small
That puts it not unto the touch
To win or lose it all.

22

Inglorious Restoration and Glorious Revolution

*In which an unprincipled king is celebrated
and his principled brother is not so lucky*

After King Charles I was executed in 1649, England became a military dictatorship. Archibald Campbell, Marquis of Argyll, and the Scottish Puritan Covenanters realised too late that they could wield more power under a weak monarch than under a military dictator. Only a month after executing the moderate Presbyterian Montrose, the Covenanters brought the uncrowned Charles II to Scotland. The new King put expediency before principles. Where his father's rigidity had brought about his execution, Charles II's moral flexibility brought him friends.

The English Puritan Council of State ordered Thomas Fairfax, the victorious general of Marston Moor, to invade Scotland. He refused, saying that the Scots had the right to appoint their own head of state. Oliver Cromwell took over and led an army north. David Leslie, the skilled commander whose professional troops had defeated Montrose's depleted volunteers at Philiphaugh, confronted Cromwell at Dunbar on Sept 3 1650. Leslie's tactics were hampered by the Presbyterian minister authorities in Edinburgh who thought they knew more about warfare than Leslie. Cromwell routed the Covenanters. John Haldane, Laird of Gleneagles, who had begun developing a fine new mansion house on his estate, was killed in the battle.

The Covenanters surrendered Edinburgh Castle to Cromwell in December 1650. They hastily crowned King Charles II at Scone, the ancient Pictish coronation site beside Perth. Argyll placed the crown on Charles's head. Cromwell, ably assisted by General George Monk, systematically took control of southern and central Scotland. On 2 August, the English army captured Perth. On 14 August, it captured Stirling. Farmers in the Auchterarder area, in between Perth and Stirling, were no more able to resist Cromwell than their ancestors could oppose a Roman legion sixteen hundred years before. Cromwell devastated the recently modernised Drummond Castle.

Charles II rallied the remnant of the Covenanting army and headed towards the English West Country where his father had enjoyed support. The son was not so successful. Cromwell defeated him at the Battle of Worcester on 3 September 1651. Charles fled to France.

The men of the Auchterarder area chose not to fight Cromwell's troops. Their wives rose up against another form of Puritan authority. In 1652, Perth Synod banned two ministers for advocating the right of a congregation to choose its own form of government. A furious mob of about sixty women from Aberuthven, led by the wife of Rev. John Graham, one of the banned ministers, chased the dignitaries of the Synod through Aberuthven, dragged them from their horses, stripped them of their cloaks and beat them with sticks. Just as in 1596, when the people of Aberuthven refused the Church Commissioners' demand that they denounce Rev. John Hamyll, the next generation also stood up for freedom of choice.

There were more old scores to settle in the Auchterarder area. In July 1654, Royalists burned Castle Campbell, which the ever-expedient Marquis of Argyll had allowed to be garrisoned by Cromwell's troops.

By then Cromwell himself had moved on to Ireland, where he suppressed Catholic uprisings. He arranged for many Catholics to be transported from rich agricultural areas to poorer land in Connaught. Many did not go quietly, but became bands of robbers, justifying their actions in the name of maintaining old traditions. The Puritans called them 'Tories', a name that persists in politics today.

Cromwell understood practical economics. Sir Henry Vane, a Puritan who had been Governor of Massachusetts in North America, became Treasurer of the English navy and invested in a massive programme of ship building. The 1651 Navigation Act boosted English shipping by requiring all imports to be carried by English ships or by ships from the country where the goods originated. The Dutch, who had become the carriers of Europe, were hit hard. In 1652 and 1653, the Dutch admiral Maarten Tromp attacked English ships until General Monk returned from 'pacifying' Scotland and killed Tromp in a sea battle off Texel in Holland.

Cromwell turned Britain into a major sea power. Colonies grew on the North American seaboard. Jamaica was captured from Spain in 1656. Cromwell signed a treaty with the French Cardinal Mazarin, receiving the Port of Dunkirk in exchange for agreeing to help attack the Spanish south Netherlands. Admiral Robert Blake destroyed the fleet of the Dey of Tunis, which had plagued Mediterranean shipping. Blake also agreed a treaty against piracy with the Dey of Algiers.

Oliver Cromwell died of malaria and other complications on 3 September 1658. His life might have been saved by quinine, but his religious prejudices made him refuse to touch 'Jesuit powder'. Cromwell's son Richard was appointed Lord Protector. He had neither his father's ability nor his appetite for government.

General Monk sensed that divisions between Parliament, the army and independent religious factions could plunge Britain into another phase of civil war. A monarchy, limited by Parliament, seemed the best option for stability. The Long Parliament, which had been called by Charles I in 1640 and gone through many radical phases, dissolved itself on March 16 1660. The Convention

Parliament took its place. It restored the monarchy and House of Lords, but remained generally Presbyterian.

Backed by General Fairfax and other moderate Puritans, Monk negotiated with the exiled King Charles II, who could be relied on to agree to anything that restored him to his throne. Charles promised religious toleration and conceded substantial powers to Parliament. He returned to London on his thirtieth birthday, May 29 1660. Richard Cromwell was allowed to retire to France. He returned to England twenty years later and lived quietly near Winchester under the name Mr Clarke.

Charles II granted a pardon to anti-Royalists, except for twenty-eight who were directly involved in arranging his father's beheading. Thirteen of them were executed. As a further gesture, the bodies of Oliver Cromwell and two of his generals, Henry Ireton and John Bradshaw, were exhumed from Westminster Abbey and hanged at Tyburn.

The body of Auchterarder's favourite son, the Marquis of Montrose, had the opposite fate to Cromwell. After execution, Montrose had been dismembered and his limbs displayed in Scottish cities as a warning to potential Royalists. After the Puritan regime collapsed, Montrose received a belated hero's funeral in Edinburgh in 1661. Those who regarded themselves as the good and great of Scotland, who had lacked the courage to follow him in life, now marched solemnly up the High Street behind his funeral bier. Soon after, Montrose's head was replaced by Argyll's on the Tolbooth spike. The unprincipled Charles II made no effort to save the equally expedient Argyll, although he was the man who had crowned him King of Scotland.

In 1660, after the Civil War, the people of Auchterarder had to pick up the pieces. They did this literally, in the case of Montrose's Kincardine Castle, helping themselves to its shattered masonry to build a new parish church. The roof of the old church, St Mackessog's, had collapsed in 1660 just after morning service. The tower of the seventeenth-century church still stands in the centre of Auchterarder, next to the old cemetery.

Aberuthven, known then as now as 'Smiddy Haugh', was famous for its metalworkers. There are records of Thomas Smythe dressing the Marquis of Montrose's fencing swords and regularly shoeing his horses including 'the grey mare, grey courser, grey hackney, the brown horse, the sorral naig, the pockmanty naig and the horse named the Grey Oliphant'. Montrose's exile and death meant a huge loss of business to Auchterarder and Aberuthven. Kincardine Castle had hosted royal visitors. Local producers and tradesmen had profited. At government level, Puritan meanness replaced Cavalier generosity. When the monarchy was restored in 1660, the local economy remained poor.

By the late seventeenth century, royal burghs' monopolies on foreign trade had been eroded. Non-royal burghs expanded. Auchterarder was unable to compete. A few major landowners dominated the town. A rental return of 1649 shows that the Barony, owned by the Drummonds, accounted for 21 per cent. Various branches of the Grahams collectively accounted for 50 per cent. Lord Rollo of Dunning accounted for 15 per cent. The remaining 14 per cent came from seventeen small landowners.

In 1662, an Act of Parliament exempted James Drummond 3rd Earl of Perth from paying dues from Auchterarder on the grounds that it was not a royal burgh, but merely a burgh of barony.

It was a political sleight of hand designed to reward Drummond, who had supported the Stewart monarchy in the dark days of Cromwell's Puritan republic. The 1662 Act left Auchterarder's royal burgh status technically unclear for nearly three hundred years, until it was reconfirmed in 1951.

Like the Grahams and the Drummonds, the Murrays generally backed the Stewart royal family in the mid seventeenth century. The Stewart kings had kept the Earldom of Atholl in their family since the fourteenth century, when David Murray was expelled. In 1629, John Murray, Master of Tullibardine, inherited it from his mother, Lady Dorothea Stewart. He died in 1642, succeeded by his son, John, 1st Marquis of Atholl. Ten years later, Cromwell's troops seized Blair Castle. When the Stewart dynasty was restored in 1660, the 1st Marquis of Atholl maintained a deft political balancing act, opposing violent revenge on the Puritan Covenanters.

Once on the throne, Charles II swiftly disbanded most of the army, removing the enforcing power of Cromwell's military dictatorship. Soldiers received arrears of pay and sought civilian jobs. Only the King's Horseguards and the reliable soldier George Monk's Coldstream Guards were retained as a standing army. Monk was made Duke of Albemarle and Commander in Chief.

Instead of promoting religious tolerance, Charles made an Episcopalian, Edward Hyde, Earl of Clarendon, his chancellor. Clarendon drove Parliament to pass the Act of Uniformity in 1662, forcing all clergymen to renounce The Solemn League and Covenant, accept the Book of Common Prayer and be ordained by a bishop. In a bloodless parallel to the Catholic-inspired massacre of 1572, about two thousand Puritan clergy were expelled from their parishes on St Bartholemew's Day, 24 August, 1662. Clarendon persecuted Roman Catholics too, trying to create a monolithic Church of England. Ironically, his own daughter Anne was married to a Catholic, the King's brother James, Duke of York, Lord High Admiral of England.

Clarendon's intolerance merely provoked both Puritan and Catholic resolve. He made himself more unpopular in England when he sold Dunkirk back to King Louis XIV of France, losing the nation's port on the European mainland. After Louis's chief minister Cardinal Mazarin died in 1661, Louis became even more autocratic. Elsewhere, the divine right of kings had become an unworkable fashion, but in France Louis XIV could say, 'L'état c'est moi' (I am the State) and get away with it.

On 21 May 1662, Charles II married Catharine of Braganza, sister of King Alfonso VI of Portugal. They had a public Protestant marriage and a Catholic secret one. It was a useful dynastic alliance. Portugal was an enemy of Spain. Catharine's dowry included Tangier in North Africa and Bombay in India, important to Britain's expanding trade.

The new 23-year-old Queen spoke no English but was dark-haired and voluptuous, a preference Charles displayed in his choice of mistresses, Louise de Kérouaille, Duchess of Portsmouth, Barbara Palmer, Duchess of Cleveland

and Nell Gwynne, who bore Charles a son, Charles Beauclerk, who was given the title Duke of St Albans. The King granted peerages to several more of his illegitimate children.

Clarendon suffered the fate of unpopular politicians. He was blamed for everything that happened during his administration. In 1665 the Plague swept through London. In 1666 the Great Fire destroyed the centre of the capital. In 1667, a Dutch fleet under Michiel de Ruyter sailed up the Medway and the Thames, destroying English ships in Chatham docks. Clarendon was impeached by Parliament and fled to France, a safe haven for most species of British political exile.

Clarendon's daughter Anne could not protect him, although she was married to the heir to the throne. Their child, Clarendon's granddaughter, Mary, born in 1662, was next in line to the throne. A second daughter, Anne, had been born in 1665. All three were to become British queens.

Charles II formed a new administration, known as the Cabal from the initials of its five leading members (Clifford, Arlington, Buckingham, Ashley, Lauderdale). The word 'Cabal' suggested secrecy, associated with the Jewish mystical Kabbalah. It also had an ironic reference to 'caballeros', the Spanish equivalent of cavaliers.

In 1668 the Cabal formed an alliance with the Netherlands and Sweden against Spain's old enemy France. In 1670, however, Charles II signed a secret treaty with the French King Louis XIV, promising to declare himself a Catholic when the time seemed right. Louis gave the hard-up Charles a handsome subsidy. By 1673, England was openly at war with the Netherlands and the Cabal collapsed.

In 1671 James, Duke of York's wife Anne Hyde died of cancer, aged thirty-four. In 1673 James married the Italian Mary Beatrice d'Esté, daughter of the Duke of Modena. She was a shy fifteen-year-old Catholic who had expected to become a nun. She became friends with her step-daughters Mary and Anne who were only a few years younger than herself. Mary of Modena did her duty and bore James a child. Unfortunately for the prospects of a Catholic succession, it was a daughter, Isabella, who died, aged five, in 1681.

Fear of Roman Catholicism swept through Britain. In 1673 Parliament passed the Test Act, requiring anyone holding a government or military post to accept Church of England communion and reject the Catholic mass. As a result, the King's Catholic brother James, Duke of York resigned as High Admiral and retreated to the Spanish Netherlands. In 1677, the new English Treasurer Thomas Osborne, Earl of Danby, who had a genius for bribery and improbable alliances, negotiated the marriage of the Catholic Duke of York's daughter Mary to the Dutch Protestant leader William of Orange.

In 1678, Danby was impeached. Anthony Ashley Cooper, Earl of Shaftesbury, rose to power as Chancellor and leader of the Country Party, opposed to the pro-Catholic courtiers, nicknamed Tories (Irish robbers) who surrounded Charles II. The Country Party became known as the Whigs (from 'whey', skimmed milk, a reference to the grim, pallid faces of Covenanters, who were sarcastically known as 'whigamoors', a white version of 'blackamoors' or Negroes).

In 1679 the English Parliament passed the Habeas Corpus Act, a safeguard against arbitrary imprisonment, which became a cornerstone of British civil rights.

Religion and civil rights remained uneasy bedfellows in Scotland. After 1660, the administration of Church affairs in Auchterarder was a mix of the old Bishopric of Dunblane and the new Presbytery of Auchterarder. Under the scholarly moderate, Bishop Robert Leighton, there was no conflict. He encouraged ministers to make their sermons 'plain and useful for all capacities, not entangled with useless questions and disputes, nor continued to a wearisome length', a view with which churchgoers then and since have much sympathy.

By the time Bishop Leighton died in 1684, militant Puritanism had become fashionable again in some areas. Then, as now, religious extremism was not confined to the ignorant. Impressionable young middle-class men were attracted to simplistic solutions. In 1684 the minister of Glendevon, the Rev. William Spence, was arrested on suspicion of involvement in a Covenanters' plot against King Charles II. Spence was tortured with thumbscrews by the fearsome Royalist General Tam Dalyell, but survived and lived for another thirty years with his opinions, if not his handshake, intact.

Many Scots found employment as mercenaries abroad. There was no shortage of opportunities, fighting with or against the English. The fluctuating balance of sea power between the English and Dutch can be seen most clearly in the little settlement of New Netherlands, begun in 1624 on the Hudson River in North America. In 1653 it grew to be New Amsterdam, a centre of the beaver fur trade. In 1664 the English captured it and renamed it New York after their High Admiral. The Dutch took it again briefly in 1673 and called it New Orange after William of Orange. In 1674 it became English again and has remained New York ever since.

Beaver fur was a valuable high fashion product. It was made into hats after being treated with a mercury compound. Hat makers suffered brain damage from inhaling the fumes, hence the expression 'mad as a hatter'. In 1670, the Hudson's Bay Company was founded to exploit the fur trade. One of its founder members was Prince Rupert, the impetuous cavalier general, whose later years were devoted to scientific research, including an improved form of gunpowder and a better way of making mezzotint prints.

Charles II tried to pacify Scotland by sending John, 1st Earl of Middleton, an able soldier, to suppress Covenanter resistance wherever he could find it. Middleton was rewarded for this dismal task in 1663 by being transferred from chilly Scotland to burning hot Tangier in North Africa, where he was made governor.

Charles II ruled Scotland through his Commissioner John Maitland, 1st Duke of Lauderdale, a man as unprincipled and expedient as the King. Lauderdale had been a Presbyterian when the Covenanters were in power, but became the letter 'L' in the restored Charles II's Cabal and switched to supporting bishops when necessary. Most notable of these was James Sharp, Archbishop of St Andrews, so notorious for persecuting Presbyterians that in 1679 he was murdered by a band of Covenanters near Cupar.

Lauderdale was the grandson of Mary, Queen of Scots' devious secretary

William Maitland of Lethington. Using his labyrinthine social connections, he was spectacularly corrupt. He skimmed off tax money for himself and his family, sold government jobs and appointed pliable cronies to the judiciary. In 1673 the Scottish Parliament was so united against him that Charles II dissolved it. It did not meet again till 1681, the year before Lauderdale died. In England, Parliament was so sick of Lauderdale that a petition was raised for the King to expel him from his presence forever. Lauderdale's bribery machine went into action and the petition failed by a single vote.

Lucy Walter, another of Charles II's mistresses, bore him James, Duke of Monmouth who grew up to be an able soldier. On 22 June 1679 he joined with John Graham of Claverhouse to rout the Covenanters at Bothwell Brig. Charles II appointed his brother James, Duke of York, back in favour during a temporary lull in the national fear of Catholics, to succeed Lauderdale as Royal Commissioner in Scotland. The Duke of York was implacably hostile to the Covenanters. So was Claverhouse, mindful of their scheming and savage treatment of his kinsman the Marquis of Montrose.

Monmouth was more conciliatory. He was recalled to England, where he was popular with Whigs but, in 1684, he fled to Holland with the Whig leader Lord Shaftesbury who had lost power to the Tories. Charles II's rule became increasingly autocratic, though he took care to cultivate the support of English cities and maintain the illusion of a rule of Parliamentary law, something his executed father had failed to do. Charles died after a short illness on 6 February 1685.

Charles II had many bastards but no legitimate children. The obvious heir to the throne was his brother James, Duke of York, who had served with distinction as High Admiral and as a commander on land. The two brothers were very different. Charles was unprincipled and slippery. He was a Catholic in secret and an Anglican in public. James was an overt Catholic and therefore, according to the Test Act of 1673, ineligible to be King. When Charles II died, James staved off opposition by promising to 'preserve this Government both in Church and state as it is by law established'. With considerable public misgivings, King James II of England and VII of Scotland ascended his thrones.

Rebellions broke out. Archibald Campbell, 9th Earl of Argyll, son of Montrose's old enemy, tried to rally anti-Catholic rebels in Scotland. He failed, largely because the Campbells now had a reputation for being as greedy and unreliable as the Stewarts. Argyll was executed for treason on 30 June 1685.

At about the same time, Charles II's bastard son James, Duke of Monmouth returned from Holland and raised an army of around five thousand men, most of them Whig supporters. On 6 July at Sedgemoor, in the West Country, Monmouth was defeated and captured by John Churchill, an ambitious soldier who had recently been given the title Baron Eyemouth in Scotland and was to become the Duke of Marlborough. Monmouth was executed on 15 July.

In October 1685, Louis XIV revoked the Edict of Nantes, ending the religious freedom that Huguenots and other Protestants had enjoyed in France since 1598. A flood of Huguenot refugees arrived in England. They were mainly craftsmen and small businessmen, an asset to British commerce, particularly to the growing silk trade in Spitalfields in London. They were no political threat to King James.

James, however, began to promote Roman Catholics to high office despite the Test Act. He appointed four Catholic peers to the Privy Council and gave protection to a Catholic judge, Edward Hales. He received the Papal Nuncio at Court and publicly celebrated mass.

In Scotland, the Catholic James Drummond, 4th Earl and 1st Duke of Perth, rose to be King James VII's Lord High Chancellor of Scotland. Edinburgh Castle was put under the command of the Catholic George, 9th Earl of Huntly and 1st Duke of Gordon. Both men owed their Dukedoms to the Catholic King.

James II and VII built up an army of around 13,000 men. On April 4 1687, without consulting Parliament, he made the First Declaration of Indulgence, which removed religious tests as a requirement for government office. This royal pronouncement had the effect of granting toleration to Puritans as well as Catholics. Some Puritans, such as John Bunyan, the author of *Pilgrim's Progress,* perversely refused to accept the King's tolerance because it was unparliamentary and smacked of the divine right of kings. Toleration of Catholics was equally unpleasing to many Church of England bishops.

By 1688, King James's autocratic manner of expressing his principles had lost him the support of Whigs, Tories and the Established Church in both England and Scotland. On June 10 1688, his Queen Mary of Modena bore him a son, also named James. The male child, who would be brought up as a Catholic, automatically became heir to the thrones, taking precedence over his much older sister Mary, who was married to the Dutch Protestant leader, William of Orange.

A remarkably broad spectrum of British interests proposed to William of Orange that he should intervene in Britain to secure the succession of his wife Mary to the English throne. King James misjudged the situation so badly that he even alienated his own army leaders, including Churchill, by stationing Irish soldiers in England.

William of Orange landed in England on 5 November 1688. He received so much support that there was no military battle to defend the old regime. William's arrival was hailed as the Glorious Revolution. It is one of the oddities of the British festival calendar that 5 November is remembered for the failed Gunpowder Plot of 1605 but not for the successful Constitutional Revolution of 1688.

On December 23, King James fled to France. He was James VII of Scotland and James II of England. Many wanted him to be James the Last, but history is never that simple. James II and VII died in France on 16 September 1701 at St Germain en Laye, where he held his court in exile. He was buried there, but his royal body was exhumed and destroyed during the republican French revolution at the end of the eighteenth century. The two rulers of rigid principle, the Puritan Oliver Cromwell and the Catholic James II and VII, were dragged from their graves. The unprincipled Charles II, who reigned between them, rests undisturbed in Westminster Abbey.

23

The Union of the Parliaments

In which religious wars continue as usual, and a failed colony
provokes constitutional reform, with a little help from bribery

Religion and empire go together. The one excuses the other. In the sixteenth and seventeenth centuries, Catholic France and its old enemy Catholic Spain built up colonies in the Americas and Asia. So did Protestant Britain and its Protestant rivals, the Dutch. The tortures of the Spanish Inquisition and the witch-hunts of the New England Puritans were tactics to enforce authority. Imperial strategy, however, made faith subordinate to military alliance.

The European imperial ambitions of Islam suffered a setback in 1571 when the Ottoman Turkish fleet was destroyed by a Christian alliance at the Battle of Lepanto. By the middle of the seventeenth century, the Ottoman Empire was on the rise again. The Holy Roman Empire was weak. In 1667, the Ukraine was divided between Russia and Poland, provoking Russian Cossacks to invite Sultan Mohammed IV and his Vizier (chief minister) Ahmed Kuprili to send an army to help them. They achieved spectacular results, forcing the weak King Michael of Poland to sign the Treaty of Buczácz in 1672, acknowledging Turkish suzerainty over the Ukraine and agreeing to grant a huge annual payment to the Ottoman Empire.

In the following year, King Michael died. The Holy Roman Emperor, Leopold I, considered many possible candidates for the Polish throne, including James, Duke of York, who had recently been forced to leave England because of his Catholic beliefs. James was not chosen to become King of Poland. Instead, twelve years later, he became King James II of England and VII of Scotland. The Emperor Leopold selected as King of Poland John Sobieski, a warrior patriot who had just defeated a renewed Turkish invasion.

The Scottish–Polish royal connection had to wait for another generation, when James VII's son, James 'The Old Pretender', married John Sobieski's granddaughter Clementina and produced 'Bonnie Prince Charlie'. In 1673, however, John Sobieski delivered a hammer blow to the Ottoman Empire when he led a Christian army to defeat the Turks who had laid siege to the great Holy Roman Imperial city of Vienna. Among those who served alongside the Catholic John Sobieski against the Turks was the Protestant grandson of the executed

British King Charles I's sister Elizabeth, Prince George of Hanover who became the British King George I in 1714.

Louis XIV of France was ambivalent about John Sobieski's success. As a leading Catholic monarch, he felt obliged to seem glad that the armies of Islam had been repelled back to Turkey. On the other hand, he was keen to prevent the Hapsburg Holy Roman Emperor Leopold I from building on John Sobieski's victory.

In 1685, Louis XIV revoked the Edict of Nantes, which had given the Protestant Huguenots freedom of worship for almost a hundred years. Thousands of skilled French artisans and tradesmen fled to Protestant England, the German states and North America.

William III, Stadtholder of Holland, recruited a regiment of Huguenot exiles to augment his army in the fight against Louis XIV. In 1686, William allied with other Protestant countries to form the League of Augsburg, surrounding France with enemies. When William and his Stewart wife Mary became King and Queen of Britain in the Glorious Revolution of 1688, Louis XIV sent French troops to Ireland to rally Catholic support for the deposed King James II.

William's Protestant army arrived in Ireland and crushed James's Catholics at the Battle of the Boyne on 12 July 1690, a date still marked annually in Ireland and Scotland by parades with loud flutes and drums. The Battle of the Boyne rankles today among sectarian supporters of Rangers and Celtic football clubs and provokes vicious assaults from bigots and pious blandishments from politicians.

William went on to subdue Ireland but, by the Treaty of Limerick in 1691, he granted freedom of worship to Roman Catholics. Four years later, however, the Irish Parliament, which had no Catholic members, annulled the Treaty of Limerick. Catholics were denied the right to buy land, carry weapons, marry Protestants or enter the learned professions. This mean-spirited decision foolishly created a huge, ill-educated underclass, given to expressing its resentments violently.

In England, the religious and constitutional settlement was much more measured. The 1689 Bill of Rights is the cornerstone of today's Parliamentary democracy. It guaranteed freedom of election and freedom of speech in Parliament. It also required the monarch to observe the will of Parliament in law-making, taxes and military matters. The Toleration Act of 1689 maintained the supremacy of the Episcopal Church in England, but granted freedom of worship to Presbyterians and other Protestant minorities. Catholics, however, remained banned from official posts and from inheriting the throne.

In Scotland, King James VII had imposed bishops to rule the Church and tried to crush the Puritan Covenanters who had sold his father Charles I to be executed. When James was deposed, the Scottish Parliament of 1689 demanded that Episcopacy be abolished. King William III, trying to reduce religious conflict, made the Presbyterian Church of Scotland the established religion, but granted tolerance to Episcopacy. It was a placatory gesture, but it created a muddle over Church property and the right to make appointments.

At the end of the seventeenth century, the Jacobite William Drummond, 2nd Viscount Strathallan used his right as a patron to keep the Parish Church in Auchterarder locked, rather than let Rev. James Mitchell, the congregation's choice, preach there. Strathallan favoured the Jacobite Rev. James Rattray, who had been banned by Auchterarder presbytery for refusing to pray for the health of King William III of Orange. Rattray stole the pulpit bible and refused to hand it back to the presbytery. Lord Strathallan eventually gave up and opened the church, though Rattray seems to have clung permanently to his stolen bible.

In 1696, the Scottish Parliament passed an Act For Settling Of Schools, requiring each parish to have a schoolhouse and schoolmaster paid for by the parish's heritors (a committee of landowners). Auchterarder had already had a parish school for a hundred years, if not more, but funding had been erratic as it often is for education.

In Perthshire, the Grahams remained loyal to Charles I's Stewart line, despite being repeatedly let down. The Marquis of Montrose's kinsman, John Graham of Claverhouse, Viscount Dundee, rallied support for the deposed James VII. These supporters became known as Jacobites (from 'Jacobus', the Latin form of James).

Claverhouse is known as 'Bonnie Dundee' or 'Bloody Clavers' depending on the historical point of view, Jacobite or Covenanter. Like Montrose, Claverhouse had the support of the huge Clan MacDonald, as much for their mutual dislike of the Puritan Campbells as for their support of James VII.

King William III sent General Hugh MacKay with an army to confront Claverhouse. On June 27 1689 at Killiecrankie in northern Perthshire, Claverhouse defeated MacKay but was fatally wounded in the battle. There was no other Jacobite commander of Claverhouse's stature. MacKay regrouped his forces and set about subduing the Highlands. In France, the great military engineer Sebastien de Vauban was building vast fortresses and town walls for King Louis XIV. William III lacked the money to do the same in Scotland, but he had General MacKay create Fort William to help garrison the unruly Highlands. It lay at the strategic road junction to the north-west, near the site of Montrose's Royalist victory at Inverlochy in 1645. Forth William was never enough on its own.

John Campbell, 1st Earl of Breadalbane was given £15,000 to distribute among clan leaders, provided they swore an oath of allegiance to King William III. The deadline was December 31 1691. Alastair MacIan, Chief of the MacDonalds of Glencoe, arrived at Fort William on the deadline day, only to be told that there was no law officer present to accept his oath. In foul winter weather, MacIan made his way across difficult country to Inveraray, where the Sheriff Depute Colin Campbell of Ardkinglas was too drunk after Hogmanay to take MacIan's oath until 6 January. Technically, MacIan had committed an offence.

The Lord Advocate, Sir John Dalrymple, Master of Stair, had served James VII but was keen to curry favour with the new King William III. Dalrymple deceived the King by failing to say that MacIan had tried to meet the deadline. Instead, Dalrymple obtained a writ from the King to 'extirpate that seat of thieves'.

On 1 February 1692, Robert Campbell of Glenlyon arrived in Glencoe with a gang of his kinsmen. The MacDonalds, observing the conventions of Highland hospitality, gave them food and shelter. During the night of 13 February, the Campbell guests murdered thirty-eight of their MacDonald hosts. The Massacre of Glencoe offended even those who were anti-Jacobite. William III sacked

Dalrymple but did not charge him with any offence. The murdered MacDonalds became martyrs for the Jacobite cause. The Campbells' reputation for treachery was reinforced and, in some parts of Scotland, has never recovered.

The other great Perthshire families had to choose whether to support the new King, William III, or fight to restore the deposed James VII. In 1662, James Drummond, 3rd Earl of Perth had been rewarded for supporting Charles II by notionally reducing Auchterarder's Royal Burgh status to Burgh of Barony. This allowed him to avoid paying higher taxes on his property, but caused a legal tangle only resolved three centuries later when Auchterarder's Royal Burgh status was verified in 1951.

His son, James, 4th Earl of Perth rose to be James VII's Chancellor in Scotland and was promoted to 1st Duke of Perth. When James VII fled in 1688, the Duke of Perth retreated to Drummond Castle then tried to flee to Ireland. He was captured and locked up in Stirling Castle, then allowed to emigrate to France where he lived in comfortable retreat with his deposed King at the court in exile in St Germain en Laye.

Like the Grahams and the Drummonds, the Murrays generally backed the Stewarts, especially since 1629 when John Murray, Master of Tullibardine, inherited the Earldom of Atholl through his mother Lady Dorothea Stewart. His son, also called John, was promoted to a Marquis but switched sides to support William III. As a result, Claverhouse lacked the Athollmen troops who had supported Montrose thirty years earlier. Ironically, Claverhouse is buried on the Atholl Estate, not far from where he was mortally wounded while winning the Battle of Killiecrankie. In 1703, John, son of the 1st Marquis of Atholl, was made a Duke. Three generations of John Murrays rose from Earl to Marquis to Duke by backing political winners.

England had fought the Hundred Years War against France from 1337 to 1453. On 13 May 1689, England declared war on France again, beginning a second Hundred Years War that lasted until 1815. William III formed a Grand Alliance of Nations, an extension of the 1686 League of Augsburg. His objective was to prevent a Jacobite revival by damaging the interests of their sole ally, King Louis XIV. William III, as Prince of Orange, brought the Protestant Dutch Republic into the alliance. Catholic Spain joined the alliance to protect the Spanish Netherlands from the French. In Central Europe, many German states also aligned against Louis XIV.

On 19 May 1692, Admiral Edward Russell, with a fleet of English and Dutch ships, defeated and destroyed a substantial part of the French navy at the Battle of Cap La Hogue.

William III could never be sure of the English nobility, especially those who had previously served James II. Even key military leaders, such as Admiral Arthur Herbert, Lord Torrington, and John Churchill, Duke of Marlborough, were of doubtful loyalty. The death of Queen Mary on 28 December 1694 left William even more isolated. They had no children. Mary's sister Anne, married to Prince George of Denmark, was heir to the thrones of England and Scotland. William came to rely increasingly on Whig politicians. The war against France dragged on, with expensive military forays into Europe.

The astute Whig Chancellor Charles Montague, 1st Earl of Halifax, borrowed money for the King by creating the Bank of England. He used the meteoric Scottish financier William Paterson to sell shares whose value depended on future alcohol tax revenues.

On 10 September 1697, by the Treaty of Ryswick, Louis XIV agreed a truce with William III, importantly recognising the late Queen Mary's sister Anne as William's heir, and not the exiled James II and VII nor his descendants. On 6 September 1701, James died in France. His son James became the Jacobite claimant to the thrones of England and Scotland. At first he had no practical support.

On 20 February 1702, William III fell and broke his collar bone when his horse stumbled over a molehill in London's Hyde Park. The King became fevered and died on 8 March, aged fifty-two. He was a reserved, dutiful man, who loved his wife, detested court intrigue and did what he thought best for his nations, Holland and Britain.

In 1296, after the Scottish King Alexander III was killed when he fell from his horse, Scotland was torn apart in a long war over the royal succession. After William III's fatal riding accident in 1702, the succession passed peacefully to Anne. She was thirty-seven and had just seen the death of the last of her seventeen children, William Duke of Gloucester, aged eleven. The other sixteen had died in infancy. She needed an heir to the throne. To guarantee a Protestant succession, the Act of Settlement in 1701 named Sophie of Hanover, daughter of King Charles I's sister Elizabeth, as Anne's heir.

There was no immediate uprising in favour of the man who called himself King James III and VIII. Jacobites consoled themselves by drinking toasts to 'The little gentleman in the brown jacket', referring to the Hyde Park mole who had unwittingly caused William III's death. Scots politicians were concerned with more urgent matters – their personal finances.

English investors and merchants had made money from trade with the colonies in the Americas and from the spice trade in Asia. The East India Company produced spectacular profits and corruption scandals. Scotland had lacked an equivalent. The Navigation Acts of 1651 and 1660 excluded Scottish ships from English-controlled ports overseas.

In 1695, William Paterson from Dumfries, who had become rich through his role in founding the Bank of England, created The Company of Scotland, trading to Africa and the Indies. Its purpose was to establish a Scottish colony at Darien in Panama in Central America, with a port that would profit from North American, South American and West Indian trade. On paper, it looked like a good idea. Private investors rushed in. Some bought the permitted maximum of £3,000 worth of shares, a huge sum. The cities of Edinburgh and Glasgow also invested the maximum.

On 2 November 1698, five Scottish ships landed at Darien. Within weeks, the colonists discovered the realities of the climate. Tropical storms, land unsuited to Scottish agriculture and isolation from supplies were compounded by rampant disease, especially dysentery. The Darien Scheme was a disaster. A second attempt was made, but fared even worse.

By 1700, most of the 3,000 Scots who had emigrated to Darien had died. The proposed port was worthless. So were the Darien Scheme's shares. Blame flew thick and fast. Scottish investors attributed failure variously to corruption, mutiny, King William III's indifference, the rival East India Company, the Spaniards, the wrath of God and, of course, the English.

How could Scottish public institutions and private investors replenish their finances? The obvious solution was to achieve a deal whereby Scottish traders could use English-run ports and to harmonise the administration of trade by both Scotland and England. This might or might not be achieved by negotiation between the Scottish and English Parliaments. The more radical alternative was to slash bureaucracy by having only one Parliament to govern Britain, with equal rights for all British investors and merchants.

A long series of bad harvests in the 1690s had made rural Scotland barely self-sufficient. Protective tariffs placed Scotland at a disadvantage in English markets. A United Parliament would open new trading possibilities and stimulate the Scottish economy. But why should England want to take on the burden of a poor Scotland? There was one very good reason – the Jacobites.

When a national economy thrives, the people are in no hurry to change their government. When both the privileged and the poor are short of money, political alternatives begin to look attractive. Scotland was poor and the Pretender James III and VIII was an alternative. He was Catholic and, sitting in exile in France, had never harmed Scotland. The current Scottish government was Protestant and had mismanaged the economy. To English eyes, James was a dangerous rallying point for Scottish disaffection and had the potential to give England's enemy France a foothold in Scotland.

Some Scots, like William Paterson, argued for a Union of the Parliaments. John Haldane, Laird of Gleneagles, supported him. Haldane had been a Director of the Darien Scheme and, by the trickery of a fellow investor Walter Herries, had been jailed in London and held personally responsible for some of the Scottish Company's debts. His fellow directors, aware that Haldane was one of the least rascally of the Darien participants, helped resolve his case, but Haldane lost a lot of money. Keen to avoid any repeat, John Haldane soon became known as 'Union Jack' because of his championing the cause of a strong British economy with a United Parliament.

Not everyone agreed. Andrew Fletcher, Laird of Saltoun in East Lothian, was no Jacobite, but he valued Scottish sovereignty, fearing that Scottish members of a United Parliament would be subservient to their English counterparts. In 1703, the Scottish Parliament passed the Act of Security asserting Scotland's independence and refusing to recognise Sophie as heir to the Scottish throne unless trade restrictions with England were removed, Presbyterianism was confirmed as the established religion and Scotland could raise its own army.

The following year, relations between the two countries deteriorated amid a blustering cacophony of nationalism. In February 1705, the English Parliament passed the Aliens Act, effectively treating Scots living in England as foreigners and imposing more restrictions on Anglo-Scottish trade. Something had to give.

The Parliaments agreed that the question of their Union had to be decided. But how? And by whom? James, 4th Duke of Hamilton, a former supporter of James II and VII, but with his Hamilton predecessors' genius for duplicity, persuaded members that Queen Anne should choose commissioners herself to arrive at a solution. Anne relied on her slippery Lord High Treasurer Sidney Godolphin for advice. He was pro-Union. Thirty-one suitably minded commissioners were appointed from both Scotland and England. Among them was Union Jack Haldane. James Douglas, 2nd Duke of Queensberry piloted the Union Treaty through the Scottish Parliament. He was rewarded with the title Duke of Dover, about as far from Scotland as possible.

The Union Treaty of 1707 removed trade barriers between Scotland and England. Scotland acknowledged Sophie as heir to the throne and received a guarantee that the Scottish Church and legal system would remain independent. England agreed to pay Scotland £398,000, known as 'The Equivalent' to offset Scotland's future share in the British national debt. England's equivalent payment also helped offset the disastrous Darien scheme losses suffered by the Company of Scotland trading to Africa and the Indies. The Company was wound up. A persuasive £20,000, paid to Scottish parliamentarians, hastened the Union of the Parliaments.

Forty-five Scottish members entered the House of Commons in Westminster. Union Jack Haldane of Gleneagles was one. Sixteen Scottish peers were elected to the House of Lords. The Commons had twenty-four Welsh members and 489 from England, of whom 293 held seats south of the Thames. Scottish peers were outnumbered nine to one in the House of Lords. The separate Scottish Parliament ceased to exist until it was recreated 300 years later as an upper tier of Scottish local government.

On 1 May 1707, some lamented the loss of the Scottish Parliament just as they had lamented their financial losses in the Darien Scheme. Others felt that Scotland had rid itself of two pestilent swamps.

ies Graham, 1st Marquis of Montrose (1612–1650), Scotland's great cavalier general and poet. Portrait by
hard Van Honthorst.

Coat of Arms of Auchterarder, Strathearn's Royal Burgh.

A CITY SET ON A HILL CANNOT BE HID

Last surviving stonework of Auchterarder Castle. King Malcolm III Canmore (c.1031–1093) had a hunting lodge here. The castle was demolished in the eighteenth century and its masonry recycled for agricultural buildings.

Cathan's Church, Aberuthven. Ruin of the extended thirteenth-century church, built on the site of a sixth-tury Christian settlement. The eighteenth-century square Montrose vault, designed by William Adam, is burial ground of Strathearn Grahams.

ibardine Chapel. Built in the fifteenth century by the Murrays, who became Dukes of Atholl.

Drummond Castle. Built in 1487 by John, 1st Lord Drummond. The seventeenth-century formal gardens are among the finest in Europe.

Innerpeffray Library. The oldest free lending library in Scotland, founded in 1680 by David Drummond, Lo Madderty. The present building was constructed in 1762 by his kinsman Robert Hay Drummond, who beca Archbishop of York. (© Jo Cound)

Thomas Graham, Lord Lynedoch (1748–1843). During the Napoleonic Wars, he was second in command to the Duke of Wellington in the successful Peninsular War, then commanded the British force in the Netherlands. Portrait by Sir Thomas Lawrence (© Perth Museum and Art Gallery, Perth and Kinross Council)

Adam Duncan, 1st Viscount Camperdown (1731–1804) and Laird of Gleneagles. Admiral who defeated the Dutch, France's allies, in the Napoleonic Wars. Portrait by John Hoppner.

LMS GLENEAGLES HOTEL
PERTHSHIRE
BY NORMAN WILKINSON.

Above. Gleneagles Hotel. Railway poster by Norman Wilkinson. Site of the first international golf competition between Britain and the USA and subsequent major tournaments, including the 2014 Ryder Cup. Location of decisive global conferences, such as the 1977 Commonwealth Heads of Government Conference, which outlawed racism in international sport, and the 2005 G8 Summit, the first genuinely global initiative to tackle man-made climate change.

Right. Henry Hall, whose Gleneagles Hotel Dance Band made the first live radio broadcast of dance music on the newly formed BBC in 1924.

THE GOLDEN AGE OF
henry hall
AND THE BBC DANCE ORCHESTRA

16 TRACKS i
THE MUSIC GOES 'ROUND AND AR
UNDERNEATH THE AR
HERES TO THE NEXT
IT'S A SIN TO TELL

Featuring VAL ROSING FLANAGAN AND ALLEN
LEN BERMAN LES ALLEN
LESLIE SARONY · DAN DONOVAN
GEORGE ELRICK · ELIZABETH SCOTT · THREE SISTERS

Hercules
and family

Above. Hercules the Grizzly Bear, star of films and TV. Voted Scottish Tourist Board Personality of the Year 1981. Pictured with his owners, wrestler Andy Robin and his wife, Maggie.

Left. Alex Salmond, current Scottish First Minister, holding a giant Coca Cola bottle with the image of the eighteenth-century populist poet Robert Burns to celebrate Scotland's Year of the Homecoming in 2009. Salmond is a master manipulator of Scottish myth. (© Andrew Milligan/Press Association Images)

Prince William, Earl of Strathearn and Countess Catharine. Prince William's grandmother, Queen Elizabeth II, is descended from Strathearn families on both her father's and mother's sides. Prince William continues si centuries of links to the Earldom of Strathearn. (University of St Andrews)

Matthew Paris's Map of the British Isles, c.1250. It shows how Scotland is perceived as having a central belt from Galloway in the west to Edinburgh in the east. Scotia Ultramarina (Overseas Scotland) is reached by Stirling Bridge. The strategic heartland of Strathearn lies under the word 'ultra'.

Coins found on the Gask Ridge, the Northern Frontier of the Roman Empire. Faustina, wife of Marcus Aurelius, Emperor AD 161–180 and Commodus, Emperor AD 180–192. (© Sue Young)

FIG. 1465.—Inchaffray Abbey. Exterior of North Gable.

Ruins of Inchaffray Abbey, the Augustinian monastic house which was a major landowner and the most dominant religious force in Strathearn during the Middle Ages, with close links to Holyrood Abbey in Edinburgh.

King Edward I (1239–1307). He quartered his troops at Auchterarder Castle, then took Scotland's 'Stone of Destiny' from Scone and placed it under his coronation chair in London's Westminster Abbey, to symbolise his authority over Scotland. In this manuscript illustration, the forceful Edward I is receiving homage from his son, the ineffectual Edward II, who lost the Battle of Bannockburn.

King Robert Bruce (1274–1329). Supported Edward I then turned against him. Won the Battle of Bannockburn 1314. With the 'Declaration of Arbroath' Bruce asked Pope John XXII in 1320 to recognise Scottish independence. The Pope told him to make peace with England. Bruce refused. Scotland fell into anarchy after his death. Statue at Stirling Castle by A. Currie.

John Knox (*c*.1513–1572). Puritan fundamentalist preacher. He won the first recognition of the Protestant faith in Scotland with the Peace of Auchterarder, 1559. His followers then rampaged from Perth across Strathearn, looting and burning churches.

Mary of Guise (1515–1560), widow of King James V (died 1542). Regent of Scotland from 1544. Pro-French Catholic fundamentalist who ratified the Peace of Auchterarder in 1559, acknowledging Protestantism as a political force in Scotland. Mother of Mary, Queen of Scots. Portrait by Comeille de Lyon.

Left. Auchterarder Parish Church Tower. Built in 1660, recycling masonry from Kincardine Castle.

Below. Kincardine Castle, home of James Graham, 1st Marquis of Montrose, who fought Oliver Cromwell's republicans and the Marquis of Argyll's puritans. General Middleton destroyed the castle in 1646 while Montrose campaigned elsewhere.

Maggie Wall's Cross on the old road from Dunning to Auchterarder. Memorial to a local woman burned as a witch in 1657.

"Maggie Wall burnt Here"
"1657 as a Witch".

Medal issued to celebrate the government victory over Jacobite rebels at the Battle of Culloden in 1746. The Presbytery of Auchterarder, which had been looted and burned by Jacobites in the previous uprising of 1716, sent a delegation to congratulate the Duke of Cumberland in 1746 for bringing peace to Scotland. Under the caption 'Justice Triumphant' the medal shows a heroic British lion defeating a Jacobite wolf.

ehovah Jireh (God will provide), carved above the door of St Andrew's Free Church, built after the 'Auchter-rder Case' (1834–43) broke up the Church of Scotland in the most wide-ranging religious reform since the Reformation.

Ba'ad's Smithy in Auchterarder, which exported ploughs worldwide in the nineteenth century, including to pioneers of the American West.

William Hally (*left*), Auchterarder provost and mill owner, who joined with Thomas Stewart (*right*), radical weaver poet, to invite the Hungarian freedom fighter Louis Kossuth to Auchterarder in 1857.

Richard Burdon Haldane, Ist Viscount Haldane (1856–1928). As Secretary of State for War, he modernised the British army before the First World War. Shown with his friend, the scientist Albert Einstein. Haldane also wrote a book on relativity.

24

Jacobite Scorched Earth

*In which we endure bad roads, see a minister hanged, visit Scotland's first
free lending library and witness spiteful losers commit a sectarian atrocity*

In the reigns of William III and Anne, the war between Britain and France
dragged on, complicated by a conflict over the Spanish succession. King Charles
II of Spain had been mentally and physically in poor health throughout his
long reign from 1665. He had no children. There were three claimants to the
succession: Archduke Charles of Austria, who was the Holy Roman Imperial
candidate; Duke Philip of Anjou who was the grandson of King Louis XIV of
France; and Joseph Ferdinand, the Electoral Prince of Bavaria. When Charles II
died in 1700, Philip of Anjou became King Philip V of Spain. The balance of
power in Europe tilted in France's favour.

In 1701, on behalf of his grandson Philip V, King Louis XIV of France tried
to expel the Dutch from the Spanish Netherlands. Naturally, King William III
of England, who was also the Prince of Orange, fought back. He sent John
Churchill, Duke of Marlborough with an army to Flanders. Marlborough was
to make a reputation for himself over the next twelve years as one of Britain's
greatest generals.

Marlborough secured Holland and made territorial gains in Germany. When
a French army threatened to capture the Holy Roman Imperial city of Vienna,
Marlborough led an army across Europe and routed the French at Blenheim
on 13 August 1704. Louis XIV's military power never recovered. Marlborough,
with the profits of war, built a splendid house in Oxfordshire, which he called
Blenheim Palace.

While Britain was engaged in Europe, the Old Pretender, the self-styled King
James VIII and III, tried to invade Scotland in March 1708. His French ship sailed
towards the Forth estuary but never landed. James caught measles, was seasick
and retreated when Admiral George Byng's fleet appeared on the horizon.

Marlborough defeated the French at Ramillies in 1706 and secured Flanders.
In 1708, he captured Lille, a key city on the route from Holland to France, after
the Battle of Oudenarde, a name commemorated in Strathearn by a farm near
Bridge of Earn. In 1709, Marlborough routed the French at Malplaquet and
captured Mons. Many Scots served Marlborough. The 1st Duke of Atholl's oldest
son John was killed at Malplaquet.

Meantime, Admirals Sir George Rooke and Sir Cloudesley Shovel captured Gibraltar, giving Britain a strategic stronghold in the Mediterranean. Minorca was added in 1708. English armies stormed into Spain, in support of Archduke Charles of Austria's claim to the Spanish crown, but local support was weak except in Catalonia.

The wars were extremely expensive. Marlborough's wife Sarah had been a close friend of Queen Anne, but the two women fell out. Anne dismissed Sidney Godolphin and other Whig ministers in 1710, replacing them with Tories, led by Robert Harley, whom she made Earl of Oxford. Marborough was relieved of his command at the end of 1711, by which time the war had spread to Canada.

In 1713, peace was agreed by the Treaty of Utrecht. Great Britain kept Nova Scotia, Newfoundland, and the Hudson Bay Territory in Canada, along with Gibraltar and Minorca in the Mediterranean. The first governor of Minorca was John Campbell, 2nd Duke of Argyll, the appointment being a reward for his military campaigns in Spain. Britain also gained a monopoly on the Negro slave trade to Spanish America. Louis XIV recognised Queen Anne and her Protestant successors in Britain, while she recognised Louis's grandson Philip V as King of Spain. As a consolation prize, the Emperor Charles VI received the Spanish Netherlands, plus Milan, Naples and Sardinia in Italy.

On 8 August 1714, Queen Anne died. Her heir, Sophie, the Dowager Electress of Hanover, had died on 8 June. Sophie's son George, Elector of Hanover, became King of England and Scotland. He was fifty-four years old and well aware of the lurking Jacobite alternative to the Protestant succession.

The Union of the Parliaments bought the loyalty of most Scottish parliamentarians. Since the united parliament in Westminster was anti-Catholic, there was no prospect of its supporting the Old Pretender's claim to the throne. In Scotland, particularly in Perthshire, the picture was much more complex.

Some families kept supporting the Stewarts, no matter how they behaved or, in the case of King Charles II, how they switched religions for political convenience. James Graham, Marquis of Montrose, had lost his life in 1650 by returning from Europe to fight for the Stewart monarchy in Scotland. His kinsman, John Graham of Claverhouse, another outstanding pro-Stewart general, had been killed at the Battle of Killiecrankie in 1689. Neither Montrose nor Claverhouse was a Catholic.

The house of Murray, however, divided its allegiances. The Duke's son William, Marquis of Tullibardine, supported the Catholic Stewarts, while his brother, Lord James, who became the 2nd Duke, supported the Protestant succession.

Another local royalist, William Drummond of Cromlix, went into exile at the same time. Unlike Montrose, he did not return until the monarchy was restored in 1660. Instead, Drummond became one of many Scottish mercenaries in Europe, rising to the rank of General in the army of the Russian Tsar Alexis I. Drummond's reputation for bravery and military skill earned him the post of Major General of Charles II's forces in Scotland. In 1686, James VII created him 1st Viscount Strathallan.

The Drummonds generally were pro-Jacobite, but not necessarily Catholic.

Rev. James Drummond, closely related to the Catholic James Drummond, 1st Duke of Perth, was parish minister of Auchterarder, then Muthill. He became Bishop of Brechin, but was expelled in the Glorious Revolution of 1688.

Scotland's religious wars were not over, especially not in Auchterarder. Political instability delayed investment in transport, housing and business infrastructure.

The Royal Burgh of Auchterarder in the early eighteenth century is well described by local author Charles Kennaway in his novel *Gentleman Adventurer* (1951): 'Situated on a ridge with its little crofts and thatched cottages lying at odd angles to one another . . . The main street was broad and, towards its centre, inclined into a pleasant square . . . to the north (of which) stood the kirk, surrounded by its old kirkyard.'

In the Auchterarder area, most men, and some women, were employed in agriculture. War and trading restrictions reduced the volume of cattle hides exported to Europe. On the other hand, more peaceful relations between Scotland and England allowed cattle to be fattened in summer in Perthshire, then herded south for sale in England. From pre-Roman times, cattle had been bred in the Auchterarder area and, as valuable moveable assets, had been vulnerable to theft. As early as 1175, the Scottish Parliament had made it illegal to buy cattle from anyone without proof of ownership.

By the seventeenth century, export taxes on cattle were an important source of government revenue. When General David Leslie defeated the Marquis of Montrose at the Battle of Philiphaugh in 1645, part of his reward was £10,000 of duties levied on exported cattle.

Many Auchterarder people supplemented their incomes with a handloom in their cottage, making woollen cloth, much of it tartan. Linen, handwoven from locally grown flax, became an alternative. Supplies of wool and demand for cloth were erratic, with no stability of income. Political stability was even less certain.

Auchterarder had no port and poor local roads. As long ago as the first century, the Romans had built a road from their camp at Bertha, north of Perth, along the Gask Ridge to ford the River Earn at Strageath, then on to their camp at Ardoch and down to the Antonine Wall at Camelon. This remained the main east-to-west road through Strathearn until the eighteenth century.

There was also a north-to-south road, today known as the Cadger's Yett footpath, which takes a high route over the Ochils into Glendevon. It was used by generations of soldiers and traders. The pass through the Ochils at Gleneagles (now the A823) was not made into a viable road until the nineteenth century, though there was a rough track on the other side of the glen. Other roads led to churches, farms and fords. For example, there was a 'coffin-walk' for funeral processions from the long-established village at the Castleton to the old church of St Mackessog's.

Throughout the Middle Ages, all these roads were largely unpaved, muddy tracks, often impossible for wheeled transport. Agricultural produce or other goods from Auchterarder had to be carried on foot, on pack-horses, or ferried down the River Earn to join the Tay near the great Celtic religious site of Abernethy.

There were no bridges over the Earn until the mid-eighteenth century. To go from Auchterarder to Perth, it was unwise for most of the year to try to ford the

Earn at Dalreoch. Those who could afford it might use the Dalreoch Ferry boat operated by the Haldanes.

There was a southern road to Perth, which crossed the Ruthven Water at the Milton, then ran east towards Dunning, crossing the Pairney Burn not far from Pairney Farm. The Pairney Bridge, built in the late seventeenth century, is the oldest surviving bridge in Auchterarder parish. From Dunning, the road kept to high ground to Forgandenny and Bridge of Earn, where it joined the main Edinburgh to Perth road.

Until the Pairney Bridge was built, the main route from Auchterarder to Perth ran north down today's Hunter Street, past St Mackessog's Church, then on to the ford at Kinkell and up to Trinity Gask to join the old Roman road, following it eastwards.

The Kinkell ford was not always safe. As late as 1783, James Bishop, the local precentor (who led psalm singing) was swept away and drowned. He had a history of drunkenness. His newspaper obituary tactfully says he was 'an agreeable preacher to all who relished the doctrines of the gospel in their primitive simplicity'. He figures in a rhyme:

Was there e'er sic a parish, a terrible parish;
Was there e'er sic a parish as that o' Kinkell?
They've hangit the minister, drooned the precentor,
Dang doon the steeple and drucken the bell.

The minister, who was hanged in 1682, was the Rev. Richard Duncan. He fell out with his kirk elders and other religious officials when they obstructed maintenance of the kirk. When the body of an unknown child was discovered, the minister was accused of adultery with his servant, Catharine Stalker, and murder of their child. He was convicted on the flimsiest of circumstantial evidence and swiftly executed hours before a pardon arrived from Perth. The church was then allowed to fall down. The expensive bell was sold to Cockpen Kirk in the Lothians. The profits from the sale were not clearly accounted for.

The Auchterarder area has had its fair share of acrimonious disputes over the neglect of public buildings. The Kinkell incident is more spectacular than most.

Small-minded barbarity and generous-spirited scholarship were close neighbours. Along the River Earn from Kinkell, David Drummond, Lord Madderty, founded Innerpeffray Library in 1680. He had married Beatrix, sister of James Graham, 1st Marquis of Montrose. Like the great Marquis, Beatrix loved reading. Soon, Innerpeffray Library lent books to people from local parishes. Remarkably, given the relative value of books at the time, they could be borrowed without charge, making Innerpeffray the first free lending library in Scotland. Even more remarkably for the time, books could be borrowed by women as well as men.

The Innerpeffray Estate passed to Thomas Hay, 6th Earl of Kinnoul, one of the Commissioners of the 1707 Treaty of the Union of the Parliaments of Scotland and England. Thomas Hay's grandson, Robert Hay Drummond, who became Archbishop of York, had the present Innerpeffray Library building constructed in 1762. Many of the books there today come from his collection.

In the early eighteenth century, Innerpeffray Library represented the latest in enlightened thinking. However, one of Thomas Hay's daughters, Margaret, married a man who would have a devastating impact on Strathearn: John Erskine 6th Earl of Mar.

Wherever there is religious conflict, there are political opportunists. The Earl of Mar, known as 'Bobbing John' both for his swaying in whichever way the winds of politics blew and for his sycophantic manners, had enriched himself as an architect of the 1707 Union. He was aware, however, of the resentment that the mainly Catholic north and west of Scotland held towards the mainly Protestant south and east.

Mar thought that France and Spain were theoretical backers of any British Catholic cause. He failed to appreciate that their theoretical backing was never converted into political success. Mar also did not realise the implications of Louis XIV's death on 1 Sept 1715. The new French King, Louis XV, was the infant great-grandson of the old king. The French ministers did not see Scotland as an immediate priority.

A previous Earl of Mar, Donald, in 1332 had stationed his troops in Auchterarder before losing the Battle of Dupplin to Edward Balliol. 'Bobbing John' was to do even worse than his ancestor.

In September 1715, Mar raised the Jacobite standard in Aberdeenshire. He led an army of ten thousand men south to camp at Auchterarder on 17 October. He then withdrew to Perth, but requisitioned for his troops a huge quantity of meal from the recent Auchterarder harvest, plus loads of coal for the field kitchens. Mar knew the area well.

Mar told his Lieutenant-General Alexander Gordon 'to search at Auchterarder, Dunning, Tullibardine, Muthill and Crieff for all the leather and made shoes which are fit for the use of the army and to seize the said leather and shoes.'

A letter from one of Gordon's kinsmen warns about what in the twenty-first century is called 'friendly fire': 'The gentlemen of the picket-guard are willing to patrol about Auchterarder but, seeing they cannot speak Irish (Gaelic) to their sentries, they may be exposed to their fire.'

In the Auchterarder area, the situation was similar to 1332, when David II and Edward Balliol, who both claimed to be King of Scotland, fought the Battle of Dupplin near Forteviot. In 1715, the townspeople and burgesses were Protestant and favoured the stability which they expected from George I. Many of the local nobility were Jacobite sympathisers, if not active supporters.

John Haldane of Gleneagles was known as 'Union Jack' for his support for the Union of the Scottish and English Parliaments in 1707, but he had some sympathy for the Jacobite cause. His patience was sorely tried when Mar's troops arrived on the Gleneagles Estate and 'shot a great many sheep and black cattle, plundered their shepherds' and tenants' houses, broke open Gleneagles closet, the granaries and took what meal they had for their subsistence.'

On 10 November 1715, the Earl of Mar held a Grand Review of his army in Auchterarder. His cavalry, with divisions of Gordons and Hamiltons, made a show of Jacobite fighting strength.

On 13 November 1715, at Sheriffmuir, between Auchterarder and Dunblane, the Jacobite Earl of Mar was met by John Campbell, the Hanoverian 2nd Duke of Argyll, a descendant of Montrose's implacable Puritan enemy. Argyll had only about three thousand two hundred troops, but forced Mar's nine thousand to withdraw after an inconclusive battle. Some Jacobite leaders were captured, including William Drummond, 4th Viscount Strathallan, who remained in prison for two years, but lived to fight again for the Jacobites and died at the Battle of Culloden thirty years later.

Astonishingly, Mar never regrouped to attack Argyll's outnumbered forces. Instead, Mar led his men back through Strathearn where they looted Tullibardine. The troops, short of food, seized any surviving sheep and threshed all remaining corn at Dalreoch and Gleneagles.

Winter set in with a vengeance. Mar's troops had eaten most of the local food. The people of Auchterarder were starving. Worse was to follow. Mar learned that Argyll had assembled a bigger army and was preparing to march through Strathearn against him. On 17 January 1716, Mar issued the following order: 'The enemy should be as much incommoded as possible . . . This can by no means be better effected than by destroying all the corn and forage, which may serve to support them on their march, and burning the houses and villages'.

On 25 January 1716 at three in the morning, Ranald, Chief of Clanranald, among the fiercest of the Jacobites, arrived in Auchterarder with three hundred men. A snowstorm was howling.

Without warning, Clanranald set fire to the thatched roofs of the houses. When the inhabitants tried to salvage their belongings, Clanranald threw everything back into the flames, except food and blankets, which they stole for themselves. As people fled from their burning houses and tried to shelter in the church, the Jacobites attacked and robbed them. Many were murdered. Others died of hypothermia.

The destruction of Auchterarder was thorough and ruthless. Lord George Murray, from the powerful house of Atholl, came from Perth to supervise. Colonel Patrick Graham commanded a Jacobite garrison at Tullibardine. On the orders of James Drummond, 2nd Duke of Perth and his savage kinsman Ludovic Drummond, the burning continued for days.

Aberuthven, Dunning, Blackford and Crieff were destroyed along with farms in between, except those owned by known Jacobite supporters. Even then, the rampaging Clanranald made mistakes, burning the wrong houses. Graham even burned Damside, near Aberuthven, and other houses belonging to his own kinsman, the Duke of Montrose. He then burned the nearby Kirklands.

In Auchterarder, Andrew Mailer, who had five children, some too young to walk, begged Colonel Graham to leave him enough fodder for one cow to provide milk for the infants. He was forced to stand and watch his house and corn being burned. Remarkably, as a title deed thirty years later for 42 High Street shows, several of Andrew Mailer's family survived the destruction.

Andrew Mailer and others signed a document called *The Late Unnatural Rebellion*, detailing the Jacobites' atrocities. Anticipating trouble, the Protestant minister's wife, Mrs Stedman, had removed the furniture from the manse and distributed it round other houses, but the Catholic Jacobites burned these too.

John Paterson, an exciseman, had his house burned along with 'a parcel of drugs'. William Davidson's house and shop, one of the few two-storey buildings in the town, were burned along with market goods, textiles and books. Weavers had their looms and tools burned. Mar's scorched earth policy was callous. His troops obeyed his orders with vindictive glee.

One of the few houses spared in Auchterarder was 'The Abbey', which stood on today's Abbey Road. It was the largest house in town and owned by Mrs Paterson, who let Jacobite sympathisers meet there before the rebellion.

The Jacobite footsoldiers burned Protestant Strathearn in 1716, thinking it would help their cause. It did not. The Old Pretender, along with Mar and the 2nd Duke of Perth, fled to France a few weeks later. They had lingered in Scotland, waiting for a consignment of Spanish gold to arrive, only to hear that the ship had been wrecked in St Andrews Bay. While the Jacobite leaders abandoned their troops, Hanoverian soldiers picked up coins from the sand.

In the Auchterarder area, many people claimed compensation from King George I, pleading that their properties had been burned because they had supported him. Most claims took seven years to settle. Some lawsuits dragged on for sixty years. Compensation became known as 'the burning money'. Some were paid at a tenth of what was claimed, on the grounds that, though the thatched roofs had been burned and house contents destroyed, the stone walls of many houses survived and could be redeveloped. Slate roofs were an expensive, but safer option. Some of these early houses, like 172–176 High Street, still stand today, though much altered. On many houses, an old roofline shows through the harling on gable ends.

Charles Kennaway, the twentieth-century novelist, did not like the reconstruction: 'As a result of the Jacobite burnings, new houses had been erected of a drab stone with roofs of equally drab slates . . . making an almost continuous street . . . Each heritor or owner, in his need to acquire every possible bit of land, had built his house or cottage up to the very edge of the road.'

He noted that, by the end of the eighteenth century, the village green effect of the kirkyard had been blocked off by 'a new girnal or storehouse . . . right on top of what had been part of the graveyard not so much earlier.'

The people of Auchterarder mostly supported the Hanoverians. On the site of the old North Crofts, half way down the High Street, stands Hanover Gardens. It owes its name, not to eighteenth-century political sympathies, but to the twentieth-century Hanover Housing Association, which provides homes for the elderly. It is historically appropriate, but name origins are not always what they seem.

Further up the River Earn, one community underwent a significant name change. After the Jacobite burnings of 1716, the name Drummond carried unpleasant connotations. Crown commissioners changed the name of Drummond village back to its informal Gaelic alternative *Crubha Cnoc* or 'Hill of Trees'. It was anglicised to Crieff, with its hill, the Knock rising above it. Other Strathearn towns retain both a formal and an informal name. Aberuthven is locally called Smiddy Haugh. Auchterarder is the Lang Toon. The burned communities struggled to recover. Scotland was not yet free of sectarian terrorism.

25

Enlightenment and Military Roads

*In which a badly worded oath sparks the Age of Reason and
we meet the forgotten man in the British National Anthem*

After the failed 1715 Jacobite rebellion, King George I's Whig ministers set about ensuring stability at home and abroad. Britain and Holland signed an alliance with their old enemy France in 1717. Soon, Austria joined to form a Quadruple Alliance.

There was no coherent alliance against them, but Spain remained a threat. So did rising states to the north and east. King Charles XII of Sweden wanted to recover the Duchies of Bremen and Verden, which had been acquired by King George I's Hanover. Russia, emerging as a major power under Tsar Peter I (The Great), threatened British trade in the Baltic. In Germany Frederick William was building Prussia into a military force.

Some Jacobites who had fled from Britain after the 1715 rebellion served in foreign armies and courts. Sir Henry Stirling, 3rd Baronet of Ardoch, served Peter the Great and married the daughter of Admiral Thomas Gordon, a Jacobite in the Russian navy.

In Britain, the lessons of the failed Scottish Darien Scheme were forgotten in 1711 when Robert Harley, the Tory Earl of Oxford, led the formation of the South Sea Company. It took over a large part of the national debt in exchange for trading privileges. Both Tories and Whigs invested heavily. The fanciful profits never materialised. In 1720, the South Sea bubble burst, ruining investors and the old Whig government's credibility.

A new Whig government emerged, led by Sir Robert Walpole, who had sold his holdings of South Sea stock at peak prices just before the crash. Walpole was Britain's first Prime Minister, remaining in office from 1721 to 1742. Southern Britain thrived under his policy of avoiding wars, promoting trade, and encouraging manufacturing and agricultural improvements. Walpole had a genius for bribery, duplicity and ensuring others took the blame if things went wrong.

Walpole fell out with John Campbell, 2nd Duke of Argyll who, after military service in Spain, Minorca and the Battle of Sheriffmuir, tried to pursue a political career in London. Argyll was as greedy and corrupt as Walpole, but less skilled in political timing and blinded by arrogance and snobbery.

King George I detested his son and heir George, Prince of Wales. Argyll the Duke wormed his way into the Prince of Wales's favour. Walpole, the commoner, had the support of the King. Argyll's career in London never reached the heights he had hoped for. Full of resentment, he gathered round him a faction of malcontents in Scotland. Argyll even compromised his Campbell Puritan traditions by intriguing with Catholic Jacobites.

When King George I died in 1727, Argyll hoped for more power. King George II, however, found Walpole indispensable. It took another fifteen years for the House of Commons to turn against Walpole, who had reluctantly agreed to go to war with Spain in 1739. By then the nation, having profited from Walpole's years of peace, was in the mood for glory. In the eighteenth, as in most centuries, glory means war. Walpole resigned in 1742 and was made Earl of Orford. Argyll died in 1743. His brother Archibald Campbell, Lord Islay, succeeded to the Dukedom. He was a more astute politician than his brother and equally capable of extending Campbell influence by whatever means he could.

In eighteenth-century Auchterarder, political influence and practical authority were not taken lightly. Not only did the lawsuits after the burning of 1716 continue for sixty years, but civil and religious law also allowed great scope for confusion and indignation.

The records of the Presbytery of Auchterarder end in 1687, just before the Revolution against the Catholic King James VII. By the time they begin again in 1703, the Bishopric of Dunblane had lost its authority. Populist Evangelism, but not extreme Puritanism, had become fashionable. Bishops were so disliked that, at a Graham funeral in Aberuthven in 1712, a local mob chased the Episcopal clergy away and the corpse had to be buried without a religious service.

In the same year 1712, the Patronage Act was passed, reinforcing local major landowners' rights to make appointments to parish churches without the congregation's approval. It was a piece of legislation doomed to create disputes, but it was not repealed until 1874.

At the time of the Jacobite burning of Auchterarder in 1716, the Rev. John Stedman, a timid preacher, was parish minister. He had been afraid to enter the pulpit for months. His place had been taken by the Rev. William Reid, minister of Dunning, who preached with a pistol at his side in case Jacobite rebels should trouble the congregation. Reid, an elderly man, died in Dunning the day before the Jacobites arrived to burn it. His parishioners hastened to bury him. The Jacobites burned his house, saying it was a pity they could not burn him with it.

In December 1716, after the destructive Jacobite leaders had fled, the Presbytery of Auchterarder met to license a new minister, Rev. William Craig. It examined him on the soundness of his faith, using a list of formal questions composed by the timid John Stedman and others. Craig refused to swear the clumsily written oath: 'I believe it is not sound and orthodox to teach that we must forsake sin in order to our coming to Christ.'

In other words, Craig believed in Christ's teaching that sinners were welcome to come to God and be sorted out. The established Church view was that sinners should make a show of repentance before the Church would touch them.

The Presbytery tripped over its own double negatives and denied Craig a preaching licence. He appealed to the General Assembly of the Church of Scotland in Edinburgh. Acrimonious debate exploded over the question of whether a sinner should be admitted to the church before he had repented his sins.

A new term, 'high-fliers', was coined for those who, like Craig, believed in a more modern, rational approach to religion. The Auchterarder Creed debate became a rallying point for free thinking in Scotland. Craig himself was an unwilling philosophical hero. All he wanted was to obtain his preaching licence. His practical frankness about working with sinners almost cost him his job. He began to retract his statement, but it was too late to stop the controversy.

Underlying the Auchterarder Creed was the conflict between local privileged patronage plus national religious and political authority on the one hand, and the right of individuals to think for themselves on the other.

The spark from Auchterarder lit debate in Edinburgh. The independent Scottish Parliament had recently been abolished. Fear of Catholic Jacobite insurrection was rife. A return to violent Puritanism was equally unattractive. By the mid eighteenth century, Scottish philosophers, like David Hume and Adam Smith, were analysing the roles of belief and authority in government. Their books show how it is counter-productive for any organisation or government to find itself on the opposite side to common sense. In Auchterarder, people already knew that.

Allied to scientific investigation, the revolution in political thought became known as 'The Enlightenment'. The debate spread to Europe and America. The French philosopher and satirist Voltaire, in his *Essaie sur l'Histoire Générale*, praised Auchterarder's most famous son, the Marquis of Montrose, for his passionate commitment to justice, and developed the central freedom issue expressed in The Auchterarder Creed debate.

By the end of the century, the concepts of individual and economic liberty had evolved sufficiently to overthrow governments. In 1776, the United States of America was formed. In 1789, France became a republic.

In 1731, the General Assembly of the Church of Scotland, prompted by Archibald Campbell, Lord Islay, voted to let heritors (local landowners) appoint ministers to parishes without the consent of the congregation as a whole. This practice became law the following year with the Act Anent Calls. As a result, groups of parishioners, who disliked the heavy hands of patronage and central authority, left or 'seceded from' the established Presbyterian Church.

In Auchterarder, a small Secession Church, funded by local people, was built in 1732 in the wynd behind the Star Hotel. It witnessed many a religious storm until its roof was destroyed in the howling gale of 28 December 1879 that blew down the Tay Railway Bridge in Dundee.

In 1776, the year of the American Revolution, the landowner patron of Blackford Church, Moray of Abercairney, presented a Mr Stevenson as minister despite the congregation's protests. Many seceded from the parish church. Auchterarder Presbytery then forbade all landowners to provide a site for seceders from both Auchterarder and Blackford to build a Secession church.

These new Seceders called themselves at first The South United Presbyterians, and held services outside in the market site behind the Star Hotel, confronting both the nearby Parish Church and the 1732 old Secession Church. They acquired a portable pulpit, called a 'tent', with a canopy and back sounding-board. This Tent Yard was a famous centre of rousing evangelism. Confusingly, the term 'tenting yard' was already used to describe land containing 'tenters', wooden frames for stretching new-woven woollen cloths on tenter-hooks to dry evenly after they had been processed in the fulling mill at the Ruthven Water.

In 1778, the South United Presbyterian congregation bought a permanent site on the other side of the High Street, behind today's Golf Inn and Baker's Wynd. It came to be known as The Relief Church. That was not the end of the matter. The question of relief from secular control over spiritual matters would explode again in Auchterarder in 1843 and cause a permanent disruption of the Protestant church in Scotland.

Just as The Auchterarder Creed opened paths for new intellectual debate in Scotland, so the burning of Strathearn made George I's government open new roads into central and northern Scotland, enabling troops to move swiftly to suppress any further Jacobite rebellion.

Some Perthshire nobles who supported the 1715 Jacobite rebellion were stripped of their powers and of their lands. John Murray, 1st Duke of Atholl, ceased to be Lord Lieutenant of Perthshire and had to resign his Dukedom in favour of his third son, James, who supported the Hanoverians.

William Murray, the Jacobite Marquis of Tullibardine, returned to Scotland briefly in 1719 with three hundred Spanish foot soldiers and George Keith, 10th Earl Marischal. The two nobles squabbled over how best to deploy their small resources. True to Jacobite form, the foot soldiers lost a battle at Glenshiel and were captured, while their leaders fled to Europe.

Unusually, the heads of the Grahams and the Campbells were on the same side. James, 1st Duke of Montrose, who was Secretary of State for Scotland, and the soldier-politician John, 2nd Duke of Argyll backed the Hanoverians, though several of their respective kinsmen joined the Jacobite army. James Graeme of Braco Castle was married to a relative of the Jacobite Earl of Mar. It was Graeme of Braco, with his knowledge of the local landscape, who carried Mar's instruction in 1716 to burn Auchterarder. The Duke of Montrose did not exact retribution on his kinsman and allowed James Graeme to remain in Braco.

One branch of the Campbell labyrinth, the MacGregors, had great influence in the cattle trade. Depending on your personal experience of them, the MacGregors were enterprising businessmen or thieves and racketeers. As early as 1611, a proclamation had been made in Auchterarder, offering a reward of £1,000 for any MacGregor chief taken dead or alive. At the Battle of Sheriffmuir in 1715, Rob Roy MacGregor and his men had promised to join the Jacobites, but waited on lower slopes near Balhaldie and, seeing that the battle was inconclusive, decided not to join either side.

Cattle were fattened on summer pastures in northern Scotland and brought south for export. By the early eighteenth century, Crieff, with its autumn 'Tryst', had become a major cattle market. From there, cattle drovers took their herds south, by the Ochil passes via Cloan and Coulshill, Gleneagles and Glendevon, to the key distribution centre at Falkirk. One of the main drovers' roads south from Auchterarder was via the Cadger's Yett, a footpath that survives today.

The drovers were superstitious. They tied a complex knot, St Mungo's Knot, into the tails of their cattle, so that the saintly protector of dumb animals would keep them from accident or witchcraft. The owners of such cattle, as they passed near the mediaeval St Mungo's Chapel in Gleneagles, would feel doubly protected.

In Auchterarder there was a regular livestock market behind today's Star Hotel until 1970. The Star was also, from the late eighteenth century, a coaching inn from where passengers and mail could be linked to London.

Drovers struggled with muddy tracks and cattle thieves. To protect trade, increase law and order and suppress Jacobites, King George I commissioned General George Wade in 1724 to survey the Highlands. Wade said no insurrection could be quelled unless new all-weather roads were built to let Redcoat troops march quickly into the rebel heartlands. Wade was given the job of constructing two hundred and fifty miles of new roads. He achieved most of it within ten years.

It was an extraordinary achievement. As a mark of respect, Wade is the only personage, other than God and the monarch, to be mentioned in the British National Anthem, whose fourth verse is:

God, grant that Marshall Wade,
Shall by thy mighty aid,
Victory bring.
May he sedition hush
And like a torrent rush
Rebellious Scots to crush.
God save the King!

In the twenty-first century, it is considered tactful to omit this verse when the National Anthem is sung on public occasions.

In addition to the military road network, a system of garrisons was planned, but most of the money was spent on building one stronghold, Fort Augustus, in 1730. It lies halfway between Fort William and Inverness and was named after King George II's younger son William Augustus. He was then only a child. Sixteen years later, all Scotland knew him as the Duke of Cumberland.

The Auchterarder area was at a low ebb after the Jacobite burnings of 1716. When the new Perth–Stirling military road was constructed in 1742, it went via Crieff and Braco, bypassing Auchterarder.

To go from Auchterarder to Stirling, the road had hardly changed from Roman times. It ran up today's Orchil Road and straight on to Ardoch to join the old Roman road leading west. Today's A9, over boggy, low-lying ground, was not constructed until the end of the eighteenth century. It began as a Turnpike (a statutory public road), linking Auchterarder to Stirling, via Blackford and Dunblane.

The route from Auchterarder to Perth was not improved until, around 1765, bridges over the River Earn were built at Kinkell, Dalreoch and Forteviot, replacing old fords. Transport of goods then became much easier.

Wade provided a road infrastructure for policing the Highlands. Who was to do the policing? The Disarming Act of 1725 forbade private individuals to bear arms. Legislation to deprive the Highlander of his broadsword, dirk, pistols and targe was as controversial as today's attempts to introduce gun control in the USA. The Hanoverian government provided an ingenious solution. Men were granted a dispensation to carry weapons if they gave military service. Ever since, Strathearn has been a good recruiting ground for the British army.

In 1725, six independent companies, later increased to ten, were appointed to 'watch' the Highlands. Several of the companies wore dark tartans. The whole force became known as The Black Watch (Am Freiceadan Dubh) as opposed to the regular army's Redcoats (Saighdearan Dearg). In 1739 these companies were amalgamated to form the 43rd Regiment. By the time the regiment was renumbered the 42nd in 1751, the Jacobite cause had been effectively destroyed in one final slaughter led by the Duke of Cumberland on Culloden Moor.

26

The Forty-Five Rebellion and the Agricultural Revolution

*In which we hear local cheers after Bonnie Prince Charlie's army
is slaughtered at Culloden, while Jacobites resort to singing sad
songs and playing cricket as their forfeited estates flourish*

Sir Robert Walpole is often called Britain's first Prime Minister, a term which he disliked. He is also known as 'The Drill Sergeant of the Whig Party', a term which amused him. By largely avoiding war from 1727 to 1739, he created conditions for investment in new methods of agriculture, which was still the main source of employment in Great Britain.

Walpole's brother-in-law, Charles, 2nd Viscount Townshend, after a career in high office that included being Secretary of State and a Commissioner for The Treaty of Union, quit politics in 1730 to devote himself to agricultural improvements at his estate Raynham Hall in Norfolk. He became known as 'Turnip' Townshend for extolling the merits of the profitable, nutritious and exotic root vegetable.

The Peace of Utrecht in 1713 had established European boundaries but the further frontiers of empires allowed more scope for conflict. In the West Indies, official British–Spanish trade was advantageous to both nations. So was the thriving contraband industry, though governments could not acknowledge it. An official blind eye was turned to smuggling until Britain's mood became more jingoistic.

In 1738, Captain Robert Jenkins told a House of Commons committee that Spaniards had boarded his ship in the West Indies and, in order to make him confess to smuggling, had tortured him and cut off his ear. The incident had happened seven years before and had been recorded in an official report, but William Pitt and a new generation of politicians now seized on it as an excuse to pressure Walpole into fighting 'The War of Jenkins' Ear' against Spain.

In 1740, the Hapsburg Holy Roman Emperor Charles VI died. The King of Bavaria succeeded him as Emperor Charles VII. He was the son of Charles VI's cousin Maximilian of Bavaria and the Polish Princess Cunigunda Sobieska, closely related to Clementina Sobieska, mother of the young Jacobite soon to be known as Bonnie Prince Charlie. The Hapsburg Empire had divided so that Charles VI's daughter Maria Theresa succeeded him to the throne of Austria. King Frederick II of Prussia promptly seized neighbouring Silesia from her. Both France and Spain supported him. The wars of the Austrian succession involved all the major European powers.

John Dalrymple, 2nd Earl of Stair, son of the Lord Advocate implicated in the Massacre of Glencoe, encouraged Parliament to vote for war against France and Spain, saying that Britain could thus expand its empire in America. The British King George II was more interested in fighting in Europe and protecting his native Hanover, but he was compromised by his family interests. His sister Sophia Dorothea was married to Frederick II of Prussia.

The Dalrymples and the Gleneagles Haldanes detested one another, especially after Patrick Haldane of Gleneagles, a shrewd lawyer, was appointed Commissioner for the disposal of Jacobite estates forfeited after the 1715 Rebellion. The Scottish legal establishment remains famous for its spiteful internal wrangling. The sharp-tongued John Ramsay of Ochtertyre near Crieff said that the nine of diamonds was called the 'Peter (Patrick) Haldane' or the 'Curse of Scotland' whenever it appeared on the card table among Dalrymple's cronies. The family ambitions were not thwarted. Haldane's son George became Governor of Jamaica.

Sir Robert Walpole resigned as First Lord of The Treasury on 2 February 1742, but Whig domination of Parliament continued, led by John Carteret, Lord Granville. He persuaded the Austrian Empress Maria Theresa to recognise the Prussian Frederick II as King of Silesia. Carteret then accompanied King George II to Europe in 1743 where the King led his troops to victory over the French at the Battle of Dettingen and drove them out of Germany. It was the last time that a reigning British monarch fought on a battlefield.

Eighteenth-century political parties were less formally structured than today. The Whigs, Tories, Country Party, Patriots and King's Friends overlapped in their policies. In 1742, the young Scottish philosopher David Hume wrote an essay on *The Parties of Great Britain*. He tried to pin down the respective beliefs of each party but, like political commentators before and since, found himself unable to do so.

Strategy, not belief, guides policy. In September 1743, by the Treaty of Worms, England formally allied with Austria. France and Spain promptly allied with Prussia and a Second War of the Austrian Succession broke out, which rapidly spread from Silesia to become the first global war, involving conflict on every continent.

In 1744, Henry Pelham succeeded Carteret as Whig leader. In February of that year there was an invasion scare when French troops gathered at Dunkirk, but a storm dispersed the accompanying French fleet. In fact, the French did not try to cross the English Channel. In April 1745 they invaded the Netherlands. A defence was rallied, using Dutch, Austrian and British troops, including Captain David Graeme of Braco, the pro-Hanoverian son of the Jacobite who had hand-delivered the order to burn Auchterarder in 1716. The 25-year-old Duke of Cumberland, younger son of King George II, led the allied army. At the Battle of Fontenoy in May 1745 he came up against the formidable general Maurice of Saxony (Le Marechale de Saxe), who defeated him. It was an experience Cumberland did not wish to repeat.

Black Watch troops served at Fontenoy. The regiment had been formed in 1739 to police the Highlands of Scotland, but King George II's new overseas commitments meant that they were deployed elsewhere. This diversion of government troops overseas led the Jacobites in 1745 to think they could stage a successful rebellion.

James, the Old Pretender, the self-styled King James VIII and III, was in comfortable exile in Rome, surrounded by flatterers and chatterers. His son, Prince Charles Edward, had the Stewart gift of appearing plausible against all common sense. He found two able Perthshire men as his Lieutenants-General. One, Lord George Murray, had seen service in 1715 and had encouraged the burning of Strathearn. The other, James Drummond, 3rd Duke of Perth, was a Catholic romantic. Other local aristocrats, like Laurence Oliphant, 7th Laird of Gask, welcomed Charles Edward to his house. In practical military terms, as in the 1725 Rebellion, the French promised aid but failed to deliver.

On 25 July 1745, Charles Edward landed in Scotland with the object of restoring his father the Old Pretender to the thrones of Scotland and England. Charles Edward raised the Jacobite standard at Glenfinnan in the Highlands. He marched south, gathering support where he could. On 12 September, the Jacobite army stopped in Auchterarder and held a military review, hoping to recruit more troops. They failed. Memories of the cruel 1716 Jacobite burning of Auchterarder made the town mainly Hanoverian in its political sympathies.

When Charles Edward moved on to Perth, Lord George Murray equipped the Jacobite troops with haversacks so that each soldier could carry his own ration of meal. Charles Edward, now known as Bonnie Prince Charlie, was more concerned with the fancy lacework of his own clothes.

Not all Scotland was as sceptical as Auchterarder. Nobles and lairds were divided, but some who had not prospered under the Whigs fanned anti-Union nationalism. Charles Edward assembled an army of around six thousand men and won the Battle of Prestonpans near Edinburgh on 21 September. He entered Edinburgh but failed to capture Edinburgh Castle. He then set off on a long march into England. He got as far as Derby, causing panic in London. Lord George Murray, however, pointed out to Charles Edward that both General George Wade in Newcastle and the Duke of Cumberland had armies, larger and more professional than the Jacobites. On 4 December 1745, Charles Edward retreated to Scotland.

The Duke of Cumberland chased Charles Edward northwards. After celebrating Cumberland's twenty-fifth birthday with an extra ration of brandy, on 15 April 1746 at Culloden, near Inverness, his troops slaughtered the Jacobite soldiers. The next day, Charles Edward, also aged twenty-five, abandoned his followers.

Two weeks after the Battle of Culloden, Auchterarder Presbytery voted to send a delegation to congratulate the victorious Duke of Cumberland. Charles Edward fled to France, then Rome, as his father had done before him, where he took to drink.

William, 4th Viscount Strathallan, who was captured at the Battle of Sheriffmuir in 1715 and imprisoned for two years, went to fight again for the exiled Stewarts, though he was sixty years old. He was killed at Culloden and is buried at Innerpeffray. His estates, along with those of other Jacobite supporters, were forfeited to the crown. James Drummond, 3rd Duke of Perth, escaped the battlefield, but fell ill after months of privation in hiding and died on board ship, fleeing to France. Lord George Murray escaped to Europe, like Bonnie Prince Charlie, and lived for another fourteen years.

When Cumberland died in 1765, King George III made his own brother, Henry Frederick, Duke of Cumberland and added the title Duke of Strathearn. Once again, Strathearn and the monarchy were closely linked.

James, the Old Pretender, died in 1766. Bonnie Prince Charlie died in 1788, but the Jacobite–Hanoverian conflict lingered in the Auchterarder area for over two hundred years in romantic fiction and children's games. Old Lady Nairne of Gask, the Jacobite matriarch, died soon after Culloden, grieving for her dead kinsmen, but Lady Carolina Nairne later wrote wistful Jacobite songs, with titles like 'Will ye no come back again?' and 'Wi a hundred pipers an a' an a''. Both she and Robert Burns wrote versions of 'Charlie is my darling'.

One of Lady Nairne's kinsmen fled to the New Forest in the South of England. To disguise his Jacobite links, he altered his name to Nyren and adopted conspicuously English ways. His son, John Nyren was a star of the Hambledon Club, England's first great cricket team. His grandson, Richard Nyren wrote the first history of English cricket.

Cricket was the death of King George II's older son, Frederick, Prince of Wales. He was a keen supporter of the newly fashionable game, where nobles led teams and gambled huge sums on match results. In 1751, Prince Frederick was hit by a cricket ball and died after an abscess formed. His son George succeeded him as Prince of Wales and became King George III in 1760, when George II suffered a stroke while sitting on his chamber pot.

The game 'Carl-Doddies' (or Charles against George) was played as late as the 1960s by children using plantain stalks to cross swords. It was a summer equivalent to conkers, played in autumn with chestnuts. In Scotland, the Jacobite rebellions have been sentimentalised, their role in sectarian atrocities largely forgotten. In Auchterarder, where Charles Stuart was once seen as a terrorist leader seeking to impose an alien faith, his image now smirks prettily on tea towels and shortbread tins.

The Whigs decided to ensure that the Jacobite menace was removed once and for all. Imposing political will by military might is a short-term solution. To destroy political opposition, a government must align the people's financial interests with its own. The Whigs' logic was straightforward. Scotland was poor and backward. If it could be made to thrive economically, nobody would invite the Jacobites to trample over their fields or loot their towns.

Before improvement could be put in place, any captured Jacobite leaders had to be dealt with. Thomas Pelham-Holles, Duke of Newcastle, and brother to the Whig Party leader Henry Pelham, promoted William Murray, a brilliant lawyer from a great Perthshire family to be Solicitor General. In 1746, Murray prosecuted captured Jacobite leaders, including the elderly Simon Fraser, 12th Lord Lovat, who tried to embarrass Murray in court with remarks about how Murray's mother was 'of great use to us in Perth' in helping the Jacobite cause. Lovat was executed.

Many of the surviving leaders kept their heads attached to their necks by fleeing to the continent. Their lands were attaindered (seized as a forfeit) by the Crown. The Whig administration appointed Crown Commissioners to redistribute the properties and oversee their management, imposing higher standards of crop cultivation.

In the Auchterarder area, the Crown took over the estates of the Catholic James Drummond, 3rd Duke of Perth. Agriculture remained the mainstay of the local economy. After the 1745 rebellion, Mr Wigh, the Crown Commissioner examining the forfeited Drummond estates, was scathing about Auchterarder's backwardness, describing the people as 'idle and poor, the farmers not thinking it necessary to thin their turnips when small, allowing them to grow until they be the size of large kail plants and then it is thought a great loss to take them up, unless in small quantities, to give to the cow. A few tenants excepted, no family had oatmeal, nor could they get any. They eat nothing better than bear (barley) meal and a few greens boiled together at midday for dinner, and bear meal pottage evening and morning.'

Forty years after the 1716 Jacobite burning of Auchterarder, the town was poverty-stricken and squalid, 'dwindled into a pitiful village', as Mr Wigh put it. 'The houses in general in this barony are in very bad order and the tenants are very far back in improvement of any kind.' Their cows were ill-fed and unfit for market. 'Their milk scarcely serves their own families.' Despite their poverty, the townspeople were, 'peaceable and honest', except that they squabbled with their neighbours over grazing.

Methods improved rapidly later in the eighteenth century. Crop rotation was better understood. Potatoes and, increasingly, turnips were grown more efficiently. Barley remained the main crop, though oats were grown too. Flax was profitable, both for lint and linseed oil and later as a supplement to animal feed. Wheat needed more fertiliser than most farmers could find. Animal manure was valuable.

On little crofts and on the pendicles of land behind the houses in Auchterarder, tenants, too poor to own a horse or an ox, ploughed their land with the cas-chrom, the ancient foot-plough. In larger fields, from the Middle Ages to the mid eighteenth century, local farmers ploughed their land with 'the old Scots plough'. It consisted of a ploughshare, the metal blade to turn the soil, mounted on a heavy wooden frame, dragged by one or two oxen. Around 1765, the Carron Iron Works in nearby Stirlingshire began to produce a 'swing plough', with a metal 'mould board' to shape the furrow more efficiently with less drag.

Henry Home, Lord Kames of Blair Drummond, the great agricultural reformer, encouraged the swing plough's inventor John Small to publish *A Treatise on Ploughs and Wheeled Carriages*. Kames himself wrote *The Gentleman Farmer*, full of practical, modernising ideas which were adopted by landowners throughout Britain and North America. Kames presented Small's ploughs to the

Blair Drummond Estate tenants. His landowning friends in Strathearn quickly adopted the new ploughs.

Despite Mr Wigh's sneers, cows sold well at the Auchterarder market. The export demand for cow hides had long since dwindled away, but new opportunities arose. Auchterarder and Blackford became famous for making good footwear, sturdy brogues. There were more specialist uses for calf skins. The Birrell family from Kinnesswood in Kinross were Scotland's premier parchment maker. They bought calf skins in Auchterarder in the second half of the eighteenth century from James Carrick, a flesher, and from William, James and Mungo Isdell. The finest parchment could be obtained by buying a pregnant cow, aborting the calf and using its delicate skin.

Much of the parchment was used by the Chancery Office in Edinburgh for the plethora of new charters and documents, generated by the revitalisation of Scotland. Even today, when governments depend on a reliable electricity supply for generating digital documents, there are charters still legally valid that began life as an Auchterarder cow.

The agricultural revolution changed the landscape and the dinner table. For the first time, people in the Auchterarder area could be reasonably confident that, although harvests were bound to vary, there would probably be enough to eat.

The Battle of Culloden on 16 April 1746 was the last pitched battle fought on British soil. It was followed by centuries of peace and prosperity at home, such as Scotland had never enjoyed before. It stands in contrast to the Battle of Bannockburn on 24 June 1314, after which Scotland collapsed into civil war and poverty before the next decade was out, followed by centuries of insecurity. In both battles, each side had Scots and Englishmen fighting as allies. Propagandists have mythologised both battles. History shows that, if a day is to be celebrated annually for bringing long-term benefits to ordinary Scottish people, it is 16 April, not 24 June.

The robust and fragrant sweet william (*Dianthus Barbatus*), popularly named after the Duke of Cumberland, today flowers uncontroversially in domestic gardens and municipal flowerbeds. It could be argued that the sweet william's colourful versatility would make a more appropriate modern symbol for Scotland than the prickly thistle adopted from the country's impoverished mediaeval past. National symbols, however, are rarely the subject of rational debate.

27

The English-speaking World Divides Again

In which old families get new jobs and we visit a Georgian ghost town, then see a successful revolution in the colonies

The Union of the Parliaments in 1707 consolidated the English-speaking world under a single legislative body. The colonies in America, India and elsewhere were subordinate to Parliament in Westminster. The British Empire had many languages. In Scotland, many of the population were bilingual, speaking Gaelic at home and English on formal occasions. Those who did not learn English were at a significant disadvantage for better-paid employment. In the Auchterarder area, almost all families spoke English in the home, though many Gaelic words were generally understood. Some Gaelic agricultural words linger in use today. For example, many older men will refer to a digging fork as a 'graip'. Some other local agricultural terms, like 'heuk' (a sickle) are regional variants of English words, in this case 'hook'.

Although the Jacobites and other disaffected minorities wanted to separate Scotland from England, the real split in the English-speaking world happened on the other side of the Atlantic Ocean. The collapse of Jacobitism in 1746 unified the British Isles against England's traditional enemy, the French. Culloden was the last military battle fought on British soil. The victorious Duke of Cumberland headed for Europe.

Until the Crown Commissioners improved the local economy after the Forty-Five Rebellion, the Auchterarder area lacked enough jobs for young people. One source of employment was the army. The area was a good recruiting ground for The Black Watch, which had been formed to guard against further Jacobite risings but was now a British Army regiment available for service throughout the world.

The next generation of ruling-class families generally recognised political reality and switched from Jacobite to Hanoverian. David Graeme succeeded his Jacobite father as 3rd Laird of Braco and served under the Duke of Cumberland in the Netherlands. He rose to become a general and also served as MP for Perthshire, defeating George Drummond of Blair Drummond in the 1764 election. Laurence Oliphant, 8th Laird of Gask, whose father had welcomed Bonnie Prince Charlie, fought for George III in the Perthshire Dragoons.

James Murray, younger son of the Jacobite leader Lord George Murray, gave loyal service to the Hanoverians, first in Saxony in the Seven Years War, then as a Black Watch Captain in America, where he was wounded at Fort Ticonderoga in 1758. After a distinguished military career, he too became MP for Perthshire. His brother George Murray became an admiral in the British navy.

Admiral George Anson had made himself a popular hero by sailing round the world from 1740 to 1744, returning with £500,000 of treasure captured from Spanish ships. As First Lord of the Admiralty from 1751, he restructured the British navy, instilling ruthless discipline and more promotion by merit, rather than by birth or mere time-serving. The poet James Thomson, a minister's son from Kelso, dedicated a poem *Liberty* in 1736 to Frederick Prince of Wales who then awarded him a pension. In 1740, Thomson, as adept with words as with Whig politics, wrote the song *Rule Britannia,* hailing Britain's maritime triumphs. He was rewarded with a sinecure job as Surveyor-General of the Leeward Islands in the West Indies. Military bands have been drumming into us that 'Britannia rules the waves' ever since.

The Whig Oligarchy, led by Henry Pelham till 1754, then by his brother the Duke of Newcastle, increased their hold on the government of Britain. In 1746, Parliament passed the Disarming Act, which banned the wearing of Highland dress. Up to that time, many cottages in the Auchterarder area had a spinning wheel or a hand loom, on which both men and women produced brightly coloured tartans, using local vegetable dyes. After 1746, looms were allowed to produce only the drab grey cloth popular in Edinburgh and other centres of the Scottish Enlightenment. The wearing of the kilt was forbidden until 1782, when the enterprising new Lord Advocate Henry Dundas, from Comrie north-west of Auchterarder, who later became Viscount Melville, had the law repealed and removed a legitimate Highland grievance.

Parliament dismantled the clan system by abolishing a chief's right to inherit a sheriffdom or conduct a court, and forbade chiefs to raise armies. The sole exception today is the Atholl Highlanders, the only remaining legal private army in Britain. Up to 1746, a clan territory's value to a chief lay in the number of men he could mobilise for war. Now the value lay in the land assets, rather than the people who lived on it.

In the north and west of Scotland where much of the land was rough grazing, unfit for arable farming, many families were driven out of their rented cottages by landowners who could make more money from sheep than from subsistence tenants. They sought work in expanding towns like Glasgow or emigrated to the colonies. In the fertile Auchterarder area, the opposite happened. The Crown Commissioners, who administered the Duke of Perth's forfeited estates, granted longer leases to his tenant farmers, encouraging them to invest in better agricultural methods. Auchterarder expanded eastwards with a long extension of the High Street called The New Feus (houses owing ground rent to the landowner), still known as The Feus today.

War in Europe continued until 1748 when the Treaty of Aix la Chapelle confirmed Silesia as belonging to Prussia and recognised Maria Theresa as monarch of Austria, with her husband Francis I as Holy Roman Emperor, succeeding Charles VII who had died in 1745. Most importantly for Britain, the Protestant Hanoverians were recognised as the nation's rightful royal dynasty. The Catholic Jacobite court in exile in France mostly retreated to Rome.

The Treaty of Aix la Chapelle was only a temporary lull in the complex struggle between European monarchs, who sought to expand their kingdoms into empires. In 1756, war broke out over British and French interests in America and India. It was the third phase of the War of the Austrian and Silesian Successions and became known as The Seven Years War.

In India, Britain had factories (trading establishments) at Madras and Bombay (now Mumbai), established by the East India Company in 1661. The French had their own factories. In 1746, the French administrator and military commander Joseph François Dupleix captured Madras, but it was restored to Britain by the Treaty of Aix la Chapelle. In 1751, Dupleix's British counterpart Robert Clive captured the French-held town of Arcot.

It took an atrocity to provoke general British public interest in the war in India. On 20 June 1756, Suraja Dowla, Nawab of Bengal, captured the English fort at Calcutta and imprisoned 146 British prisoners in a tiny, airless space. The following day, only twenty-three were still alive. Robert Clive avenged the atrocity by recapturing Calcutta and killing the Nawab of Bengal at the Battle of Plassey on 22 June 1757. Mir Jaffir became nominal ruler, but Clive proceeded to control Bengal and received enormous bribes and money skimmed from taxes. In 1760, Colonel Eyre Coote routed the French at the Battle of Wandiwash, after which French influence in India dwindled. 'The Black Hole of Calcutta' remains today in the English language as a metaphor for cramped, miserable conditions.

Clive returned to England in 1760, became Baron Clive and went back to India in 1765 to revive the fortunes of the East India Company, which had become chaotic after he left. He introduced reforms and returned to England in 1767. Five years later, Clive was accused of corruption by a Parliamentary select committee, which then conceded that he had given Britain 'great and meritorious services'. He suffered from depression, became an opium addict and committed suicide in 1774.

In North America in 1749, the French established Fort Rouillé, where Toronto stands today, and built a fort at Niagara. They held Detroit and, in 1753, built Fort Duquesne, controlling the strategic Ohio Valley. A 22-year-old American-born Lieutenant Colonel George Washington successfully attacked a French force on 27 May 1754. The French fought back, defending Fort Duquesne, and defeated the English General Edward Braddock at the Battle of Monongahela in 1755. For seven years, war ebbed back and forth in New York State and Ohio. In 1758, at the French Fort Ticonderoga, near the Canadian border, the British Commander James Abercromby lost heavily to the French Commander in Chief in North America, Louis Joseph, Marquis de Montcalm. James Murray, son of Lord George Murray, was wounded in action.

In 1759, the young soldier James Wolfe led a daring attack on the French stronghold of Quebec in Canada. He took the city but was killed in battle along with the French leader Montcalm. The following year, Montreal surrendered to the British, who now controlled the St Lawrence River, vital for trade and military manoeuvres. The British captured Fort Duquesne in 1758 and renamed it Pittsburgh, after William Pitt, who was now leading the Whig administration. At sea in the West Indies, Admiral George Rodney captured Martinique, Grenada and St Lucia.

The Seven Years War at first went badly for Britain in Europe. In 1756, the French captured Minorca. Admiral John Byng, son of Admiral George Byng who had chased the Old Pretender and his Jacobites away from the Forth estuary in 1708, was held responsible for Minorca's loss. A furious King George II had Byng shot on the deck of his own ship, the *Monarque,* 'pour encourager les autres' (to encourage the others) as the sardonic French writer Voltaire put it.

In 1757, King George II was angry again when his son the Duke of Cumberland, victor of Culloden in 1746, was forced to surrender at Klosterseven, allowing the French to occupy his native Hanover. In 1758, however, the tide turned in Europe. The French were driven out of Hanover. In 1759, Admiral Edward Boscawen, known as 'Old Dreadnought', inflicted a heavy defeat on the southern French fleet in Lagos Bay in Portugal. In the same year, Admiral Edward Hawke blockaded the northern French fleet in Brest for months, depriving French colonies of supplies. He then destroyed the fleet in a daring battle in Quiberon Bay and was made 1st Baron Hawke.

In the following century, Hawke's equally fearsome descendant Martin, 7th Baron Hawke, captained the Yorkshire County Cricket team for nearly thirty years and dominated imperial cricket in the Edwardian era. In the grand imperial manner, Lord Hawke's Yorkshire team-mate Sir Stanley Jackson, captained England at cricket in 1905 and became Governor of Bengal in 1927. Unlike Robert Clive, whose tenure as Governor of Bengal brought him opprobrium and suicide, Stanley Jackson became Chairman of the Conservative Party and died in peaceable old age in 1947, the year that India gained its independence from Britain.

The Treaty of Paris in 1763 brought the Seven Years War to an end. In Europe, Britain regained Minorca and with it a strategic base in the Western Mediterranean. In North America, Britain gained Canada and the Ohio Valley, opening up expansion to the west. Spain, which had entered the war on France's side in a Bourbon family pact, ceded Florida to Britain and received Havana in Cuba in exchange. In the West Indies, Britain gained Grenada, St Vincent, Tobago and Dominica. In India, France was allowed to retain trading stations at Pondicherry and elsewhere, but their fortifications were demolished.

By the time the Seven Years War ended, Britain had a new king, George III, who succeeded his grandfather in 1760. The new king's father Frederick, Prince of Wales, had his life cut short by a cricket injury in 1751, the same year that some British people claimed their own lives were cut short by eleven days when Britain abandoned the Julian calendar, which had been devised by the Roman Emperor Julius Caesar. Britain adopted the Gregorian calendar, named after Pope Gregory XIII who had introduced it in many European countries as early as 1582. To bring Britain into line and remove accumulated calendar errors, the day after 2 September 1751 was 14 September. The former New Year's Day of 25 March was dropped in favour of I January, so that the legal and calendar years were the same.

At the end of a war, thousands of unemployed battle-hardened soldiers are released into their native streets. Governments try to avoid rebellion by finding something for them to do. The Seven Years War was no different. Auchterarder had the potential for growth. In 1763, when the war ended, Boreland Park, part of the Drummond lands forfeited to the Crown after the failure of the Jacobite rebellion in 1745, was designated for the use of about 140 war veterans, most of whom became self-employed handloom weavers.

The experiment was a failure. Most of the ex-soldiers, accustomed to regular pay, disliked the instability of supply and demand for hand-woven cloth and moved away. Known as the 'Colony of Boreland Bog', the houses were crammed close together. As a report on the annexed estates said, 'The access to these houses is very inconvenient, not having enough space to make a sufficient broad road, and the soldiers cannot let a chicken out of their houses but in their own or neighbour's corn.' Only a fragment of the settlement remains today. In Edinburgh, the Georgian New Town remains the city's most desirable property. By contrast, Auchterarder's Georgian housing experiment is a barely visible ghost town.

Names matter. The title 'Colony of Boreland Bog', devised by government officials, did not help sell the project. In Edinburgh's New Town, private sector developers encouraged the middle classes to buy into the royal Hanoverian aura of George Street, Queen Street, Princes Street, Charlotte Street and Frederick Street. In 1811, the novelist Sir Walter Scott, wanting to build an impressive house by the River Tweed, bought a site called Clarty Hole and quickly renamed it Abbotsford. Even today, Gleneagles Hotel sold building sites on newly named Queen's Crescent for £1 million each. They would be worth less if the old name, White Muir Bog, had been kept.

Boreland Park was the first major expansion of the town for centuries. When Auchterarder was burned by the Jacobites in 1716, it extended only from the Townhead down as far as the crossroads between today's Hunter Street and Abbey Road. Hunter Street, then called Powhillock Road, led to St Mackessog's Church. The Castleton was a separate village.

Webster's census of 1755 shows the total population of Auchterarder parish, with Aberuthven and outlying farms, as 1194. Until the twentieth century, most houses were rented, rather than owned by their occupants. High Street houses had pendicles of land behind them, where a cow could be grazed and kail or other crops grown. There were wynds between the houses, but no significant side street except to the Castleton weavers' village. A track ran down today's Ruthven Street to Ruthven Water and the Milton, through lands formerly belonging to the Abbey of Inchaffray.

The Forty-Five Rebellion both alarmed local tradesman, mindful of the destruction of 1716, and alerted them to the possibilities of profitable public works contracts when the Rebellion was crushed. 'Brotherhood' was a byword of the era. It could mean the practical encouragement of mutual interests, or just an excuse for alcohol and elaborate rituals, depending on the individuals concerned. In 1745, the Masonic Lodge St John Number 46 received its charter and has played an active part in the Auchterarder community ever since.

The big clan families of the area did not yet invest in building grand new houses for themselves, although there was general peace and prosperity locally after 1746. The Drummonds' land was forfeited and, though the Duchess of Perth clung to Drummond Castle till 1750, the house was not significantly improved for another sixty years. The Grahams were short of ready money. The Murrays were fragmented and let Tullibardine Castle fall into ruin, though they preserved the nearby fourteenth-century chapel and persuaded the Crown Commissioners to allow some of James Drummond, Viscount Strathallan's forfeited lands to be bought by other members of his family. The Campbells concentrated their ambitions on the West of Scotland and Edinburgh.

It was left to the Haldanes to set the pace for distinguished house building in the Auchterarder area. Around 1750, Mungo Haldane, elder brother of Patrick the Commissioner, remodelled Gleneagles House with two neo-classical wings, intending to build a grand central block. The grand part never happened, no doubt to the relief of subsequent owners who would have had to maintain it. The scheme was later completed as a model of elegant restraint. Two huge gate columns at the end of the drive give a hint of what might have been. Later in the century, another Haldane house, Foswell, was rebuilt, again with a combination of elegance and restraint.

William Pitt, as Secretary of State, skilfully guided the Whig government in the early years of the Seven Years War. In October 1761, John Stuart, Earl of Bute, replaced him. Bute's flagrant corruption led to his becoming Prime Minister in May 1762, then provoked anti-Scottish demonstrations and caused his dismissal in April 1763. He left the country in debt. Pitt's colleagues, led by George Grenville, introduced new taxes to milk the colonies, especially America. Pitt opposed the policy, believing it would provoke revolt among people, like George Washington and Benjamin Franklin, who had been invaluable loyalists in driving the French out of North America. Pitt was right, but the tax-hungry Grenville replaced him at the head of the Whig government.

In 1764, the Sugar Act and the Colonial Currency Act increased the colonies' revenue burden. In 1765, the Stamp Act imposed an official charge on all legal and commercial documents, almanacs, playing cards and dice. The Stamp Act caused riots in Boston and passionate debate in colonial assemblies, leading to the Stamp Act Congress in New York in October 1765, when delegates from nine colonies sent a Declaration of Rights and Liberties to King George III.

The Stamp Act was repealed in March 1766, but followed by a more sweeping piece of legislation, the Declaratory Act, forced through by Charles Watson-Wentworth, Marquis of Rockingham, the new Whig leader. The Declaratory Act said that the British monarch and Parliament had the right to impose laws and taxes on the colonies without consulting their local legislatures. As William Pitt predicted, the Americans reacted badly. 'No taxation without representation' became the byword of grievance.

In poor health, William Pitt, now the Earl of Chatham, resigned from office in 1768.

In 1767, the Chancellor Charles Townshend, grandson of 'Turnip' Townshend who had quit politics for agricultural experiment, introduced legislation that imposed taxes on glass, paper, painters' colours and tea imported to the colonies. Relations deteriorated. In the Boston Massacre of 1770, British troops killed several people in a brawl that got out of hand. As a conciliatory gesture, Parliament abolished the taxes on glass, paper and painters' colours but continued to levy taxes on tea. It was too late. On 16 December 1773, local citizens disguised as American Indians raided ships in Boston Harbour, dumping their cargoes of tea overboard. Parliament reacted to 'The Boston Tea Party' by closing the Port of Boston and passing the Massachusetts Government Act, which deprived the people of most of their chartered rights.

The American colonists began to organise serious resistance. On 5 September 1774, the First Continental Congress met at Philadelphia. All the British American colonies, except Georgia, took part. The Congress sent an ultimatum to Westminster, threatening trade embargoes unless grievances were settled. The new Prime Minister, Frederick, 8th Lord North proposed reconciliation, but King George III called the American political activists 'traitors' and launched an attack on Massachusetts.

North was both weak and arrogant. He and General George Gage, Governor of Massachusetts, underestimated the strength and organisation of the Americans. On 19 April 1775, Gage's troops were driven out of Concord and defeated at the Battle of Lexington. A Scottish-American, Ebenezer Munro of the Lexington Militia, fired 'The shot heard round the world' at Lexington. A British Scot, Major John Pitcairn immediately fired back. His pistol, made in the famous pistol-manufacturing town of Doune, fourteen miles west of Auchterarder, is now in the Lexington Museum.

On 10 May, the second Continental Congress met at Philadelphia and soon created the Continental Army with General George Washington as Commander in Chief. On 4 July 1776, the American Congress issued the Declaration of Independence, a model of restrained eloquence and confident compassion, drafted by Thomas Jefferson. Several of the signatories to the Declaration of Independence were of Scottish descent, including Jefferson, who was descended from King Robert Bruce.

William, 5th Viscount Howe on land and his brother Richard, 1st Earl Howe at sea used reinforcements from Britain to fight against Washington. On 7 October 1777, the American General Horatio Gates forced a large British army under General John Burgoyne to surrender at Saratoga in upstate New York. It was a turning point of the American War of Independence. Burgoyne was transferred to Ireland where he combined being Commander in Chief of the armed forces with writing successful light comedy. Gates quarrelled with Washington and was transferred to the South. He left the army, freed the slaves on his Virginia estate and retired to New York.

In 1779, the American War crossed the Atlantic, when Captain John Paul Jones harried ships along the British coast. Jones was originally a Scot from Dumfriesshire, the embodiment of the successful Scottish mercenary. He is regarded as a liberator and founder of the American Navy, but also served as an admiral to the totalitarian monarchs, Catherine the Great of Russia and the French King Louis XV. When Jones died in 1792, however, he was buried as a hero of the French Revolution.

On 19 October 1781, Charles, 1st Marquis Cornwallis surrendered his army of seven thousand men to George Washington at Yorktown in Virginia. It was a blow from which the British cause in America never recovered. Cornwallis was appointed Governor General of India, where he was more successful. He managed to contain the famously cruel Sultan Tipu of Mysore, though Tipu was not finally dealt with until the formidable General Sir David Baird from Comrie, north-west of Auchterarder, killed him at the Battle of Seringapatam on 2 May 1799.

The French Admiral François Joseph de Grasse helped the Americans at Yorktown by blockading the port. In 1782, France captured all the British possessions in the West Indies, except Jamaica, Barbados and Antigua, although Admiral George Rodney captured de Grasse and his fleet near Dominica. In the same year, a combined French and Spanish fleet captured Minorca, but General George Augustus Eliott, 1st Baron Heathfield, successfully defended Gibraltar, firing red hot canon balls at the Spaniards. Eliott came from the tiny town of Stobs in the Scottish Borders from where Auchterarder's German prisoner-of-war labour was administered during the First World War.

On 3 September 1783, Britain, France and Spain, exhausted and impoverished by war, signed a peace treaty in Paris. The new nation, the United States of America, was officially recognised, though it took until 1789 for its constituent states to sort out constitutional issues and elect George Washington as its first president.

Just as it does from war zones today, news of imperial battles reached Auchterarder through newspapers and by word of mouth through those who had relatives serving at the front. Communication travelled by ship, taking weeks or months, rather than today's instant satellite reports. At family level, the impact is the same.

28

The Pax Britannica and the Industrial Revolution

In which the British King and the French nation go mad, but local Strathearn girls brighten up

It is one thing to occupy foreign countries with soldiers and another to administer an empire. A local majority needs a sound economic reason to tolerate a ruling minority imposed from afar. The Romans built their empire by doing deals with local leaders and offering foreign peace as an alternative to home-grown or civil war. The Pax Romana (Roman Peace) gave protection and collected taxes. The Roman Empire broke up because its central administration became too unwieldy and greedy and its military capacity did not grow in line with the expanding borders, which it had to defend. The historian Edward Gibbon published the first volume of *The Decline and Fall of the Roman Empire* in 1776, the year the American colonies declared independence. The book had a great impact. Britain's ruling classes did not want the British Empire to go the way of its Roman counterpart.

The Pax Britannica suffered a shock when the new American republic was formed. The Americans' grievance had been 'No taxation without representation,' demanding a say in determining their own economy. In the same year, 1776, the Scottish economist Adam Smith published *The Wealth of Nations*. He advocated cutting government regulation and bureaucracy to let private initiative create trade and new enterprise. His liberating ideas appealed to rising politicians like the brilliant debater Charles James Fox, who opposed government coercion during the American War of Independence, and to William Pitt, son of the Earl of Chatham who had skilfully led Britain through the early years of the Seven Years War.

Frederick, 8th Lord North, whose arrogance had underestimated the intelligence and resolve of the American leaders, resigned as British Prime Minister in 1782, but then formed a coalition with his adversary Charles Fox, trying to cling to power. The coalition failed after a year. In December 1783, William Pitt the Younger, aged only twenty-four, became Prime Minister. The 1774 general election removed 160 of the old Whig oligarchy, which had become deeply unpopular with an electorate sickened by smug, greedy politicians. Pitt was a scholarly young man of conspicuous integrity who represented a fresh option. Although he came from a Whig background, he is the father of 'laissez-faire' Tory policy.

Pitt the Younger successfully introduced reforms. In 1784, the India Act made the British administration of India more coherent by giving the Governor General considerable local powers but making him responsible to a Parliamentary Board of Control. It brought to an end the arbitrary rule of the East India Company and governors like Warren Hastings, who was impeached by Parliament soon after. Hastings, like his predecessor Robert Clive, had in some ways served the Treasury well. For example, he brought in large revenues from the opium trade. Parliament acquitted Warren Hastings after a seven-year-long legal process, which ruined him financially.

In 1770, another continent opened up when Captain James Cook landed in Botany Bay in Australia. To provide a labour force in the vast, thinly populated country, the Pitt government established Port Jackson as a penal colony. Enterprising criminals served their time then made lives for themselves in the new town of Sydney and further afield. When transportation ended in 1840, New South Wales was flourishing.

In 1786, Pitt made a commercial treaty with France, based on free-trading principles. British manufactured goods flowed out and French wine flowed in. He cut public spending by reducing the cost of borrowing. He did this by introducing a clear tendering process, replacing the haphazard generous interest rates paid to Whig financier cronies. Pitt also introduced an effective audit system for public accounts and set about reducing the national debt, which had grown dramatically during the American War of Independence. In 1788, Britain formed a Triple Alliance with Prussia and Holland, aimed at balancing the power of France and protecting Sweden from Russian aggression in the Baltic.

Pitt's right-hand man in Scotland was Henry Dundas, who came from a Scottish Whig legal family. Dundas had vociferously supported Lord North's American War policy and became Lord Advocate in 1775 and Keeper of the Signet for Scotland in 1777. A man whose political scruples were in inverse proportion to his ambition, Dundas transferred his allegiance to Pitt and was made President of the India Board of Control. He turned his attention to home affairs and became Secretary of State for the Home Department. In 1784, Dundas introduced a Bill to restore the Scottish estates forfeited after the Forty-Five Jacobite Rebellion. Dundas owned a huge estate, north-west of Auchterarder, near Comrie, over which his monument towers today. In 1802 Henry Dundas was made Viscount Melville and Baron Dunira.

Many working people detested Dundas as a repressive Tory. His effigy was burned in Perth on 6 November 1796 in a republican riot. John Murray, 4th Earl of Atholl calmed the mob, shouting, 'Liberty and equality!' to show that not every aristocrat supported Dundas and that workers' families, made poor by wartime inflation, deserved respect.

Henry Dundas's influence was so labyrinthine that he was nicknamed 'King Henry the Ninth'. He went on to become Secretary of State for War, Treasurer of the Navy and First Lord of the Admiralty. Dundas's 1784 Bill benefited his Strathearn neighbours, the Drummonds. Captain John Drummond, a descendant of the disgraced Duke of Perth, obtained the estate and the title Baron Drummond. Andrew John Drummond, who would have inherited the title of Viscount Strathallan had it not been forfeited, became a general in the British army.

Another Andrew Drummond, brother of William, 4th Viscount Strathallan who died at Culloden, founded the Charing Cross Bank in London in 1717 and profited by making large loans to the British government. The Drummonds stayed close to the source of government power. In one case, it was rather too close. Edward Drummond was accidentally shot dead in 1843 by an assassin's bullet intended for Prime Minister Robert Peel as the two walked from the Charing Cross Bank.

Communication is essential for good administration. The economic growth of the Pitt and Dundas era required an upgrade of the postal service in Perthshire. In the mid eighteenth century, a walk or ride from Auchterarder to Perth was a long, slow expedition. A journey to Edinburgh was an event that many local people never experienced. On the other hand, since Roman times, some local nobles, traders and scholars travelled internationally as a matter of course.

For centuries, letters were carried by servants or trusted messengers. The King's mail was mainly used for official business. From 1683 there had been a post office in Perth, but letter carriers charged rates that excluded all but the very rich. After 1750, Turnpike Road and Bridge legislation provided far better surfaces and bridges. Tolls were charged, usually by the local landowner. In 1763, an Edinburgh–London mail coach service began. By 1767, coaches ran separately from Edinburgh to Perth and to Stirling. A direct Perth–Stirling link was needed.

After a bridge over the River Earn was built at Dalreoch around 1765, a new Crown Post Office was proposed, to be located in Auchterarder, to take advantage of a new direct road between Perth and Stirling. The people of Crieff opposed the plan, fearing their town, of similar size to Auchterarder, would be marginalized. George Haldane of Gleneagles argued the case for the Auchterarder route and won the support of the British Postmaster General, Francis Freeling. The case for the Crieff route was argued by David Smythe of Methven and Sir Patrick Murray of Ochtertyre, near Crieff. Ironically, Haldane, Murray and Smythe were all closely related.

Auchterarder or Crieff? The decision was made at the highest level in the British Government, under the influence of Henry Dundas. His best friend locally was Sir Patrick Murray. Not surprisingly, in 1793 Crieff, not Auchterarder, was awarded the new Crown Post Office, which brought substantial new business. Auchterarder was sidelined. For centuries, the town had been unable to grow because it lacked a good transport infrastructure to the port of Perth. Dundas's Crown Post Office decision meant that the ancient Royal Burgh missed out again.

King George III had been a significant political force during the American War, but in November 1788 he became agitated and delusional. It is likely that he suffered from porphyria, a genetic disorder. At first it seemed that George, Prince of Wales, an extravagant dandy and friend of Pitt's rival Charles Fox, would become Regent and hand power to the Whigs. Pitt, however, skilfully saw the 1789 Regency Bill through Parliament, which recognised the Prince of Wales as Regent but curbed his powers. The King temporarily recovered, and remained in generally good mental health for another twelve years before he slid into insanity again.

In France, there was madness of another kind. Like Britain, France had incurred huge debts in the American War of Independence. Unlike Britain, France's method of government had scarcely evolved since the Middle Ages. Britain had two Houses of Parliament, the Lords and the Commons, which moderated one another and regulated the King. France was still ruled by autocratic royal command, operated by a host of privileged courtiers and a higgledy-piggledy accumulation of local laws. The French justice system was slow and erratic.

Pitt was able to improve Britain's financial outlook with the support of both Houses of Parliament. King Louis XVI of France had only the cumbersome Estates General, in which self-interested nobles and clergy persistently frustrated reforms proposed by the middle classes. On 17 June 1789, the middle class members of the Estates General broke away to form a separate National Assembly. Some nobles and clergy who supported reform joined them. On 14 July, amid rumours that the King and supporters of the old regime would suppress the National Assembly, an angry mob stormed the Bastille prison in Paris, murdered its governor and freed those locked up inside. They were convicted criminals, not political prisoners, but the freeing gesture became a symbol for 'Liberté, Egalité, Fraternité' (Liberty, equality, brotherhood), the effective emotional slogan for the French Revolution, retained ever since by the French state.

Events moved fast. On 4 August 1789, Marie Joseph, Marquis de Lafayette, a noble who believed in republicanism and had served with George Washington in America, proposed a Declaration of Rights, using the American Declaration of Independence as a model. Lafayette was a moderate. As commander of the newly formed National Guard, he protected the royal family from an angry mob, mostly women, that marched to Versailles on 5 October.

Once a revolution begins, opportunists of all kinds seek to gain by it, inflaming the fears and grievances of the masses. There were peasant riots across France. In the rush for equality, mobs failed to distinguish between good landowners and bad ones. The new National Assembly seized control of France and restructured both national and local government, dividing the country into eighty-three Departments. Hereditary titles and rights were abolished. The judiciary was reorganised.

Maximilien Robespierre, a fanatical Puritan lawyer from Arras in the north of France, led the Jacobins, a political club, named after the Dominican monastery that they had commandeered in the Rue St Jacques in Paris. Articulate, energetic and obsessive, Robespierre rose to power, backed by a network of Jacobin clubs throughout France. He was appointed Public Accuser, an office that he used to condemn his adversaries. Georges Jaques Danton, another lawyer, led the Cordeliers Club, which was even more extreme. A big man with a loud voice, he thundered revenge on the old regime, aided by his club-mate, the pamphleteer Jean Paul Marat.

On 20 June 1791, King Louis XVI fled from Versailles with his Queen Marie Antoinette and their family. They were captured and imprisoned. On 20 April 1792, France declared war on Austria and Prussia. The French campaigns went badly. The moderate General Lafayette was impeached and fled. He was captured by the Austrians who kept him safe until 1796.

The captive King Louis XVI agreed to constitutional reforms, but the revolution was out of control. New assemblies appeared and were rapidly replaced. On 21 September 1792, the French monarchy was abolished. On 21 January 1793, the National Convention had the King executed after a vote, carried by a majority of only one. His family was also executed. A reign of terror began. Executions of aristocrats and moderates became public entertainment. Hatred of monarchy extended to opening ancient royal tombs, exhuming the corpses and destroying them. Nationality did not matter. The revolutionaries dug up and disposed of the body of the exiled Catholic King James VII of Scotland and II of England.

France became a rogue state with new institutions alien to the rest of Europe. The French Republic replaced worship of the Christian God with the Goddess of Reason whose statue was installed in Nôtre Dame Cathedral in Paris. A new calendar was created, with New Year's Day set on 22 September, the day the Republic was founded. The French Revolution began to devour itself. Marat was murdered in 1793. Robespierre and Danton were executed in 1794.

In 1795, a new French government, the Directory, tried to address the collapse of the French economy from which investors had fled. Commerce had become chaotic amid rampant inflation. Lazare Carnot reorganised the French military, appointing Napoleon Bonaparte to lead an invasion of Italy.

William Pitt believed in diplomacy to secure prosperity, not war to promote expensive glory, but he could not keep Britain out of the European conflict. National sentiment was more divided than earlier in the eighteenth century when the Scottish poet James Thomson's motif 'Britannia rules the Waves' captured the public imagination. The acerbic pamphleteers John Wilkes and the republican Thomas Paine criticised British government institutions. The eloquent Edmund Burke alienated his Whig friends, particularly Charles Fox, with his 1790 *Reflections on the French Revolution*, which advocated strong measures to suppress radical views in Britain.

The English Lakeland poet William Wordsworth went on a walking tour in France in 1790, well before the reign of terror, and returned full of revolutionary zeal. He wrote in his long poem *The Prelude:* 'Bliss was it in that dawn to be alive, and to be young was very heaven.' Like most literary radicals, he later became conservative but in the 1790s his words romanticised revolution. The Ayrshire poet Robert Burns also flirted with republican notions, writing an 'Ode on General Washington's Birthday'. Burns had a genuine gift for poetry and an even greater gift for self-promotion. He was willing to toady to those who could help him out of his perennial self-inflicted financial problems.

Burns's life contradicts his poetry. He planned to emigrate to Jamaica and work as an overseer of plantation slaves, but wrote populist egalitarian sentiments like 'A Man's A Man for A' That'. He was a failed tenant farmer but marketed himself as an inspired ploughboy in an age that idolised noble savages and peasant genius. His ruthless ambition is best expressed in 'To a Mouse' and 'To a Mountain Daisy', where he sheds crocodile tears while crushing anything in his path. Famously vain, mock humble and irresponsible with women and alcohol, he flattered his way into local jobs as an excise officer. He was appointed to be an exciseman in the Dunblane area west of Auchterarder but died in 1796 before he could take up the post. Robert Burns is a prime example of an unpleasant individual producing genuinely great poetry, notably his comic work and his songs. As the hypocrite's hypocrite, Burns has been the much-quoted darling of generations of Scottish politicians.

Burns had a fine ear for language and an excellent command of formal English, but his best poems follow the fashion for idealised rustic sentiment, which grew as a contrast to the harsh realities of the industrial revolution. The first cotton mill in Scotland powered by a water wheel was built in Penicuik in Midlothian in 1778. Others followed rapidly. The New Lanark scheme in 1778 employed 1,300 workers. By 1785, there were giant mills at Stanley on the Tay and at Deanston on the Teith. Both offered more profitable employment to weavers than their old-technology jobs in nearby Auchterarder. In the Auchterarder area, industrialisation was slow and modest.

Modesty did not form part of one thriving Scottish industry. Political revolutions tend to be violently Puritan. The French Revolutionary leaders suppressed any literary and artistic works that they thought were salacious. Glasgow printers filled the gap in the French market by exporting cheap pornography, with woodblock illustrations that were crude in skill and subject matter.

In Strathearn, there was a rather more cheerful manifestation of feminine allure. Tartan had been banned after the Jacobite Rebellion but, fortunately, it is hard to stop young Scottish women from wearing lively colours. It was noted in the First Statistical Account for Crieff Parish that, 'About 1780, female servants and others of that rank first began to wear ribbons. Now, instead of the grave and solid productions of the country, the gay cloths, silks, muslins and printed cottons of England adorn on Sundays almost every individual'. Henry Dundas lifted the ban on tartan in 1782.

The Statistical Accounts give the first comprehensive picture of life in Scotland. The account for the Auchterarder area was written in 1793 by the local minister, Andrew Duncan, who had the old Parish Kirk renovated in 1784 and extended in 1811. The Statistical Account shows a population of '805 males and 865 females; 798 reside in the villages of Auchterarder, Boreland Park and Miltown and 872 in the country.' Mr Duncan noted that the birth rate was dropping because young people were leaving the area. They went to find jobs in the boom towns of the Industrial Revolution: Perth, Dundee, Edinburgh and particularly Glasgow.

Up to the mid eighteenth century, most local weavers worked with wool. Some made linen from flax grown locally for both its fibres and its linseed oil. With the growth of the British Empire in the Americas, cotton became a desirable fabric.

Throughout the eighteenth century there was a waulkmill at the foot of today's Abbey Road, for fulling (processing) and dyeing the yarn used by handloom weavers. Throughout Scotland there was concern about river pollution caused by 'steepers of lint'. Court actions were brought against mill owners, including the Auchterarder Waulkmill, under environmental legislation dating back to the sixteenth century.

The Board of Annexed Estates in Perthshire set up schools for teaching sewing and knitting. Mrs King's School in Auchterarder operated from 1775 to 1783, with an annual class of over thirty girls. They learned plain and fancy sewing and had the option of a course in knitting woollen stockings. Many of the girls have names of families who had been in the area for centuries: Drummond, Fenton, Graham, Hally, Mailer.

By 1793, Auchterarder had a suburb beside the Ruthven. Milton, or Mill Town, had four corn mills, three lint mills, two oil mills, plus a paper mill and a fulling mill. There was not enough year-round water-power to drive the wheel of a big cotton mill. It took another sixty years before steam engines made the Milton a practical site for cotton mills.

The Crown Commissioners had a granary built to hold unsold produce from markets from one week to the next. This evolved around 1790, with later remodelling in 1830, into Girnal House, Auchterarder's oldest remaining public building. In 1831, a steelyard for weighing goods was constructed in front of the Guardhouse, which stood where the Aytoun Hall stands today. Later, a borough workshop was added near the site of today's Public Library.

Coal had replaced wood as the fuel of choice and was brought from mines at Blairingone and Dollar on roads through Glendevon or over the Ochils, by the Cadger's Yett from Tormaukin to Coulshill. Peat was still cut, especially on the slopes above Foswell.

In the twenty-first century, climate change and unstable weather cause anxiety. It was always so. The 1793 Statistical Account for Auchterarder notes that the River Earn sometimes ruined crops by overflowing its banks at harvest time in September and October.

Apart from the water mills at the Milton of Auchterarder, there were other mills on the Ruthven, notably at Drumtogle, east of Aberuthven. Larger mills had funnel-shaped kilns where corn was dried before it was ground. In 1786, Andrew Meikle invented the powered threshing machine. The power usually came from horses, walking in a circle around 'horse gins', in round buildings with conical roofs and wide openings for carts. These buildings were a common feature of the Strathearn farm landscape till the late twentieth century. Now only a few survive.

In 1793, the distillery at the Milton had two 40-gallon stills. At the same time, the Rev. Andrew Duncan wrote of local health, 'The disorder, which has been most prevalent and fatal for some years past, is a fever of the nervous kind.'

In Auchterarder, by the time of the 1793 Statistical Account, horses were commonly used for ploughing, instead of oxen. There were over a hundred ploughs in the Auchterarder area, many of them designed for teams of four horses, the rest for two. There were also about two hundred and fifty single-horse carts. The roads were not yet wide or stable enough for a two-horse cart.

Aberuthven, because of the number and quality of its smithies, had long been known as 'Smiddy Haugh'. In Auchterarder, the main smithy was Baad's Smithy beside the Ruthven Water. It grew in the nineteenth century to manufacture ploughs for export, particularly to Canada and Australia where Scottish pioneers were establishing farms.

Almost every farm reared horses, for both farm work and transport, plus black cattle whose milk yield and beef were better than Highland cattle. Sheep flocks were growing as farmers began to rear their own lambs rather than purchasing them from markets in southern Scotland. Blackface (Linton) sheep, with better wool and mutton yields, replaced the smaller, silky-fleeced Highland sheep. In some parts of Scotland, landowners evicted small farmers and turned the land over to sheep grazing. In the Auchterarder area, with its rich arable land demanding a steady supply of labour, forced emigration was less of a problem.

Voluntary emigration was a different matter. Many Scots took advantage of the opportunities opening in the Americas. George Haldane, whose father Patrick had been a Commissioner for the sale of the estates of Jacobite leaders after their atrocities in Strathearn, became Governor of Jamaica. There was plenty of scope for young men who joined the army or navy to fight for Britain as Napoleon rose to power in France.

Scotland had immigrants as well as emigrants. Many Irish Catholics left the poverty and repression of their native land to seek jobs in Scotland's booming industrial towns. Some supporters of the fallen French monarchy fled to Scotland. Among them was Charles-Philippe, Count of Artois, who was the youngest brother of the executed King Louis XVI. In Paris and Versailles, the Count of Artois had gained a reputation as the most extravagant and irresponsible member of the Bourbon royal family. He had lavished vast sums of public money on entertainment and interior decoration.

By the time he arrived in Leith on 6 January 1796, the Count of Artois was deeply in debt and a political embarrassment to the British government. Henry Dundas arranged for Artois to be housed in Holyrood Palace within the boundaries of a traditional debtors' sanctuary. Artois gathered round him a variety of Scots who were fond of French culture. Several were Stewart sympathisers who had lived in France after the failed 1745 Jacobite rebellion. Among them was General Andrew John Drummond of Strathallan who had grown up in France and could speak formal court French, military English and the robust broad Scots of Strathearn.

Britain no longer feared a Stewart Catholic invasion. In the long gallery at Holyrood, the Count of Artois and his friends created a little chapel and heard mass without provoking any significant opposition. Meantime, Europe was becoming a running battlefield as Napoleon's imperial ambitions grew.

29

Foreign War and Domestic Peace

*In which Britannia still rules the waves, Europe is
reshaped and grand houses are built in Strathearn*

The Battle of Culloden, on 17 April 1746, was the last pitched battle between two armies on British soil. Since then, governments have taken the view that war is a sport best played with no home games. There is always plenty of scope for war on the global circuit. Modern weaponry makes it a bad option to lure enemies into your home territory.

The Carron Ironworks, established in 1759 near Falkirk, south of Stirling, manufactured a new generation of manoeuvrable, easily fired artillery. The carronade, an accurate naval cannon, gave British ships superior fire-power for their perennial wars against the French. Good local supplies of coal and ironstone, with easy access to transport on the River Forth, made Carron an ideal location for this Anglo-Scottish company. After a difficult cash-flow start, the Carron Ironworks won big contracts.

Across the English Channel, France needed a strong leader after the chaos of the French Revolution. Of the ruling classes, lawyers and soldiers make their money by engaging in disputes. France had tried rule by lawyers, Robespierre and Danton, with disastrous consequences. Now it was a soldier's turn. In 1796, the Directory, the latest in a rapid series of French governments, appointed a Corsican general, Napoleon Bonaparte, to attack the Austrians in Italy. France had changed from a monarchy to a republic, but it had not changed its traditional enemies, Britain and the Holy Roman Empire.

In 1796, Napoleon defeated an Austrian army at Millesmo and Lodi in northern Italy. He captured Milan and extracted large payments from Pope Pius VI, the Dukes of Parma and Modena and the King of Naples in exchange for a truce. In April 1797, he agreed a truce with the Austrian Archduke Charles, brother of the Holy Roman Emperor Francis II. Within a month, Napoleon broke the truce by invading Venice. It was a bargaining point. On 17 October by the Treaty of Campo Formio, Austria acquired Venice, but ceded the Dutch Netherlands (Belgium) to France.

Napoleon won land victories, but Britannia still ruled the waves. On 19 August 1796, by the Treaty of San Ildefonso, Spain joined France with a view to attacking England and Ireland. Portugal remained on Britain's side. On 14

January 1797, a Portuguese frigate, commanded by a Scottish captain called Campbell, saw a large Spanish fleet off the coast of Cape St Vincent. Admiral Sir John Jervis outmanoeuvred and defeated the Spaniards. Jervis was made Earl St Vincent. Poor pay and conditions caused part of the British fleet to mutiny in the summer of 1797 Richard, 1st Earl Howe, First Lord of the Admiralty, who had seen long service in American and French wars, quelled the mutiny by persuasion rather than violent retribution. Only a few ringleaders were executed, but morale remained volatile.

Amid this discontent, Admiral Adam Duncan had the unenviable task of defending Britain's east coast against the Dutch fleet, part of the French coalition. Duncan, a fair-minded man, calmed his sailors and attacked the Dutch off the coast of Holland, destroying most of their ships at the Battle of Camperdown on 11 October 1797. Duncan was made Viscount Camperdown. He was sixty-six years old, had seen long naval service and retired to look after the Gleneagles estate which he had inherited from his Haldane mother. Adam Duncan was married to Henry Dundas's niece, which gave him a career advantage, but he owed his success in battle to naval skill, not family connections.

In 1798, Napoleon occupied Rome, captured Pope Paul VI and proclaimed a Roman republic. He then invaded Switzerland and created the Helvetic Republic. Now that France had defeated Austria, could Napoleon invade England? An army gathered in Boulogne in April 1798, causing consternation in Britain and a rush to enhance coastal defences. The invasion never came. Instead, Napoleon sailed from the southern French port of Toulon with an army, which captured Malta on 12 June and landed in Egypt, capturing Alexandria and Cairo.

Just when it seemed Napoleon was invincible, a new British hero appeared. Horatio Nelson had distinguished himself at the Battle of Cape St Vincent. On 1 August 1798, as Admiral of the Mediterranean fleet, he sailed into Aboukir harbour near Alexandria and destroyed the French fleet at the Battle of the Nile. The following year, Napoleon withdrew his army from Egypt and returned to France. Nelson was made Baron Nelson of the Nile. Latin was still the language of scholarly wit. An anagram of 'Horatio Nelson' soon circulated: 'Honor est a Nilo' (Honour is from the Nile).

Adam Duncan was a steadfast commander. Horatio Nelson was a daredevil maverick. To the public, he embodied the bravery and glamour necessary for winning wars. Because of his celebrity status, Nelson got away with contrariness that was punished in others. In July 1799, he disobeyed orders to bring ships to defend Minorca. Admiral John Byng had been executed on the deck of his ship in 1756 for failing to protect Minorca, but Nelson was merely censured by the Admiralty. By 1801, Nelson was a hero again after his daring victory at Copenhagen over France's allies, the Danes.

Prime Minister William Pitt elevated Admirals John Jervis, Adam Duncan and Horatio Nelson to the peerage, but he was also lavish in giving titles to those whose service to the nation was not obvious. Aware of how the French Revolution had become a bloodbath, Pitt suppressed any signs of republicanism in Britain. In trying to maintain the status quo, he opposed reforms that were politically inevitable.

Slavery had become a hot political issue. To those with even the least belief in liberty, slavery was repugnant. It was, however, hugely profitable. The sugar plantations of the West Indies depended on slave labour and, Pitt felt, once one started down the road of new freedoms, liberty could run amok. The legality of slavery in Britain had become unclear ever since a ruling in 1772 in the case of the escaped Negro slave James Somerset, whom his owner wanted to export from Britain back to the West Indies. The silver-tongued Chief Justice William Murray, 1st Earl of Mansfield, who had earlier vigorously prosecuted the Jacobites to compensate for his own family's Jacobite sympathies, ruled that slavery was 'odious' and there was no law to support the practice in England. On the other hand, there was no law to prohibit slavery.

James Somerset was freed, but slavery persisted, particularly in the West Indies. Lord Mansfield retired to his home, Scone Palace outside Perth, with a reputation for verbose ambivalence, characteristic of what Strathearn people call 'the wind of the Murrays'. He died in 1793. In 1778, Henry Dundas supported the case of a Scottish slave, Joseph Knight, in a case similar to Somerset's. In 1792, Dundas persuaded Parliament that the slave trade be 'gradually abolished'. Pitt chose not to make it happen quickly.

Pitt at first resisted granting equality to Catholics in Ireland, where their rights had been curtailed ever since William of Orange's 'Glorious Revolution' in 1688. In 1800, Pitt changed his mind, fearing that, without equal rights, Irish Catholics would be ripe for French-inspired revolt. King George III disagreed. On 1 January 1801, the Parliaments of Great Britain and Northern Ireland were united, creating the United Kingdom, but with no emancipation for Catholics. Pitt resigned as Prime Minister in February 1801. Within weeks, the King lapsed into insanity, which persisted until his death in 1820. Roman Catholics in Ireland were not emancipated until 1829.

The Prime Minister of the new United Kingdom, Pitt's close colleague Henry Addington, had to deal with problems at home and abroad. On 9 November 1799, Napoleon had become First Consul of France. In effect, he was the military dictator of a country that had changed its form of government several times in a violent decade. Napoleon imposed order with clear military discipline. He founded the Bank of France. He created a civil service to collect taxes, replacing the old, corrupt, private 'tax farmers'. He reformed the judiciary. Napoleon then returned to Italy and routed a new Austrian army at Marengo on 14 June 1800.

Britain and France were both yet again impoverished by war. Addington and Napoleon agreed the Peace of Amiens in March 1802, by which Britain officially recognised the French republic. Britain agreed to leave Egypt, but kept Ceylon (Sri Lanka) and Trinidad. France agreed to leave Rome and Naples.

Britain also agreed to give Malta back to the Knights of St John. Instead, it retained it as a strategic naval base in the Mediterranean. Napoleon also broke the Peace of Amiens by invading Italy and Switzerland once more. On 18 May 1803, Britain declared war on France yet again. It was a France whose institutions were increasingly modernised and stable. Napoleon improved the education system and allowed the Christian Church, banned by the French Revolution, to function again. On 18 May 1804, Napoleon was made Emperor of France. It was a hereditary title. Napoleon's dynasty now replaced the Bourbon King Louis XVI, executed in 1793.

The week before Napoleon became Emperor of France, William Pitt returned as Prime Minister of Britain, replacing the lesser statesman Henry Addington, who was made 1st Viscount Sidmouth. Napoleon gathered a huge army in Boulogne, facing the English coast, but repeated the strategy of 1798 and invaded elsewhere. He took command of the French army in Germany and forced a 30,000-strong Austrian army to surrender at Ulm on 17 October 1805, then captured Vienna.

Britain needed a victory and it got one. On 21 October 1805, Lord Nelson shattered the combined French and Spanish fleets at the Battle of Trafalgar, half way between the Spanish naval base of Cadiz and the Straits of Gibraltar.

Nelson was mortally wounded on the quarter deck of his flagship, the appropriately named *Victory*. He received a hero's funeral in St Paul's Cathedral in London. A tidal wave of national pride rippled across Britain. In Dundee the great clock maker James Ivory, who made fine long-case clocks for the well-to-do, topped these imposing timepieces with a bronze medallion of Nelson, rather than the local hero Admiral Adam Duncan, owner of the Gleneagles estate and victor of Camperdown only a few years before. Glamour sells merchandise.

Napoleon retaliated in central Europe. He won a dazzling victory over the combined Austrian and Russian armies at Austerlitz on 2 December 1805, after Prussia decided to stay out of the conflict. On 15 December, France made an alliance with Prussia and gave it Hanover, the ancestral home of the British Georgian monarchy. Austria was humiliated. By the Treaty of Pressburg on 26 December, France received Piedmont, Parma and Piacenza in Northern Italy, while Austria gave up the rest of its Italian Empire to the new Kingdom of Italy, whose king happened to be Napoleon. Pro-French Bavaria received much of Austria's remaining German Empire. On 6 August 1806, the last Holy Roman Emperor, Francis II, gave up his crown, becoming Francis I of Austria instead. A European institution, which had been founded by Charlemagne a thousand years before, ceased to exist.

William Pitt did not live to see the end of the Holy Roman Empire. He had a powerful brain, but a weak body and was often in poor health. Distressed by Austerlitz, he died on 23 January 1806. His great Parliamentary contemporary Charles Fox died on 13 September. William, 1st Baron Grenville became Prime Minister. The following year, after decades of campaigning by William Wilberforce and the Methodist preacher John Wesley, the slave trade was abolished throughout the British Empire. This did not mean slaves had to be freed, only that they could not be sold. It took until 1833 for slave ownership to become illegal.

The twin cults of Nelson and Napoleon created a bizarre phallic competition. In London's Trafalgar Square, a giant column was erected with a statue of Nelson on top. In the Place Vendôme in Paris, the French erected a huge imitation of the Roman Emperor Trajan's column, topped with a statue of Napoleon. To emphasise the imperial nature of Napoleon's column, it was clad in bronze recycled from guns captured from the Austrians and Russians and magnificently worked with bas-reliefs depicting Napoleon's victories. Britain did not go to the expense of such detailed artwork. Instead, sixty years later, the nation commissioned Sir Edwin Landseer to sculpt four mighty bronze British lions near the base of Nelson's column. Imperial gestures have a way of backfiring. Napoleon's grandiose statue was replaced several times and Trafalgar Square became a handy assembling point for generations of anti-government demonstrations.

Henry Dundas was forced to resign in 1805, after a commission of enquiry found systemic malpractice in the navy's finances. Dundas was impeached, but later acquitted, with the help of his influential nephew-in-law, Henry Cockburn, a particularly polished pillar of the Edinburgh legal establishment. Dundas, now Lord Melville, went on wheeling and dealing until his death in 1811.

Napoleon saw himself as the reconstructor of Europe. Having already given Hanover to Prussia, he negotiated with Britain to make Hanover British again. It was nearly a hundred years since the Elector of Hanover had become King George I. By now, Britain had bigger imperial priorities. Prussia, however, was furious that Napoleon felt he could give and take away territory as he pleased. Frederick III's military power was a pale shadow of his predecessor Frederick II the Great, but the myth of Prussian might on the battlefield persisted at home. It was soon shattered. Prussia went to war with France and was routed at the Battle of Jena on 14 October 1806. Russia came to Prussia's aid, but Napoleon contained their attack at the Battle of Eylau on 7 February 1807.

Napoleon announced a ban on British imports to Europe. It was unenforceable. It was also not in Napoleon's interests. His soldiers at the Battle of Eylau wore greatcoats made in Leeds and shoes from Northampton. Portugal refused to enter Napoleon's trade war against Britain. Napoleon then invaded the Iberian Peninsula and made his older brother Joseph King of Spain. A mild man, under his younger brother's thumb, Joseph Bonaparte had already been made King of Naples in 1806. He now let Napoleon give the throne of Naples to Joachim Murat, an able general who had enhanced his career prospects by marrying Napoleon's sister Caroline.

France's military and financial resources were stretched thin. In July 1808, a popular uprising chased the new King Joseph out of Spain. Britannia ruled the waves. Now it was time for action on land. Into Portugal sailed Arthur Wellesley, a younger son of the Irish Earl of Mornington. Wellesley had seen service in Europe and India, where his brother Richard was Governor General. He had been given command of the forces at Seringapatam over the head of a more senior officer, General Sir David Baird from Comrie, north-west of Auchterarder. Wellesley had taken credit for the defeat of the ferocious Tipu Sahib in 1799, although, unlike 'Oor Davie', he was not involved in the fighting. Baird was seen as the hero, Wellesley as the master of logistics.

Wellesley went on to be an efficient campaign leader in India and had returned to become a Member of Parliament and Secretary of State for Ireland in 1807. Now he resumed his military career. As in India, Wellesley in 1808 was not the senior officer but, after the death of Sir John Moore at the Battle of Corunna on 16 January 1809, Wellesley was given command. He scored victories at Talavera in 1809, Busaco in 1810 and captured Almeida, the last French stronghold in Portugal. In 1812, he advanced into Spain and Captured Ciudad Rodrigo, Badajoz and Madrid.

Meantime, as Napoleon's dynastic ambitions grew, he lost sight of the military strategies that had brought him to power. The contrast in self-images is obvious in the portraits that he commissioned. The 1796 portrait by Antoine-Jean Gros shows a slim sword- and banner-wielding soldier. The bombastic 1810 portrait by Jean-Auguste-Dominique Ingres shows a fat, gorgeously robed emperor, holding multiple sceptres. His vanity prevented him from seeing that he looked like a parody of the seventeenth-century Louis XIV, 'Le Roi Soleil' (The Sun King). Napoleon divorced his wife Josephine, who was from the old French nobility, and in 1810 married the superiorly titled Archduchess Marie Louise, daughter of the Austrian Emperor Francis I. Ironically, Napoleon had previously stripped his father-in-law of the title of Holy Roman Emperor. Titles and dynasties mattered to Napoleon. When Marie Louise bore a son, Napoleon made him King of Rome.

In 1812, Napoleon invaded Russia. It was a disaster. On 7 September at the Battle of Borodino, both sides suffered huge losses. The French advanced to Moscow, only to find that it had been burned by retreating Russian troops. Napoleon sent the offer of a truce to the Russian Emperor Alexander I, who did not reply. Napoleon lingered in Moscow as the Russian winter set in. Eventually, his army retreated to France in straggling disorder, lacking food and adequate clothing and harried by constant attacks. Of the 600,000 men that Napoleon took to Russia, fewer than 100,000 survived.

Whether in war or sport, one heavy defeat for the top team gives hope to the rest. Wars of liberation broke out across Europe to shake off French domination. In Britain, however, Wellesley felt that Spencer Percival, who had become Prime Minister in 1809, did not provide enough funding for military campaigns. Percival had to deal with a depleted domestic economy, struggling under Napoleon's trade embargoes. A bankrupt broker, John Bellingham, shot and killed Percival in 1812, making him the first British Prime Minister to be murdered. Surprisingly, there have been no others. His successor, Robert Jenkinson, 2nd Earl of Liverpool, gave Wellesley more help. A restrictive Tory at home and a liberal free trader abroad, Liverpool stayed in office for fifteen years. In 1813, Wellesley advanced into Spain and on 21 June won the Battle of Vittoria. He then drove the French out of Spain and led his army into France.

Britain obtained troops and sailors where it could. In the Auchterarder area, as in many rural communities, the army presented good career possibilities for both officers and men. In foreign campaigns, local soldiers were recruited, especially in Spain and Portugal. The dreaded press-gangs of the British navy pressed reluctant able-bodied men into service, especially if they were easily outwitted when drunk in a seaport. The British navy pressed thousands of American citizens into service, causing great resentment in the American capital, Washington.

On 19 June 1812, America declared war on Britain, hoping to seize Canada while Britain was preoccupied in Europe. The Americans captured Toronto, but withdrew when British reinforcements arrived. On 25 July 1814, Sir Gordon Drummond defeated an American army near Niagara and burned the city of Buffalo with its strategic Black Rock Naval Yard. On 24 August 1814,

General Robert Ross captured Washington and burned the White House and Capitol buildings.

The United States had its victories too. On 29 December 1812, the US warship *Constitution* blasted the British frigate *Java* into surrender off the coast of Brazil and went on to score other triumphs at sea. The *Constitution*, affectionately known as 'Old Ironsides', remains today in Boston as a symbol of American sea power. On 5 July 1814, at the Battle of Chippewa, the British General Phineas Riall, seeing soldiers in drab grey uniforms, thought they were a non-professional militia. They were not. They were regular soldiers, commanded by General Winfield Scott, who routed the British. Scott's men were dressed in grey because the military contractor had run out of blue cloth. To this day, the full dress uniform of the US Military Academy at West Point is grey, to commemorate the victory at Chippewa.

The astute third President Thomas Jefferson had made the Louisiana Purchase from an impoverished France in 1803. New Orleans became a melting pot of French, Spanish, Negro and White American culture. On 8 January 1815 at the Battle of New Orleans, General Andrew Jackson forced the British to retreat to their ships, inspiring a popular folksong and his later Presidential campaign. On 14 December 1814 with the Treaty of Ghent, Britain and the United States of America ended their war. People had been killed. Ships and towns had been destroyed, but territories stayed as they were when the war started.

Britain's losses in the American War of 1812–14 were small compared to Napoleon's losses in his Russian campaign. The nations of Central Europe rose against him. On 18 October 1813, a combined Austrian and Prussian army subsidised by Britain and with corps from Bohemia, Silesia and Wurtemburg, defeated Napoleon at the Battle of Leipzig in eastern Germany. The allied coalition crossed the Rhine and advanced into France. The Dutch, who had been under French rule since Napoleon ousted their Austrian overlords, asserted independence and expelled the French administrators.

On 12 March 1814, Wellesley advanced from Spain. He seized the port of Bordeaux, essential to the French wine trade. On 31 March, the allies conquered Paris. On 11 April, Napoleon abdicated as Emperor of France. He was sent to be Emperor of Elba, a small island between Italy and his native Corsica, with a handsome annual salary paid by France.

Soon after Napoleon's defeat, one of his great military adversaries announced his retirement. General Thomas Graham, whose final command was over the allied forces in the Netherlands, was sixty-five and had been created 1st Baron Lynedoch after an outstanding career. He came from Balgowan, over the Gask Ridge from Auchterarder, and was descended from Sir William Graham of Kincardine who married King Robert III's daughter Mary.

Thomas Graham's early life was that of a well-connected country gentleman. In 1774, at the age of twenty-six, he married eighteen-year-old Mary, daughter of Charles Shaw, 9th Lord Cathcart. Graham commissioned Thomas Gainsborough to paint her portrait. The elegant 'Mrs Graham' is one of the best-known paintings in the Scottish National Gallery. Through his wife, Graham was related to other great Perthshire families, the Murray Earls of Mansfield and Duke of Atholl, against whose cricket team he scored most runs in a match in 1785, one of the earliest full scorecards recorded in Scotland. He also found himself related to Lady Hamilton, Lord Nelson's flamboyant mistress.

When his wife died of tuberculosis in 1792, Thomas Graham immersed himself in public service. In 1794, he raised the 90th Regiment, known as The Perthshire Volunteers, and became Member of Parliament for Perth. He fought against Napoleon in Spain and rose to be second in command to the future Duke of Wellington. At first their personal relationship was strained. Wellington was an Irish Tory. Graham was a Perthshire Whig. By the time Graham founded a military gentleman's club in 1815, later to become the United Services Club, Wellington was among the first to join.

Napoleon's former supporter Charles Maurice de Talleyrand, a statesman of unusual deviousness and cynicism even for that profession, devised the terms of Napoleon's capitulation. A great survivor, he had thrived as the Abbot of St Denis under the old French monarchy, then drafted the French Revolutionary Bill of Rights in 1789 and despoiled the Catholic Church. As a diplomat, he had been instrumental in spreading distrust and division among the nations allied against Napoleon. He advised Napoleon against invading Russia and, after that disastrous campaign, seemed to be the voice of moderation and progress when Napoleon fell from power. Talleyrand had the gift of knowing how to trim his sails the instant before the wind changes direction.

Who was to replace Napoleon as French head of state? Napoleon had reformed France's central and local governmental structure. This created the possibility of restoring the French monarchy, but without its old autocratic powers. Authority would lie with democratically elected representatives, not the king. It was a system that worked in Britain, where government continued smoothly under Prime Minister Lord Liverpool and Foreign Minister Robert Stewart, Lord Castlereagh, who had a reputation for tactical duplicity equal to Talleyrand. The mad King George III was safely tucked away. His son George, Prince Regent, romped gaudily in Bath and Brighton, a convenient butt for political satire.

A limited monarchy seemed a wise choice for France. Louis XVIII was made king. He was the elder of the two surviving brothers of King Louis XVI, executed in the French Revolution, and had lived in exile during the Napoleonic wars. From 1807 to 1814, he had been housed at Hartwell in Buckinghamshire. Louis XVIII's younger brother, Charles-Philippe, Count of Artois, spent most of the Napoleonic wars in comfortable exile in Holyrood at the expense of the British government, who curbed his spectacularly lavish tastes. When Louis XVIII became King of France, Artois became his Lieutenant General and returned to his old extravagant ways.

On 8 June 1815, after complex negotiations at the Congress of Vienna, where Talleyrand was the oil in the machinery of diplomacy, the boundaries of Europe were redrawn. Austria recovered lost territory and gained Milan and Venice. Prussia received Saxony, Westphalia and part of Poland, but ceded other territory to Bavaria and Hanover. Russia gained part of Poland. A new Kingdom of the Netherlands was created, comprising Holland and the former Austrian Netherlands (Belgium). Poland, partitioned repeatedly since the eighteenth century, was reduced to boundaries that reflected much of the Duchy of Warsaw, with the Russian Tsar as king. The proud old Poland, of Bonnie Prince Charlie's Sobieski ancestors, was now a weak fragment.

The Congress of Vienna restored the old Bourbon monarchy in Spain. Sweden retained Norway, which it had gained from Denmark the previous year. Britain kept Malta as a Mediterranean base, Ceylon (Sri Lanka) important for Asian trade, and the Cape of Good Hope on the strategic southern tip of Africa which it had seized from the Dutch. The settlement was intended to provide lasting peace. In fact, it ignored the rising trend for unification in Italy and Germany and freedom movements elsewhere.

While the rest of Europe was debating in Vienna, Napoleon was not quite finished. On 20 May 1815, he landed with an army of 1,500 men on the sparsely populated south coast of France, near where the Film Festival city of Cannes thrives today. He marched north, rallying more troops, and entered Paris on 20 May. He ruled for a hundred days. On 25 May, the coalition of Britain, Austria, Prussia and Russia agreed to confront him with a combined army under the command of Arthur Wellesley, who had recently been created 1st Duke of Wellington.

On 18 June, Wellington crushed Napoleon at the Battle of Waterloo in Belgium with the aid of the Prussian General Gebhard Blücher. Wellington then had to restrain Blücher from sacking Paris. Napoleon abdicated again on 22 June. This time, he was sent as a prisoner of war far away to the island of St Helena in the South Atlantic where he died on 5 May 1821.

The Auchterarder area did not suffer the invasion panic attacks that gripped coastal Britain during the Napoleonic wars. Major landowners invested in new homes, grand classical villas with no fortifications. The Haldanes had begun the trend as long before as 1750, with their remodelling of Gleneagles House. After Admiral Adam Duncan's victory at Camperdown in 1797, the house was given a commemorative avenue of graceful lime trees that remains today.

David Graeme, MP for Perthshire, who owned a sugar plantation in the West Indies named after his great kinsman Montrose, remodelled Braco Castle in the later eighteenth century, adding an elegant Georgian wing. In 1801, Laurence Oliphant of Gask commissioned Richard Crichton, a pupil of Robert and William Adam, to build a neo-classical mansion. In doing so, he left 'The Auld Hoose' of Gask, celebrated by his Jacobite songstress kinswoman, Lady Nairne.

Drummond Castle near Muthill slid into disrepair after the Forty-Five Rebellion. After the all-embracing Henry Dundas, as Secretary of State for the Home Department, restored forfeited Jacobite estates to their former families in 1785, James Drummond, 1st Baron Perth of Stobhall, began repairs. He also obliterated the thirty houses of an estate village, built to house Hanoverian troops after the Forty-Five, drowning this unpleasant memory in the scenic new Drummond Loch near the main drive to the castle. His daughter, Clementina Sarah Drummond, who married Peter Burrell of the Willoughby d'Eresby family, made major modernisations and improvements to a home that had seen much violent change in Scotland over the centuries.

The Cavalier Marquis of Montrose's Kincardine Castle had been shattered by

Cromwell's artillery and its stones recycled in 1660 to build the parish church of which the tower still stands in the old cemetery in the centre of Auchterarder. In 1805, the Kincardine estate owner James Johnston commissioned the great Dunblane architect, James Gillespie Graham, to build a fashionable Gothic castle, complete with ornamental battlements and turrets, none of it intended for real defence.

Auchterarder High Street changed too. The crushing of the Jacobites and the stable economy created by the Crown Commissioners removed the need for fortified buildings in Strathearn. For the first time in history, householders could invest in their properties with little fear of looting and burning. Quarries near Auchterarder provided good stone. Slates replaced thatched roofs. It was not just new houses that changed the local landscape. The 'Dule Tree' near Kincardine Mains farm, where the Grahams had strung up malefactors, had fallen into disuse. The Auchterarder town gibbet at Gallowhill also ceased to be required once Perth Sheriff Court sat in judgement on all capital offences.

Auchterarder Castle was pragmatically demolished in the late eighteenth century. Its masonry was recycled to construct useful agricultural buildings. It had been the site of King Malcolm Canmore's hunting lodge in the eleventh century, and had housed King Edward I's troops before he took Scotland's Stone of Destiny from Scone in 1296. Now its stones sheltered farm animals, grain and ploughs instead of armed men.

30

Public Water and Public Land

In which Scotland changes its image and Auchterarder justifies its name

Scottish soldiers had variously fought for Britain, America, France, Prussia, Sweden, Austria and other nations in the first decades of the nineteenth century. A mercenary career was one thing. National identity was another.

The Union of the Parliaments in 1707, followed by the suppression of the Jacobites and British triumphs abroad, created an awareness of belonging to a nation whose representatives from across the country assembled in the English capital. To call a Scot 'English' did not necessarily raise the hackles that it does now. David Scott MP for Perthshire said in 1808, 'We commonly, when speaking of British subjects, call them English, be they English, Irish or Scots.'

To outsiders in the early nineteenth century, Scotland had a contradictory reputation. The influential English essayist and lexicographer Samuel Johnson made a tour of Scotland in 1773 and wrote scathingly about primitive, insanitary people eking out a miserable existence in a cold, wet climate. His comments were written at the height of what came to be known as the Scottish Enlightenment, when philosophers like David Hume and Adam Smith gained international reputations. Edinburgh New Town, designed by James Craig, nephew of the 'Rule Britannia' poet James Thomson, created an elegant haven for the capital's officer classes. Edinburgh New Town prided itself on being a model of culture and civilisation. It still does.

The contemporary Auchterarder new town Colony of Boreland Bog, designed for the rank and file rather than for the officer class, was a poverty-haunted failure whose last ruins are crumbling. Johnson's acid *A Tour of the Western Isles* was published in 1775. A year later, Adam Smith quit Edinburgh for Johnson's cosy London clubland. He was only enticed back to Scotland by the salary of Commissioner of Customs, an ironic job for the father of laissez-faire economics.

For centuries, the perception of Scottish history was coloured by the twenty volumes of *Rerum Scoticorum Historia*, completed by the treacherous Puritan publicist George Buchanan shortly before his death in 1582. In the seventeenth century, the great antiquarian Robert Sibbald brought a more clinical evidence-based approach to Scottish historical writing. Sir John Clerk of Penicuik continued this rationalist approach, establishing a more coherent picture of Scottish history since Roman times.

In 1759, William Robertson published *A History of Scotland 1542–1603*, giving a more balanced account of the Scottish Reformation than Buchanan's rant. In 1776, David Dalrymple, Lord Hailes, from the legal family that engaged in a mutual dislike with the Auchterarder Haldanes, published the first volume of *The Annals of Scotland from the Accession of Malcolm Canmore*, but never finished his project.

The scholarship of Sibbald, Clerk, Robertson and Dalrymple had less popular appeal than the colourful fantasies of James MacPherson, who invented 'Ossian', a Gaelic bard, whose poems told the tragedy of a once heroic culture overwhelmed by modern society. *Fingal*, published in 1762, captured the British need for romantic escapism from the realities of costly wars with France. MacPherson escaped from Scotland, and from a scholarly outcry about the authenticity of the poems he claimed to have translated, by becoming Surveyor General in Florida and then a merchant with the East India Company. He later became an MP in Cornwall and paid to be buried in Westminster Abbey, perpetuating the Ossian myth.

Scotland needed a writer who could combine the reputable scholarship of the best antiquarians with the exciting drama of the populists. It was Scotland's good luck to have the right man in the right place at the right time. Walter Scott, who was Sheriff Depute of Selkirk, began his writing career by collecting and editing *The Border Minstrelsy*, published in 1802. Having steeped himself in folklore and in the gripping techniques of traditional ballads, Scott wrote his own long narrative poems. *The Lay of the Last Minstrel* 1805, *Marmion* 1808 and *The Lady of the Lake* 1810 were international best-sellers. They captured the romance of Scotland without MacPherson's fakery.

When fashion changed and readers preferred novels to long poems, Scott published his first novel *Waverley* in 1814. In the preface he wrote, 'There is no nation which, in the course of half a century, or little more, has undergone so complete a change as the Kingdom of Scotland.' His prolific output of novels sold worldwide and created the image of a romantic, heroic Scotland, with the added qualities of good humour and generous spirit.

Walter Scott's confident light touch in his fiction was combined with a genuine scholarship and pride in Scottish history. He scored a spectacular publicity coup for Scotland when he helped arrange King George IV's visit to Edinburgh in August 1822. British monarchs had, with some reason, avoided visiting Scotland for nearly two hundred years. George IV, who succeeded his father George III in 1820, had no such fears.

A flamboyant dandy who had pranced round southern England as Prince Regent, George IV saw Scotland as an opportunity for gorgeous pageant. He equipped himself with fantastic Highland Dress costumes, replete with fancy sword and pistols, diamonds, emeralds, rubies and pearls, sixty-one yards of royal satin plaid, thirty-one yards of royal plaid velvet, seventeen and a half yards of royal plaid cashmere with silver buckles and other trimmings galore. Sir Walter Scott formally presented the King with a silver St Andrew's cross, gifted by the ladies of Edinburgh.

The middle classes, with their love of aping their superiors, especially if they are cartoon figures, came flocking to Scotland and to tartanry. *The Fair Maid of Perth* 1828 drew visitors to the town from around the world. By the time Scott died in 1832, the international image of Scotland had changed from a dangerous bog to a heathery paradise. In his *Tales of a Grandfather*, his last great work, published between 1828 and 1830, he did what no Scot had done before. He made real Scottish history fun to read.

Scott did not minimise conflicts. There were plenty of them in his time. The wars with France brought victory, expense and prisoners. In Perth, a huge jail was created for French prisoners of war. Conditions appear to have been reasonably humane. Some prisoners carved ornaments from wood or old soup bones and sold them to local people at the prison gates. Captured officers were often quartered with families in Perth. Like many Italian and German prisoners in the Second World War, some were in no hurry to go home to fight for a political regime they disliked.

In 1819, when Scott published his *Legend of Montrose*, Auchterarder people hoped to benefit from this publicity for the town's most famous son. It was not to be. Overworked and in poor health, Scott took the easy option of churning out an action-packed saga with the Great Marquis as a background figure rather than a carefully developed central character. The novel is mainly set among military exploits far from Montrose's home town.

The population of the Auchterarder area rose to around 3,600 by 1818, of which about one third were children. Auchterarder itself had about 2,600 people. Aberuthven had about three hundred. The landward area accounted for the rest.

The 1789 Act for Making Turnpike Roads in Perthshire improved the east-west Perth to Crieff road, but was of little help to Auchterarder until 1814. Then, after seven years of committee meetings, local landowners agreed to create a Turnpike Road to the south, today known as the A823, along the east side of Gleneagles and Glendevon. They also agreed to extend it northwards to connect with the Crieff to Stirling road near Bishop's Bridge.

Shares were sold in the new Turnpike Road with profits to be made from tolls. Sir Patrick Murray of Ochtertyre took the lead. He was backed by, among others, three local military heroes who took time away from defeating the French to argue for the new road: Admiral Duncan of Camperdown and Gleneagles; Thomas Graham of Balgowan near Gask, who became Lord Lyndoch; and Sir David Baird, victor of the Battle of Seringapatam in India and fresh from triumphs in the Spanish Peninsular War. Another supporter was the Earl of Kinnoull, who was later to fall foul of many Auchterarder people in the Great Disruption of the Kirk. The A823 through the Ochils, connecting the Highlands to the Lowlands, was completed around 1822.

Scotland's new romantic image and potential tourist trade were not the main reasons for building the road. The real motivation was to get coal. Coal imported from the ports of Perth and Stirling was expensive. There was cheaper coal to be had from the coalfields of Blairingone, but the roads through the Ochils were poor. Carts could carry a load of only five hundredweight, equivalent to the weight of four medium-sized men. When the new Turnpike Road was built, it was suitable for bigger carts, drawn by two horses, carrying loads five times greater than before. The price of coal in Auchterarder fell by a quarter, helping the local economy.

Coal came north to Auchterarder. On the return journey south, the carts carried slates from Aberuchill, Glenartney and Glenalmond to provide roofing for expanding Edinburgh and Fife towns. The new Gleneagles Turnpike Road also brought limestone from Roscobie and Lathalmond near Yetts of Muckart to provide cement for the house-building boom.

Although local working conditions and business opportunities improved in the late eighteenth and early nineteenth centuries, there was an increasing awareness of fortunes to be made overseas. For example, over twenty people from Auchterarder, plus a further fifty from the surrounding area, emigrated to Delaware County in upstate New York in the 1830s. Others settled throughout the British Empire.

Locally, officialdom and entrepreneurial spirit clashed as they always do, sometimes with comic effect. The Treasury earned, and still earns, a substantial income from excise duty levied on whisky. Smugglers and illicit distillers were constantly at war with the excise men or 'gaugers'. Perthshire's new roads and bridges were a boon both to smugglers and to the troops who tried to catch them.

The best-known local encounter is the Battle of Corriemuckloch, on 21 December 1823, when a party of Scots Greys rode from Auchterarder with the local excise man to intercept smugglers who were carrying a cargo of whisky from hidden stills, north of Amulree, to Crieff for Hogmanay.

They clashed at Corriemuckloch near the Sma' Glen. Nobody was killed. Troops carried off as many barrels as they could, leaving the rest to be collected later. Not surprisingly, the remaining barrels disappeared and their evidence vanished down the throats of local people at Hogmanay. Both sides claimed victory.

Whisky, taxed or not, was plentiful. In contrast, Auchterarder, the town whose name means 'the well-watered place on the high ridge', lacked a reliable water supply.

The town's first church, St Mackessog's, was built low down by the Kirkton Burn at the foot of Powhillock, probably in the late sixth century. A small settlement grew up nearby. Higher up, on the same north side of the Auchterarder ridge, King Malcolm III Canmore built Auchterarder Castle in the eleventh century. In its courtyard lies a sixty-foot-deep well, rediscovered in 1984, providing an all-year-round water supply.

On the south side of the Auchterarder ridge, the lands belonging to the Abbey of Inchaffray benefited from the Lochy Burn and the Ruthven Water. As the town developed in the Middle Ages, the wells along the High Street dried up in summer. Water had to be carried from the Ruthven.

For several months each year in the early nineteenth century, most of the town was literally high and dry. For a piped supply, it was unrealistic to pump water uphill from the Ruthven, the Kirkton or the castle. Could it be piped downhill from springs at the edge of the Common Muir? This extended west from the town gallows, just north of today's St Margaret's Hospital, Public Park, Golf Course and Cemetery all the way to where the A9 Bypass now runs. Committees had met for centuries, wondering what to do. Nothing had resulted.

The Common Muir had always belonged collectively to the townspeople, who used it for grazing animals and for recreation. It was quite separate from the lands of the Barony of Auchterarder, which had been forfeited by the Jacobite Duke of Perth after the 1745 rebellion, but restored to the Drummonds in 1784. Lord James Drummond promptly sold the Barony of Auchterarder in two lots. John Malcolm Esq. bought the lands of Castlemains. The Hon. Basil Cochrane, who had profited from service with the East India Company, purchased the rest of the Barony.

Basil Cochrane was related to Admiral Thomas Cochrane, eldest son of the 1st Earl of Dundonald. Admiral Cochrane, like Admiral Duncan of Gleneagles, was a hero of the Napoleonic Wars. He became a radical Member of Parliament, fighting corruption in public service and tabling the first parliamentary motion for universal suffrage.

Ironically, this advocate of public good was caught up in a stock market swindle and jailed for a year. The First Lord of the Admiralty, John Jervis, Earl St Vincent had a low opinion of Thomas Cochrane and his family: 'The Cochranes are not to be trusted out of sight. They are all mad, romantic, money-getting and not truth-telling.'

Admiral Cochrane's Auchterarder relative, Basil, certainly had no scruples about the common good. In 1808, Basil Cochrane claimed the Eastern Commonty, part of the Common Muir of Auchterarder, on the grounds that Auchterarder was no longer a royal burgh and therefore the townspeople had no rights to the Eastern Commonty.

There appeared to be no date at which Auchterarder had ceased to be a royal burgh, although it had certainly failed to pay its dues to Parliament on several occasions. An Act of Parliament in 1696 stated that landowners of burghs of barony could take over common land, whereas landowners of royal burghs could not. Did that entitle Cochrane to grab the Eastern Common Muir?

Cochrane's case was hotly disputed in court. Local lawyer Robert Mailer, supported by townspeople such as David White and Robert Smitton, who had exercised rights on the Common Muir, took the lead against Cochrane. In 1812, fearing that Basil Cochrane might take control of a potential water supply, the people of Auchterarder tried to raise public subscriptions to pay for a pipeline across the Common Muir. They failed to raise enough money. Only two hundred yards of pipes, made from hollowed spruce and larch trees, were laid.

In 1831, a new water committee was set up, chaired by William Thomson, blacksmith at Baad's Smithy, a substantial manufacturer of ploughs which came to be exported throughout the British Empire. The new committee consulted Adam Anderson, then rector of Perth Academy and a future professor of Natural and Experimental Philosophy (Science) at St Andrews University. Anderson had recently designed a radical solution to Perth's disgusting water problems. He devised a scheme for Auchterarder, tapping the plentiful wells at Crook o' the Moss, which lies on today's PGA Centenary Golf Course, at the opposite side of the A9 from the entrance to Gleneagles Station, a road still prone to flooding.

A good plan is one thing. Making it happen is something else. Captain Marriot Chadwick Aytoun of Glendevon, who had a sound grasp of engineering from his days in the Royal Horse Artillery, took the initiative to see the scheme through at great personal expense. Some major landowners also contributed funds.

Captain James Hunter, a descendant of Sir William Montifex of Auchterarder Castle who had owned the Barony of Auchterarder in the fourteenth century, brought history full circle by buying Basil Cochrane's part of the Barony of Auchterarder in 1831, though the question of ownership of the Eastern Common Muir dragged on until 1860 when an Act of Parliament was passed, vesting the Common Muir in Commissioners for the benefit of the whole community. Hunter wanted the new water scheme to be successful. He donated some funds on condition that the supply went as far as the splendid new house he intended to build, Auchterarder House, on Powhillock Road (now named Hunter Street). Hunter also developed the Feus, extending Auchterarder eastwards.

James Johnston of Kincardine, on whose land the Crook o' the Moss Wells lay, simply wanted to charge the town for the water. He signed a bond in 1833, granting the town permanent access to the water supply.

At first, there was a single water pipe with a few taps at intervals along the High Street. The first branch pipe to a house was laid in 1831. Within a year, another ninety houses had an indoor tap. Many poorer householders took buckets to draw their water from iron stand-pumps. These pumps remained in use till the mid-twentieth century.

The successful water scheme provided up to 72 gallons per minute, delivered through cast-iron pipes. It required building aqueducts across low-lying ground, one of which can still be seen near Greenwells on the Gleneagles PGA Centenary Course.

In thanks for implementing Adam Anderson's plan, the townsfolk presented Captain Aytoun in 1832 with a silver punchbowl, made by the Edinburgh silversmith Andrew Wilkie, embossed with scenes of the landscape from where the water flowed.

The town also arranged for a grand civic dinner in Captain Aytoun's honour. Unfortunately, there was no venue big enough to hold all the dignitaries and other guests. Five simultaneous dinners were held in separate locations, with messages of congratulation circulated between each. In contrast to the unwieldy civic dinner, the practical Captain Aytoun donated two fat oxen, which were butchered and distributed to local poor families.

The need for a good-sized Town Hall was obvious, so in 1851 the town discussed making a more substantial tribute to Captain Aytoun's energy and public spirit. Aytoun died in 1854. Despite the efforts of mill-owner William Hally and lawyer William Young, the local Aytoun Memorial Committee dithered for years.

The tribute finally arrived in 1872 when public subscription bought the site next to Girnal House and paid for the Perth architect Charles Robinson to design a handsome town hall, faced in best Bannockburn stone, in the latest Venetian Gothic style. The estimated cost was £1,600. The actual cost was £3,000, built mainly by Peter Anderson, a local builder who was beset by union labour conflicts. It was named the Aytoun Memorial Hall and remains the building that defines the town.

The Aytoun Hall was built at the same time as two other celebratory monuments: the William Wallace Monument near Stirling and the Statue of Liberty outside New York City. All three suffered long delays, furious arguments about funding and conflicts with the workforce. Two are towering symbols of national triumphalism with no practical local use. The third, the Aytoun Hall, was generously designed to serve the local community.

The Statue of Liberty and the Wallace Monument were handsomely restored with central government funding in the late twentieth century. In contrast, the Aytoun Hall suffered from decades of inadequate local government maintenance. Only in 2005, with the national flag-waving G8 Summit Conference of World Leaders in Auchterarder's Gleneagles Hotel, was the Aytoun Hall allocated national funding for repairs. It then took the building's owners Perth & Kinross Council a further seven years to do the necessary refurbishment work.

Back in 1872, by the time the Aytoun Hall was named, Auchterarder's water supply was already inadequate for the rapidly growing town. Lacking anyone with Captain Aytoun's drive and persistence, it took until 1904 for an additional supply to be piped from Duchally on the slopes of the Ochils.

Adam Anderson's water scheme and Marriot Aytoun's application transformed Auchterarder, just as Perth was belatedly taken out of the evil-smelling Middle Ages by Adam Anderson's water scheme there. Perth never paid Adam Anderson for all his work in designing a successful water scheme. Auchterarder did.

The 1831 Water Committee chairman William Thomson's son, John, set up an engineering business in Glasgow and helped develop a modern water supply for St Petersburg in Russia. By coincidence, two centuries later, the G8 Summit Conference was held in 2005 in Auchterarder, and in St Petersburg the following year. Water supplies, with their key role in both climate change and global poverty, were central to these G8 agendas.

Auchterarder's new water supply was for domestic and light commercial use. For many centuries, flour mills and other mills had used the Ruthven Water to power their wheels. Industrial use of water for weaving looms came when William Hally set up a mill in an old malt barn at the Castleton in 1836. *The Second Statistical Account* of 1837 notes a 'woollen manufactory of shawls and blankets' by the Ruthven Water.

The Royal Burgh of Auchterarder won its battle for a good water supply and to save its Eastern Commonty. It lost an equally valuable land asset. The town also had a Western Commonty, which ran from the Muirton (which is more correctly called the Muir of Kincardine) west along the road towards Braco. It included the White Muir and lay entirely in Blackford parish. The Western Commonty was bordered by three great estates, owned by James Moray of Abercairney, James Drummond of Strathallan and the Kincardine Estate. In 1817, these landowners applied to the Sheriff Court in Dunblane to be allowed to carve up the Western Commonty between them, citing the controversial 1696 Act of Parliament as their justification.

For the Eastern Commonty, there were several wealthy Auchterarder businessmen to oppose Cochrane and Hunter. For the Western Commonty, there were only a few crofters at The Muirton. The Dunblane Sheriff Court chose as arbiter two other major landowners, Anthony Murray of Dollerie and

John Monteath of Duchally. Not surprisingly, the court found in favour of the big estates. Small parcels of land were given to the Muirton crofters. The common good for the Western Commonty was abolished.

Unlike the Eastern Commonty case, which was taken all the way to the Court of Session and resulted in the 1860 Act of Parliament in favour of the whole community of Auchterarder, the Western Commonty decision in Dunblane was never appealed to a higher court.

These two legal decisions have had a dramatic impact on Auchterarder today. For example, on the Eastern Commonty lie St Margaret's Hospital, The Public Park and The Cemetery. It also includes the site of Auchterarder Golf Course, which provides the main source of income for the Auchterarder Common Good Fund. On the former Western Commonty lies Gleneagles Hotel and Golf Courses, an entirely private enterprise. If the land on which the multi-million Gleneagles leisure industry operates were still owned by the townspeople, its rent income would transform the community.

Auchterarder's new water scheme was fairly quickly followed in 1842 by a Gas Works, which provided lighting for houses and shops and also street lighting. For heating and industrial use, gas remained much more expensive than coal. William Hally built a huge mill by the Ruthven in 1872. It was not until 1910 that it replaced steam power with a gas plant.

Meetings to develop the water supply were held in several venues, including the Town School and the Masonic Lodge. The Masons held considerable influence over the construction industry throughout Scotland in the nineteenth and twentieth centuries. They had evolved from the great trade guilds of the Middle Ages, designed to set standards and protect the interests of their members, always looking to secure contracts for public works.

In Auchterarder, the Masonic Lodge St John Number 46 received its charter in 1745. After the crushing of the Jacobite rebellion and the reconstruction of the rural Scottish economy, there was plenty of public work to be had. Though the Lodge's rites were secretive, its public face was an accepted part of community life. In 1872, the foundation stone of the Aytoun Hall was laid with full Masonic honours and a time capsule, containing coins and newspapers of the day.

Improved roads and a reliable water supply made Auchterarder blossom. By 1837, James Aitken in *The Second Statistical Account* could write, 'The situation of the town is high and more than ordinarily healthful,' and, 'the inhabitants of Auchterarder may be regarded as in circumstances of more than usual comfort.' The population of Auchterarder parish leaped from 1,670 in 1791 to 3,315 in 1836.

Land ownership had changed dramatically since the sixteenth century when the Grahams and the Drummonds between them controlled nearly three quarters of Auchterarder's tenancies. In 1835, the Barony of Auchterarder owned by Captain James Hunter accounted for 22 per cent of the town's rental roll. Graham of Inchbrakie accounted for 21 per cent. The remaining 57 per cent was divided among 43 different owners.

In 1837, the main manufacturing industry in Auchterarder and Aberuthven was weaving cotton brought from Glasgow. There were over five hundred handlooms. By the Ruthven there were thirteen mills of different kinds.

Agriculture continued to improve, with new breeds of stock, including Ayrshire cows for dairy, Teeswater cattle for beef, and Leicester sheep for wool. Land was better managed. James Aitken wrote approvingly, 'Scarcely is there a field without a drain.' There was a Saturday market, mainly for grain. The Parish Agricultural Association staged an annual ploughing match. The town had a veterinary surgeon.

As the town grew and prospered, so opportunities for doctors increased. One Rev. Dr John King, who was minister of the Relief Church from 1806 to 1837, attended to both physical and spiritual health. By 1837, there were five medical practitioners in the parish. They could avail themselves of the leeches to be found in the ponds at Damside, south west of Aberuthven. James Aitken notes that these are 'the genuine medical leech *Hirudo medicalis*, larger and more vigorous than those imported into this country' and 'preferred by the people in the neighbourhood to foreign leeches.'

A sure sign of prosperity is the arrival of lawyers to participate in squabbles or to protect rights, depending on your point of view. In 1793, Auchterarder had only one lawyer. In 1837, there were six lawyers and a banker.

There were twenty-one inns in Auchterarder and two in Aberuthven. Not surprisingly, the town needed a policeman. Constable Archibald Stewart was appointed to Auchterarder in 1847, but only after the Burgh Police Act of 1857 was a police house with a prison cell built, around 1870, on the north-east corner of Hunter Street, handy for the Railway Hotel and other hostelries near the Feus.

In 1837, *The Second Statistical Account* lists ten major landowners. It also lists '5 fatuous persons, 1 blind and 6 deaf and dumb.' They all had their opinions when the clash between the townspeople and aristocratic patronage came to a head with 'The Auchterarder Case', which changed Scottish society forever and had cultural repercussions throughout the British Empire and the USA.

31

The Spirit of Reform

*In which democracy becomes fashionable and we see the
established church keep its hierarchy but lose its congregation*

God and the King remained the ultimate powers to be feared in eighteenth-
century Britain, though there was much debate about how religious and regal
authority should be administered. By the early nineteenth century, the madness
of King George III and the extravagant ineptitude of his heir George IV and his
brothers brought the monarchy into disrepute.

Locally in Auchterarder, the royal castle where mediaeval kings like
Malcolm Canmore and Edward I had exercised their authority had become an
inconvenient ruin. Its new owner, John Malcolm, who claimed descent from
Malcolm Canmore but had bought the land from the Drummonds in the late
eighteenth century, demolished the castle and used the stone for sturdy farm
buildings that remain in use today. Only the outline of the ramparts and a little
folly constructed from old masonry remain as evidence of royal power.

Politically, power lay with Parliament. Lord Liverpool's Tory administration
lasted from 1812 to 1827. It brought the French wars to an end with Napoleon's
defeat at Waterloo in 1815, but dealt with the economic slump that follows any
expensive military victory by adopting harsh policies that drove many families
to the point of starvation.

To protect farmers' incomes, the government introduced a Corn Law in
1815, banning lower-priced imports and driving up the cost of food. The new
law immediately provoked riots among weavers in Perth. The increasing use of
machinery in agriculture and industry changed the labour market. Many soldiers
and sailors, no longer needed for war, found it hard to secure employment. The
Foreign Enlistment Act of 1819, which forbade British subjects to serve in foreign
armies, increased their problems. For hundreds of years, Scots had been well
paid as mercenaries overseas before returning home. Now, service to a foreign
government meant giving up British citizenship. Some chose to emigrate. Some
remained resentful at home.

Income tax, introduced as a temporary wartime measure, was never abolished
and, despite protests, became the core of every subsequent government's personal
taxation policy.

Bribery and nepotism were rife at all levels of government, national and local.

The advocate Henry Cockburn called Edinburgh Town Council, 'omnipotent, corrupt and impenetrable.' In the early nineteenth century, election fraud went largely uncontrolled. Protestors faced being accused of disloyalty to a nation made paranoid by fear of French invasion. New newspapers appeared, arguing for reform. *The Dundee Advertiser* was founded in 1801, and *The Aberdeen Chronicle* in 1806. By the time the Edinburgh *Scotsman* was first published in 1819, politicians found it harder to get away with the scare-mongering that had been acceptable in wartime.

In 1819, Lord Archibald Hamilton succeeded in prompting a parliamentary inquiry into the affairs of Scottish burghs, which revealed how ruinous corruption had been in the cities of these three reforming newspapers. In the same year, however, magistrates in Manchester brutally suppressed a public demonstration, which became known as the Peterloo Massacre. Henry Addington, Lord Sidmouth, who had been a brief and undistinguished Prime Minister after Pitt in 1802, was Home Secretary in Lord Liverpool's Tory Government. Sidmouth and Robert Stewart, Lord Castlereagh, reacted to the public outrage after Peterloo by forcing through even more repressive legislation. Six new acts curtailed the liberty of the individual and the freedom of the press.

The new legislation deepened the government's unpopularity. Castlereagh was so hated that, when he committed suicide in 1822, a large crowd gathered to cheer and jeer at his funeral procession to Westminster Abbey.

A younger generation of Tories, like William Huskisson, George Canning and Robert Peel, adopted more democratic policies to allay public hostility. Huskisson believed in Adam Smith's principle of free trade, which had been abandoned when the Corn Law was introduced in 1815. As president of the Board of Trade from 1823, Huskisson lifted many restrictions that had been imposed in wartime. British shipping increased by 45 per cent over the next twenty years. Ironically for a promoter of modern transport, he was knocked down and killed by a train at the opening of the Liverpool and Manchester Railway in 1830.

George Canning, who had been wounded in 1809 in a duel with his Tory colleague Castlereagh in one of history's more spectacular party splits, was a political adventurer who adapted his beliefs to keep up with popular opinion. He was a wartime conservative, but argued for repeal of the Corn Law in the 1820s. As Foreign Secretary after Castlereagh's suicide, Canning recognised political reality in supporting the USA President James Monroe's 1823 doctrine, forbidding European states to interfere in transatlantic disputes, effectively recognising the independence of Portugal's former colony Brazil and Spain's former colonies, Argentina, Mexico and Colombia. He also supported the Greek independence movement against their Turkish overlords. On 27 October 1827, a combined British, French and Russian naval attack destroyed the Turkish fleet at the Battle of Navarino. Canning succeeded Lord Liverpool as Prime Minister in 1827 but died soon after.

At a time of changing international boundaries and demand for political reform, Britain needed a steady hand as Prime Minister. There was none steadier than the Duke of Wellington, a national hero after defeating Napoleon at Waterloo in 1815. Wellington liked plain speaking and discipline but disliked change. As Prime Minister from 1828 to 1830 Wellington represented the last of the old era. As an Irishman, he was acutely aware of the anger and potential revolution among Roman Catholics who were excluded from public office and suffered centuries of poverty after a succession of English and Scottish Protestant land grabs. With some reluctance, Wellington saw through the Roman Catholic Emancipation Act in 1829. Instead of pacifying Ireland, the act gave Daniel O'Connell's independence movement greater hope for further political success. In Scotland and England, Wellington was increasingly seen as a figure from the past and an obstruction to necessary reform.

Across the English Channel lay evidence of what could happen if reform was not addressed. The restoration of the monarchy in France, after Napoleon's defeats in 1814 and 1815, did not secure stability. King Louis XVIII acted with the autocratic presumptions of his Bourbon predecessors. When he died in 1824, his younger brother, the Count of Artois, became King Charles X.

The new French king, who had spent most of the Napoleonic Wars in exile in Holyrood Palace at British expense, tried to overrule the French Parliament and curb freedom of the press. He was forced to abdicate on 2 August 1830. By 20 October, he had retreated back to Edinburgh, confident that he could sponge once more on the romantic Francophile notions of Scottish conservatives. The elderly novelist Walter Scott was sympathetic, but the general public saw the French ex-king as a spendthrift who had been expelled from his native land with good reason. He lingered in Holyrood for two years with a small reactionary Catholic clique before moving to Prague where he died in 1836.

King Charles X of France fell from power because his royal will and resources were weaker than those of his Parliament and voters. In Britain, King George IV was just as extravagant as Charles X, but had the Duke of Wellington to steer him away from most head-on clashes with Parliament. George IV died on 24 June 1830, a few weeks before Charles X fled from France. Both kings had failed marriages, scheming mistresses and no legitimate heirs.

George's brother, the Duke of Clarence, became King William IV. He was bluff, hearty and French-hating, like the cartoon character John Bull. He rid himself of much of his brother's expensive clutter and court rigmarole, which he found distasteful and out-dated. He liked to walk in London and did not disdain to talk to passers-by.

William IV began as he intended to continue. In 1820, George IV's coronation, with lavish banquets and pageantry, had cost £240,000. Ten years later, King William IV's coronation cost only £30,000. It would have been even less, but he reluctantly agreed to the traditional ceremony and procession which gave the public something to cheer. He refused to authorise payment for prolonged feasting and fancy costumes for hangers-on.

The arch-traditionalist Duke of Wellington felt that the new king was letting the nation down by failing to stage a display of Britain's pomp and glory. Charles, 2nd Earl Grey, who replaced Wellington as Prime Minister in November 1830, agreed with the old Duke, but had more urgent matters to consider. Reform was in the air. King William, though unimpressed by flummery, was no radical. He feared that revolution might spread from France to Britain.

Britain did not have a written constitution. Its method of government had evolved over the centuries by lurches of political necessity. The Union of the Scottish and English Parliaments in 1707 did not unite or reform their legal systems, which were a vast accumulation of precedent and expediency designed to enforce the will of the king and his government.

When the Republic of the United States of America was founded in 1776, it adopted a written constitution that presumed the will of the people to be paramount. In Britain, the divine right of kings had evaporated with the Glorious Revolution of 1688, but legislative power still lay with a small group of aristocrats, supplemented by nouveaux-riches. The political philosophers Jeremy Bentham from London and James Mill from Montrose popularised the idea of democracy as 'the greatest good for the greatest number'. Known as utilitarianism, this principle had obvious appeal to the increasingly literate and well-informed masses. For the British government, the problem was how to grant more equality without abolishing the political structure that kept them in their jobs.

Prime Minister Earl Grey united Whig reformers like John, 1st Earl Russell with liberal Tories such as Henry, 3rd Viscount Palmerston, both of whom were Englishmen who had studied at Edinburgh University. They prepared a Bill to reform the electoral system and parliamentary representation.

Parliamentary constituency boundaries had not changed to reflect the mass population movements of the industrial revolution. Boom cities, like Manchester, Birmingham and Leeds, had no Members of Parliament. Like Perth, Dundee and Aberdeen, they were represented by a member from a nearby rural area. In England, there were thirty-five constituencies, with very few voters, returning seventy members.

Most of the population was not allowed to vote. Practice varied, but largely depended on ownership of significant property. The 1811 roll of county electors in Scotland shows eight counties, each with fewer than thirty voters. Only nine counties had more than one hundred voters. Corruption was rife. Some seats in the Commons were as much controlled by peers as their seats in the Lords. British businessmen working overseas, especially for the East India Company, enhanced their status by buying votes and securing a seat in Parliament.

In 1832, after two attempts foiled by arch-conservatives, the Reform Bill was passed by Parliament. Constituency boundaries were changed to give more equal representation. Scotland received eight new seats. Locally, the town of Perth was given its own seat, while Auchterarder continued to be represented as part of rural Perthshire.

Because of its separate legal system, Scotland required its own Reform Bill. The 1832 Reform Act (Scotland), like its English counterpart, gave the vote to all householders owning properties rated above £10 per annum. To give the vote to middle-class tenant farmers, any tenant with a nineteen-year lease paying £50 per year also had the vote. By December 1832, the Scottish electorate had increased from 4,500 to 65,000 out of a population of about two million.

Earl Grey, with his alliance of aristocratic Whigs and liberal Tories, had staved off revolution by enfranchising the middle-class males who are most likely to manage revolution successfully, as they had in France and America. Politically, there was as yet no need to give the vote to women or the working classes.

Further reforms followed swiftly. In August 1833, slavery was abolished, though it persisted in Jamaica until 1840. The Factory Act of 1837 set a minimum age of nine for factory workers and required owners to provide two hours of education per day for children under twelve.

In contrast, the Poor Law Amendment Act of 1834 was not the humanitarian reform it might have been. It abolished the expensive old system of parishes handing money to the unemployed on the basis of the size of their families. This forced the unemployed to seek casual labouring work for a pittance. It was Adam Smith's laissez-faire economics at its crudest. It provoked political discontent, especially because of the contradiction that the Corn Laws, an equally crude form of protectionism, kept the price of food high.

Scotland did not have a reformed poor law for another decade, by which time Britain had seen a succession of short-lived governments. William Lamb, 2nd Viscount Melbourne was Prime Minister briefly in 1834, uniting Tory and Whig moderates, but was replaced by Sir Robert Peel for the first few months of 1835.

Robert Peel came from a compassionate tradition. His father, also called Robert Peel, had carried through the Health and Morals Act in 1802, which improved conditions for apprentices in factories. Peel himself, as Home Secretary, had established the London Police Force in 1829, whose officers were nicknamed 'Peelers' or Bobbies' after their founder. By April 1835, Melbourne was Prime Minister again, promising further orderly reform.

The political establishment had reformed parliamentary elections and representation, without revolution. Could Scotland's religious establishment achieve calm reform? It had never done so before and was not about to do it now.

Once again, Auchterarder was at the centre of controversy and change. 'The Auchterarder Creed' of 1716, with its notion of freedom of choice for the individual, had stirred up international controversy and gave new focus to questions about who should have authority over the people's beliefs.

During the eighteenth century, a 'Relief' Church was established in Auchterarder. It and other small groups were regarded merely as minor irritants by the established Presbyterian Church of Scotland, which retained much of the style of patronage of the pre-Reformation Catholic Church. As in the sixteenth century, resentment over abuse began to simmer.

The French Revolution was militantly atheist. The brothers Robert and James Haldane of the Gleneagles family believed that social justice could be achieved by Christian principles. In 1798, they formed The Society for Propagating The Gospel At Home, whose evangelical preachers were plain-spoken and practical. The established Church of Scotland sneered at their populist missionary zeal and spread rumours that the Tabernacles set up by the Haldanes were the equivalent of French Revolutionary Jacobin clubs. They were not. They were congregations of people with a revived Christian faith.

The Haldanes promoted the concept of lay preachers as well as ordained clergy. They helped shape the Congregationalist Church, though they later became Baptists. More importantly, their plain faith influenced Christian reform movements worldwide, including the Dutch Reformed Church in South Africa and the Réveil movement in Geneva, once home to John Calvin.

Robert and James Haldane belonged to a Christian tradition in Auchterarder that emphasised plain worship, bowing down to God but not necessarily to those who made appointments in God's name.

The vexed question of authority came to a head in Auchterarder in 1843 with 'The Great Disruption', which finally split the Presbyterian Church in Scotland into many warring sects, some of which continue to this day.

Private landowners had taken over from bishops the right to make local church appointments. The patron for Auchterarder parish was Thomas-Robert Hay-Drummond, 10th Earl of Kinnoull. The Earls of Kinnoull had been beneficial to cultural life in Strathearn through Innerpeffray Library. They had also a malign influence through their kinsman 'Bobbing John', the Jacobite Earl of Mar who burned Strathearn in 1716.

The 9th Earl of Kinnoull expressed himself by erecting a folly, a fake Rhineland ruined tower, looking down on the River Tay high above the east end of today's Friarton Bridge. The 10th Earl preferred genuine conflict to fake ruins.

In 1834, he proposed the Rev. Robert Young as the new minister of Auchterarder. The congregation did not like Young's long sermons, nor the way he read them. Out of Auchterarder's population of 3,000, only two people, Michael Tod and Peter Clark, formally supported Young.

Kinnoull was asked to make some other choice, preferably Rev. James Aitken, who had been acting minister and wrote the Second Statistical Account for Auchterarder in 1837. Kinnoull refused to have his judgement questioned and took the matter to the courts. Aitken went off to the Laigh Church in Kilmarnock.

Abstract philosophical debate about free-thinking was one thing. Handing over the right to make decisions was another. The 1832 Reform Act had swept away many opportunities for electoral abuse and corruption. Not everyone approved. The Duke of Montrose was an outspoken opponent of electoral reform. When he died in 1836, some Aberuthven villagers jeered as his funeral procession made its way towards the fine Montrose Mausoleum, designed by William Adam in 1736. A mourner whacked a villager with an umbrella and a fight broke out, in a repetition of the fisticuffs at a previous Aberuthven Graham funeral in 1712.

The Reform Act of 1832 rankled with its opponents for the rest of their previously privileged lives. Local lawyer A.G. Reid, author of *The Annals of Auchterarder*, called the Reform Act a 'contagion'.

Another local lawyer, William Young, founder of generations of Auchterarder lawyers, provosts and town clerks, enthused about the Reform Act giving the vote to more Auchterarder people. William Young was the son of a tenant farmer in Madderty, well aware of the former powerlessness of those who did not own land. He was not related to the unfortunate Rev. Robert Young.

The 'Auchterarder Case', as it came to be known, dragged on through the courts until the House of Lords in 1839 ruled that, as the law stood, the congregation had no rights in the choice of its minister. In 1842, the House of Lords went even further and said that the Rev. Robert Young was entitled to damages, which he calculated at £10,000. This was an enormous amount, considering that a labourer in Auchterarder earned about £20 per year.

Did the people of Auchterarder meekly submit to the combined authority of Established Church and State? They did not. The Auchterarder Case split the Church of Scotland. On 18 May 1843, some 450 ministers walked out of the General Assembly in Edinburgh to form a new Free Church of Scotland.

Why is the Free Church called 'free'? The Scottish Court of Session's verdict of 1838 was that the appointment of a minister to the established Church of Scotland was a civil matter, not a religious one, therefore the Earl of Kinnoull could appoint whomever he liked to Auchterarder Parish Church. In order for a congregation to be free to choose its minister, it had to free itself from the established Church of Scotland.

In 1843, architects Cousin & Gale began work on a Free Church, St Andrew's, on the High Street, with no obligations to Lord Kinnoull or any other landowner. Its statement of intent is clearly visible above the door: *Jehovah Jireh* (God will provide). St Andrew's was designed by Andrew Heiton, who then went on to design Cloan for the Haldanes and devised other distinguished houses in Perthshire and elsewhere.

Rev. Robert Young, whose appointment had caused all the controversy in 1834, turned out to be a mild-mannered man who remained as minister of a much-reduced congregation in the Parish Church until 1865. By the end of the nineteenth century, the Parish Church, in the old cemetery, was in poor condition. Members of the congregation fainted because of the foul stench rising from the vaults. In 1905 it was replaced by a new building further down the High Street, the Barony Church, designed by Honeyman & Keppie, who employed the innovative architect Charles Rennie Mackintosh.

The pre-Reformation font from St Mackessog's was transferred to the Barony Church, as were two Parish Church bells dated 1754.

St Andrew's Church's bold slogan *Jehovah Jireh* proved rather too optimistic. The building became the Gleneagles Furniture Centre when the divided congregation reunited in 1983, for financial rather than religious reasons. The Barony Church was renamed the Parish Church, taking the town in a 1,500-year full circle.

The mid nineteenth century saw a burst of independent church-building in Auchterarder. In 1849, the South United Presbyterians, from The Tent Yard near the old Parish Church, built The Blackford and Auchterarder Relief Church behind today's Golf Inn, which was its manse. Later known as the West Church, it was demolished a century later after its congregation merged with St Andrew's.

The Rev. George Jacque was minister of the Relief Church in Auchterarder for fifty-eight years. He lived in the Relief Church Manse, built in 1837 and remodelled along with the church in 1849. He saw the Great Disruption and its after-effects, and remained a popular figure in the area. He was an eloquent and witty preacher who wrote both hymns and comic verse.

Around 1890, another church sprang up near the top of Montrose Road. Known as Trinity Church, it was a collaborative effort by various groups of Seceders from the established Church of Scotland, who combined as The North

United Presbyterians. It only lasted until 1913, when it merged with the West Church, home of the South United Presbyterians. However, Trinity Church's main contribution to local history was still to come. It became The Drill Hall, used by troops and then as the base for the Home Guard in World War II and the Territorial Army until the 1960s.

It would be misleading to say the Great Disruption was a conflict between the aristocracy and the common people. In many cases, they were on the same side. In Aberuthven in 1836, local people disrupted the funeral of the arch-conservative Duke of Montrose, but a few years later his kinsman, the public-spirited Major George Drummond Graeme of Inchbrakie, gifted the ground for a Free Church built in 1852, with a manse, school and schoolhouse. He also paid for all the construction materials. The building work was done by local voluntary labour.

Major George Graeme was eleventh in line from the great Marquis of Montrose and, like many of the Grahams, had a distinguished military career. He played a key role at the Battle of Waterloo in 1815. The church he provided in Aberuthven served the parish for over a hundred years, until the manse was sold in 1963, some years after the parish was linked to Gask. It was later linked to Dunning. Aberuthven Church was sold as a private house. A new smaller church was built behind the school.

After the Great Disruption of 1843, other fragments of the old established Church of Scotland built their own buildings and worshipped in their own ways. Free churches came and went. Only the United Free church, set back from the High Street near Montrose Road, survives today. It was built in 1893 by the Auchterarder Evangelistic Society. The local UF congregation was granted use of the building from 1929 to 1936, and then bought it outright.

The Emancipation Act of 1829 had granted greater equality to Catholics. In 1879, Our Lady of Succour was built on the Castleton, near the site of the mediaeval Castle of Auchterarder.

The Episcopal Church, often caricatured as the Church of England in Scotland, built a fine church in 1896, designed by Ross & Macbeth, and took the religious history of Auchterarder full circle by naming it St Kessog's, after the first Christian foundation in the town. It has elegant stained-glass windows by Charles Kempe of London. Previously, the St Kessog Mission Building had occupied the old Sheddan's School. It has since served several functions, including being the Unionist Rooms in the mid-twentieth century when political conservatism was locally strong. Today, it is the Scout Hall.

The Rev. Edward Reid, son of James Reid, the locomotive magnate of Auchterarder House, funded the building of this new St Kessog's. Edward Reid later served as Bishop of St Andrews, Dunkeld and Dunblane until he died in 1938.

In 1921, near to St Kessog's, Bishop Reid bought Castlebrae, which had been built in 1887 by William Mallis, the local shoe manufacturer. Given the repeatedly explosive nature of religious controversy in Auchterarder, it is perhaps not surprising that it took over fifteen hundred years of Christianity for a bishop to choose to live in Auchterarder. Castlebrae is now a Police Federation convalescent home.

The Reids were great benefactors to Auchterarder. Edward Reid's brother, Andrew, gifted the organ to St Kessog's and, in a generous ecumenical gesture, gifted an organ to the West Church and installed a stained-glass window in memory of his parents in the present-day Parish Church. The Reids also gave land for the Roman Catholic Church. Most importantly, in 1926 Andrew Reid funded St Margaret's Hospital, in memory of his parents. By the end of the nineteenth century, there were seven churches in the parish.

The Auchterarder Case and its consequent Great Disruption radically altered the structure of society in Scotland. It did not abolish patronage or privilege, but it gave others the confidence to walk away from it if they had the means to do so. The Great Disruption also marked the end of the Church's dominance of society. Secular bodies began to take control of education, poor relief and other services.

Just as the Peace of Auchterarder in the sixteenth century first legally recognised the Protestant cause in Scotland, and the Auchterarder Creed of the early eighteenth century sparked the debate on free-thinking that evolved into the European Enlightenment, so the Auchterarder Case of the nineteenth century had a global impact.

For centuries, Scots had gone abroad to fight and to trade. Now there was a new career option. From 1843 the vast majority of Scottish Christian missionaries, to the countries of the British Empire and beyond, formally adopted the principles that had been first spelled out in Auchterarder. Like the early Celtic missionaries who had come to Scotland with St Columba, nineteenth-century Scots missionaries were largely from vigorous new denominations that had reacted against the establishment.

Their teaching still resonates today, interpreted in many ways. For example, it became a tenet of USA foreign policy that existing authority may be overthrown in the name of righteous intervention.

The right to freedom of thought and expression have always been fiercely debated in the Auchterarder area. As long ago as the seventh century, there were local squabbles about the way church affairs should be run. It would be unwise to think that these debates are over.

32

The Coming of the Railways

In which the teenage daughter of the Duke of Strathearn inherits the throne,
while we see a steam-powered social revolution, and anticipate a working canary

In October 1834, the Houses of Parliament were destroyed by fire. Only the mediaeval Westminster Hall and the cloisters of St Stephen's Chapel escaped. The cause was not a revolutionary attack, like the failed Gunpowder Plot of 1605, but a burning of out-of-date office records which went spectacularly wrong.

Out of the ashes rose the buildings that symbolise London today, with the distinctive clock tower housing Big Ben, whose chimes give authority to today's news headlines. Sir Charles Barry, assisted by the brilliant young Gothic Revival enthusiast Augustus Welby Pugin, designed the new Houses of Parliament. Parliament accepted the architectural proposals in 1836. It took thirty years to complete the work.

Parliament had been reformed. Now it was rebuilt. In 1837, as work began, another institution reinvented itself. King William IV, last of the Hanoverian kings who had ruled Britain since 1714, died. In his last few days, as his heart and lungs grew weaker, he announced that he wanted to live to see another anniversary of the Battle of Waterloo on 18 June. Plain-spoken, sentimental, French-hating and stubborn to the last, he got his wish. He died two days later.

His eighteen-year-old niece succeeded him to the throne. She was the only child of George III's fourth son, Edward Duke of Kent and Strathearn. He was a harsh disciplinarian and a hypocritical spendthrift. He died of a fever when his daughter was only eight months old. She shared the Christian name of her mother, Victoria of Saxe-Coburg, sister of the Belgian King Leopold I. Little was expected of the youngster but, as Queen Victoria, she became Britain's longest-reigning monarch and gave her name to the most successful era of British prestige and culture.

Lord Melbourne became the new queen's trusted friend and mentor. She also received guidance in a kindly, practical correspondence with her uncle, the Belgian king. Small, energetic and astute, Victoria quickly understood the political issues of the day, as seen from several perspectives. Her grasp of the mechanisms of government disconcerted Sir Robert Peel, whose Tories brought about the fall of Melbourne's Whig administration in 1839. As previous Prime

Ministers had done, Peel requested the resignation of the current Ladies of the Royal Household, intending to install his own political place-women. Victoria refused. Peel resigned on a point of principle, expecting Victoria to back down. She did not. Instead, she invited Lord Melbourne to form a new government.

The new queen was no old-fashioned autocrat, but she would not let herself be bullied. Politically, she was caricatured as favouring the elderly Whig oligarchy. The truth was more complex. She needed the companionship of someone her own age. She fell in love with her cousin, Prince Albert of Saxe-Coburg Gotha, who was a few months younger than her. He was elegant, hard-working and liked practical jokes. He also had a strong sense of duty and a lively interest in modern culture and industry. Victoria and Albert married on 10 February 1840. The following year, Lord Melbourne resigned as Prime Minister, forced out of office by a vote of no confidence carried by the new Tory majority in Parliament. Albert, as Prince Consort, had no formal role in the machinery of government, but his wide-ranging interests, energy and calm encouragement were invaluable in helping Victoria deal with party politicians.

The Reform Act of 1832 had helped the middle classes. Its passing prompted a working-class demand for equal rights. In 1838, the People's Charter was published, demanding that all men be given the vote. One Chartist leader, William Lovett, had proposed that women should be given the vote too, but his colleagues told him that such a ridiculous demand would damage the credibility of the Chartist movement. There were Chartist riots, particularly in industrial towns. At the same time, two middle-class radicals, John Bright and Richard Cobden, formed the Anti-Corn Law League to abolish restrictive trading practices and reduce food prices.

Robert Peel became Prime Minster for the second time in September 1841. The nation's finances, having barely recovered from the enormous costs of the Napoleonic Wars, were heavily depleted by a new war in Afghanistan. It began in 1837 as a British attempt to counter Russian influence, but degenerated into an expensive muddle, with thousands of casualties, as all wars in this difficult terrain tend to become. Peel withdrew British troops from Afghanistan in 1842.

On 20 January 1843, Peel and his Secretary Edward Drummond, of the Strathearn family, were walking from Drummond's family-owned Charing Cross Bank in London, when Daniel M'Naghten from Glasgow leaped at them with a gun. Peel was unharmed. Edward Drummond was shot dead. At the trial, evidence was produced that M'Naghten was what today would be called a paranoid schizophrenic. He was therefore not sentenced to death, but committed for life to an asylum for the insane.

Amid disquiet over the lack of a hanging, a Parliamentary debate led to the formation by the Law Lords of the M'Naghten Rules, which gave the first clear legal definition of insanity. The M'Naghten rules stated that a plea of insanity could only be accepted if the accused's 'disease of the mind' prevented him from understanding what he was doing or knowing it was wrong.

Peel's government was helped by fine weather and good harvests in the early 1840s, but plunged into crisis in the Irish potato famine of 1845. Blight destroyed the staple food of Irish peasants. Thousands died. Peel reluctantly persuaded his divided Tory cabinet to repeal the Corn Laws and allow cheap imports of grain to help the starving. The cabinet decision was leaked to *The Times*, probably by George Gordon, 4th Earl of Aberdeen, which published the momentous news on 4 December 1845 before Parliament had been told. Peel felt obliged to resign as Prime Minister but his Tory colleagues could not agree on a replacement, so he continued at the head of the government. The Corn Laws were abolished on 15 May 1846. The aged Duke of Wellington saw the Bill through the House of Lords, putting sympathy for his native Ireland above his Tory protectionist instincts.

The Whigs were by now a spent force electorally, unable to form a viable opposition, although several of their leaders remained influential. The Tories obliged the nation by warring among themselves and splitting into two parties from which voters could choose. Peel resigned on 29 June 1846. John, 1st Earl Russell, the Whig grandee who had introduced the 1832 Reform Bill and came round to supporting the repeal of the Corn Laws, became Prime Minister. He headed a largely Tory protectionist cabinet, egged on by rising stars like Benjamin Disraeli. The free-trade Peelites, including future Prime Ministers Lord Aberdeen, Spencer Compton Cavendish, who became 8th Duke of Newcastle, and William Gladstone, formed a new political party, which evolved into the Liberals.

Prominent among the new Liberals was the Scot James Broun-Ramsay, 10th Earl of Dalhousie, who had been Peel's President of the Board of Trade and had retained his office in 1846 under Russell in order to implement the regulations that he had devised for Britain's expanding railway system. A year later, Dalhousie, aged thirty-five, became the youngest Governor General of India. He promoted railway building on a massive scale to open up and modernise the sub-continent.

Railways were first created in Britain to haul minerals. In the mines and above ground, iron tracks were laid so that ponies and horses could haul wagons more efficiently. The first wagons to carry passengers appeared on the little Oystermouth Railway on Swansea Bay in South Wales in 1806. The introduction of steam-driven engines transformed the railways. On 27 September 1825, a crowd marvelled to see a steam engine pull trucks of coal and a wagon with passengers from Stockton to Darlington in north-east England. The following year, two Scottish lines were opened to haul coal: the Dalkeith and Edinburgh Railway and the Monklands and Kirkintilloch Railway.

The railways spread fast. New companies attracted investors. By the late 1830s, industrial Central Scotland had several lines. To create a coherent network, big companies swallowed up little ones. The 1831 Glasgow and Garnkirk evolved into the giant Caledonian Railway. The Monklands Railways combined with Edinburgh and Glasgow Railway to become the North British.

Victorian business enterprise exploited new technology. The Reform Act of 1832 gave a political voice to the middle classes. Written communication remained a privilege for the rich. From the 1830s, a daily stagecoach from Perth to Glasgow stopped at the Star Hotel in Auchterarder, carrying parcels and mail. However, the cost of sending a letter from Scotland to London had risen to over a shilling (5p). Members of Parliament and senior officials could send letters at public expense and often let their chums use the service free. The mail service was a jumble of contrary local practices.

Rowland Hill from Worcestershire led the movement for postal reform, proposing a clear, standardised service. He succeeded. From 10 June 1840, the middle classes could afford to express themselves by letter. A new nationwide flat rate Penny Post (0.4p) was a boon to business and gossip. Families, which scattered in search of work, could communicate.

In 1842 the London to Newcastle postal service switched from road to rail. In 1847 the service was extended north to Edinburgh. Freight and mail were profitable. Comfortable railway carriages were designed to attract paying customers away from the old horse-drawn stagecoaches. When Victoria came to the throne in 1837, the journey from Edinburgh or Glasgow to London took two full days, bumping along rough roads. In winter, it could take much longer. By 1848, with the opening of the West Coast railway route, passengers could arrive at their destination in only twelve hours.

Railways reached Auchterarder in 1848 with the opening of the Scottish Central Railway between Stirling and Perth. A line was proposed to run north of the Ruthven Water, close to the town, but some townspeople opposed it. Instead, Auchterarder Station was built near Kincardine Woods, an inconvenient mile south of the town, a decision regretted ever since. Nevertheless, tourists poured in and agricultural produce poured out.

In 1856, another station, Crieff Junction (now Gleneagles Station), was built a mile south-west of the town to serve a new branch line, which ran through the Strathallan Estate, stopping at Tullibardine and other small stations on the way to Crieff. Local lawyer A.G. Reid noted that this station could have been sited much nearer to Auchterarder, but for local apathy. Railway companies were aggressive entrepreneurs. By 1865 the Caledonian Railway had bought up all the railway companies in the Auchterarder area.

The Caledonian Railway era promoted tourism, branding Crieff, 'The Montpellier of Scotland' and marketing Auchterarder Golf Course, opened in 1892, on railway posters. The town left in ruins by the Jacobites was now a smart tourist destination.

At the east end of the High Street soon after 1848, the Railway Hotel (now the Craigrossie Hotel) was built with a colourful sculpture of a locomotive above the entrance. It stands opposite Abbey Road, which leads down over the Ruthven to Auchterarder Station.

Not every railway enterprise was successful. After stone was quarried from a site just south of today's public park to build the massive railway viaduct across Kincardine Glen, it was thought that there might be a coal seam in the same area. Railway engines needed huge quantities of coal and any local source was potentially valuable. A Coal Bore was dug in the 1840s, but proved impractical when it hit two powerful springs of water. The Coal Bore remains visible today, as a little hollow near the Gelly Burn and the big Granny Stane.

The digging was not wasted. A hundred years later, the Town Council tapped one of the springs to bring pure water and fun to the paddling pool in the Public Park. 'Health and Safety' paranoia, which swept through public service in the late twentieth century, turned the paddling pool water off again.

The Auchterarder area had a more significant impact on the mining industry.

The distinguished physiologist J.S. Haldane, of the Gleneagles family, was called to investigate the Tylorstown Colliery Disaster in the Rhondda Valley in Wales in 1896. Described as 'a medical detective' by *The Times*, J.S. Haldane worked out that the greatest loss of life in the mines was caused, not by explosion or lack of oxygen, but by carbon monoxide poisoning. A practical man, Haldane taught miners to take canaries or mice, in portable cages, down the mines, which would show the ill effects of poison gas long before it became dangerous to humans. His brilliantly simple system saved many lives.

The coming of the railways had brought a building boom to Auchterarder. Some grand houses had already been built in the early nineteenth century.

James Drummond, later 8th Viscount Strathallan, commissioned Robert Smirke in 1817 to remodel Strathallan Castle in classical style. Smirke, an accomplished watercolour painter as well as an architect, visited and recorded the Parthenon and other buildings in Greece in 1803. Like Robert Adam, Smirke used classical columns for the façades of his public buildings and grand country houses, such as Strathallan. Smirke had already designed the County Buildings facing the Tay in Perth and went on to build The British Museum and other public buildings in London.

In 1831, Captain James Hunter commissioned Auchterarder House from the architect William Burn, a passionate antiquarian with a fondness for crow-stepped gables and strapwork balustrades. It was built on Powhillock Road, which ran from the eastern edge of the town to St Mackessog's Church, beside the Kirkton Burn. The road was later renamed Hunter Street.

Around 1840, Gillespie Graham, who had married Margaret Graham of Orchill, remodelled The Old House of Orchill with fantastic Gothic and Jacobean detail.

William, 9th Viscount Strathallan was an early photographer. His first surviving photograph shows him in front of Strathallan Castle in 1842. The Castle still has a photographic darkroom with red glass, which he built in 1860. Soon after, he moved his family to Machany House. Strathallan Castle was rented. One tenant, Colonel James Reid Stewart, an ironmonger from Glasgow, replumbed the castle and built a turbine house near Mill of Machany, making Strathallan Castle one of the first houses in Scotland to have an electricity supply.

In 1849, William Young, who had developed from a radical lawyer into a prosperous businessman and civic dignitary, employed the Perthshire architect Andrew Heiton to build Belvidere (now Ochil Tower School), a confident, elegant house off the High Street, looking towards the Ochils. William Young was also the agent for the Union Bank of Scotland and founder of generations of Auchterarder lawyers and activists on behalf of the town.

By 1855, architectural fashion had changed. Queen Victoria's Scottish Baronial extravaganza at Balmoral set the tone for Cloan, another Haldane house, which was remodelled by the versatile Andrew Heiton with French château detail.

In 1869, Alexander Mackintosh, an Edinburgh advocate, commissioned the promising young architect William Leiper to build Coll Earn House, its Scottish Baronial turrets balanced by light, airy Arts and Crafts windows. Leiper went on to win international acclaim for his handsome Sun Life Building on West George Street, Glasgow, and the extraordinary colourful Templeton's Carpet

Factory on Glasgow Green. At Coll Earn House, Mackintosh's daughters, Dorothy and Emily, discreetly portrayed in a stained-glass window designed by Daniel Cottier, still shine down.

In 1887, William Mallis whose boot and shoe factory had thrived behind Shepherd's Wynd, built a fine villa, Castlebrae, nearby. It is now a Police Federation Convalescent Home.

In 1882, William Leiper returned to build Ruthven Towers (now a nursing home) on Abbey Road as a fine Scottish Baronial home for the owner of Hally's Mill at the foot of the road.

Beside mill-owner William Hally's splendid warehouse (now Watson Hogg's) a row of villas grew along New Street, later named Montrose Road after the seventeenth-century cavalier hero. The largest of these villas is Drumcharry, built by the lawyer A.G. Reid, who wrote the *The Annals of Auchterarder,* published in 1899.

The Auchterarder area had never seen such a volume of high-quality, confident building. Work was provided for local tradesmen. The huge houses required large staffs to maintain them. The rich were doing rather well. Some others were not.

33

Industrial Magnates and Radical Weavers

In which we see more revolutions, visit an exhibition and
see a factory owner and a radical worker acting in harmony

Ever since the Glorious Revolution of 1688, the role of the British monarch has increasingly been as the symbolic figurehead of the ship of state, not as the captain. A few of these figureheads, like George IV and Edward VIII, have been short-term gilded effigies, but constitutional stability has its advantages. Long-serving monarchs, with a broad perspective and energetic sense of duty, like Queen Victoria and Queen Elizabeth II, have been invaluable to the ever-changing politicians who have tried to navigate Britain through troubled times.

In France, the revolution of 1789 set the precedent for constitutional instability. In quick succession came the bloodthirsty First Republic, the Napoleonic Empire, the restored Bourbon King Louis XVIII and his brother King Charles X, who was forced to abdicate in 1830.

To replace Charles X, the French chose the eldest son of Louis Philippe, Duke of Orleans, who had been a hard-drinking gambler and member of the Bourbon royal family. He had changed his name to Philippe Egalité (Equality) in a rush of revolutionary fervour. Although he voted for the execution of King Louis XVI, he was sent to the guillotine in 1792 along with his royal relatives. His son, also named Louis Philippe, escaped from the French revolution and drifted through Switzerland, the USA and England before settling in Paris, retaining the populist Egalité surname. In 1830, Louis Philippe was made Lieutenant General of France and then was crowned king.

Just as in Britain, there was great pressure for electoral reform in France in 1830. The Reform Act of 1832 granted democratic power to the British middle classes, making it against their interests to indulge in revolution. King Louis Philippe did the opposite in France, introducing increasingly repressive measures. He lasted as long as 1848 only because the French were equally suspicious of his rival Louis Napoleon from the alternative French royal house of Bonaparte. In February 1848, King Louis Philippe fled to England and lived discreetly as 'Mr Smith', just as Richard Cromwell became 'Mr Clarke' when he was forced to abdicate as Lord Protector of England in 1659 and fled to France.

In December 1848, Louis Napoleon was elected President of France to popular acclaim. Like his predecessors, he seemed to offer modern democracy. Like them, he changed his ways. By 1851, he had alienated the Constitutional Assembly. On 2 December 1851, with the help of the French army, he declared himself Emperor Napoleon III.

Instability in France was good for a Britain that was more united than ever. The 400-year-long Stewart dynasty's erratic intrigues with France against England had been finally crushed with Bonnie Prince Charlie's defeat at Culloden in 1746, an event hailed by the Presbytery of Auchterarder. During the Napoleonic Wars, there was no significant Scottish support for France.

Peace and the railways brought Scotland and England even closer. Students so admired the progressively reformed British constitution that Robert Peel became the first Prime Minister to be elected Rector of Glasgow University. The main beneficiaries of the new national harmony were industrial magnates and traders. The repeal of the Navigation Acts in 1849 reduced freight charges and increased British mercantile trade. Both Perth and Dundee had improved their docks in the peaceful period after the Napoleonic wars. Now raw materials flowed from across the British Empire to be turned into profitable merchandise.

John Pullar, a Perth weaver, had built up a business in the late eighteenth century, cashing in on the new demand for waxed green cotton cloth for umbrellas. His company survived the downturn caused by Napoleon's blockades of British ports, and flourished with the arrival of railways. In 1851, distribution became cheaper with cut-price railway parcel rates to London. The reshaped company, John Pullar and Son, Silk Dyers, went from strength to strength. Pullars developed a huge factory in Mill Street in Perth, employing over 400 by the time they received a royal warrant from Queen Victoria in 1856. Sadly, today the building no longer generates wealth for the local economy, but houses hundreds of local authority officials whose salaries are paid from public funds.

Dundee became known as 'Juteopolis' in the mid nineteenth century. Bales of jute were shipped from India and turned into sacking and other fabrics for industrial and agricultural use. Until plastic sacks appeared in the mid twentieth century, jute was the packaging material used for delivering essential bulky goods, ranging from potatoes to coal.

All this international trade required new ships. Glasgow had become a centre of Scotland's coal and iron industries, well placed for shipbuilding. John Wood of Port Glasgow built Henry Bell's revolutionary steamship the *Comet* as early as 1812. The Clyde was dredged to create new shipyards at Govan, Whiteinch and elsewhere. Clydeside became famous for its sturdy, ocean-going steamships.

Auchterarder, far inland, had a different industrial development. The banning of Highland Dress, after the 1745 Jacobite rebellion, forced handloom weavers to abandon their traditional craft skills and instead make cheap, dull grey cloth for city dwellers. In Auchterarder, the woollen industry declined until tartan came back into fashion.

In Auchterarder in the late eighteenth and early nineteenth centuries, handloom weavers worked on contract to merchants who supplied them with machine-spun cotton yarn to turn into cloth. Many houses on Auchterarder

High Street had a weaving shed attached, and enough land to graze a cow and grow some potatoes and kail.

The experiment at Boreland Park in 1763, where veterans of the Seven Years War were allocated housing with cheap rents, was a mixed success. Many took jobs as weavers, disliked the working conditions and left the area.

The victory at Waterloo in 1815 ended the wars with France, but the cost of war brought a downturn to the British economy. Unemployment increased. Handloom weavers struggled to survive, working long hours and supplementing their income with any other work they could find.

Their lot improved when King George IV revived the demand for tartan in his 1823 visit to Scotland. It increased enormously twenty years later, when Queen Victoria built her Scottish fantasy at Balmoral. She wrote enthusiastically about life in rural Scotland in her holiday journals, which became best-sellers when they were published. Scottish cloth, rugs and shawls were must-have items.

Around 1840, William Hally set up a business at Boreland Park. He bought wool, contracted handloom weavers to make it into cloth, and took the finished product to Glasgow by cart. When the railways arrived in 1848, William Hally was quick to use them to bring flax and yarn from the docks in Dundee. He stopped taking finished cloth by cart to Glasgow. Instead he dispatched it from the new Auchterarder Railway Station. In 1863, he took over an old malt barn in the Castleton and employed weavers himself. This was the first industrial weaving mill in Auchterarder. William Hally became a successful businessman and Provost of Auchterarder.

Business boomed. By 1869, Hally's Castleton Mill had 150 power looms, driven by a steam engine. Tweeds, shirting, shawls and handkerchiefs sold well. On the corner of Montrose Road, Hally built a big warehouse, which in 1948 became Watson Hogg's. It is now part of Gleneagles Knitwear, still an independent Hally family business.

In 1872, William Hally built a 25-power-loom mill at Ruthven Vale on the south side of the Ruthven, where the water supply was better than at the Castleton. Ruthven Vale was quickly extended to take in all the work previously done at his mills in the Castleton and at Dallerie in Crieff. Castleton Mill closed in 1880. By 1892, Hally's Ruthven Vale Mill had 540 looms, producing 80,000 yards of cloth per week, mainly woollen shirting and pyjama cloth. Ruthven Vale Mill switched from steam power in 1910, installing a gas plant. The factory maintained its weaving output till the 1960s and produced knitwear until 1996.

In Auchterarder, more new mills sprang up by the Ruthven Water at the foot of Abbey Road on lands that had previously belonged to the Abbey of Inchaffray. The water was not used to power a mill-wheel, but to supply the boilers for massive steam engines. One company, Peter Young's Mill, failed quickly. Others became a crucial part of the local economy, drawing workers from miles around.

Auchterarder's other leading mill entrepreneur was James White, who built a factory in the 1840s at Kinnoull Place on the North Crofts. It was known as Factory Wynd. Today, it is Hanover Place. It held only hand looms. In 1877, he replaced it with White's Mill, also known as Glenruthven Mill, on the north side of the Ruthven Water, opposite the much larger Hally's Mill. White bought 100 looms from the Anderson Foundry in Glasgow. The mill produced high-quality fabrics, tartans, worsteds, silk, taffeta and fine poplin.

In about 1919, James White's son, Robert, purchased a second-hand steam engine, reputed to have come from a steamboat that had been operating since the 1820s and had carried the composer Mendelssohn on his famous voyage to Staffa and Fingal's Cave. Victorian technology was durable.

By the time Glenruthven Mill was remodelled in 1979, it had the last working textile steam engine in Scotland, its sixty power-looms producing fine cotton cloth for the bespoke shirt makers of London's Jermyn Street, and Hathaway in the USA, plus lightweight woollen cloth for upmarket brands like Jaeger. It closed in 1983, unable to compete with cheaper foreign imports.

Britain's economic expansion in the first decade of Queen Victoria's reign gave Britain an unrivalled mercantile confidence and authority. Albert, Queen Victoria's Prince Consort, took the lead in organising an event 'to give the world a picture of the point of industrial development at which the whole of mankind has arrived and a new starting point for further exertions'. The Great Exhibition of 1851 was housed in a giant new building made entirely of glass and iron, designed by Joseph Paxton. The Crystal Palace was built in Hyde Park in London and displayed an astonishing array of manufactured goods, machinery, sculpture, painting, raw materials and environmental information. Six million visitors to the Great Exhibition marvelled at how the new Steam Age united art and science.

The Great Exhibition drew displays from all over the world, but visitors were left in no doubt that the host nation was the global leader in trade and industrial innovation. Many of the goods were at a price that the middle classes could afford. Scottish exhibits ranged from fashionable Paisley shawls and Edinburgh fine silver to magnificent carpets and pottery from Glasgow.

British prestige was at its height. In Central and Eastern Europe, old regimes began to totter. Hapsburg Austria was no longer the power it had been when it ruled the Holy Roman Empire. It lost ground in Italy in 1849 when the new French president Louis Napoleon sent an army to occupy Rome. Pope Pius IX fled. Count Johan Joseph Radetzky battled to hold Lombardy and Venice for Austria. Giuseppe Mazzini led a campaign to unite Italy and drive out both the French and the Austrians. A movement to unite Germany was also growing, led by the Prussian King Frederick William IV and the astute statesman Otto von Bismarck.

The new young Austrian Emperor Franz Joseph I suppressed an independence movement in Hungary in 1849. The Hungarian freedom fighter Louis Kossuth escaped to Turkey, which was itself struggling to hold on to its old empire. Tsar Nicholas I of Russia described Turkey as 'the sick man of Europe' and, on the pretext of protecting the rights of Greek Orthodox Christians in the Turkish Empire, invaded Moldavia and Wallachia in early July 1853. The invasion threatened all European trade on the River Danube. In response, Austria massed troops on its eastern frontier. On 5 October 1853, Turkey formally declared war on the Russian invader. To prevent Russia gaining a port on the Black Sea with access to Mediterranean trade, Britain and France, now allies after centuries of enmity, sent a joint fleet to the Dardanelles on 22 October. Russia replied by destroying a Turkish fleet at Sinope on 10 November. The allied fleet sailed into the Black Sea on 4 January 1854, ready for action.

The confidence and sure touch of the Great Exhibition only three years before was now sadly missing in the British government. Lord John Russell's administration had given way in February 1852 to a new government led by the conservative orator Edward Stanley, 14th Earl of Derby. He lasted less than a year before a coalition administration led by George Gordon, 4th Earl of Aberdeen took office in December 1852.

Faced with the crisis in Turkey, Aberdeen's government dithered. France, especially after Napoleon III declared himself emperor in 1851, was much more inclined to action. Eventually, Britain agreed to send troops to the Crimea on the north shore of the Black Sea to besiege the Russian-held port of Sevastopol. Fitzroy James Somerset, 1st Baron Raglan, who had lost his sword arm at the Battle of Waterloo in 1815, led the British force. Lord Raglan combined with French Marshall St Arnaud to defeat the Russian Prince Alexander Menshikov at the Alma on 20 September 1854. Disaster followed at Balaclava on 25 October when the Light Brigade lost two thirds of its men to Russian artillery in a foolhardy cavalry charge. The poet Alfred Tennyson commemorated the epic blunder in thunderous verse. 'The Charge of The Light Brigade' was taught to schoolboys to demonstrate the difference between wasteful arrogance and sound imperial authority.

There were many who questioned imperial authority itself. Not everyone in Britain earned a share of the economic boom. Auchterarder had its share of poverty, particularly among the seven hundred handloom weavers who worked there in the mid nineteenth century. In Scotland, weavers have had a long tradition of radical politics. Low pay, monotonous work, and arbitrary changes in product demand combined to make weavers regard the moneyed classes with sarcastic scepticism or open hostility.

Thomas Stewart (1827–1902) was an Auchterarder weaver who used his considerable intelligence, energy and sardonic humour to poke fun at snobbery and sycophancy. In a poem, 'The Queen's "Visit" to Auchterarder in 1849', he describes how townsfolk dressed up in their Sunday best and walked to Auchterarder Station to gawp at Queen Victoria, but

> She comes! She comes! Our gracious Queen!
>   For see the train's in view;
> She came and passed – but ne'er was seen.
>   The train like lichtnin' flew.

Tom Stewart was not a negative protestor. He made things happen. In 1857, he and other Auchterarder men, including Provost William Hally, arranged a visit to Auchterarder for the great Hungarian freedom fighter, Louis Kossuth. A carriage was hired from the Star Hotel to bring Kossuth from Auchterarder Station. Tom Stewart delivered a formal welcome. Kossuth was a major European celebrity and a political activist who favoured nationalism and republicanism. It was a daring and remarkable achievement to bring him to Auchterarder. It is perhaps even more remarkable that, at a time of acute class-consciousness, Hally, the mill-owner, and Stewart, the radical weaver, worked together to make it happen.

When the Prince of Wales was married on 10 March 1863, the people of Auchterarder decorated the town with flags and bunting. Three triumphal arches were built across the High Street. At night, there was a firework display. Tom Stewart made an alternative demonstration. He printed in large illuminated letters on his window blind:

Down with Kingcraft and Flunkeyism.
Stand up for rights of labour.

The same day, *The Perthshire Advertiser* reported, 'Many workers are leaving the district in consequence of the scarcity of work. Webs are getting scarce and wages low. We do not recollect of seeing our town in such a miserable state as at present. Weavers, especially those who have families depending on their labour, are looking forward to the summer months with fear and trembling.'

The American Civil War was raging, cutting off exports from the cotton fields of the South. Sadly, six weeks later, Tom Stewart and his family had to leave Auchterarder to find work in Glasgow, where he lived for the rest of his life.

The radical inheritance of Auchterarder weavers lived on. Ewan MacColl, whose mother came from Auchterarder weaving stock, was a singer-songwriter who led the mid-twentieth-century folk song revival, celebrating working class values. His anti-establishment lyrics could hardly be more different from Lady Caroline Nairne's earlier sentimental local Jacobite songs, though MacColl's 'The First Time Ever I Saw Your Face' is as tender a love ballad as anything Lady Nairne wrote.

Another descendant of radical nineteenth-century Auchterarder is Tony Benn, caricatured for his 'loony left' politics, but an astute Secretary of State for Energy from 1975 to 1979 during the early years of the North Sea oil boom. Benn's great-grandfather was Peter Eadie of Auchterarder, who invented the 'ring-traveller', a weaving device to twist textile fabrics and guide them on to the bobbin to make a flawless yarn. Eadie was born at The Muirton in 1837 in the first few weeks of Queen Victoria's reign. He is a good example of the enterprising Scottish Victorian engineer, working abroad then returning to Scotland. Peter Eadie was famous for his scathing socialist wit and became Provost of Paisley, a large town full of radical weavers, in 1905.

In the nineteenth century, some men became very rich through railways. James Reid began as an apprentice blacksmith in Ayrshire. He rose to become the owner of the huge Hyde Park North British Locomotive Works in Springburn in Glasgow, which built engines for railways throughout the British Empire.

He became President of the Institution of Engineers and Shipbuilders and chairman of Glasgow's Tramway Company. Like other industrial magnates, Reid wanted a prestigious country mansion. He bought Auchterarder House, employing one of Glasgow's leading architectural firms, Burnet Son & Campbell, to remodel the front and interior in a Jacobean style. He suffered a tragic blow in 1882 when his eldest son, aged 24, was killed in a hunting accident.

Reid was also a patron of the arts. He became president of Glasgow's Fine Arts Institute. While other industrialists chose the safer option of buying 'old masters', he built up a superb collection of works by contemporary painters like Constable, Turner and Corot. When James Reid died in 1894, aged 72, his sons donated his collection to Glasgow Art Gallery. He was also commemorated in Springburn by a statue sculpted by Goscombe John, one of the greatest of the New Sculpture artists, whose modern realism had replaced late Victorian pompous stodge. As noted above, in The Great Disruption chapter, James Reid's sons, Edward and Andrew, were also generous benefactors to Auchterarder.

From the middle of the nineteenth century, Auchterarder had a more diversified economy. It was no longer just the market town for the surrounding agricultural area. At their peak around 1900, the mills employed about 450 women and 250 men. The rest of the population worked mainly in trades or agriculture. For women, domestic service in the new big houses was a major source of employment. The number of shops rapidly increased, but office workers were few.

Auchterarder had a thriving boot- and shoe-making factory in the nineteenth and early twentieth centuries, run by the Mallis family. By 1860, Auchterarder had two tanneries. William Mallis's factory had a steam engine to power leather-cutting machines. It lay behind today's Shepherd's Wynd, where he also provided a hall for the use of local Black Watch volunteer soldiers. Most boots were made for the local market, but at the end of the century a contract was won for boots for soldiers fighting in the Boer War in South Africa.

The town also had distilleries at the Ruthven Water and a substantial brewery, Carmichael's, at Newton Feus.

Alongside successful private enterprise, the Co-operative Movement sprang up to provide poorer people with good food and household goods at lower prices, plus the benefits of co-ownership in the form of dividends, based on how much an individual spent. The Co-op 'divvy' still exists, though now in electronic form.

The first Co-op in Auchterarder was the Baking Co-operative in 1846. The Auchterarder United Co-operative arrived in 1860 after the Feus was developed. The Provident Co-operative came to the Townhead in 1866, followed by the City of Perth Co-operative in 1871. Later, Aberuthven gained a Co-op, known as 'The Store', handily beside the bus stop on the south side of the main street.

These societies merged until finally in 1955 the national Scottish Co-operative Wholesale Society was formed. Not until well after the Second World War did most wealthier local families patronise the Co-op. Today, it would be absurd to avoid it on social or political grounds.

34

Victorian Valour
and Public Services

*In which we smell a military mutiny caused by fat, hear three wars to protect Britain's
drug trade, and see very local government efficiently run by very local people*

The Crimean War in the 1850s, like the Afghan Wars in the 1840s, was expensive
in lives and money. British troops suffered appalling conditions after a storm in the
Balkans on 14 November 1854 wrecked ships, with huge loss of military supplies,
clothing and food. Casualties from the Battle of Inkerman on 5 November were
kept in such overcrowded misery in Scutari and other military hospitals that
Nurse Florence Nightingale led a campaign for army sanitation reform. Her
book *Notes on Nursing* in 1859 set the standard for improved training for nurses.

In January 1855, Lord Aberdeen's dithering coalition government fell. Henry
John Temple, 3rd Viscount Palmerston, became Prime Minister and pursued a
more aggressive policy to bring victory in Crimea. On 9 September 1855, the
Russians destroyed the main buildings in the port of Sevastopol and then withdrew
their troops. On 30 March 1856, the Treaty of Paris brought the Crimean War
to an end. Britain, France, Austria and Russia agreed that the Black Sea should
be neutral and that the River Danube should be free for trade. The Turkish
European Empire survived intact until December 1861 when Moldavia and
Wallachia united to form the independent principality of Romania. The original
pretext for the Crimean War, the protection of Christians in the Islamic Turkish
Empire, was forgotten. Like any religious minority, the Christians' position was
precarious. Massacres of Christians in Bulgaria in 1876 and in Armenia in 1894
were deplored in the West but unavenged.

As one war ended, another began. The Governor General of India, James
Broun-Ramsay, 10th Earl, 1st Marquis of Dalhousie, was an energetic young Scot.
He organised road and railway building across the sub-continent. Four thousand
miles of recently invented telegraph system connected the provinces as never
before. He opened the Indian Civil Service up to all British subjects, regardless
of race. Christian missionaries, many of them Scots in the robust, independent
tradition that had spread after the Auchterarder Case and Great Disruption of
1843, set up churches in India. Charles John Canning, son of the liberalising

politician George Canning, succeeded Dalhousie as Governor General of India, just when Dalhousie's policies were meeting serious local opposition.

Throughout any empire, native populations are torn between potential economic advantages offered by their foreign overlords and the familiar customs of their former local rulers. Some Indian princes welcomed the British Empire. Others stirred up rivalries between Hindus, Sikhs, Moslems and Christians. Early in 1857, several Sepoy soldiers in the Punjab refused to touch ammunition for their new Enfield rifles, because they believed the cartridges were greased with a mixture of fat from cows, an animal sacred to Hindus, and fat from pigs, an animal regarded as unclean by Moslems. These previously loyal soldiers were imprisoned as mutineers.

On 10 May 1857 at Meerat, other Sepoys mutinied, freed the eighty-five imprisoned Sepoys and marched south-west to Delhi, where others joined the revolt. The cartridge-grease cultural offence crystallised all the resentment against British rule that had been building up for years. Within weeks, the Indian Mutiny threatened to become a national uprising.

Nana Sahib became the mutineers' leader. On 4 June 1857 he massacred a thousand men, women and children in Kanpur, after promising them a safe conduct from the city. Nana Sahib then besieged the British Residency in Lucknow, which held out till it was relieved on 17 November 1857 by Sir Colin Campbell, who had previously led the Highland Brigade to victory at the Alma in the Crimea in 1854. Campbell then recaptured Kanpur on 6 December 1857. After months of guerrilla warfare, Nana Sahib disappeared, probably into hiding on what is today the Afghanistan–Pakistan border region. In recognition of his military leadership, Colin Campbell, the son of a Glasgow carpenter, was made Baron Clyde in 1858.

At the heart of Campbell's forces was the Black Watch, which served with him at the Alma and Sevastopol. Strathearn was a recruiting ground for the Black Watch ever since the regiment was formed in 1725 to keep the peace in the Highlands after the Jacobite rebellion and burning of Auchterarder. Local soldiers served throughout the British Empire, returning with an international perspective.

Queen Victoria created a new medal in 1854 to honour soldiers who had shown the highest level of bravery. The Victoria Cross is the opposite of a flashy decoration. Quiet, almost dull-looking, it carries the words 'For Valour' and remains today the most highly regarded and rarely bestowed award for heroism. Eight Black Watch soldiers won the Victoria Cross during the Indian Mutiny.

The Governor General earned the nickname 'Clemency Canning' for his moderation after the Indian Mutiny was suppressed. In August 1858, the Crown took over the old East India Company, an early example of the nationalisation of a large industry. Canning became an earl and first Viceroy of India, acting under the guidance of a new British government department. In 1877, to mark forty years as Queen of the British Empire, Victoria was proclaimed Empress of India.

Palmerston's government had ended the Crimean War and dealt with the Indian Mutiny, but it fell in February 1858 because of events nearer home. On 14 January 1858, outside the Paris Opera House, an Italian nationalist activist, Felice Orsini, threw a bomb at the French Emperor Napoleon III, whom he believed was obstructing the unification of Italy. Napoleon III survived, but ten bystanders were killed and many injured. Orsini had given passionate political speeches in Britain. The bomb was made in Birmingham. Palmerston presented a Conspiracy to Murder Bill, aimed at those he saw as foreign terrorists sheltering in Britain.

The previous year in Auchterarder, the Hungarian activist Louis Kossuth had preached national unification to an appreciative audience that valued British unity. Across the centuries, Auchterarder people have been deeply suspicious of those who seek to curtail civil liberties in the name of public order. Others felt the same. The Conspiracy to Murder Bill was flawed and panicky. On 18 February 1858, Parliament threw out the Bill, when public opinion saw it as an attempt to pander to the French and to suppress free speech. Palmerston resigned.

The Earl of Derby returned as Prime Minister but lasted only until June 1859, when Palmerston became Prime Minister again, powerfully aided by William Gladstone as Chancellor and Lord John Russell as Foreign Secretary. Their first task was to deal with the authorities in China who were interfering with Britain's profitable opium trade. The Victorians, with their zeal for information, were generally matter-of-fact about the medicinal and recreational uses of opium. A children's book of the period, *Eva And Her Playmates* by C.M. Smith, gives instructions on how to make narcotics from the opium poppy.

The East India Company began importing opium from China in the late eighteenth century, bribing officials in Canton (Guangzhou) to ignore their Peking (Beijing) government's ban on the trade. The enterprising Scottish trading company Jardine Matheson thrived on the opium trade. Successive British governments supported drug smuggling, causing scuffles in the China Sea, which escalated into war between Britain and China in 1841. The Treaty of Nanking (Nanjing) 1842 ceded Hong Kong to Britain and opened Shanghai and Canton to British and other overseas trade.

A Second Chinese War broke out in 1856, when officials seized the *Arrow*, a British-registered lorcha, a boat of the kind used for drug smuggling and kidnapping young Chinese men to work as coolies in the West Indies and other colonies. Palmerston ordered the bombardment of Canton. As in the Crimean War, British and French fleets worked together. The treaty of Tientsin (Tianjin) on 29 June 1858 introduced the regulation of the opium trade and gave Britain diplomatic representation at Peking and key Chinese ports.

The agreement did not last. The Third Chinese War broke out in June 1859. Palmerston, ever aggressive, sent James Bruce, 8th Earl of Elgin to attack Peking. He burned the Summer Palace on 12 June 1860. The Chinese government agreed the Treaty of Peking two weeks later with further concessions to British trade.

George Chinnery, who died in 1852, was a raffish, opium-smoking artist who made hundreds of sketches of life in Chinese ports, especially Canton and Macau. He painted oil portraits of merchants, officials and European visitors. Chinnery kept exotic mistresses in China and Calcutta, and a British wife, who tried to keep her distance from his moods and debts. Chinnery was closely related to the lairds of Gleneagles, whose main family line adopted the surname Chinnery Haldane and, in the twentieth century, produced another flamboyant artist, the Edinburgh society photographer Brodrick Chinnery Haldane.

Having given an air of legitimacy to Britain's opium trade in China, Palmerston's government turned to matters in Europe. The nationalist movement in Italy was gathering strength, led by the politicians Giuseppe Mazzini and Count Camillo di Cavour and the guerrilla leader Giuseppe Garibaldi. France and Austria fought and conspired with each other to defend their Italian territories. In May 1860, Garibaldi and his thousand Red Shirts seized Sicily and Naples from the French.

In May 1861 at Turin, a parliament representing most of Italy recognised the Sardinian King Victor Emmanuel II as king of a united Italy. Austria clung on to Venice until 1866. The French remained in Rome until 1870, when they withdrew in the midst of a crisis in France itself. Palmerston, despite Queen Victoria and Prince Albert's Austrian sympathies, supported the unification of Italy, just as he believed in a United Kingdom at home.

In 1860, the unification of Germany also took a step forward when the Zollverein, a commercial union of German states led by Prussia, adopted a policy of free trade, excluding Austria. After years of intrigue, Prussia routed Austria at the Battle of Sadowa on 3 July 1866. The astute and ruthless Prince Otto von Bismarck advanced the claims of the Prussian King William I to be Emperor of all Germany. Hungary, afraid of the growing might of Germany, recognised the Austrian Emperor Franz Joseph I as King of Hungary in 1867. Palmerston did not live to see the shift of power in central Europe. After winning a General Election earlier in the year, he died on 18 October 1865. In Scotland, he has one curious legacy. He is the only Prime Minister to have a senior football club ground named after him, Palmerston Park in Dumfries, home of Queen of the South.

Queen Victoria was sympathetic to both Austria and Prussia and torn between their interests. On 14 December 1861, she lost her most trusted advisor, her husband Prince Albert. Exhausted with overwork from the intense thoroughness he put into his many projects, he caught typhoid fever and died soon after. He was only forty-two. Queen Victoria was distraught. She went into mourning, always dressed in black and became increasingly reclusive.

Wars in Afghanistan, Crimea and China had cost Britain dearly. William Gladstone, as Chancellor, tackled the national debt in 1860 by raising the level of income tax and keeping other taxes high. By 1865, his policy had been so successful that, to popular acclaim, he halved the level of income tax and reduced taxes on tea and sugar.

Gladstone was a believer in mass education. In order to make books more affordable, he introduced a Bill in 1860 to abolish the tax on paper, but the House of Lords threw it out. Gladstone then included the repeal of paper duty as part of his 1861 Budget. The Lords did not wish to precipitate a crisis by opposing the Budget. Gladstone had his way. Ever since, each British government has included its financial proposals in comprehensive budgets, usually annually, rather than as many separate parliamentary bills. Tax-free paper made it possible for publishers to print thousands of copies of cheap editions of books, ranging from evangelical theology to popular science and fiction of all kinds. Cheap paper also meant cheap newspapers and more competitive journalism, a phenomenon that subsequent generations of politicians have cursed more often than they have blessed.

Many of today's national institutions were shaped in Victorian Britain. At their best, the twin concepts of civic duty and improvement of public facilities could be harnessed to private enterprise for genuine local good. The 1833 Municipal Reform Act gave Scottish ratepayers a greater say in electing local administrations, which had the right to decide how a town should be run. The life-threatening powers of mediaeval barons were long gone. Ownership of the Barony of Auchterarder, now divided between John Malcolm and Basil Cochrane, brought only the rights of a landlord.

Today's Tudor Café, on the north-west side of the High Street, has the old coat of arms of Auchterarder above its door. It shows the town's biblical motto 'A City Set On A Hill Cannot Be Hid' (Matthew 5:14). In the nineteenth century, the building was the meeting place of the Heritors, landowners and senior members of the Parish Church, who formed the equivalent of a town council. They were responsible for maintaining the church, manse and public school. They also nominated parish ministers and appointed schoolmasters.

The Heritors were involved in most local policy matters, including roads. In practice, landowners paid for road-making out of their own pockets, if they felt it was in the interests of their estates or if money could be made from tolls. Shortly after 1822, the Haldanes of Gleneagles paid for today's A823 from Yetts o' Muckhart through Glendevon as far as Loaninghead, where it crosses today's A9. From that point, the Murrays of Tullibardine picked up the construction bill until the road approached Muthill and the Drummond estate.

The Auchterarder Muir Improvement Act (1860) vested ownership of the Common Muir in Commissioners to manage and improve the land. They allocated areas for a public park and a burial ground, large enough to meet the needs of the expanding Victorian town and still in use today. They also set aside an area for a new market, though the market behind the Star Hotel in the town centre continued until 1970. The Muir Commissioners used profits from land rents to maintain the town's water supply and drains, pave the streets and provide funding towards a town hall and public library. The Muir Commissioners and the Heritors worked closely together.

The Heritors also administered relief to the poor in conjunction with the Kirk Session. This involved providing only 'outdoor relief', enough to keep the destitute alive and encourage them to go away. The 1845 Poor Law (Scotland) Act encouraged institutional 'indoor relief'. In 1863, The United Combination Poorhouse of Upper Strathearn was built at the western edge of the Common Muir of Auchterarder. Ten parishes, from Crieff to Forteviot, subscribed to maintain beds in the 'Poor's House', later called The Strathearn Home. The building still stands today, but has been redeveloped for private housing.

In accordance with Victorian moral principles this was not a dumping ground, but well built to provide 'a house of refuge where inmates should receive liberal and sympathetic treatment'. It housed men and women, elderly and orphans, Protestants and Roman Catholics.

Many stayed briefly, until their health or family circumstances improved. Itinerants from other parts of the country were accommodated, though their expense was less welcome. A telegram refers to the problems of housing 'a girl of feeble mind' until it could be determined where she came from. The Strathearn Home's Parochial Board consisted of men of substance from each parish, including Viscount Strathallan for Blackford, and Murray of Dollerie for Crieff. William Young, the able Auchterarder lawyer, was much involved in running an institution that showed the community's compassion and practicality.

The Strathearn Home was regarded as a good model. In 1864, the same architect, James Campbell Walker, was employed to design the Atholl and Breadalbane Poorhouse at Logierait. There were also cheap, privately run lodging houses for people with low incomes, notably The Ludging Hoose, a bleak tenement at the Townhead in front of today's Glenmaller house, and another rooming house in Shepherd's Wynd where Rafford now stands.

Graham Whitelaw, Conservative MP for Perth 1892–95, was the tenant of Strathallan Castle. He bought land on Orchil Road and, after many delays, a home was built for the poor of Auchterarder, Blackford and Trinity Gask parishes. When he died in 1928, he bequeathed £6,000 for the running of the Whitelaw Home. Decades later, when this home closed, its funds were merged with the Mailer Trust and used for Glencairn House.

The 1892 Burgh Police (Scotland) Act provided for more democratic town councils. Auchterarder set one up in 1894. It met in a new council chamber added to the Aytoun Hall in 1902 to commemorate the Coronation of Edward VII and paid for by public subscription. The Heritors, who had administered the town for centuries, were redundant. Their meeting place was sold. For much of the twentieth century, it was David Treasurer's Fruit and Vegetable Shop. Unlike the old Heritors, the new elected town councillors were generally neither major landowners nor churchmen. Instead, they were mostly tradesmen, some, like the mill owner William Hally, both wealthy and imaginative.

The public staircase to the 1902 council chamber is in the Aytoun Hall. The councillors' own access to the chamber was through a robing room in Girnal House. On the staircase up to the robing room, they installed the most important artwork in Auchterarder, the massive bronze bas-relief 'Homer' by the English 'New Sculpture' artist Harry Bates. The inscription reads, 'His speech flowed from his lips sweeter than honey. Iliad Book 1. 124.'

At first glance, this looks like a self-deprecating joke about the honeyed words of local councillors and officials. Go back to the classical source, however, and you find the line refers to the quarrel that led to the Trojan War. The inscription is double-edged. It pokes fun at glib civic dignitaries, but warns that local disputes can escalate into global conflict.

Those who installed 'Homer' had witnessed the Great Disruption of the Kirk, a culture-changing event that began in Auchterarder. The flood of Scottish missionaries from the Free Churches set the moral tone of much of the English-speaking world for generations to come. The inscription beneath 'Homer' was a reminder to councillors to do their duty. In the refurbishment of 2009–11, 'Homer' was relocated to a corridor.

Within a year, the newly constituted Auchterarder Town Council had to tackle a serious health threat. On 2 February 1895, a fifteen-year-old girl staying in the Ludging Hoose was diagnosed as having smallpox. She had recently worked in a rag store in Glasgow, which had been the source of an epidemic there. The Ludging Hoose was evacuated and much of its furnishings burned.

The girl was quarantined in a moveable hospital, brought from Crieff, set up on the Common Muir. She was effectively treated for two months, given new clothes and her fare paid back to Glasgow. Prompt action prevented a local epidemic, but the cost of closing and refurbishing the Poor House, and providing isolated nursing and other care for the girl, caused the Council rates to be increased.

Taxes are never popular. When Auchterarder adopted the Burgh Police (Scotland) Act in 1894, local people were concerned about the cost of employees' salaries under the new Council. Andrew Deuchars, an Auchterarder tinsmith, gasfitter and town councillor, wrote a doggerel lament:

> The scavenger, the inspector and surveyor maun be paid,
> And the man to licht the lamps at nicht – my friends, I am afraid
> That fivepence ha'penny in the pound is sure to be ower sma'
> To pay for work that maun be done in the burgh area.

Deuchars also fought against 'the demon drink'. In 1894, a Good Templar Hall opened in Abbey Road in Auchterarder as an alternative to the Aytoun Hall for public events. It had a temperance policy, but was not opposed to all fun. Both it and the Aytoun Hall showed silent films as soon as they became available. It is easy to mock the Victorian Temperance Movement and its solemn insistence that temperance and abstinence are the same thing, but they addressed a genuine social problem. The hall is currently a nursery school.

The most robust manifestation of the Temperance Movement, The Salvation Army, is widely respected for providing direct, uncomplicated help to distressed people who have been failed by officialdom. In Auchterarder today, the Salvation Army's brass band music, particularly around Christmas, is accompanied by the sound of local people's coins dropping into collection tins.

The town council was admirably led by Provost William Hally, who set an example by personally donating 100 tons of coal for the unemployed and poor in the bad winter of 1895. He also managed, in 1899, through the Town Council, to persuade William Kempt, General Superintendent of the Caledonian Railways, to provide cheap tickets for mill workers in the autumn holidays.

In 1895, Royal Mail pillar boxes appeared on the High Street. In 1899, the town was linked to the national telegraph system. Just as new legislation made the Heritors redundant in 1892, the Auchterarder Town Council Confirmation Act in 1903 transferred the powers of the Common Muir Commissioners to the Town Council.

Late Victorian Auchterarder still had the mediaeval town market, old Parish Church and the school at its centre, although 'The Lang Toon' was becoming even longer with the development of workers' houses to the east and middle-class villas to the west. In addition, by the end of the nineteenth century, Auchterarder had a row of four buildings which played a major part in the town's civic life. Three still retain their roles: The Aytoun Hall, Girnal House and the Masonic Hall. The fourth, the Medical Hall, housed John Stewart's Dispensary until the late twentieth century.

35

Democracy at Work and Play

In which we see American slaves, Irish rebels, Sudanese dervishes, more voters, schoolteachers, exotic animals, harvest bows and, by jingo, blazing flambeaux

In the mid nineteenth century, while Germany, Italy and other European nations were adopting unified national identities, the United States of America was breaking in two. The northern states were industrialised. Their workers were paid. The southern states were rural with huge cotton and tobacco plantations worked by slaves. In Britain, slavery had been formally discredited as long before as 1772, when the Perthshire lawyer Chief Justice William Murray, 1st Earl of Mansfield, ruled that there was no law to support slavery. It took until 1833 for Parliament to abolish slavery in Britain. British companies continued to depend on importing American cotton and tobacco produced by slaves.

In the early twenty-first century, most British people wear clothes made in Asia by families working in poverty. For the same commercial reasons, Britain tended to back the South when war broke out in the United States, though the official stance was neutral. On 6 November 1860, Abraham Lincoln was elected President of the United States. He believed that the USA was a federal republic whose states were collectively bound by laws made by Congress and the Senate in the capital Washington D.C. Lincoln favoured the abolition of slavery. In February 1861, the southern states broke away to form the Confederate States of America, with Jefferson Davis as President, believing that each state had the right to determine its laws and to enforce slavery if it so wished.

War broke out. On 13 April 1861 the Confederates captured Fort Sumter in Charleston harbour and on 21 July defeated the Federals at the First Battle of Bull Run, driving them away from the Confederate capital, Richmond, Virginia. President Lincoln ordered the blockade of Confederate ports, damaging their trade to Europe and creating a sudden supply crisis, both for British industrial mills and for independent weavers.

In reply in 1862, the Confederates commissioned the warship *Alabama*, built at Birkenhead near Liverpool in England. The Federal ambassador protested to the British Foreign Secretary Lord John Russell. In an expedient muddle, the British government ordered the *Alabama* to be detained, but she sailed away with a largely British crew to inflict severe damage on Federal vessels until the

Federal cruiser *Kearsage* sank her on 19 June 1864. William Gladstone, the British Chancellor, stirred acrimony by saying that the Confederate president Jefferson Davis 'had made a nation'. British anti-slavery opinion was outraged. After long legal battles, the British government paid £3 million in compensation for the damage caused by the *Alabama* and other British-built vessels.

While Gladstone was showing his sympathies for the rural slave-owning American Confederacy, one of his pet projects was taking shape in rural Perthshire. Gladstone admired prestigious English public schools like Eton and Harrow and disliked the more democratic Scottish Presbyterian way of education. He joined with the Scottish Tractarian James Hope to found Glenalmond College, ten miles north of Perth, where young gentry could receive an Episcopal education in a cloistered setting. Begun in 1843, the splendid hall in Glenalmond's tranquil quadrangle was built between 1861 and 1863 just as the guns were thundering in the American Civil War.

The Victorians believed in Christian virtues, though the precise definition of these virtues remained elusive. Perthshire gained a Presbyterian counterpart to Glenalmond in 1860, with the construction of Morrison's Academy in Crieff. It was endowed by Thomas Morrison from nearby Muthill who had become a successful Edinburgh businessman. Both Glenalmond and Morrison's Academy believed in 'muscular Christianity', a chilly combination of vigorous sports and rote education enforced by corporal punishment. It was a formula with enduring appeal to parents. As a result, the author of this book received a robust Victorian education almost a century later, being required to sing songs like *The British Grenadiers*, celebrating Empire-building warfare, and *The Campdown Races*, a jolly image of life in the American Confederacy.

At first the Confederate armies were victorious but on 7 April 1862 they were forced to retreat south after the Battle of Shiloh. The Federal President Abraham Lincoln issued a proclamation on 22 September 1862 freeing all slaves, although he was not in a position to enforce emancipation in the South. On 13 July 1863, the Confederate General Robert E Lee was defeated at the Battle of Gettysburg. Federal Generals Ulysses S Grant and William T Sherman relentlessly drove the Confederates further south, burning the commercial centre of Atlanta on 2 September 1864. On 9 April 1865, General Lee surrendered, ending the American Civil War. On 14 April, the victorious President Abraham Lincoln was shot dead by an assassin in a theatre. The new American President Andrew Johnson began the task of reconstruction and reconciliation, pardoning most of those who had fought for the Confederacy.

Scots fought on both sides of the American Civil War. The Federal blockade cut off the supply of cotton, forcing Auchterarder weavers, like the radical Tom Stewart, to leave forever to find other employment in Glasgow and elsewhere. The American Civil War brought to an end two centuries of independent weavers in the Auchterarder area. The textile industry continued to thrive in the mills, where owners had the money and marketing ability to source new raw materials and outlets.

British Prime Minster Lord Palmerston had curbed his aggressive instincts by adopting an officially neutral stance in the American Civil War. When

Palmerston died on 18 October 1865, his Foreign Secretary Lord John Russell became Prime Minister. He had been Prime Minister before, from 1846 to 1852. This time his Liberal Government did not last as long. In July 1866, the Conservative Earl of Derby returned to be Prime Minister for the third time, having defeated Russell's Reform Bill, a measure aimed at giving the vote to more of the population.

On 18 March 1867, the Conservatives introduced their own Reform Bill, hastened by Trade Union demonstrations and public unrest. The Chancellor, Benjamin Disraeli, a flamboyant orator, persuaded Parliament to give many more householders the vote and to reallocate some Parliamentary seats from small towns to growing cities. The Second Reform Act became law on 6 August 1867. It was a necessary addition to the 1832 Reform Act, but still left most of the rural classes and all women without a vote in elections. Gladstone was furious that his great rival Disraeli had helped himself to Liberal policies and passed them off as Conservative. In 1868, Parliament passed a similar Reform Act for Scotland. Lord Derby stepped aside to let Disraeli become Prime Minister in February 1868.

By December 1868, the Liberals were back in power with Gladstone as Prime Minister. He struggled with the problem of Ireland, where the Roman Catholic majority was disadvantaged compared to the Protestant minority. Poverty had driven many Irish Catholics to North America. In New York and other cities the Fenian movement, named after the old Irish militia, grew with the purpose of disrupting the British Empire wherever possible and forcing greater 'home rule' for Ireland.

A small Fenian invasion of Canada in 1866 was easily suppressed but, combined with alarm at the growing power of its neighbour the USA after the American Civil War, made the various Canadian colonies seek more security. As long before as 1840, Upper and Lower Canada had been united to give a voice to both English- and French-speaking colonists. In 1867 the Dominion of Canada created a federal union. The Fenians turned to launching terrorist attacks in England. Gladstone's attempts to make Irish landowning and religious practices less confrontational failed to eliminate discontent on both sides.

In industrial Scotland, where thousands of poor Irish immigrants competed for jobs, religious tensions grew and remain to this day. Rural Auchterarder attracted few immigrants. Roman Catholics were tolerated but viewed with suspicion by families that had grown up with tales of atrocities in the Jacobite burning of Auchterarder in the previous century. The landowning classes had long since embraced the Presbyterian or Scottish Episcopal Churches. Local perception was generally that wealthy, cultured Catholics might exist in France and Italy, but that the Catholics in the Auchterarder area were the remnants of Gaelic peasantry or ill-educated Irish.

The British Empire had grown rich on trade with the Americas and Asia. With the abolition of slavery in America, Asia and Africa became increasingly important sources of cheap raw materials for Britain's factories. The shipping route to Asia went round the southern tip of Africa where there was a long established British colony of the Cape of Good Hope. The increasingly ambitious Napoleon III of France looked at British trade with envy.

In the early 1850s the Khedive of Egypt, Mohammed Said, secured French finance to build a railway from Alexandria to Suez with a view to cutting a canal to link the Mediterranean and Red Seas and provide a much quicker shipping route from Europe to Asia. British banks also lent money, although Prime Minister Palmerston opposed the Suez Canal scheme. In 1863 Ismail, the new Khedive, took advantage of the demand for Egyptian cotton generated by the American Civil War supply shortages, and invested the profits in public works schemes to modernise the country and improve transport of all kinds. The Suez Canal opened on 17 November 1869, by which time Palmerston was dead and French and British governments were attempting co-operation in Suez.

In July 1870, Napoleon III's ambitions drove him to declare war on Prussia, which he saw as a dangerous continental rival. His perception was right. His military judgement was not. Prussia, with its astute Chancellor Prince Otto von Bismarck and disciplined army developed by Count Helmuth von Moltke, routed the French at the Battle of Sedan on 1 September 1870. The Prussians besieged Paris, which was reduced to starvation and surrendered on 28 January 1871. Napoleon III fled to Britain, as his predecessors Louis XVIII and Charles X had done. France became a republic again with Adolphe Thiers as first President of the Third Republic. On 18 January 1871, King William of Prussia was proclaimed Emperor of all Germany.

The German Emperor's son and heir Frederick was married to Queen Victoria's eldest daughter, also called Victoria. When Gladstone's government fell in 1874, the new Prime Minister Benjamin Disraeli pointed out that when Frederick became Emperor his wife would be an Empress and therefore outrank her mother. Disraeli had Queen Victoria take the title Empress of India on 1 May 1876. The British Empire now had an empress in name as well as reality. Disraeli was rewarded with the title Earl of Beaconsfield.

Titles mattered. In 1874, to enhance the Royal Family's formal links with Ireland and Scotland, Queen Victoria made her third son, Prince Arthur, 1st Duke of Connaught and Strathearn. Dormant since her father's death, the old Earldom of Strathearn, once owned by Grahams and Stewarts, was again a royal title. The new 1st Duke of Strathearn lived until 1942. In his 92-year-long life, both the British Empire and Strathearn changed out of all recognition.

The British Empire was a machine of interdependent parts. In Egypt, whose cotton was essential to the mills of Auchterarder, the Suez Canal's future became uncertain. The governing structure of Egyptian territories was complex. The Khedive of Egypt owed tribute to the Sultan of Turkey, but was the superior of General Charles Gordon, the British Governor General of the Sudan, which Egypt had conquered in 1822. In November 1875, Khedive Ismail, unable to sustain the national debt he had incurred by massive spending on transport infrastructure, sold his shares in the Suez Canal to Britain, making it the largest shareholder in the canal.

As British influence grew, so did Egyptian and Sudanese nationalist movements, determined to eject foreign rule. Britain sent troops. France did not. Gladstone's Liberals returned to power in April 1880. On 15 September 1882, Sir Garnett Wolseley defeated an Egyptian uprising and occupied Cairo. The Mahdi

Mohammed Ahmed, a Moslem spiritual leader, led an independence movement in the Sudan. His dervish army slaughtered General Gordon and his troops in Khartoum on 26 January 1885.

On 29 October 1888, the leading European powers agreed, by the Suez Canal Convention, to keep the canal open to all shipping both in peace and war. It was an empty gesture. All sides pursued their national interests. Not until 2 September 1898, when General Horatio Herbert Kitchener defeated the Mahdi's successor Khalifa Abdullah at the Battle of Omdurman, did the Suez Canal's future become clear. The French also reluctantly withdrew from the Nile region, making the Suez Canal Convention workable at last.

Queen Victoria's popularity, which waned when she became reclusive after Prince Albert's death in 1861, rose again when she was skilfully marketed by Disraeli as a unifying mother figure to the disparate nations of the Empire. In Strathearn, there was local pride in the heroism of Black Watch soldiers in the Sudan and tales of more battles in Afghanistan and in the 1872–74 Ashanti War in the Gold Coast (now Ghana). To general approval in 1877, Disraeli sent a fleet to confront the Russians in the Balkans. Gunboat diplomacy was the order of the day, giving rise to the term 'jingoism' from the popular song:

> We don't want to fight,
> But, by jingo, if we do,
> We've got the men, we've got the ships
> And we've got the money too.

No matter how competent its leaders, no government remains popular for long once it faces the realities of exercising authority. The Ballot Act of 1872 introduced secret voting in Parliamentary and local elections, making it more difficult to bully voters. Disraeli was voted into and out of office until he was defeated by Gladstone for the second time in 1880 and died the following year. Gladstone further extended the franchise by the Third Reform Act of 1884, which gave the vote to county tenants and lodgers paying over £10 annual rent. This gave many agricultural labourers and others in Strathearn the right to vote for the first time.

Parliament still thought women were unfit to express sensible political views. Not so the Auchterarder Literary Association, which staged debates on current topics. On 6 March 1871, it debated 'Ought females to be allowed to vote for Members of Parliament?' Despite Auchterarder's early enthusiasm, it was not until 1918 that Parliament granted women over 30 the right to vote. Equal voting rights for men and women in Britain did not arrive till 1928.

In June 1885, the new Conservative leader Robert Cecil, 3rd Marquis of Salisbury succeeded in ousting Gladstone's Liberals from power. His administration lasted only seven months before Gladstone returned for an even shorter period. In July 1886, the Marquis of Salisbury became Prime Minister again and sailed the nation through choppy political waters until July 1902. His Conservative regime was only out of office for three years when the Liberals, led by Gladstone from August 1892 to March 1894 and the Earl of Rosebery till June 1895, gained the public's confidence again.

Gladstone had been forced to resign in 1886 when his own party revolted against his plans to grant 'home rule' to Ireland. National unity expressed itself spectacularly in 1887 with mass celebrations of Queen Victoria's Golden Jubilee. Across the British Empire there were parties in public parks, lavish pageants and music from military bands, cheered through flag-bedecked streets. Millions of commemorative mugs and tea towels were produced, a fashion which continues to this day whenever a royal occasion presents a marketing opportunity.

Many towns created lasting memorials to Queen Victoria's Golden Jubilee. In Auchterarder, a tall Jubilee Cairn was built at the western edge of the town, where the Orchil Road led across the Common Muir. The cairn is inset with large curling stones, engraved with mottoes like *Persevere to the end*, embodying the Victorian spirit. In 1897, Queen Victoria's Diamond Jubilee produced even more enthusiastic celebrations, at a time when patriotic fervour was enhanced by Britain's war with the Dutch-speaking Boers in South Africa.

By the end of the nineteenth century in Auchterarder, everyone was expected to be literate. There was a great appetite for newspapers and books. 'Improving literature', such as history, science or art, appealed to some. 'Penny dreadfuls', garish fiction, appealed to others. Education had always been a major issue for both rich and poor. From the seventeenth to nineteenth centuries, the rich had private tutors and completed their education with foreign travel on 'The Grand Tour' of Europe. In Auchterarder, poor weavers, like miners elsewhere, on the one hand placed a high value on working to give their children the education and qualifications for middle-class jobs, and on the other hand had a great spirit of radical comradeship among themselves.

In the Middle Ages, education was in the hands of priests. After the increase in printed books and the Reformation of the Church in 1560, more people wanted to read and write. By 1610, Auchterarder had a school beside the old Parish Church where the War Memorial stands today. In the eighteenth century, there was a Parish School, a single room in a cottage at the gate of the old Parish Church, shared with a weaver's shop, with the schoolmaster living above. Schoolmasters were paid, usually badly, by landowners and the parish. School fees were too much for poor families.

In 1811, John Sheddan of Lochie established John Sheddan's Charity School, separate from the Parish School, endowing it with the rents from Barnet's Croft on the south side of the town, for the free education of twelve poor children.

At first he let the Kirk Session administer the rents but, when they abused the system by renting Barnet's Croft to two of their own members, Sheddan revoked his Deed of Trust and set up a new body of School Governors to be chosen by the householders of the parish, with no interference from the Kirk. Sheddan, mindful of Jacobite atrocities, which had reduced the town to poverty, also excluded Roman Catholics from the school's board of trustees. Sheddan was religious, but he made a clear distinction between the principles of religion and the principles of the men who operate a church.

In 1837, there were seven schools, including the Parish School (by the old Parish Church), Townhead School (on Castleton Road), and Sheddan's School. The local literacy rate was impressive. James Aitken, in *The Second Statistical*

Account, writes 'We do not think there are any above six years of age who cannot read and very few grown up who cannot write'. Other schools came and went. Anyone could call him- or herself a teacher and give lessons. Those who paid the fees quickly found out who could teach. This practice exists today in private music lessons and extra tuition to supplement schoolwork.

Education in Scotland was a higgledy-piggledy jumble of local arrangements until the Education Act of 1872, which set up School Boards for all parishes. By the end of the nineteenth century, local lawyer A G Reid could write that in 1875 Auchterarder acquired 'a palatial building which cost about £5,000 to erect and which might be sufficient for a small university. There is a staff of ten teachers and the annual cost of the establishment is about £900.'

In Victorian times, education and recreation went together, guided by 'muscular Christianity', and the Latin motto *Mens sana in corpore sano* (A healthy mind in a healthy body). From 1872, school attendance was compulsory from age five to thirteen, except that children over ten could be 'half-timers' if they had local jobs. The Auchterarder mills had many 'half-timers'. Some children under ten worked in the mills, especially if they came from a distant parish and had no birth certificate.

The school emphasised the 'Three Rs': reading, (w)riting and (a)rithmetic, but was flexible enough to take advantage of any educational opportunities. For example, the school's logbook for July 8 1887, Queen Victoria's Golden Jubilee Year, records that children were given a half-holiday when Fosset's Circus came to town. Long before TV, the circus gave children the chance to see exotic animals.

The Victorians had a passion for knowledge. For the first time, large numbers of the working classes saw education as a realistic way to finding a better job. The expanding British Empire created thousands of administrative posts and professional opportunities. By the time the Scottish social reformer Samuel Smiles wrote his best-seller *Self Help* in 1859, Auchterarder people had already taken the initiative.

Education was not confined to the young. By 1837, there was a 'Mechanics Institute' in Auchterarder, with a programme of lectures on literary, scientific and moral subjects. Peter Smeaton and his son William, of Woodside, on the slopes of the Ochils, established a public library in Auchterarder in 1855, for the use of the people of Auchterarder, Aberuthven, Blackford, Dunning, Gask, Glendevon and Trinity Gask. Tom Stewart, the radical weaver poet, noted that the trustees of the Kirk Session sat on the Smeatons' bequest for many years, without buying any books, until a public meeting was called and the trustees announced that they intended to proceed without delay.

Tom Stewart was delighted that the American steel magnate Andrew Carnegie, who came, like Stewart, from a Scottish weaving family, donated £1,000 for a new Public Library. Carnegie was prompted by the formidable and well-connected Elizabeth Haldane of Cloan, who served as library secretary for forty years.

In 1885, with improvements in 1896, the new library was installed and merged with the Smeaton Library upstairs in the Institute, a refurbishment of the Girnal

House, next door to the Aytoun Hall. The Institute offered not only a Library and Reading Room, but also a Lecture Hall with a lively series of events. Upstairs, it also had a Billiard Room and Recreation Rooms. Last, but not least, both hot and cold baths were available.

In the 1890s 'flickers', the first moving pictures, were shown in fairground tents, then in public halls. The Aytoun Hall and the Good Templar Hall in Abbey Road screened films in the silent era.

Some local traditions lingered from mediaeval and even pagan times. Auchterarder, like many towns, had a procession of burning torches on New Year's Eve. Today, only Comrie's Flambeaux survives in Strathearn. Until 1904, Auchterarder's Flambeaux was a spectacular Hogmanay encounter. On one side were the Headiers who met at the Gelly Dub, near today's St Margaret's Hospital, after drinking at The Luggie, a pub at the top of Castleton Road. The other side, the Footiers, gathered in the Feus after drinking at the Railway Hotel.

Both sides were equipped with long wooden poles, sometimes 'borrowed' clothes poles. These were bound with scraps of cloth, donated by the Provost William Hally from his mill, and soaked in tar from the gasworks at the Feus. Each side lit their flambeaux from bonfires at the Townhead and the Common Loan, then marched towards one another to meet as midnight struck on the Aytoun Hall clock. They then competed to be first to insert a flambeau in the iron ring in front of the Hall, usually intended for tethering horses. This annual competition was, to put it kindly, robust. For the sake of public order, numbers were eventually reduced to twelve on each side.

At Hogmanay, in addition to pub alcohol, many local people drank 'Treacle Peerie', a potent, seasonal home-brewed beer. Some roamed the High Street in pantomime-style costumes. Cross-dressing was popular. 'Harald Blacktooth' was a favourite female role. Superstition demanded that houses, including chimneys, should be thoroughly cleaned on New Year's Eve so that the devil's helpers could not shelter in the dirt from one year to the next.

In contrast, Christmas was barely observed. It was not a statutory holiday for farm labourers. It was a middle-class indulgence until it became a mass-marketing opportunity in the mid twentieth century. Easter was celebrated by rolling Easter eggs, real hardboiled eggs, brightly painted, to mark the rolling away of the stone from Jesus's tomb. Chocolate Easter eggs appeared in the twentieth century.

At Hogmanay (31 December), Candlemas (1 February), Beltane (1 May) and Hallowe'en (31 October), some householders laid a long bar of iron across their thresholds. They believed that 'cauld iron' was the one thing that Satan and his legions would not cross, even on those nights when they were most active.

Hallowe'en, before it became Americanized at the end of the twentieth century, was a curious mix of children's games like 'dooking for apples' and trying to eat, blindfold, a treacle-smeared pancake dangled from the kitchen pulley. Underneath, there lurked old pagan superstitions, particularly in the guisers, dressed up as mischievous spirits.

'The three luggies' was a local Hallowe'en game for girls. A luggie is a wooden drinking bowl with handles sticking out like ears. It gave its name to the Victorian Townhead pub. In the game, one luggie was filled with clean water, one with dirty water and one left empty. Girls were blindfold and made to choose. Clean water meant they would marry a good husband. Dirty water meant a bad one. An empty luggie predicted a life of spinsterhood.

Another local Hallowe'en ritual was 'the fathoming of the stack' to protect hay from evil. Earlier in the autumn, men made harvest bows, by plaiting two stalks of corn into elaborate shapes. They gave them to their girlfriends, or even to their wives.

The nineteenth century saw great developments in local organised sport. Curling became fashionable, but a curling pond, dug at the Gelly Dub, never held enough water to be reliable. Why is it called the Gelly Dub? *Dub* is the Gaelic word for a small pond. *Geallaidh* means white or shining water. It sounds cheerful, but, as a grim pun, it was locally pronounced 'Gally Dub', referring to the nearby town gallows, past which the water flowed.

In a three-day burst of collective enterprise in January 1830, local voluntary labour, aided by some subscriptions, dug a curling pond at the Blindwells, at the south-west corner of the Common Muir. It was called Loch Common. Its embankments survived, though ravaged by moles and rabbits, until the 1980s, when it vanished under the A9 Bypass. The only lasting reminder of local curling sits in the curling stones set into the 1887 Jubilee Cairn on the Orchil Road.

Football grew in popularity through the nineteenth century. Local leagues were formed. Clubs came and went quickly. Auchterarder had Victoria, Fairmuir, Vale of Ruthven and Auchterarder Thistle. Clubs sometimes were named after the colour of their shirts. It was a brave opponent who sniggered at the name Auchterarder Primrose or Dundee Violet. Primrose players were generally not timid little flowers, and Violet was nicknamed 'Dundee Violent' as their players vented the frustrations of their day-jobs in the jute mills.

Cricket blossomed in Victorian times. The Parish School logbook of 1878 notes 'The Rifle Corps has been disbanded and cricket is now all the rage.' A scorebook of 1889 records a match between the weavers of Ruthvenvale Terrace and the Greenwells team from the Common Muir, the equivalent of Footers and Headiers. The match was played at Greenwells, near the source of Auchterarder's water supply. Another, larger, cricket ground was developed in the triangle of the Common Muir, between Orchil Road and the line of the Gleneagles to Crieff railway. A lofted drive for six could land the ball on the rails.

Both cricket and the railway lasted about the same time in Auchterarder, succumbing to economic pressures in the 1960s. All that is left is a narrow grass gully showing where the track ran past the ground's western edge.

On 22 January 1901, Queen Victoria died. Her reign, from 1837, is the longest of any British monarch, though the present Queen Elizabeth II (1952–) is catching up. Both of these long-lived queens have a powerful sense of duty allied to great energy. They share the ability to see the big picture and focus on long-term goals, rather than short-term success or failure. Both also have a much greater and sharper sense of humour than is usually recognised. Both have provided that mix of distanced majesty and genuine interest in the welfare of ordinary people that tourists and businessmen love and makes republicans gnash their teeth in frustration.

36

The Edwardian Era

*In which men temporarily stop shooting one another and shoot wildlife
instead, while women reveal their ankles and burn down houses*

The raw material of history does not consist of neat crop rows, but symbiotic
entanglements. The death of the reclusive, black-dressed elderly widow, Queen
Victoria in January 1901 and the accession of her 59-year-old, cigar-smoking,
fashionably dressed son King Edward VII changed the face of the British
monarchy, but not the thrust of British politics. Edward VII was a bon viveur
with a taste for sport and mistresses, but he was no political lightweight like the
previous two male monarchs, William IV and George IV.

Edward VII followed his mother's successful strategy of trying to maintain
good relations with the royal houses of Europe, including the blustering
Kaiser William II of Germany. Edward had long been fond of France and was
instrumental in agreeing the Entente Cordiale, a commercial and military
agreement with France, signed on 8 April 1904. The two nations, which had
been enemies for nearly a thousand years, became allies.

Edward VII also made a point of being a visible Emperor. He had visited India
in 1875–76, just before his mother took the title Empress of India. When he
returned as Emperor, he was entertained with spectacular sporting events, such
as a kheddah or capture of wild elephants in Mysore in February 1906.

King Edward VII loved field sports, especially shooting. Local estates, which
had once been the strongholds of warlike nobles, became country houses with
moorland playgrounds for the aristocracy. Their visitors' books reveal how
international these house parties were, reflecting the extent of the British Empire
and its allies. For example, Lionel, Lord Tennyson, grandson of the Poet Laureate
Alfred, Lord Tennyson, shot his first stag on the Drummond Estate near Muthill.
Lionel Tennyson had grown up in Australia, where his father was Governor
General, and went on to captain England at cricket.

Robert Cecil, 3rd Marquis of Salisbury, bridged the Victorian and Edwardian
eras as Prime Minister. For most of his premiership, he was also Foreign Secretary,
seeing no need to appoint some other politician to the post. He viewed the
British Empire as a global complex of opportunities for enterprising businessmen,
educators and administrators who should be given responsibility for getting

on with their jobs. As a result, the aristocracy continued their privileged town and country ways, the middle classes enjoyed growing prosperity, but the poor struggled on low wages.

The poor had their champions. Robert Cunninghame Graham, known as Don Roberto for his adventures in Argentina, was a charismatic descendant of the mediaeval Earls of Menteith and Strathearn. Elected to Parliament in 1886, he was the first Chairman of the Scottish Parliamentary Labour Party, which he founded with his miner–journalist friend Keir Hardie in 1888. Don Roberto's scathing attacks on the exploitation of the working classes were an embarrassment to the Liberals, who had marketed themselves as champions of reform. With the formation of the Independent Labour Party in 1893, the Liberals saw working-class voters, whom they had fought to enfranchise, desert them for the vigorous new party, which also attracted aristocratic intellectuals.

It is the paradoxical mark of success of any political party that it transforms itself from reforming zeal into reactive bureaucracy. Don Roberto became disillusioned with the Labour Party. In 1928, he became the first leader of the National Party of Scotland, the forerunner of the Scottish National Party. He regarded nationalism as 'the first step to internationalism, the goal which every thinking man and woman must place before their eyes.' He died in 1936, long before the SNP had evolved into a credible government machine.

Don Roberto attacked the grasping complacency that had seeped into the British Empire. At the height of Queen Victoria's Golden Jubilee in 1887, he condemned British policy in South Africa, where the discovery of gold on the Witwatersrand in the Transvaal had brought a flood of British immigrants, turning Johannesburg into a lawless boom town. The Transvaal was an independent state, whose President Paul Kruger led the white population of Dutch-speaking Boers.

In 1890, Cecil Rhodes, an Essex entrepreneur who had made a fortune from South African diamonds, became Prime Minister of Cape Colony, south of the Transvaal. The previous year, Rhodes had founded the British South African Company. In 1893, with the compliance of the Portuguese, Rhodes's company seized the vast tribal lands of the Matabele and Mashona, calling the new territory Rhodesia. To give an air of legitimacy, the new capital city was named Salisbury after the British Prime Minister.

The Boers in the Transvaal were now surrounded on three sides by British-controlled provinces. On their ocean frontier, they lacked a viable port.

Rhodes wanted a British united South Africa. The Boers wanted a Dutch-led federation. Tensions grew. Backed by Rhodes, on 31 December 1895 Dr Leander Starr Jamieson, the colonial administrator of Mashonaland, led six hundred troops of the British South Africa Company to raid Johannesburg. Their pretext was to protect uitlander (foreigner, meaning British) women and children. The Boers forced Jamieson to surrender on 2 January 1896. An embarrassed British commission of enquiry censured Rhodes, who resigned as Prime Minister of Cape Colony. Three years of uneasy peace followed. Britain increased pressure to create a Union of South Africa and the Boers sought Germany's aid to prevent it.

War exploded on 11 October 1899, when the Boers advanced to attack Ladysmith, aiming for the port of Durban on the east coast. They then attacked

Kimberly and Mafeking on the western border of the Transvaal. Britain sent shiploads of troops but the Boers, wearing khaki clothing and avoiding pitched battles, inflicted severe losses on the brightly uniformed British forces. Many Perthshire men in the Black Watch were killed on 10 and 11 December 1899 at Magersfontein when the Boers intercepted the Highland Brigade.

Britain sent more troops. Sheer weight of numbers defeated the Boers. British generals Frederick Roberts, Horatio Herbert Kitchener, Redvers Buller and John French became household names. Colonel Robert Baden Powell defended Mafeking for 218 days. News that Roberts had relieved Mafeking on 18 May 1900 was greeted with hysterical rejoicing in Britain. 'Mafeking Night' parties became legendary for over-indulgence. On 1 September 1900, Britain formally annexed the Transvaal. The Boer War lasted two more years, with Boer guerrillas skilfully using their knowledge of the terrain to inflict casualties on British troops. On 31 May 1902, peace was finally agreed at Vereeniging. Roberts and Kitchener received earldoms. Baden Powell received a peerage much later, not for his Mafeking heroics, but for founding the Boy Scouts in 1908. His sister Agnes founded the Girl Guides two years later. Both organisations embodied the ceremonious, battling patriotism of the Boer War.

Having seen the Boer War to its end, Lord Salisbury retired as Prime Minister on 11 July 1902, calmly passing on the premiership to his Scottish nephew Arthur Balfour. Salisbury was a hard act to follow. Balfour was unable to prevent divisions in the Tory party, particularly over the question of modernising the armed forces and regulating the flood of cheap foreign imports. King Edward VII disliked the presumptuous Balfour. The nation's voters also grew tired of Tory grandees.

On 5 December 1905, the Liberals, led by fellow Scot Henry Campbell-Bannerman, swept the aristocratic Balfour's party out of office. The new Prime Minister displayed the characteristic guile of the Campbells, but without the blue blood of the Argylls. The Liberals were as internally divided as the Tories, but Campbell-Bannerman was adroit in holding his party together. As MP for the neighbouring constituency of Stirling, he was always in the public eye in Strathearn, where his cabinet colleague Richard Burden Haldane from Auchterarder viewed him with distrust.

On 5 April 1908, Campbell-Bannerman resigned because of ill-health and died three weeks later. The Liberals continued to govern. Herbert Henry Asquith, a lawyer like Haldane, became Prime Minister and remained continuously in office for eight years and eight months, longer than any Premier since Lord Liverpool a hundred years before. The chancellor David Lloyd George introduced a programme of social reform. The Old Age Pension Act in January 1909 provided a means-tested pension for people over seventy. The National Insurance Act in December 1911 gave assistance in time of illness and unemployment, financed by mandatory contributions from both the employee and the employer. The Liberals also restructured taxation in 1909 to raise more money from income tax, inheritance tax and private investments. This 'People's Budget' of 1909 heralded the end of the era of lavish aristocratic house parties.

King Edward VII died on 6 May 1910, succeeded by his son George V, a solid, reliable man. He inherited his father's energy and sense of duty, but not his gift for maintaining international peace through personal diplomacy. In Britain, it was still assumed that Britannia ruled the waves, despite the fact that the new nation of Germany was manufacturing a huge navy. British merchant shipping could use the Suez Canal as a secure route to its Indian Empire.

On the far side of the Atlantic, American engineers cut a canal through the Isthmus of Panama, overcoming the local problems of climate, disease and huge expenses which had ruined the Scottish Darien Scheme two centuries before. The USA effectively controlled the Panama Canal, which allowed shipping to pass between the Atlantic and Pacific Oceans without having to round the dangerous Cape Horn far away at the tip of South America. The Panama Canal was opened to shipping on 15 August 1914.

Set on a bracing Scottish hill, far from the pestilent swamps of Panama, Auchterarder was expanding. Captain Aytoun's water supply from Crook o' the Moss was no longer sufficient for the town's needs. In 1904, a new water supply pipe was laid from a spring near Duchally, providing a much greater volume. The source was high enough in the Ochils to allow water to be piped, not just to Auchterarder, but up to standpipes in the Muirton, though most Muirton houses did not have indoor taps until the 1930s.

In Victorian Britain, the bicycle was seen as a potential threat to morals. It made young ladies more mobile, and also made their pedalling ankles visible to young men. The Edwardian era was more liberated and more realistic. Bicycles were costly and available only in city shops until the 1920s, when David Henderson's cycle shop was established on Auchterarder High Street, at Castle Wynd. It became Henderson Bros Motors, selling motor cycles, then cars and tractors as well.

The first motor cars appeared in Auchterarder during the Edwardian era. The town was just far enough from Edinburgh and Glasgow to be a desirable destination in a day's journey. The railways had already promoted the attractions of the area. The Lang Toon of Auchterarder tempted speed-obsessed motorists to exceed the 10 mph speed limit. These 'scorchers' hurtled through the town at speeds nearing 20 mph, the maximum allowed on out-of-town roads since 1904. In September 1910, a police speed trap in Auchterarder caught four vehicles, including one driven by a motor engineer from Warwickshire who made the mistake of trying to bribe the police sergeant. The other drivers were fined £1 each. The corrupt Englishman was fined £5.

Women sought political freedoms as well as bicycles. Though members of the Auchterarder Literary Association had debated and agreed in 1871 that women should have the vote, they were far ahead of general British public opinion. The Women's Social and Political Union, founded in 1903 by the redoubtable Mrs Emmeline Pankhurst, organised huge public rallies in support of female suffrage. In 1906, it launched a campaign of disruption of public events. The suffragettes were often young, articulate, good-looking and ruthless. Seeking publicity for their cause, they targeted several West Perthshire mansions. Orchil Castle was firebombed in 1912. Not till 1918 did Parliament grant some women the right to vote, provided they were over 30 years old. Below that age, women were still presumed to be unable to form a valid opinion of politicians.

Sport was less controversial. Locally, football thrived. Auchterarder Thistle even travelled to Ibrox to meet the mighty Glasgow Rangers in the Scottish Cup. Rangers won and went on to capture the trophy. Yet more sporting facilities were developed, with Auchterarder's first Bowling Club established in 1903 on land up Castle Wynd.

The great sporting success story of Auchterarder is golf. The first recorded Auchterarder golfer is Scotland's Cavalier hero, James Graham, 1st Marquis of Montrose. He attended St Andrews University and is documented playing golf the day before his wedding in November 1629. Golf became more generally popular in the nineteenth century. Locally, it took off dramatically in 1892 with the construction on the Common Muir of a seven-hole Auchterarder Golf Course, soon increased to nine holes. A clubhouse was built by 1913. Today, Auchterarder Golf Club provides the main source of income for the Auchterarder Common Good Fund.

It was not till 1979 that Auchterarder Golf Course was extended to eighteen holes, but in 1910 it was good enough to capture the imagination of Donald Matheson, General Manager of the Caledonian Railway, who holidayed in Auchterarder and dreamed up the idea of a magnificent golf-based hotel to which his railway could transport socialites from all over the world. Matheson already knew the area well. He acquired a site on the White Muir on a ninety-nine-year lease, and made plans to build Gleneagles Hotel. In 1914, the First World War brought all such leisure plans to an abrupt halt.

37

The First World War

In which we meet a great army reformer and many local heroes

When tensions grew between the British and German Empires in 1905, Richard Burdon Haldane of Cloan was appointed Secretary of State for War. His home lies close to Kincardine Castle, home of the seventeenth-century James Graham, 1st Marquis of Montrose, one of Britain's greatest military strategists. R.B. Haldane was no general but he had a profound understanding of political reality and of how outdated the British army had become in organisation and equipment.

R.B. Haldane was a political liberal who had been a student in Germany and made many friends there. However, he had the foresight to remodel and strengthen the British army to match the Germans. He developed the Expeditionary Force and founded the Territorial Army, which held its first exercises at Cloan in 1908. At first, King Edward VII supported Haldane's reforms, despite loud opposition from the deeply traditionalist Lord Frederick Roberts. Later, the King referred to Haldane as 'a damned radical lawyer and a German professor'. Haldane and his cabinet colleagues knew that Edward VII could be blunt in his opinions of a politician's character, while still valuing what he might deliver for the national good. Haldane's reforms went ahead. He was created 1st Viscount Haldane and became Lord Chancellor in 1912.

During the Edwardian era, Germany's huge investment in warships gave the rest of Europe cause for concern. Germany formed an alliance with its German-speaking neighbour Austria and with Turkey. Britain, France and Russia led an opposing alliance, which came to include Belgium, Italy, Romania, Greece, Serbia and Japan. The United States of America remained neutral.

Throughout history the Balkans has provided violent clashes of cultures. In 1908, Austria annexed Bosnia and Herzegovina, angering neighbouring Serbia. On 18 October 1912, Greece, Serbia and Bulgaria attacked Turkey, trying to drive the Ottoman Empire out of Europe. On 30 May 1913, a peace conference in London ended the First Balkan War, but on 29 June Bulgaria attacked her former Greek and Serbian allies in order to gain more territory. The Second Balkan War was quickly over. Romania and Turkey joined with Greece and Serbia to defeat Bulgaria. On 10 August the Treaty of Bucharest brought an uneasy peace. All sides were dissatisfied with the complex territorial settlement.

R.B. Haldane had visited Germany on 8 February 1912, trying to improve relations between the two countries. Kaiser William II ignored his plea to cut back on warship building. War came, not as a direct clash between the military giants, but as a hideous logical conclusion to their alliances with smaller nations. On 28 June 1914, the heir to the Austrian throne, Archduke Franz Ferdinand, was shot dead by a student, Gavrilo Princip, in Sarajevo, the capital of Bosnia. The Austrian government claimed that Serbia had colluded in the assassination and on 28 July declared war on Serbia. Russia's alliance with Serbia brought her into the war. France's alliance with Russia brought her in. Britain, with her new *entente cordiale* with France, felt obliged to join the conflict. On 4 August 1914, after Germany invaded Belgium, Britain declared war on Germany. Over the next four years, the war escalated into a global conflict, with fifty different declarations of war between nations.

It was exactly 200 years since King George I, from the German-speaking branch of the Stuart dynasty, became monarch of Britain and soon defeated an uprising by the Jacobites, the French-allied branch of the Stuarts, who burned the Auchterarder area in a scorched earth policy as they retreated. Now in 1914, Britain was allied with the French against the Germans. King George V tactfully changed the British royal family name in 1917 from the German Saxe Coburg Gotha to the very English-sounding Windsor, which conjured up an image of an ancient indestructible bastion appropriate to a nation at war.

German troops swept across Belgium and occupied Brussels on 20 August 1914. They quickly pressed on into eastern France. Britain was seized by righteous indignation and jingoistic frenzy. The new War Minister Lord Kitchener, who had ended the Boer War by hurling thousands of men at the small ill-equipped Boer army, adopted the same strategy against the military might of Germany. The difference in scale required a British army vastly greater than Haldane's new professional Expeditionary Force and Territorial Army. Posters of the fiercely moustached Kitchener appeared across the country with his finger pointing straight at passersby, demanding ' Join your country's army!' Hordes of young men, with no grasp of warfare but with a well-schooled sense of imperial duty and pride, quit their factories and offices to volunteer.

New recruiting centres sprang up across Britain. The urge for victory swept away the civilised functions of peace. In Dundee, an enlightened Edwardian committee had converted the old West Poorhouse into a modern geriatric hospital with a children's wing attached. In August 1914, the building was taken over for an army recruiting centre and barracks, where Fergus Bowes Lyon raised troops for the 5th Black Watch. The Governor Robert Grossart desperately tried to place the patients elsewhere. He and his family had to leave the Governor's House with no time to pack. They found temporary accommodation with relatives. Soldiers pilfered their possessions.

As a gesture intended to be kind, Fergus Bowes Lyon sent flowers, cut from the dispossessed Governor's garden, to the Governor's young daughter Dorothy who was the same age as his own sister Elizabeth. He also took Dorothy's pet dog Toodles to be the battalion mascot. Fergus Bowes Lyon was killed the following year at the Battle of Loos. His sister Elizabeth grew up to marry the future King George VI. Dorothy Grossart grew up to marry Allan Bell who, after a distinguished military career, exchanged the army for the Church of Scotland. He later became minister of Aberuthven and Gask parishes and Major in command of the Territorial Army unit in Auchterarder where Lord Haldane had organised its first field exercises.

In the first months of war, 90,000 British soldiers were rushed across the English Channel. On 23 August at Mons in Belgium, the slaughter on both sides began as the Germans were prevented from reaching the coast. The First Battle of the Marne from 5 to 12 September stopped the Germans from marching to Paris and set the precedent for battles lasting weeks or even months. It soon became obvious that the old tactic of infantry charges while the enemy were reloading their guns was now suicidal. Both sides were equipped with machine guns, not muskets. On the Western Front in France and Belgium, troops dug networks of deep trenches in which to shelter from enemy machine guns, snipers and heavy artillery.

On the Eastern Front of the First World War, Russian troops attacked Germany, only to be defeated at the Battle of Tannenberg, 26–30 August 1914. Other battlefronts opened up across the world. The war spread quickly to Africa, where former Boer Generals Jan Smuts and Louis Botha now fought for the British Union of South Africa against German colonies in East Africa. In the Balkans, the fighting that had triggered the wars escalated with landings at Gallipoli to fight the Turks. To public dismay, the Allies failed to take Constantinople and were withdrawn. Mesopotamia (modern-day Iraq) saw a British Indian army advance but fail to capture Baghdad.

Trench warfare soon became a way of life on the Western Front. The First Battle of Ypres from 30 October to 24 November 1914 was inconclusive. The Second Battle of Ypres from 25 April to 25 May 1915 saw the first major use of chemical warfare, when the Germans used chlorine gas to force French troops into blinded, choking retreat. Soon after, the French fought back, gaining a strip of land north of Arras, six miles long and three miles wide at a cost of 400,000 casualties. At first, Field Marshal John French commanded the British Forces on the Western Front. From December 1915, he was replaced by Field Marshal Douglas Haig, who was a decade younger, but already in his fifties. The generals were old. The casualties were young.

The British copied the Germans and used chlorine gas at the Battle of Loos from 25 September to 8 October 1915, during which Fergus Bowes Lyon was killed. Other new military technology was deployed. On 4 February 1915, the Germans announced a submarine blockade of Great Britain. On 7 May, a German submarine sank the luxury liner *Lusitania* with the loss of 1,198 lives, including 139 Americans. President Woodrow Wilson, who had previously maintained a neutral stance for the USA, now condemned German policy in a note to Kaiser William II. On 5 June, Britain's War Minister Lord Kitchener was drowned when his ship HMS *Hampshire* was torpedoed on a secret mission to Russia. The astute David Lloyd George became War Minister.

The war took to the air. American brothers, Wilbur and Orville Wright, had made the first aeroplane flight on 17 December 1903. As with all new inventions, governments were quick to see a military application. Within weeks of war breaking out in August 1914, German aeroplanes raided Paris and by December they flew across the Channel to attack Dover. British pilots responded by attacking German airfields in Düsseldorf, Cologne and Friedrichshaven. Small biplanes, equipped with machine guns, engaged in aerial combat. From January 1915, huge Zeppelin airships dropped bombs on southern England. The gas-filled Zeppelins made easy targets. By the end of the war, only seven survived out of the German fleet of eighty. Fighter-plane pilots became the stuff of schoolboy heroic fiction, most notably 'Biggles', the quintessential, resourceful modern warrior created by Captain W.E. (William Earle) Johns.

Italy declared war on Austria on 23 May 1915 and became entangled on the Balkan Front. In Egypt, French and British forces repelled Turkish advances towards the Suez Canal. The killing was on such a scale that it was no longer possible to secure sufficient volunteers for mortal combat. On 6 January 1916, the British Parliament passed the Compulsory Service Bill. Now all able-bodied men were required to be deployed wherever the war needed them. On 21 February, the Battle of Verdun began. It lasted inconclusively all year. On 1 July, the Battle of the Somme began. By the time it ended on 18 November, the Allies had advanced seven miles, with British losses of over 400,000 men and French losses of 200,000. The Germans lost 500,000 men on the Somme, some killed by a new British weapon, tanks with mounted machine guns.

At sea, the mighty new German High Seas Fleet fought the British Grand Fleet at the Battle of Jutland on 31 May and 1 June 1916. Each side lost six ships and claimed victory. As long as there were more men to send to war, no side would admit defeat. In January 1916, the British Military Service Act conscripted unmarried men aged between eighteen and forty-one. In May, married men were also called up.

As is usual in wartime, it was considered unpatriotic to voice doubts about national leadership, although change was obviously needed. On 4 December 1916, the long-serving Prime Minister Herbert Asquith resigned as leader of the wartime coalition government. Lloyd George became Prime Minister. He opened secret negotiations with the new Austrian Emperor Charles I, who had succeeded his long-lived grand-uncle Franz Joseph II on 21 November 1916. It proved impossible to reach a territorial settlement by diplomacy, the Italians being the main obstacle to agreement.

Lloyd George scored a diplomatic coup when British intelligence officers intercepted and decoded a message from the German Foreign Secretary Arthur Zimmerman to the German embassy in Mexico, which showed that Germany was prepared to wage war on American commercial shipping. On 6 April 1917, the USA declared war on Germany. It took another year for their troops to play a major role.

Ypres had seen almost continuous fighting. Field Marshal Haig ordered an offensive on 31 July 1917. By 10 November, there were another 400,000 British casualties with only five miles of territory gained around Passchendaele. War weariness set in. The ruinous financial cost of the war and the vast scale of bereavement began to over-ride jingoistic ambition. On the Eastern Front, the

Russian monarchy fell in a communist republican revolution in April 1917. The new Russian government party, called the Bolsheviks, led by the charismatic orator Vladimir Ilyich Lenin, agreed peace terms with Germany on 15 December 1917.

In France, an energetic new Prime Minister, Georges Clemenceau, took office on 16 November 1917. At sea, British Prime Minister Lloyd George's policy of building destroyers to protect convoys of merchant ships, and using depth-charges to destroy German submarines, reversed earlier German successes. Germany fought back with a huge offensive on the Western Front from 21 March 1918. Their progress was checked at the Second Battle of the Marne from 15 July to 17 August when American troops made a significant contribution.

The Russian Revolution of 1917, with the execution of Tsar Nicholas II and his family, sent a shiver of horror through other European monarchies, just as the bloody French Revolution had done in 1789. The Emperor Charles I of Austria, faced with republican movements in Hungary, Czechoslovakia, Yugoslavia and Austria itself, saw his government agree an armistice with the Allied powers on 3 November 1918 and abdicated on 12 November. The ancient Hapsburg Empire was divided into independent republics. The Turkish Empire also collapsed. On the Palestine front, British General Edmund Allenby took Jerusalem on 9 December 1917 then, with Arab assistance, took Damascus and Beirut. The new Turkish Sultan Mohammed VI agreed an armistice with the allies on 30 October 1918.

The German Empire was the last to fall. On the Western Front, Allied forces slowly advanced in the summer of 1918. As in Russia and Austria, a republican movement in Germany grew in strength. On 3 November 1918 in Kiel, German sailors mutinied. On 7 November, a republican revolution broke out in Munich. On 9 November, Kaiser William II abdicated and fled to Holland. On 11 November at 11 am, the newly formed German Republic agreed an armistice. The First World War was over, leaving nearly a million British servicemen dead and over two million wounded. France, Russia, Germany and Austria each suffered even greater losses.

About a quarter of the 2,500 population of the Auchterarder area was directly involved in military service during the First World War. Over a hundred were killed overseas, higher than the national average, reflecting the area's tradition of military service. There was a sense of pride in being the founding home of the Territorial Army. Lord Haldane had followed his military reforms with a term of three years as Chancellor, managing the British economy in the early years of the war.

R.B. Haldane's preference for diplomacy over armed conflict was well known. His reputation suffered at the hands of the ambitious right-wing chauvinist Alfred Harmsworth, Lord Northcliffe, who owned the *Daily Mirror*, *The Times* and *Daily Mail*. Haldane resigned as Chancellor in 1915. Northcliffe came to direct British propaganda later in the war. Horatio Bottomley MP, the jingoistic editor of *John Bull* magazine, drummed up hysterical anti-Haldane feeling. Bottomley soon succumbed to the temptations of his professions and was jailed for fraud.

R.B. Haldane was not as flamboyant as Lloyd George but he was shrewd, methodical, calm and practical. Others were responsible for the military tactics that caused such terrible loss of life. Haldane's tragedy was that he developed an efficient army, hoping that it would be a deterrent to war. It was not.

During the First World War, Haldane applied his practicality locally. He established an Auxiliary Hospital at his own home, Cloan. He also brought German prisoners of war to the Gleneagles Estate to build Frandy Reservoir in the Ochils above Glendevon. The new water supply was for Dunfermline and the new Naval Dockyards in Rosyth, which came to play a significant role in destroying German sea power. Rosyth also saw the surrender of the German High Seas Fleet on 21 November 1918. The ships were taken north to Scapa Flow in the Orkneys, where their crews remained as prisoners of war. On 21 June 1919, the German Admiral Ludwig von Reuter gave the order to scuttle the ships so that they could not be taken over by the British navy.

During the First World War, Auchterarder was an Agricultural Depot, Code Number STBS (AU), for prisoner-of-war labour, directed from the army camp at Stobs in the Borders. The Auchterarder depot administered six satellite Agricultural Groups, based at farms in Strathearn. Anderson's Stables in the Feus became a depot for the Transport Section of the Seaforth Highlanders. Horses played an essential role in the First World War. The army purchased them locally and also imported them from overseas. The mills in Auchterarder quickly adapted their production lines. Instead of tartans and smart shirting, khaki flowed from the looms to clothe British troops.

Of the local men who lost their lives in the First World War, some died outright, like James Archibald from Aberuthven, a Private in the Royal Highland Regiment, killed at the Battle of the Somme in 1916, and his brother Donald, a Private in the Argyll and Sutherland Highlanders, killed at Arras in 1917. Others, like James Alexander from Cloan, a Private in the Cameron Highlanders, were gassed in the trenches and returned home to die soon after in military hospitals. Some, like William Cairns from Aberuthven, a Private in the Black Watch, survived the horrors of Gallipoli in 1915, only to be killed in France in 1918.

Many of the dead were young volunteers, swept up by the surge of national pride in 1914 to 'Fight for King and Country' and 'Defend plucky little Belgium'. Others were career soldiers. Lawrence Oliphant Graeme of Aberuthven Lodge, one of the Graemes of Inchbrakie who had been generous benefactors to Aberuthven Church and School, served in the army for twenty-four years. He became Lieutenant Colonel 1st Battalion Queen's Own Cameron Highlanders. He was killed in France in 1916.

Some became prisoners of war, like Norman MacDonald of Coll Earn, a Captain in the 9th Royal Scots. He was captured in France in 1915 and held in Germany for three years. When he was released in November 1918 at the end of the war, he served in Holland, repatriating other prisoners of war.

Most served in the army, but some, like David Dewar, from Auchterarder High Street, joined the Navy. He served as a telegraphist on British coastal stations. Others, like John Brown from the Feus, joined the brand new Air Force. He served as an air mechanic in India. Lord Haldane's nephew Graeme served in the navy and saw action at Gallipoli and the Battle of Jutland.

The 6th (Perthshire) Battalion of the Black Watch had many men from the Auchterarder area. On 30 July 1916 they attacked German lines at High Wood near Arras. In eleven days fighting, the battalion suffered 350 casualties, about one third of their strength. Captain John Hally, who commanded C Company, was killed. He was replaced by Major Thomas Young, of the Auchterarder lawyer family.

Major Young kept a notebook during his service in Northern France in 1916. It is a matter-of-fact account recorded in the midst of horrific trench warfare. His grandson Will Young published this notebook privately in 2010 to raise funds for the Black Watch Museum in Perth.

Sometimes T.E. Young's notebook includes statements by other officers, some of them local Auchterarder men. For example, on 31 August 1916, Lieutenant Q. McLaren reports on an attempt to raid the German lines:

About 2.05 a.m. the Germans started using gas shells which came close to us. We noticed the smell of gas and put on our helmets (with gas masks). Finding we could not see with our helmets on, I decided to wait there. We were about 15 yards in front of our parapet. In the meantime one man had been gassed and sent back. We waited until 2.30 a.m. and as the gas was then much better we started off. As the first man got to our listening post about 50 yards out, I heard a bomb burst behind us and found 6 or 7 men wounded. Just as I had got back from seeing what had happened, a shrapnel shell burst and wounded 3 men. As the (raiding) party was now disorganised owing to the casualties, I decided to give up. All the wounded men have been brought in.

A few weeks later, Lieutenant McLaren was killed. Major T.E. Young reports:

October 26. 29 men under 2nd Lieutenants D Cable and Q McLaren made an unsuccessful raid on trenches opposite Tipperary Avenue, gap having been made the previous evening by Bangalore Torpedoes. Some minutes before the barrage was due to start, and immediately men left the trench, rocket fired by enemy towards his rear. Enemy at once opened machine-gun fire on gap in his wire and at several points threw bombs into his own wire. 2nd Lieutenant McLaren reached enemy wire but was killed trying to remove a chevaux de frise (a wooden structure with metal spikes) which had been placed in the gap. Surprise being impossible the party retired. Other casualties – 3 wounded.

Local women served in many different roles, often medical. Mary Elizabeth Haldane of Foswell served first at St Leonard's Hospital in Edinburgh, then in military hospitals in France. Margaret Anderson from Auchterarder was a staff nurse at military hospitals in the Eastern Mediterranean. Margaret Deuchars from Auchterarder served first in Aberdeen Military Hospital, then in the 30th General Military Hospital in France.

The No. 4 Perth Voluntary Aid Detachment, with its Quartermaster, Major T.E. Young's wife Nessie, recruited large numbers of local women, mainly for hospital work. Some women served far afield. Elsie Minty of Cloan stayed where she was, and became Sister and Masseuse in the Cloan Auxiliary Hospital throughout the war. Strathallan Castle, which had been bought in 1910 by the Yorkshire businessman Sir James Roberts, was used as a Red Cross convalescent home, treating, amongst others, Belgian soldiers.

After Germany formally capitulated 'at the eleventh hour', 11 a.m on 11 November 1918, there was a determination in Auchterarder to commemorate the sacrifice of so many local people. A War Memorial, bearing the names of the dead, was built in the Cemetery on Auchterarder High Street and unveiled in 1921. Aberuthven and Tullibardine built their own War Memorials. Throughout the British Empire, War Memorials were built, most of them with bronze plaques or sculptures mounted on massive stone plinths.

The First World War was marketed as 'the war to end all wars'. Now global politicians had to sit round the conference table and try to justify that glib claim.

38

The Roaring Twenties and After

*In which a new world order emerges, and we see alcohol banned, the Gleneagles
Hotel arrive with the Jazz Age, and the first golf match between Britain and the USA*

On 18 January 1919, a peace conference began in Paris, with representatives from
twenty-five of the victorious Allies of the First World War. On 28 June, they
signed the Treaty of Versailles, which set out terms for post-war reconstruction.
Germany was obliged to pay for the damage done during the war. The poverty-
stricken new German Republic was given thirty years to pay the debt. Resentment
rapidly grew among the new generation of German politicians who felt that
they were being punished for the policies of the German monarchy, which
they themselves had abolished. Nationalism and Socialism were the driving
philosophies of the new German populist party. Its rabble-rousing spokesman
Adolf Hitler had a genius for invoking traditional German symbols and values
and blending them with a mystical self-righteousness. The name of the National
Socialist Party was soon shortened to The Nazis by the rest of the world.

Austria, which also had abolished its monarchy, was forced to recognise the
independence of Czechoslovakia, Hungary, an enlarged Poland and the new
Yugoslavia, which was formed from an uneasy union of Balkan states. In the
Middle East, Syria became a French protectorate. Mesopotamia (today's Iraq)
became a British protectorate as did Palestine, where Jews and Arabs shared
an uncomfortable co-existence. A new nationalist movement in Turkey, led by
Mustapha Kemal, opposed to both the old Sultanate and the Allied settlements,
gathered in strength.

The horrors and crippling cost of the First World War made the Allies look
for a way to resolve future international conflicts by diplomacy rather than
military force. To achieve this, on 29 April 1919 the Covenant of the League
of Nations was signed. All member states were given equal voting rights in a
General Assembly, while an Executive Council was created with representatives
from Britain, France, Italy and Japan, with Germany and Russia added later. A
permanent secretariat was established in neutral Switzerland. The number of
participating nations grew, but the USA refused to join, feeling that its newly
won position as the world's most powerful economy might be hindered by
being only one of many round the conference table. Perversely, the USA, which

regarded itself as the world's leading democracy, was unwilling to participate in a democratic League of Nations.

Given inevitable political conflicts, the League of Nations needed an outstanding diplomat as its head. The League elected, as its first Secretary General, Sir Eric Drummond, 16th Earl of Perth, from the Strathearn aristocratic family that had woven its way through centuries of conflict. Drummond remained Secretary General until he retired in 1932, leaving the concept of a League or Union of Nations as an established feature of international politics.

France and the USA had long been republics. By the end of the First World War, Germany, Austria and Russia had also abolished their monarchies. Why did Britain keep its monarchy when nationalism and socialism swept away royal families elsewhere? The short answer is that Britain had reduced the power of its monarchs centuries before, when King Charles II was welcomed in 1660 as a head of state responsible to Parliament, after ten years of the hideously repressive Cromwellian republican experiment. In the eighteenth and nineteenth centuries, British monarchs were seen as prestigious figureheads, some more admirable and magnificent than others. Real economic, social and military policy was dictated, not by the British monarch, but by elected politicians.

Unlike the removal of autocratic regimes in Russia, Germany and Austria, to abolish the British monarchy after the First World War would have made no real difference to how the country was run. It would simply have meant that politicians grabbed royal property and administered it at public expense. On the other hand, the King was a genuine national asset. In wartime, George V was seen as a sturdy, reliable head of state, whose presence encouraging the troops was a symbol of British continuity and triumph over foreign adversaries. In Strathearn, an important source of recruits to the Black Watch, King George V enjoyed further popularity as Commander in Chief of the Regiment.

Nationalism and socialism were not revolutionary unifying forces in Britain as they were elsewhere, but ideologies to be accommodated within the existing framework of government. The exception was Ireland. Ever since the seventeenth century Plantation of Ulster, the underprivileged Catholic majority had resented the dominant Protestant minority. The Home Rule for Ireland movement had gathered force in the nineteenth century but had become frustrated by endless debates that failed to find a way to grant more local Irish democracy without compromising the United Kingdom.

On 20 April 1916, in the middle of the First World War, Sir Roger Casement, an Irishman who had served in the British diplomatic service, returned to Ireland in a German submarine to help lead an armed revolt. British troops crushed the Easter Rebellion after a week of bloodshed in Dublin and elsewhere. Casement was executed as a traitor on 3 August. For the cause of Home Rule for Ireland, the homosexual, German-assisted Casement was not the sort of leader to win British public sympathy. Nor was Padraig Pearse, the incendiary Gaelic revivalist whom the rebels chose as leader of a proposed provisional government in the Easter Rebellion. He was shot along with Casement. The astute Sinn Fein leader, Eamon de Valera, led pressure for Irish Home Rule. Civil war broke out in 1919.

In 1921, the British government ended the war by partitioning Ireland into

Northern Ireland (6 counties) and Southern Ireland (26 counties). The Catholic South became the Irish Free State and evolved into a republic in 1949. Northern Ireland remained part of the United Kingdom. In 1922, the Sinn Fein supporter Erskine Childers, who wrote *The Riddle of the Sands*, became the last British novelist to be executed for political activities. In contrast, his party leader de Valera, except for short periods out of office, became Prime Minister, then President of the Irish Republic until 1973. The partition of Ireland in 1921 instantly created a movement for reunification. The toxic mix of nationalism and sectarianism bedevils Ireland to this day.

In the industrial cities of Scotland, where there was a large Irish population, events in Ireland were closely watched and help given to both sides. However, Scottish political uprisings came, not in the form of violent separatism, but in strikes for higher wages. In 1915, engineers on Clydeside, engaged in building ships for the war effort, downed tools and demanded a wage that kept pace with wartime inflation. Their articulate leader, John Maclean, after the communist revolution in Russia in 1916, was regarded by the British establishment as a potentially dangerous leader of a Red Clydeside, which might provoke Irish-style rebellion in Scotland. In the Auchterarder area, like most of rural Scotland, the problems of Clydeside felt more remote than the daily news of local young men killed or wounded in France and Belgium.

Scottish nationalism was low on the agenda for Strathearn, where Catholic rebellions were a thing of the past. The rebel burning of Strathearn in 1716 had been avenged by the Battle of Culloden in 1746, the last pitched battle on British soil, after which the Protestant government seized the estates of rebel leaders. Crown Commissioners then imposed agricultural reforms to benefit the local population, creating peace and prosperity. In 1716, James Drummond, 2nd Duke of Perth, was a rebel leader. Two hundred years later, his kinsman Sir Eric Drummond, 16th Earl of Perth, was the trusted British diplomat chosen as first Secretary General of the League of Nations.

For Strathearn after the First World War, Scottish nationalism was an intellectual curiosity, not a political practicality. The journalist Christopher Grieve, who reinvented himself as the poet Hugh MacDiarmid, enthusiastically embraced fashionable ideologies of communism and nationalism. During a childhood illness, he had read his way through John Jamieson's *Dictionary of the Scottish Language*, acquiring a vast vocabulary of words from different centuries and widely varying regions of Scotland. He stirred these words together and called the mixture Lallans, proclaiming it to be the true language of Scotland, although many of the words had never previously been uttered in the same sentence. MacDiarmid had a great ear for sound and rhythm. Contemporary intellectuals had to acknowledge that his verse sounded good and were reluctant to admit their ignorance of much of his vocabulary. Later, MacDiarmid stood as a Communist candidate in Strathearn in the 1964 General Election and lost his deposit.

Lallans fitted into the fashion for synthetic languages that grew with the mood for international harmony after the First World War. Global synthetic languages, such as Esperanto and Volapük, enjoyed some support but were deemed impractical by most educators. The Irish playwright Bernard Shaw donated funds to promote Esperanto, but never adopted it in his own work, preferring to make money from writing in English. Lallans survived as an intellectual construct for an element of the Scottish literary establishment but never attracted the readership of works in genuine regional Scots.

A more real contribution to language is Sir James Wilson's *Lowland Scotch as Spoken in the Lower Strathearn District of Perthshire*, published in 1915. Wilson records the distinctive vocabulary and syntax of the area, with scholarly and sympathetic attention to accent and sense of humour. It remains the best guide to the way locally educated people speak today, although vocabulary has evolved considerably because of new mass media. Today, most local people are bilingual, using dialect for pithy speech and globalised English for formal language. The author of this book recently asked a habitually punctual bus driver why he was running late one afternoon. The reply was, 'A bogie cowpit ower a dyke ayont Loaninheid,' an admirably succinct way of saying that traffic flow on the A9 had been temporarily restricted by an accident involving a tractor trailer upended over a wall beyond the Loaninghead junction.

As Wilson showed, the language in Strathearn was rich. By 1918, the country was poor. The national debt at £8 billion was ten times the level of 1914. Much of the debt was owed to the USA. Victory in the First World War was followed by an economic slump. Postwar depression is a repeated pattern in history, but still comes as a surprise to victors. There was now no demand for military khaki cloth from the mills in Auchterarder and a much-reduced demand for the sort of materials made before the war. During the First World War, while men fought overseas, women filled traditional male jobs in business, factories, agriculture and public services. Their work was recognised in 1918, when women were at last given the vote, but only if they were over the age of thirty. In the nineteenth century, successive Reform Acts had extended the franchise to more and more men. In the 1918 Fourth Reform Act, all men over the age of twenty-one were given the vote. It soon became apparent, in homes shared by young couples, that women in their twenties did not lack voluble political opinions. It took until July 1928 for women over twenty-one to be given the same voting rights as men.

In the 'Khaki Election' of 14 December 1918, the newly enlarged electorate gave Lloyd George's coalition government a vote of confidence. By October 1922, amid rising unemployment, miners' strikes and other industrial unrest, the coalition fell apart. The Liberal Party split between the followers of Lloyd George and those of Asquith. Andrew Bonar Law, a Canadian-born Ulster Scottish Conservative with an honest reputation, became Prime Minister. He had little chance to make much of the job. He was already suffering from throat cancer and resigned on 20 May 1923. He died a few months later. Stanley Baldwin became Prime Minister, leading a cabinet full of Tory grandee egotists. He managed them well, but the nation was in the mood to give new blood the chance to solve Britain's problems. Baldwin lost a General Election that, on 22 January 1924, brought a Labour Party government to power in Britain for the first time.

Richard Burdon Haldane, the Auchterarder man who reformed the British army before the First World War and then served as Chancellor, had quit the internecine wrangling of the Liberal Party, and joined the Labour Party, seeing it as the way forward. In 1924, the new Prime Minister, Ramsay MacDonald, gave Haldane a second term as Chancellor, with the task of rebuilding the economy. That autumn, without consulting his Chancellor, MacDonald promised substantial financial aid to communist Russia. The public saw it as putting MacDonald's ideological sympathies ahead of Britain's national interest. On 7 November 1924, the Conservative Party, led by Stanley Baldwin, swept back to power. He remained in office for five years, surviving a General Strike in 1926 when almost half of Britain's six million trade unionists downed tools for ten days in a generally unsuccessful attempt to make employers pay higher wages.

In Strathearn, the agricultural economy struggled. So many men had been killed in the war that there was a national shortage of skilled labour. New ideas were tried. Raspberries, first introduced locally in 1907 at Drumtogle, east of Aberuthven, were profitable. After the First World War, the fields around Aberuthven and Shinafoot were covered in raspberry canes and, at summer picking-time, by a swarm of Irish migrant workers, tramps, boys from Glasgow borstals and any local people who wanted to earn quick money. The potato harvest was a more orderly affair. Cheap labour was achieved by giving schoolchildren a holiday from school. Most adult potato pickers were women, but children worked alongside them, closer to the ground and with more supple backs. Even today, the autumn school mid-term is referred to as the 'tattie holidays'.

The Education (Provision of Meals) Act of 1906 meant that 'necessitous children' received food, which their parents might otherwise not afford. Poor Law relief had always been denied to 'the able-bodied poor' but this had to be amended by emergency legislation when jobs became so scarce after the First World War. 'Broken men', penniless war veterans, some with severe disabilities, drifted through Strathearn as tramps. After the war, to provide more affordable rented properties, council housing schemes were developed down Abbey Road and Canmore Place.

During the twentieth century, most Auchterarder provosts lived in substantial villas on the west side of town or on Montrose Road. Only once did a provost live in the working-class end of town, the Feus. He was Edward Wright. His term of office, shortly after the war, was marked by a dramatic, brief transformation.

To show solidarity with the deprivation suffered by ordinary people at home in the First World War, King George V gave up drinking alcohol till the war was over. Unlike many who survived the war, the King remained a moderate drinker. The Temperance Movement campaigned to combat the scourge of alcoholism. On 29 May 1921, Auchterarder voted to close all public house bars. Alcohol could now only be served in hotels to 'bona fide travellers'. Not surprisingly, there was an unprecedented burst of enthusiastic travel from Auchterarder to Aberuthven and Blackford.

R.M. Mitchell wrote a pamphlet, published by the self-appointed National Citizens Council. He said that until 1921, 'During the fruit picking season, the flotsam and jetsam of the underworld of the cities made the town a veritable circle of the Inferno.' In 1922, he could say smugly, 'Rarely is a drunk person to be seen in the streets during the week. Even on Saturdays they are a rare species of animal.'

It did not last. In 1923, the vote was reversed, and Auchterarder became 'wet' again. Only the Luggie, the Headiers' pub at the corner of Castleton Road, was a permanent casualty of the Prohibition years. By the next decade, moral fashion had changed so much that the town elected a new provost, David Martin, who ran a brewery in Perth.

The Temperance Movement had some high-profile political victims. Winston Churchill, as First Lord of the Admiralty in the early years of the First World War, had reorganised the navy just as Haldane had reorganised the army. Churchill had a taste for fine wines. To his horror, in the 1922 General Election, the Prohibitionist candidate Edwin Scrimgeour, locally known as Neddy, ousted him as Member of Parliament for Dundee. Churchill attributed Scrimgeour's success to the votes of the newly enfranchised women jute mill workers, who saw alcoholism rife amongst their unemployed ex-soldier husbands and sons.

In Auchterarder, the Temperance Movement inspired the refurbishment of the Aytoun Hall and Girnal House between 1922 and 1924. The Public Library was moved downstairs to a larger space at the back of The Institute. Upstairs, the billiard room was extended and room provided for draughts and other table games. An attractive tearoom was added to make the buildings even more the centre of community activities. Sadly, these facilities, which were well used by both the young and the elderly, were allowed to fall into decay by the end of the twentieth century. The last remnants were finally removed in 2009.

Post-war Auchterarder was a curious mix of ancient and modern. It still had a 'town drummer', who read official notices loudly in the street, a survival of a mediaeval custom. The last town drummer was James Soutar, who had been a semaphore signaller in the First World War. Elsewhere in the world, the sound of drums meant something very different. The jazz age of 'The Roaring Twenties' was sparkling. Short-skirted Art Deco glamour flourished in Paris, New York and London. It arrived, improbably, in rural Scotland with the construction of a single building, Gleneagles Hotel, which stands on what had been the Western Commonty of Auchterarder until James Drummond of Strathallan acquired it controversially in 1817, removing the ground from the common good.

Unlike neighbouring Crieff and Dunblane, Auchterarder had never cashed in on the Hydropathic boom of the Victorian era. The town had hotels, but they were functional rather than fashionable. All this changed when Gleneagles Hotel opened in June 1924. The hotel was the brainchild of Donald Matheson, General Manager of the Caledonian Railway Company, who had acquired the site on the White Muir of Auchterarder in 1913, on a ninety-nine-year lease, but had been unable to develop it fully during the First World War (1914–1918).

Donald Matheson, aware that Auchterarder already had a reputation for excellent golf, hired champion golfer James Braid to design the King's and Queen's Courses for the new hotel. Matheson stayed in charge of the project when the Caledonian Railway was taken over by the London, Midland and Scottish Railway in 1923.

The golf course was ready before the hotel. The cairn opposite the clubhouse bears the inscription 'Gleneagles Golf Course. Opened in 1919 – the year of peace after the Great War'. In June 1921, against a backdrop of hotel construction, the course staged the first international golf competition between Great Britain and the United States.

Donald Matheson took a personal interest in the design of the hotel. After the war, Matthew Adam of the Caledonian Railway Divisional Engineer's Office revised the original plans. The exterior of the building is solid but surprisingly unassuming, given the bold nature of Matheson's project. Its architecture neither dared to follow in the florid grand manner of Victorian railway hotels, nor embraced the new clean lines of modernism. The interior, in contrast, was supremely confident. The designer, Charles Swanson, embellished the walls with plasterwork swags and enlivened the main public spaces with Baroque and Rococo detail, modified to fit the new Art Deco taste. Scott Morton & Company fitted their patent Valtor dance floor in the ballroom.

From the start, Gleneagles Hotel was astutely promoted internationally. The press hailed it as 'the Playground of the Gods'. The newly formed British Broadcasting Company (BBC) broadcast the Opening Ball at Gleneagles as the first national transmission of dance band music. Celebrity bandleader Henry Hall continued to broadcast from the hotel for many years. The glamorous free publicity was invaluable. Although a railway hotel, Gleneagles attracted the latest in air travel novelty. In 1926, Mr and Mrs Alan Butler flew their own aeroplane from Suffolk, landing on the golf course, to spend the weekend. In 1929, a Gleneagles Air Rally drew amateur pilots with golf-bags lashed to their aircraft.

Across the Atlantic Ocean, the American economy was booming. Not so many decades before, Americans had copied British manners and customs. Now the British saw the United States as modern and glamorous and copied American fashion and manners. Prince Edward, heir to the British throne, was so enthralled by the American way of life that the New York cartoonist Miguel Covarubbias published a book entitled *The Prince of Wales and Other Famous Americans*.

Baldwin's reward for piloting the British economy through the difficult 1920s was to be voted out of office. On 5 June 1929, Ramsay MacDonald's Labour Party returned to power. In December of the same year, the American stock market suffered a collapse of confidence, after a decade of reckless borrowing and wild speculation. The Wall Street Crash shook America's allies as banks collapsed and the Great Depression set in. By July 1931, there were two million unemployed in Britain. MacDonald's Labour cabinet resigned, but he continued as leader of a coalition government, which in December 1931 introduced protective tariffs and agricultural subsidies. Free trade, on which the British Empire had thrived, had to be abandoned to prevent serious civil unrest.

Despite the General Strike of 1926, and the global Market Crash of 1929, Gleneagles Hotel thrived as a luxury holiday resort for British socialites and wealthy Americans, who could dress up in fashionable, colourful golfing costumes all day, and drink equally fashionable, colourful cocktails in the evening.

Gleneagles Hotel provided much needed employment for local people. It also brought an army of casual workers, at first from the depressed West of Scotland, then from all across Europe. The hotel opened each year at Easter and closed at the end of October. The wealthy clientele understandably fluttered south to the French Riviera rather than expose their legs, clad in the new postwar short 'flapper' skirts, to the rigours of an Auchterarder winter. Not until 1982, with the development of the Country Club, did Gleneagles Hotel open all year round.

Cleverly, the LMS Railway Company provided sites for new prestigious homes next to Gleneagles Hotel, trying to attract nouveau-riche money to offset the cost of constructing the hotel. Caledonian Crescent was developed in the 1920s with a series of fine Arts and Crafts style houses, most of which still survive.

The Auchterarder rich did not spend all their time dancing the Charleston at Gleneagles Hotel. Some applied themselves to the needs of the community. Andrew Reid, son of the railway magnate James Reid of Auchterarder House, provided funds to build St Margaret's Hospital, a modern airy building designed by architects Stewart and Patterson, to complement the acute medical care provided by Perth Royal Infirmary. The Town Council granted land for the new hospital, but reserved mineral rights in case coal or other valuable material should be found underground.

The local Member of Parliament, the formidable Katharine, 8th Duchess of Atholl, opened St Margaret's Hospital in 1926. Although a member of the Conservative Party, she later supported the left-wing coalition against General Franco's fascists in the Spanish Civil War, earning her the name 'The Red Duchess'. Compassionate and outspoken, she was popular in Auchterarder.

Kitty Atholl was flamboyant and forthright. R.B. Haldane, who became Labour Leader in the House of Lords, was quiet, measured and scholarly. Haldane combined his political career with his passion for science. He became a friend of Albert Einstein and wrote *The Reign of Relativity* in 1921. Haldane's sister Elizabeth became a nurse and managed the Edinburgh Royal Infirmary. As the drive for women's rights gathered pace, in 1920 she became the first woman Justice of the Peace in Scotland.

The Haldanes were gaining a reputation as left-wing intellectuals. J.B.S. Haldane was a distinguished biologist who wrote key papers with J.S. Huxley, and was active in the British Communist Party, chairing the editorial board of the *Daily Worker*, until he revolted against 'Stalinist interference in science'. J.B.S. Haldane also wrote humorous poetry, delighting in unlikely Noel Coward-like rhymes. When he was dying of cancer of the rectum, he wrote a funny and poignant piece, advising others to seek treatment quickly, beginning, 'I wish I had the voice of Homer / To sing of rectal carcinoma.'

Naomi Mitchison, daughter of J.S. Haldane, the scientist who had fought for better conditions in the mining industry, was a tiny, flamboyant feminist author, whose novel *The Bull Calves* is an evocation of post-Jacobite Strathearn.

The Haldanes had remained in Gleneagles for centuries. Other estates changed hands in the early twentieth century. Sir James Roberts, a Yorkshire wool merchant and newspaper owner, bought Strathallan Castle in 1911. Locally, Sir James celebrated his golden wedding in 1924, by building Strathallan Hall at Tullibardine for the benefit of the community.

He did not forget his Yorkshire roots. As a boy in Haworth he had listened to sermons by the Rev. Patrick Bronte, who outlived his three famous novelist daughters, Charlotte, Emily and Anne, and his other three children. James Roberts had also met Charlotte Bronte and her husband, the curate Rev. Arthur

Nicholls. In 1927, James Roberts gave funds for a new rectory at Haworth and, having acquired the Old Parsonage, once the Bronte family home, donated the title deeds to the Bronte Society to the delight of romantic fiction enthusiasts.

Throughout the turbulence of the First World War and 1920s, King George V remained popular, except to the political far left, which wanted to seize crown assets, and to the far right, which wanted violent repression of protestors. King George V, gruff and formal, embodied Britain's glorious past and had a good sense of what would be good for the future. In 1935, he let it be known that he did not want communities to waste money on too much pomp and ceremony to celebrate his Silver Jubilee but to do something of more enduring value. Just as his grandmother Queen Victoria's Jubilees were celebrated by the building of civic halls and fountains with practical troughs for horses, so King George V saw that there was a need to preserve green spaces in towns. Britain is full of Victoria Halls and George V Jubilee Parks.

In the 1930s, the Auchterarder area had a population of just over three thousand people. There were plenty of recreational possibilities for those who lacked the funds to enjoy Gleneagles Hotel. Auchterarder Golf Club thrived, as did the town's Football, Cricket, Bowling and Tennis Clubs. The town's Literary Association, however, which had been active since Victorian times, drawing substantial audiences to the Aytoun Hall, faded away as people chose to stay at home and listen to the newly fashionable radio. Most houses had radios before they had electricity. Householders took the huge batteries to Peter Miller's electrician's shop in the High Street to be recharged with acid bubbling in the greenish glass cells.

In the late nineteenth century, Strathallan Castle had become one of the first houses in Scotland to have its own generator for electricity. For most properties, a public supply line was needed. Electrical supplies came, like the railways, in the form of small companies, which merged later. The 1926 Electricity Supply Act established a National Grid to link power stations. In the same year the first 33Kv supply line in Scotland was laid, from the Scottish Central Electric Power Company's mains at Bridge of Allan, to supply Gleneagles Hotel. This was negotiated by the Grampian Electricity Supply Company, which could then offer householders a good, but expensive, electrical supply. It was not until after the Second World War that most houses had electricity installed.

By 1930, Auchterarder had electric street lamps. The old gas lamps had gone and, with them, the evening ritual of the lamplighter doing his rounds with a small flame at the end of a pole.

Around 1927, just in time for 'talking pictures', Peter Crerar, who also ran a cinema in Crieff, opened the Regal Cinema in Auchterarder. Before the days of television, the Regal was the place to see, not only British and American films, but also Pathé Newsreels, which made global events come alive as never before. The Regal carried on, to the delight of family filmgoers, courting couples and – on Saturday matinees – hordes of children until 1963. The building now houses Stanley and Sons Antiques.

George V's Silver Jubilee was celebrated throughout the British Empire, which had undergone a major constitutional change. In 1926, the Imperial

Conference, recognising the rise of nationalism and socialism worldwide, tried to forestall independence movements in Britain's Dominions by announcing a new level of democracy. Great Britain and its Dominions were now 'autonomous communities within the British Empire, equal in status, in no way subordinate to one another . . . united by a common allegiance to the Crown and freely associated as members of the Commonwealth of Nations.' Canada, Australia, South Africa and most other Commonwealth countries were generally content with the new relationship but in India the republican movement gathered in strength, led by the charismatic ascetic Mohandas Gandhi.

In Strathearn, there was an awareness of empire similar to, if not greater than, the average person's knowledge of world affairs today. Most families bought a daily newspaper. Radio and cinema news were novelties that commanded attention. Teenage boys received Christmas presents like *The Empire Annual* or *Engineering Wonders of the World*, whose huge print runs spread an image of progress and harmony. George V's death on 20 January 1936 prompted respectful national mourning, with a sense that the new King Edward VIII would bring a bright, youthful future to the Empire. It was not to be.

Edward's passion for all things American extended to the twice-divorced Wallis Simpson, whom he proposed to marry. Public opinion was divided between those who felt the King should be allowed to marry whom he pleased and those who believed that, as the head of the established Churches, Edward must show moral leadership and marry a royal virgin. The nation struggled amid economic depression. Ramsay MacDonald's Labour government had collapsed in July 1931, but he survived as Prime Minister of a coalition government until 7 June 1935 when Stanley Baldwin's Conservative Party swept back into power.

Confronted with Edward VIII's intention to marry a double-divorcee, Prime Minister Baldwin advised that the nation would see it as a dereliction of his royal duty. The King's marriage must preserve the majesty of the Crown. Edward made a dignified and passionate speech on radio, announcing his abdication from the throne in order to marry the woman he loved. He left Britain, never to return, spending the rest of his life on the far side of the Atlantic and in France. On 10 December 1936, his younger brother became King George VI.

The new King was married to Elizabeth Bowes Lyon, descended from the Lyon family of Strathearn. The nation warmed to the way the new Queen changed the face of the monarchy by revealing something of the domestic side of royal life. George VI was shy with an awkward stutter. He had neither the gruff, soldierly presence of his father George V nor the gadabout Jazz Age glamour of Edward VIII. Instead, with the help of his Queen, George VI was portrayed as a modern family man with two attractive little daughters, Elizabeth and Margaret, and a powerful sense of duty to be the King the nation needed. In Auchterarder, George VI's coronation was celebrated with flags and bunting in the High Street and a pageant in the park.

Elsewhere in Europe, there was no such cheerful stability. The Nazi party in Germany, led by Adolf Hitler, attracted followers among ordinary people who resented the punitive financial measures imposed by the Treaty of Versailles after the First World War. On 14 October 1933, Germany withdrew from the League of Nations, and on 16 March 1935 announced that it would develop a large army in contravention of the Versailles Treaty. On 7 March 1936, Germany occupied the Rhineland and in March 1938 annexed Austria.

In Italy, the party of National Socialism was called the Fascisti. The name was taken from the fasces, a symbol from the ancient Roman Republic, showing a bundle of sticks bound together so that they were collectively unbreakable. Benito Mussolini's Fascist government in Italy introduced a massive programme of public investment in roads and other infrastructure. Germany did the same and proclaimed its new classical public buildings and highways with a fanfare of cleverly orchestrated propaganda. Its Nazis were also characterised as fascists. Fascism represented harsh militaristic Puritan intolerance. Britain had tried it once, briefly, in the seventeenth century under Cromwell and had no wish to repeat the failed experiment. In the United States of America, President Franklin Roosevelt introduced a similar huge public investment programme called The New Deal, but without obvious militarism. Communist Russia, with dictator Joseph Stalin leading the Union of Soviet Socialist Republics, produced grandiose schemes and even more grandiose propaganda, brutally enforced.

Communism and fascism had too much in common to coexist comfortably. Their rival forces clashed in Spain where civil war broke out in July 1936. Germany and Italy supported General Francisco Franco's Fascists. Communist Russia helped Spain's Socialists. As Europe slid towards another World War, Britain and France dithered. Baldwin retired soon after George VI's coronation in May 1937, having successfully protected the monarchy but failed to match Germany's massive rearmament programme. Into the Prime Minister's role slid Baldwin's Conservative colleague Neville Chamberlain, son of Joseph Chamberlain, the influential Victorian radical imperialist from Birmingham. Neville Chamberlain's political rise had establishment inevitability about it.

National and local politics figured large in daily conversation in Auchterarder. While councillors met in the Aytoun Hall, the informal 'Auchterarder Parliament' met across the road at Helm Eadie's saddler's shop at 88 High Street. In a heady atmosphere of old pipe smoke and new leather, local worthies would drop in to express their blunt opinions of politicians and officials. Councillors seeking re-election ignored the views of the 'Auchterarder Parliament' at their peril.

Prime Minister Neville Chamberlain believed that conflict could be resolved by diplomacy. His policy was to keep Britain out of trouble by appeasing fascist and communist leaders. In September 1938, after Germany decided to dismantle neighbouring Czechoslovakia, Chamberlain met Hitler in Munich. He returned, waving a piece of paper to the press, and announced that Hitler had promised 'peace with honour'. In reality, Hitler had bought time to prepare to expand the German Empire by invading Poland, which he did on 1 September 1939. It became obvious, even to Chamberlain, that Germany's ambitions extended westwards as well as eastwards. On 2 September, France and Britain sent diplomatic notes demanding that Germany withdraw its troops from Poland immediately. Hitler did not reply. On 3 September 1939, Britain and France declared war on Germany.

39

The Second World War

*In which we see an Auchterarder granny help bring the USA
into the fight against the Nazis, and meet one of the Dam Busters*

The First World War had been justified as 'The war to end all wars'. It was not.
By the early 1930s, it was obvious to political realists that Germany's imperial
ambitions were again beyond the bounds of international diplomacy. After
Britain declared war on Germany on 3 September 1939, there was no sudden
outburst of fighting. For seven months there was a 'phoney war'. The British
government waited and watched while Germany and Russia agreed to divide
Poland between them on 28 September 1939. Large numbers of Poles escaped to
the Auchterarder area.

On 9 April 1940, German troops occupied Denmark and invaded Norway.
On 10 May, German armies invaded the Netherlands, Belgium and Luxembourg.
At last, British Conservative Prime Minister Neville Chamberlain did something.
He resigned. Winston Churchill became Prime Minister. He was a Conservative
too, but a comparatively recent one. Just as Lord Haldane had left the failing
Liberal Party for Labour, so Churchill had quit the Liberals for the Conservatives.

Churchill was regarded as a maverick who never had the confidence of
the old British establishment. He had argued in the 1930s that Britain should
strengthen its armed forces. Ramsay MacDonald, Stanley Baldwin and Neville
Chamberlain had ignored his advice, leaving Britain dangerously exposed to a
massively rearmed Germany. Now the nation saw Churchill as the right man to
deal with the crisis. He formed a coalition government and immediately sent a
large expeditionary force to Belgium.

In anticipation of German air raids on cities, many children were evacuated
from their homes and sent to live with families in the safer countryside. Large
local buildings were pressed into action. Strathallan Castle became home to
Laurel Bank Junior School for Girls, evacuated from Glasgow. Laurel Bank
Senior School was based in Auchterarder House.

In 1939, Gleneagles Hotel served as a dispersal centre for evacuated children.
They arrived bewildered, clutching gas masks, to stay with families in the country
till the war was over. The hotel then became a military hospital with a specialist
RAF Psychiatric Unit after the heroic success of the Battle of Britain in 1940.

Wards were labelled A to L, with about ten hotel rooms per ward. The main dining room became Ward C, a convalescent ward with 80 beds. The little service train, which normally shuttled laundry and other supplies between Gleneagles Hotel and Gleneagles Station, now carried medical supplies and was equipped for dealing with emergencies for badly wounded patients while they were brought up to the wards or operating theatres. Later in the war, Gleneagles Hotel served as a rehabilitation centre for injured miners who, as workers in 'reserved occupations' essential to the war effort, had similar status to soldiers for medical treatment.

Churchill became Prime Minister too late to halt Hitler's charge across northern Europe. Queen Wilhelmina and her Netherlands government fled to London. German tanks and armoured cars swept across France. On 26 May 1940, Belgium surrendered to Germany. The French army provided little resistance, leaving the British expeditionary force hopelessly exposed to the vastly bigger German armies. On 25 May, Churchill ordered a retreat. In a brilliantly organised operation using hundreds of little civilian boats, soldiers were evacuated home across the Channel from Dunkirk. Not all escaped. The entire 51st Division was captured at St Valery and marched to Germany as prisoners of war.

Anne Cessford, a teacher at Laurel Bank School and an enthusiastic Scottish Country Dancer, learned that her brother had been captured. Later, she received a smuggled message from him, containing a code, which turned out to be a new Scottish Country Dance, composed to keep up the spirits of his comrades in internment. Miss Cessford taught the schoolgirl evacuees the new dance at Strathallan Castle. Today, the Reel of the 51st has become a staple of Scottish country dancing, performed to celebrate the indomitable spirit of the Scottish regiments.

Britain needed more troops quickly. On the north side of Auchterarder High Street, where the new Community School stands today, Nissen huts, with their characteristic corrugated iron roofs, were swiftly built and new recruits billeted for training and reforming the 51st Division.

On 10 June 1940, Italy joined its National Socialist ally Germany and declared war on Britain and France. Gleneagles Hotel had a large contingent of foreign workers, as it does now. In mid June, Italian and German catering staff were rounded up as potential security risks and locked into cabins on board the merchant ship *Arandora Star*, bound for Canada. Although it sailed under the international Red Cross flag, the ship was torpedoed by a German U-boat. The internees had no chance of escape. A whole generation of local catering expertise was drowned.

On 13 June, the Germans seized Paris. A new French Premier, Henri-Philippe Pétain, negotiated an armistice on 22 June, whereby the northern two-thirds of France was subject to German control. Bordeaux and the French Mediterranean ports of Toulon and Marseille remained free, while Pétain's puppet government withdrew to the spa town of Vichy far to the south of Paris. On 5 July, the Vichy government severed relations with Britain.

At home, Local Defence Volunteer units were founded in May 1940. They consisted of men aged between eighteen and sixty-five who were in day jobs essential to the war effort or were unfit for overseas combat. In July, the LDV was renamed the Home Guard, caricatured as the ill-equipped 'Dad's Army', but full of military expertise and practical local knowledge. In Auchterarder, the Home Guard was based at the Drill Hall on Montrose Road, where the Territorial Army developed a formidable stock of weapons and conducted regular training sessions.

In the build-up to the Second World War, Sir Eric Drummond, 16th Earl of Perth, who had retired in 1932 as the first Secretary General of the League of Nations, became Britain's chief adviser on foreign publicity. After war was declared, this hardened into an effective propaganda campaign, using many of the best contemporary writers and artists, co-ordinated by the Ministry of Information. Celebrated cartoonists, like Fougasse (Cyril Kenneth Bird) and Giles (Carl Ronald Giles), used wry humour to produce posters to keep up morale at home, much more effective than the grim bluster of their Nazi counterparts.

Just as his father had been a visible reassuring presence in the First World War, King George VI took pride in remaining in London, refusing to retreat to the safer countryside, even when Buckingham Palace was bombed in the Blitz. He and his Queen Elizabeth, descended from the Lyon family of Strathearn, gained great popularity by visiting bomb-damaged areas and talking to survivors. The royal family was still formal and the ways of the court mysterious, but the King and Queen were seen as genuinely sympathetic people, not remote figureheads. Their older daughter and heir to the throne, Princess Elizabeth, later endeared herself to the nation by obviously enjoying the comparative freedom of servicing vehicles as a member of the Auxiliary Territorial Service (ATS) as well as being the dutiful royal princess on public occasions.

The greatest asset to British morale was the Prime Minister. Churchill had a magnificent gift for sonorous language, combined with truculent determination and blunt realism. In Parliament and on the radio, he made speeches that exhorted the nation to greater efforts and gave praise to servicemen. His magisterial, rumbling voice stood in contrast to Hitler's strident barking. He was well aware that his two-fingered 'V for Victory' salute was not far removed from the traditional British vulgar gesture, and enjoyed its exuberant rudeness to the enemy.

On 8 August 1940, Germany began an intensive aerial bombing campaign, the Blitz, intended to destroy airfields and industrial sites throughout Britain. In Scotland, the docklands of Clydebank were the most important target. All Scottish cities were potentially vulnerable to the Luftwaffe, the German air force. As in any war, civilians were killed and non-military sites were hit. In November 1940, a bomb fell in the garden of Fernbrae Nursing Home in Dundee, where the writer of this book was born later in the war. Bombing raids were usually conducted at night when German bombers made less visible targets for anti-aircraft guns on the ground. To make it harder for the bombers, Britain imposed a blackout. Streetlights were switched off and all buildings were required to use thick curtains that prevented light from escaping. German navigators had to rely on maps, rather than ground-level aids.

Britain fought back. New modern fighter aircraft, Hurricanes and Spitfires, were manufactured as quickly as possible to attack German bombers and their accompanying fighters. In the Battle of Britain in the autumn of 1940, hundreds of young pilots were killed, but German losses were even greater. On one day, 16 September 1940, 185 German aircraft were destroyed. The sheer size of the Luftwaffe kept the Blitz going until June 1941.

The German submarine blockade of the British coast, begun on 17 August 1940, almost eliminated imports of food, creating severe shortages, especially in cities. The government launched a 'Dig for Victory' campaign, encouraging people to grow their own vegetables. Owners dug up suburban lawns and flowerbeds and planted vegetables. In rural Strathearn, most householders already had a kitchen garden. Many kept hens. When food rationing was introduced, Strathearn families were generally better equipped to cope than those in cities.

For the first years of World War II, the USA refused to join Britain in the fight against Nazi Germany. The American Ambassador to London, Joe Kennedy, father of the future President John Kennedy, was of Irish Catholic stock and remained bitter towards the British government over 'The Troubles' in Ireland. He advised the USA to remain neutral like the new Republic of Ireland. At the same time, American government loans to Britain were running out.

President Franklin Roosevelt sent his personal security adviser, Harry Hopkins, to Britain to assess the situation and to advise him whether to support Britain against the Nazis. On 18 January 1941, in the North British Hotel (now the Millennium Hotel) in Glasgow's George Square, Harry Hopkins had dinner with the British Prime Minister, Winston Churchill, and Tom Johnston, Secretary of State for Scotland.

After the meal, Hopkins delivered a speech, quoting the Book of Ruth from the Bible: 'Perhaps I may say in the language of the old Book to which my grandmother from Auchterarder and no doubt your grandmother too, Mr Chairman, paid much attention: "Wheresoever thou goest we go and where thou lodgest we lodge, thy people shall be our people, thy God our God, even unto the end".'

Churchill was moved to tears. Hopkins went back to the USA and presented a report to President Roosevelt, arguing that American support for Britain was urgently needed to defend global democracy. Harry Hopkins' determination to defend the land of his Auchterarder grandmother was more persuasive than Joe Kennedy's 'wait and see' neutrality. On 11 March 1941, the United States Congress passed the Lend-Lease Act, giving President Roosevelt powers to grant economic aid, goods and services to nations whose defence was in the US interest. In effect, this meant Britain. By December, over a million tons of food had been delivered. Atlantic convoys of Merchant Navy ships, protected by destroyers and cruisers, kept Britain supplied.

Who was Harry Hopkins' grandmother? She seems to have been born into an Auchterarder family called Wannan in the early nineteenth century, married a Perth man called Hopkins and emigrated to the USA. To her grandson Harry and to a free Europe, she meant a great deal.

On 22 June 1941, Hitler invaded Russia. It was the same arrogant mistake that Napoleon had made in 1812. The 2,000-mile-wide Eastern Front was too big, even for Germany's huge armies. On 13 July, Britain and Russia signed a mutual aid charter. Building on Harry Hopkins' report and the Lend-Lease Act, on 14 August, Churchill and Roosevelt signed the Atlantic Charter, agreeing the importance of defending the sovereign rights of nations that had suffered occupation. Soon after, Churchill agreed to support American interests in the Pacific in the event of war with Japan, which was aligning itself with Germany and Italy. On 7 December 1941, the Japanese air force bombed the US naval base at Pearl Harbor in Hawaii. On 11 December, the USA entered the Second World War as a formidable military power.

The battlefields of the First World War consisted of men in trenches pounded by ponderous artillery. By the time of the Second World War, fast army lorries, armoured cars and tanks made troop deployment much more mobile. As Hitler's armies demonstrated in May 1940, it was possible to outflank opposing forces and advance hundreds of miles within days. Newly developed large aircraft could deliver bombs over far greater distances than shells fired from ground-based artillery.

Taking the tactical value of speed a stage further, David Stirling, from Keir, fifteen miles west of Auchterarder, devised a plan to create small units of the bravest and most skilled men to be flown or dropped by parachute to strike key targets. Like Churchill, David Stirling was seen as a maverick. The more orthodox members of the military establishment disliked him, but he was given permission to form the Special Air Service in 1941. At first its units operated in North Africa and the Middle East, but over the years the SAS developed a reputation as Britain's most ruthlessly effective assault troops. Today, David Stirling is commemorated by a bronze statue, showing him standing in his military duffel coat, facing the hills behind the ancient pistol-making village of Doune near his Keir home.

The newly reformed 51st (Highland) Division avenged the disaster of St Valery by its victories in North Africa in 1942, particularly in helping halt the progress of German Field Marshal Erwin Rommel at the Battle of El Alamein on 23 October. On 8 November, more American and British forces landed in North Africa to drive out the Italian and German invaders. The Highland Division, including the 1st Black Watch, advanced to Tripoli and Tunisia. By May 1943, the Allies had control of North Africa. The pipes and drums of the Highland Division marched through Tunis in a victory parade. Meantime, the 2nd Battalion of the Black Watch saw service further east, protecting the Suez Canal.

On 10 July 1943, the Allies invaded Sicily. Two weeks later, the Italian dictator Benito Mussolini resigned. Marshal Pietro Badoglio replaced him, abolished Mussolini's Fascist Party, and agreed an armistice with the Allies on 3 September 1943. The Fascists fought back. A German army advanced south to Rome, freed Mussolini on 12 September and set him up as leader of a puppet government. After months of heavy fighting in Italy, the Allies entered Rome on 4 June 1944, but German troops remained in other parts of Italy until the end of April 1945, when Mussolini was captured and executed by Italian anti-Fascists.

The Highland Division fought in the olive groves of Sicily in 1943 and was then withdrawn to prepare for an even bigger assault on the enemy. On 6 June 1944,

British, Canadian and American ground forces in 4,000 landing craft, backed by 600 warships and 10,000 aircraft, landed on the beaches of Normandy in Northern France. These D-Day landings forced the German occupying armies to retreat. The Highland Division retook St Valery, hailed by local celebrations. They pressed eastwards with other Allied forces. On 24 August, the Germans withdrew from Paris. On 2 September, the Allies took the Belgian capital Brussels. By October, the Black Watch was fighting on German soil.

Germany was also under attack from the east where the Russians, having crushed German armies in the long Battle of Stalingrad during the winter of 1942–43, regained control of western Russia then drove across Poland the following winter towards the German capital Berlin.

Germany's Luftwaffe had failed to subdue Britain despite the damage wreaked by the Blitz. Britain fought back with bombing raids of its own. Most famous of these are the Dam Buster attacks of 1943, in which 'bouncing bombs' were skimmed across the Mohne and Eder Lakes in the industrial Ruhr to destroy dams and flood crucial German infrastructure. Squadron Leader James Smith of the RAF 617 Dam Buster Squadron is commemorated on the War Memorial Gates in Auchterarder High Street Cemetery. He was a meteorologist as well as a pilot and gave essential weather advice to the Dam Busters' leaders Barnes Wallis and Guy Gibson.

Britain hit Germany with saturation bombing attacks on Essen and other industrial cities early in 1944. German aircraft factories were destroyed, leaving many fighters and bombers grounded without spare parts. They were sitting targets for the next wave of Allied bombers. Throughout 1944, Germany was unable to give her ground troops adequate air support. In 1944, American General Dwight Eisenhower became Supreme Commander Allied Expeditionary Forces. His success brought him the presidency of the USA in 1952.

On 7 February 1945, Churchill, Roosevelt and the Russian leader Joseph Stalin met at Yalta in the Crimea to plan the final defeat of Germany. On 1 May, Russian troops entered Berlin to find that Hitler had shot himself on 30 April. A new German government was hastily formed under Admiral Karl Dönitz, who sought an armistice. On 7 May, German military commanders were summoned to Reims in eastern France where they signed an unconditional surrender. On 8 May, towns across Britain celebrated VE Day (Victory in Europe). The streets of Auchterarder were lined with flags. This time, there was no talk of a 'war to end all wars'.

As in the First World War, many prisoners of war were sent to the Auchterarder area, mainly for agricultural work. A barbed-wire enclosure was created behind the School, as a holding compound. Those regarded as low security were allocated to local farms. Many German and Italian prisoners had been unwilling conscripts into the Fascist armies and had no wish to escape from Scotland. One German prisoner of war, Kurt Steinle, later became an electrician and popular community councillor in Auchterarder.

Despite American food aid and increased military success, food rationing remained in Britain. The 1944 allowance per person per week was: 4 oz (113 g) bacon and ham; 8 oz (226 g) sugar; 2 oz (56 g) tea; 1 s 2 d worth (6 p) meat; 4 oz

(113 g) margarine; 2 oz (56 g) cooking fat; 2 pints milk; 1 egg per 2 weeks; 12 oz (340 g) sweets per 4 weeks. Clothes and other goods were also rationed. Even in years after the war, oranges were a rare treat and at least one small local boy, familiar with pictures of pineapples from books, was surprised by their texture, years later, when he first handled one. He had expected them to be more like the hand grenades that his father had let him touch.

During the war, the Nazi submarine blockade meant that sugar could no longer be easily imported from the West Indies. The same thing had happened in the First World War and a subsidy had been introduced in 1925, encouraging Scottish farmers to grow sugar beet to be processed at a factory in Cupar in Fife. Local sugar-beet production reached a significant level only after the Second World War made it a necessity. Some shops made their own sweets. Dempster's Confectionary in Auchterarder produced toffee in tin trays. The proprietor broke up the hard toffee with a little silver hammer and weighed out the pieces in accordance with ration book regulations. Fortunately for small boys and girls, there were always little splinters of toffee, which the proprietor allowed to escape the rules. Rationing continued long after the war was over. Clothes rationing lasted from 1941 until 1949. Food rationing went on until 1953.

VE Day did not end the Second World War. By the summer of 1942, the Japanese had overrun the Philippines, Malaya, Burma and the Dutch East Indies. Hundreds of thousands of Allied troops and civilians were put into forced labour camps. Over a quarter of them died of disease and malnutrition in construction schemes like the Burmese Railway. Over the next three years, although they suffered heavy losses, American ground and naval assaults recaptured the Pacific battle zones. In 1945 America was within attacking distance of Japan itself.

President Franklin Roosevelt, most of whose political career had been conducted from his wheelchair after suffering paralysis from 1921, died in April 1945, three weeks before VE Day. His Vice-President Harry Truman became President and decided that, rather than subject American troops to a long war of attrition on Japanese soil, he would use the newly developed atomic bomb to terrify Japan into surrender. On 6 August 1945, the Allies dropped an atomic bomb on Hiroshima, destroying half the city and leaving thousands of survivors permanently damaged by radiation. Soon after, Nagasaki suffered the same treatment.

On 10 August, Japan capitulated. On 26 August, American forces landed in Japan. The Japanese Empire, which had extended into China, was dismantled. An empire in growing ascendancy, the Union of Soviet Socialist Republics, led by Joseph Stalin's Russia, declared war on Japan on 8 August and invaded Manchuria. Within weeks, almost a million Japanese occupying forces in China surrendered to the Allies. The Japanese government signed a formal treaty of surrender on 2 September 1945, which became known as VJ day (Victory over Japan).

Many young people from the Auchterarder area served in the Second World War. Casualties were not as heavy as in the First World War, but, by the time of victory in 1945, the names of more dead soldiers had to be added to the War Memorial. At the old High Street Cemetery, new wrought-iron gates were installed to commemorate the dead. Along with Dam Buster James Smith, more than half of the local servicemen killed served in the RAF. Others served in the Argyll and Sutherland Highlanders, the Black Watch, the Cameronians, the Commandos, the Royal Artillery and the Seaforths. The Treaty of Versailles peace settlement after the First World War had failed to prevent another global conflict. Could the politicians in 1945 do any better?

The Second World War changed Britain's social structure. The old hierarchical strata were increasingly seen as irrelevant. The 92-year-old Arthur, 1st Duke of Strathearn, died in 1942. His grandson Alastair succeeded him, but died the following year without an heir. The mighty Earldom of Strathearn, which had grown out of the Kingdom of Fortriu and was central to forming a united Scotland, was now only a historic name. Within a few decades, however, Auchterarder, the town set on a strategic ridge, would enter a new era and witness events of even greater global significance.

Strathearn was too important for its royal title to lie dormant for long. In 2011 Prince William, next in line to his father Charles, Prince of Wales as heir to the thrones of England and Scotland, was created Earl of Strathearn.

40

Postwar Regeneration

*In which sectarian faiths divide the world, the Welfare State arrives, the Royal
Burgh thrives again and a small boy develops a low opinion of official reports*

Within seven weeks of the end of the Second World War, a new international
body, The United Nations, was created to replace the old League of Nations.
The world's most powerful nation, the USA, had never joined the old League,
which fell apart after the rise of National Socialism. The United Nations was
formally established on 24 October 1945 with fifty-one founder countries, rising
to nearly two hundred today.

The UN had a new headquarters in New York City, replacing the Geneva base
of the League of Nations. It demonstrated a new political culture in which the
old imperial European nations held less power. The UN is designed to maintain
world peace, but the five members of its Security Council, China, France, Russia,
Britain and the USA, can each veto any decisions made by the General Assembly.

After 1945, the world was again divided into opposing doctrines. Instead
of the Islam versus Christianity or Protestant versus Catholic conflicts of the
past, the new faiths were not religions promising a better life after death, but
economic theories promising instant rewards. The USA and Western Europe
were capitalist. China, Russia and the rest of the Soviet Union were communist.
Neither theory was new. The Scottish economist Adam Smith, in *The Wealth
of Nations* published in 1776, had advocated capitalism with its emphasis on
free trade and private initiative. The German Jew Karl Marx wrote the bible
of communism, *Das Kapital*, published in 1867, in exile in the British Museum,
emphasising the need for coherent central government regulation.

As with all faiths, capitalism and communism were re-interpreted by politicians.
Communist dictators, like the Russian Joseph Stalin and the Chinese leader Mao
Zedong, led oppressive regimes that perpetuated mass poverty in the name of
equality. In the West in the 1940s and '50s, capitalism allowed much greater
economic benefits for an increasing middle class, but let the rich get richer with
the poor left far behind. Stalin's death in 1953 reduced terror within Russia.
International tension remained high.

Shared faith does not mean shared political alliance. Just as Catholic France
and the Catholic Holy Roman Empire were bitter enemies for centuries, so
communist Russia and China fell out. The Western European capitalist nations

held an envious grudge against the richer USA. Despite differences, in 1949 the USA and Britain joined with twelve other European nations to form the North Atlantic Treaty Organisation (NATO), building a huge arsenal of nuclear weapons. The Soviet Union did the same. A long Cold War set in, characterised by blustering speechmaking. After the example of Hiroshima, there was a worldwide fear of nuclear devastation on a global scale as scientists devised increasingly destructive new weapons.

Winston Churchill had been the inspirational leader of Britain's wartime coalition government. In the general election of July 1945, although the Conservative Churchill remained personally popular, the nation chose a Labour government led by Clement Attlee, who had been the coalition's Deputy Prime Minister. Attlee correctly judged that the British people were prepared to accept his policies of national austerity to pay off wartime debt, provided that social issues were fairly tackled. The postwar Labour government tried to create a humane blend of the state control doctrines of communism and the private enterprise of capitalism. This socialism was easily championed or vilified by those with narrow viewpoints.

Britain was desperately short of housing at affordable rents. Labour introduced a massive programme of local council-house building. Healthcare was expensive. The vigorous young Health Minister Aneurin Bevan created the National Health Service in 1947, with free care for all funded by a National Insurance scheme. Labour nationalised the floundering railway, coal, gas, electricity and steel industries. Education was reformed, giving poorer children access to better schools. The school-leaving age was raised from fourteen to fifteen in 1947 to create a better-qualified workforce. Attlee's policies were brave and well-intentioned. They genuinely improved social conditions and enhanced equality. They also created a culture of inert dependency on the state and inflexible nationalised industries that resisted modernisation and became an unsustainable burden on the economy.

The Auchterarder area is a good example of how the new socialist policies worked out in practice. After the war, the Auchterarder area retained its ethos of communal practicality, unthinkable to the standardised, heavily regulated world of the twenty-first century. For example, in January 1945 when the new Aberuthven minister, the Rev. Allan Bell, arrived after a snowstorm, local children were given time off school to clear the manse drive for his furniture vans.

In 1950, the population of the Auchterarder area was still just over three thousand. The need for postwar regeneration was recognised in the Tay Valley Plan of 1950. It noted that in Auchterarder 'one quarter of the young people leave the locality to find employment'.

The youth of Aberuthven were regarded as less enterprising, having 'rural outlook and upbringing. Many have no apparent desire to better themselves.' The author of the book you are holding was in a class of 'mixed infants' at Aberuthven Primary School at the time. Many of his contemporaries grew up to lead more useful lives than the compilers of official reports who sneer at the very people whose taxes finance officialdom.

The Tay Valley Plan led to the construction of large numbers of council houses on the south side of Auchterarder, adding to those built down Abbey Road before the war. The biggest new scheme was the Rossie Place development on the old South Crofts. They were modern, light and airy compared to the Victorian housing stock, much of which had become damp and dingy. The new council houses had affordable rents. Home ownership generally remained an upper- and middle-class privilege until the 1960s.

The Auchterarder writer James Kennaway was internationally acclaimed for his ability to show the nuances of social change. He captured the tensions between the old British imperial traditions and the new desire for a more equal society in his novel *Tunes of Glory*, which was made into an influential film, starring Alec Guinness and John Mills. James Kennaway died of a heart attack at the wheel of his car in 1968, when he was only forty.

Many of Kennaway's novels and film scripts drew on his Auchterarder childhood. However, perhaps the best novel ever set in Auchterarder, *Gentleman Adventurer*, was written not by James Kennaway but by his father. Charles Kennaway was a local lawyer, active in public affairs, who became President of the Scottish Branch of the National Association of Auctioneers, Estate and House Agents. *Gentleman Adventurer* is a rip-roaring yarn set in the Jacobite Rebellions, full of historical and topographical detail about Strathearn.

One of the old Auchterarder families produced a scholarly writer who wrote about previously neglected aspects of Scottish history. A.R.B. Haldane produced three definitive works: *The Drove Roads of Scotland*; *New Ways Through the Glens*; and *Three Centuries of Scottish Posts*. He also wrote perceptively about the local countryside in *The Path by the Water*.

The town market behind the Star Hotel was active during the 1950s. On Friday and Saturday mornings, the Star Wynd was barricaded for sheep sales, run by Hay Auctioneers of Perth. Before the war, people going to the Town Laundry on the Star Wynd sometimes moved the barricades slightly. Sheep then squeezed through and wandered down the High Street.

After the Town Laundry closed in 1938, sheep had to find their own ways of escaping. They often did, rambling past the frontage of the spooky, disused Secession Church (1813–1953). Its roof had been wrecked in the Great Storm of December 1879, which caused the Tay Railway Bridge disaster and William MacGonagall's lament. Another local church had lost its roof that 1879 night, when the storm blew down a tree on to the little chapel of Gleneagles House. Unlike the Secession Church, it was later beautifully restored.

Gleneagles Hotel reopened in 1947, refurbished after its wartime service as a hospital. When the railways were nationalised soon after, Gleneagles remained a luxury flagship of the new state industry. The menus were as lavish as ever, though The Ministry of Food, which continued rationing for many years after the war, restricted Gleneagles diners so that 'not more than three courses in all may be partaken of at any one meal'.

With railway nationalisation, something of the spirit of enterprise was lost and the interior of Gleneagles Hotel for many years came to look comfortably shabby, rather like the great ocean-going liners, the *Queen Mary* and the *Queen*

Elizabeth, which had also seen better days. Despite belonging to an unglamorous nationalised industry, Gleneagles Hotel retained its reputation as an international-class resort.

Gleneagles Hotel guests, seeking luxury goods, were a potential source of revenue for Auchterarder shops. In 1948 R. Watson Hogg opened a high-class outfitters' shop in the building at the top of Montrose Road, originally built by mill-owner William Hally in the 1860s as a warehouse for the jute, flax and linen brought to Auchterarder Station from the Dundee Docks. Bertie Hogg thriftily used his middle name, Watson, for business purposes, so that the carved stone initials 'W H' on William Hally's Victorian warehouse frontage, now stood for Watson Hogg.

Watson Hogg's elegant premises on the High Street were internationally renowned for cashmeres and other fine cloths, but locally Bertie Hogg was constantly cut down to size by youths jeering 'Who killed Kerr's cat?' recalling an accident when he was an errand boy on his bicycle. In 1993, William Hally's great, great, great-grandson, Richard bought the building to make it again part of the Hallys' woollen business.

After the Second World War, Auchterarder again became a prestigious holiday destination, but the town's Royal Burgh status had become uncertain. Even in the Middle Ages, there were periods when Auchterarder, lacking a port to boost its economy, failed to fulfil its statutory duties as a Royal Burgh. After the Union of the Scottish and English Parliaments in 1707, the people of Auchterarder had been unable to pay the dues owed by a Royal Burgh.

In the nineteenth century, the landowner Basil Cochrane had tried to get his hands on the Eastern Common Muir on the spurious grounds that Auchterarder's Royal Burgh status had lapsed. He was unable to get away with his attempt, but other landowners in 1817 controversially took possession of the Western Commonty, including the White Muir where Gleneagles Hotel now stands. The town, however, retained both its Eastern Common Muir and its royal title.

Auchterarder Town Clerk Robert Young and his unrelated successor Kenneth Young, an able historian from the long-established local legal family, led the campaign to have Auchterarder officially recognised again. On 28 September 1951, Auchterarder was reconfirmed as Strathearn's Royal Burgh. It was founded in the twelfth century. At no point had its status lapsed, but reconfirmation gave due recognition to the town's historical importance. The town whose name means 'the well-watered place on the ridge' now flourished a handsome Royal Burgh coat of arms.

Ironically, in the same year a hot, dry summer led to a failure of the water supply from Duchally. In the late 1950s, to provide a bigger, more efficient supply for Strathearn, a dam was built to raise the level of Loch Turret, north-west of Crieff. Auchterarder received the new supply in 1960.

Massive hydro-electric schemes, which had been delayed because of the Second World War, now brought electricity to most homes. At first, appliances were very expensive in relation to incomes, which remained low, as in all rural areas.

After the National Health Service was created in 1947, every person had the right to be on a general practitioner's list for free consultation. There were two sudden changes to child health. The first was a huge demand for free NHS glasses, transforming the educational possibilities for poorer children with bad eyesight.

The second change was that large numbers of dentists deserted the previous free school dental service to set up their own more profitable practices as subsidised NHS dentists. In the Auchterarder area, there were no school dentists just at the time when wartime rationing of sweets was about to end. The combination of inadequate school dentistry and joyous return to sugar can be seen in the mouths of many older people today.

Even after food rationing ended, the schools were still mobilised for many years as collection points for rose hips, picked by children for pocket money, which were processed in factories into sickly, but vitamin-rich syrup. Similarly, the autumn mid-term break saw willing – and less-willing – children earn money by picking potatoes in 'the tattie holidays'. Most families would pick wild brambles and make jam, a practice which remained widespread until the local advent of mass pesticides and cheap fruit imports in the 1970s.

Auchterarder School offered no education beyond the minimum school-leaving age, raised from fourteen to fifteen in 1947. Education was reformed, through 'grant-aiding', to allow children in the Auchterarder area, if they did well in the primary school 'Qualifying Exams', to have free secondary education at the previously private Morrison's Academy in Crieff. This gave an alternative to the state-owned Perth Academy, which also offered a good education up to Sixth Form level for academically ambitious children from the area.

Laurel Bank School, evacuated to Auchterarder during the Second World War, returned to Glasgow in September 1944, leaving Auchterarder House vacant. St Margaret's School from Edinburgh took up the lease, because their school boarding house had been taken over by the army as an ATS Hostel. St Margaret's School remained in Auchterarder till 1956.

Morrison's Academy in Crieff, when it became 'grant-aided', brought the children of less prosperous families to sit as day pupils beside boarders, who were the children of tea and rubber planters or colonial administrators. Education at Morrison's in the 1950s retained a strong Victorian imperial flavour. School reading books contained tales of colonial heroics. In music lessons, children sang military songs like *The British Grenadiers* and *Hearts of Oak*.

At Morrison's in the 1950s, children were also taught to sing *D' Ye Ken John Peel*, a rousing invocation to fox-hunting. In a curious blend of innocence and insensitivity, teachers made children sing songs from the nineteenth-century slave-owning American South, like *Polly Wolly Doodle* with the line 'I jumped upon a nigger 'cos I thought he was a hoss (horse).' At home, children were instinctively more modern. They tuned into the new independent station Radio Luxembourg and listened indiscriminately to the white American rock and roll of Elvis Presley, Buddy Holly and Gene Vincent and their black counterparts Little Richard, Fats Domino and the Platters.

In school playgrounds, while girls skipped and played counting games, small boys re-enacted war. The 'baddies' were either the Nazis, who lingered for decades as the embodiment of evil, or the 'Commies' particularly after war broke out in Korea in June 1950, with Britain and the USA sending troops to defend South Korea against communist North Korea. The war lasted only a year, but reinforced international prejudices.

After the First World War the British Empire had begun the transition from a network of dominions ruled from London to a Commonwealth of more equal nations. After the Second World War, Britain recognised that it must grant full independence or face nationalist revolutions around the world. On 20 February 1947, India became an independent nation. With the intention of avoiding religious conflicts, a new nation of Pakistan was created from the mainly Islamic regions of northeast and northwest India. The two halves of Pakistan were over 1,600 km apart and fell into civil war, resolved on 16 December 1971 when East Pakistan became the separate nation of Bangladesh.

In 1948, the Federation of Malaya was formed from smaller states and evolved into fully independent Malaysia in 1957. Some new nations cut their ties with the British Commonwealth. Burma left in 1947. The Republic of Ireland left in 1949.

The predominantly white English-speaking former colonies of Canada, Australia and New Zealand remained stable allies within the British Commonwealth. Africa was much more troubled. Over the following decades, Kenya, Uganda, Tanzania and South Africa evolved more violently. Rhodesia split into Zambia and Zimbabwe.

The British public generally welcomed the welfare state created by Attlee's Labour government, but became impatient with its austerity policies, particularly rationing. Drab 'Utility' clothing and plain 'Utility' furniture seemed old-fashioned when the 1951 Festival of Britain in London displayed a colourful array of new fashions, products and technology. Like the Great Exhibition a hundred years before, it was a confident statement of Britain's ingenuity and manufacturing capacity. Winston Churchill's Conservative Party was returned to office in October 1951 in a mood of national optimism.

On 6 February 1952, King George VI died of cancer. His 25-year-old daughter became Queen Elizabeth II. She and her husband, Prince Philip, Duke of Edinburgh, a distinguished naval officer and keen amateur sportsman with a reputation for not suffering fools gladly, seemed to embody modernity. The Coronation on 2 June 1953 was an excuse for thousands of families to buy their first television set in order to watch the pageantry of the glamorous New Elizabethan Age. A team of Commonwealth climbers, led by John Hunt and Edmund Hillary, conquered the summit of Mount Everest, the world's highest mountain, days before the coronation. On 6 May 1954 Roger Bannister ran the first four-minute mile. Food rationing ended on 3 July 1954. Everything seemed to be going right for Britain.

It could not last. The elderly Churchill retired on 6 April 1955, replaced as Prime Minister by his Conservative colleague, the urbane Anthony Eden. On 26 July 1956, the Egyptian President Abdel Nasser nationalised and seized the Suez Canal. Eden, with the aid of France but without securing the support of the USA, bombed Egyptian military targets on 3 October and retook the Suez Canal. Eden found himself condemned by the United Nations and the USA for his precipitate attack. Britain withdrew from the Canal Zone on 23 November.

Humiliated, Eden resigned on 9 January 1957. Another upper-class Conservative colleague, Harold Macmillan, became Prime Minister. In the Auchterarder area, the Suez crisis disrupted fuel supplies around harvest time. Many farmers had replaced their horses with tractors and modern agricultural machinery after petrol rationing ended in 1950. It was a lesson in the vulnerability of new technology.

Macmillan was an astute statesman with a sharp sense of humour that at first endeared him to the press. He seemed capable of restoring Britain's prestige in the world. On 25 March 1957, France, Germany, Italy, Belgium, the Netherlands and Luxembourg formed the European Economic Community, the forerunner of today's EU. Britain, however, did not consider itself to be part of Europe, but the leader of a global Commonwealth of Nations.

In 1957, Macmillan was widely quoted as saying, 'Most of our people have never had it so good', as the economy expanded and the welfare state thrived. In the Auchterarder area, it was not that simple. The textile trade struggled. The mills employed fewer people. Only the American market expanded significantly. By 1960, Gleneagles Knitwear was sending 80 per cent of its products to the USA.

The postwar years saw traditional agriculture become increasingly mechanised, with fewer men employed. New ideas were needed. The area made a substantial contribution to new bio-science in the 1950s, when Sir James Denby Roberts at Strathallan and John Marshall at Dalreoch led the way in producing, on a commercial scale, 'virus-free' stocks of potatoes, bred from individual clones from the Rothamstead Laboratory. By 1962, Rev. Dr William Morrice, writing in *The Third Statistical Account*, could say about local labourers, 'The increase in people from Ireland is due to the large potato business done in the district.'

The churches in Auchterarder regrouped. In 1955, St Andrews Church (now The Gleneagles Furniture Centre) joined with the West Church (now demolished), which lay behind today's Golf Hotel. The Barony Church eventually became the only Church of Scotland in Auchterarder and was renamed the Parish Church in 1983. With diminishing and ageing congregations, other church unions took place in Strathearn. Aberuthven was linked first to Gask, then to Dunning.

Dr Morrice attributed declining church attendance to the influences of unemployment, war, television and golf, adding, 'Bus parties on Sundays contribute to a general unsettlement. The Sunday peace is gone.' It had been gone for some time. A previous minister, writing *The First Statistical Account* in 1783, had lamented the wearing of 'the gay cloths, muslins, silks and printed cottons of England' on the Scottish Sabbath. Dr Morrice did not know it, but Sixties Britain was about to become much more garish.

41

The Swinging Sixties

*In which we see a communist poet set the rules for today's
party political broadcasts, and the first man walks on the
moon while Queen Victoria still jingles in British pockets*

The Cold War between communist Russia and the capitalist West continued to dominate politics in the 1960s. The Russian leader Nikita Khrushchev blustered in the United Nations. The American President John F Kennedy, who replaced the old war hero Dwight Eisenhower in 1960, added to the war of rhetoric. Remembering Kennedy's ambassador father Joseph, who had delayed the USA's entrance into the Second World War, British politicians were wary of the new American President and his glamorous entourage, nicknamed Camelot.

Since the Second World War, military success had depended on domination of the skies. Both sides invested in fleets of heavy bombers and huge unmanned guided missiles capable of delivering a nuclear holocaust. On 4 October 1957, Russia made a further technological advance, launching Sputnik I, the first satellite to orbit the earth and transmit radio signals. The United States entered into a costly 'space race' with Russia to land the first man on the moon, a project of negligible strategic value, but enormous prestige. Soon, satellites came to be regularly launched for surveillance, scientific exploration and communication.

At ground level in Britain, communication improved when, on 5 September 1959, it became possible to make a long-distance phone call without going through the operator. Auchterarder, like other towns, gained an automatic telephone exchange. The government called the new system 'Subscriber Trunk Dialling' or STD, provoking giggles in the medical profession to whom STD meant 'Sexually Transmitted Diseases'.

On 13 August 1961, communist East Germany built a huge concrete barrier across Berlin to stop disillusioned citizens from escaping to capitalist West Berlin. The Berlin Wall became a symbol of communist paranoia and repression. During the Cold War, there were endless rumours of spying by all the nations involved. In June 1963, one of these rumours flared into a scandal that brought down the Macmillan government. Britain's Secretary of State for War, John Profumo, lied to Parliament about his affair with call girl Christine Keeler, who was also involved with a Russian diplomat.

The press uncovered an underworld of prostitution, drugs, slum landlords, gangsters, sleazy osteopaths and foreign agents, which overlapped with the glamorous world of Britain's social and political elite. Harold Macmillan, already in poor health, resigned as Prime Minister on 10 October 1963. He was succeeded by the 14th Earl of Home, a descendant of Alexander, 1st Lord Home who led King James IV's army to victory at Sauchieburn in 1488.

Home renounced his peerage in order to sit in the House of Commons. A constituency seat had to be found for him. William Leburn, Conservative MP for Kinross and West Perthshire, had just died. Their by-election party candidate George Younger, from the Scottish brewing dynasty, was persuaded to step aside in favour of his party leader who ran as Sir Alec Douglas-Home. Younger later became an MP elsewhere and was rewarded with the job of Secretary of State for Scotland and other cabinet posts. In the 1963 by-election, Sir Alec won easily. For the first time, Strathearn had Britain's Prime Minister as its MP.

In the general election the following year, Sir Alec Douglas-Home was challenged by, among others, C.M. Grieve, better known by his pen name, the poet Hugh MacDiarmid. He had been a vociferous Scottish Nationalist but, when its party leaders failed to share MacDiarmid's own high opinion of himself, he became a Communist, embarrassing his new party by praising the late Russian dictator, Stalin. MacDiarmid's attempt to stage a Communist rally in Auchterarder was met with complete local indifference, but had important consequences for television.

When Sir Alec swept to victory, MacDiarmid blamed television and petitioned the Election Court in Edinburgh to declare the election void, on the grounds that Sir Alec's party-political broadcasts gave him an unfair advantage. The Court rejected his petition, ruling that Sir Alec's party-political broadcasts, as Prime Minister, were a matter of public information. That was not the end of the matter.

At the time, the BBC and Independent Television allocated broadcasting time to the Conservative, Labour and Liberal parties in proportion to the number of seats they held in the Commons. The MacDiarmid case, after the failed communist rally in Auchterarder, highlighted the bias in favour of the party in power. As a result, broadcasting arrangements were changed to allow airtime to minority candidates. Today, party-political broadcasts cause a power surge on the National Grid as viewers experience a sudden need to go away and put the kettle on.

Television was now the preferred medium for news and entertainment. From the mid 1950s independent television channels were allowed to compete with the BBC. In 1961, Grampian Television began broadcasting to the north of Scotland and later expanded to cover Perthshire. Two decades previously, the attractions of the radio had helped kill the Auchterarder Literary Association. When people chose to sit in front of a small screen, the cinema went into decline. The Regal closed in 1963 and became Stanley and Sons' Antiques.

As memories of wartime receded, a wave of nostalgia arrived in the 1960s and '70s. The antiques trade boomed. Many shops opened in Auchterarder, selling old furniture and ornaments that had been despised as old-fashioned during postwar regeneration. The desire for bright new goods also gathered force, particularly among the young. The older generation, accustomed to thrift, continued to wear sturdy tweeds, worsteds and woollens. Women darned holes in socks and turned their husbands' worn shirt collars to prolong the life of the garment. The 'baby boomers', born from 1946 to 1950, rejected their parents' 'make-do-and-mend' philosophy. They wore bright synthetic fabrics. To male delight, young women's skirt lengths shortened to above the knee. Garish nylon shirts and blouses did away with the need for ironing and gave off static sparks when couples embraced.

Cheap transistor radios replaced wooden cabinet wireless sets. British pop music echoed around the world, particularly after the Beatles appeared in 1963. Music set the tone for the language of approval. 'Swinging', a Black American jazz term, meant 'good and lively'. 'Groovy', from the grooves on vinyl records, meant much the same.

Auchterarder was still a rural economy with low wages. When cars became more affordable in the 1950s, family mobility and business increased. Roads were widened and pavements were laid in streets that previously had only muddy verges. Developments in England gave a foretaste of what was to come. On 5 December 1958, a section of the M6, Britain's first motorway, was opened. In the following year, the M1 between London and Birmingham effectively began the motorway age. The Mini, a cheap stylish British car symbolising modernity, also appeared in 1959. On 12 September 1960, the Ministry of Transport (MOT) introduced safety checks on older vehicles.

Young people's horizons widened. In the Auchterarder area, fed by television and a host of new magazines, people from poorer families had an increasing awareness of ways of life different from agriculture, shop-keeping and the mills. More privileged families had always enjoyed a more international outlook but, from the 1960s, most people could reasonably hope to buy foreign food in shops and to have foreign holidays.

Large numbers of educated young people left the area in search of better jobs. Many went to London or overseas, particularly to the USA, Canada, Australia and New Zealand. The 'brain drain' of the 1960s was, in its way, as damaging to community development as the loss of young men in wartime. One particularly unfortunate result of emigration was that the expanding public sector, lacking candidates with the most initiative and best qualifications, gave jobs to less able people who rose in seniority as older managers retired and gave local authorities a reputation for incompetence.

For those who remained in Strathearn, television coverage of football had a negative impact on support for local teams. Traditionally, people from the Auchterarder area supported their local senior team, St Johnstone in Perth. When it became possible to watch more glamorous clubs like Rangers and Celtic on TV, many fans switched from their local allegiance and, as petrol and public transport became increasingly affordable, headed for Glasgow to watch football.

In April 1961, Auchterarder people suddenly became Dunfermline Athletic supporters. A local boy, Ron Mailer, who captained the club, played in the side that beat Celtic 2–0 in a replay to win the Scottish Cup. He came from the Auchterarder family whose name goes back to the Middle Ages when they were chain-mail makers. That win made the reputation of Dunfermline's new young manager, Jock Stein, who went on to manage Celtic, making them the first British side to win the European Cup, then managed the national Scottish team in one of its most successful eras.

Auchterarder Public Park was briefly transformed once a year when the circus came to town, to the delight of children and the alarm of dog-walkers, whose pets panicked at the growls of exotic animals in flimsy-looking daytime cages. For some years up to the mid twentieth century, Auchterarder also held its own Highland Games. The only remaining hardy perennial event in the Public Park is 'The Shows', the travelling fairground heady combination of glitter and giggles, Ferris Wheel engine oil and candy floss.

'The Shows' are a gaudy triumph of free enterprise. In contrast, the nationalised railways lost money as successive governments preferred to invest in the new motorways. The government commissioned Dr Richard Beeching to evaluate the railways. His 1963 report recommended that unprofitable lines should be scrapped. Protestors argued that the new policy ignored social and environmental factors. In 1964, the line from Gleneagles Station to Crieff was closed. In an arrogant move to ensure that future governments could not reverse the decision, tracks, stations and equipment were dismantled.

Gleneagles Station was kept open and continued to bring golfers and other tourists to Gleneagles Hotel, which belonged to the nationalised British Railways. In a particularly bizarre decision, which showed that the line closers of British Railways did not consult their hotel management colleagues, British Railways invested in a huge new railway hotel at St Andrews and then promptly closed the railway line to the golfing town.

On 22 November 1963, the United States President John F. Kennedy was shot dead by the assassin Lee Harvey Oswald, who was murdered soon after while in police custody. A commission of inquiry failed to dispel theories of communist plots and right-wing conspiracies. Kennedy's assassination shook the confidence of the West, which had begun to take stability and economic growth for granted. The new American President Lyndon Johnson was a shrewd politician in dealing with rising tensions between traditional White America and the rising Black middle classes, promoting equality while marginalizing extremists. In Strathearn, where black faces were rarely seen except on TV, opinions on racial harmony tended to be over-idealistic or crudely xenophobic.

President Johnson was less adept at foreign policy, allowing the United States to become increasingly bogged down in a civil war in Vietnam, where the Chinese and Russian communist-funded North fought the American-funded South. The USA sent so many troops that it ran out of professional soldiers and forcibly drafted civilians. One young Strathearn man, a British citizen working in New York in the 1960s, had to fight a long legal battle to prevent being drafted to fight in a war in which Britain refused to participate.

By 1968, the Vietnam War was so unpopular with American voters that Johnson did not stand again as President. His Democratic party lost to Richard Nixon's Republicans. Nixon withdrew US troops from Vietnam, accepting humiliating military defeat for the USA, but scored a diplomatic coup by opening relations with Mao Zedong's secretive communist China.

Although Sir Alec Douglas-Home won a resounding victory in his own
Kinross and West Perthshire constituency, his Conservative Party lost the 1964
general election to the Labour Party. The new Prime Minister, Harold Wilson,
and his Home Secretary, Roy Jenkins, reformed much of Britain's old moral code.
Labour allowed consenting adults to indulge in homosexual practices without
fear of prosecution. Labour also legalised abortion of unwanted foetuses, under
medical conditions. Labour abolished the death penalty for murder and passed a
Race Relations Act, encouraging equality. Some religious leaders, who resented
the State's interference in moral issues, vigorously opposed these reforms.

In 1961, the contraceptive pill went on sale in Britain, allowing families the
freedom to plan the number of children they wanted. It became available on
prescription to unmarried women as well, prompting some angry allegations that
the government was endorsing sex outside marriage.

Harold Wilson judged the general desire for reform correctly. Labour won
the general election in March 1966. In the following year, however, a new force
appeared for the first time in the British Parliament when the Scottish Nationalist
Winifred Ewing won a by-election in Hamilton, an area whose industrial decline
Labour had been unable to prevent.

In 1969, Harold Wilson lowered the voting age from twenty-one to eighteen,
expecting that younger voters would support socialist policies and be enough to
defeat his Conservative rivals, many of whom like Sir Alec Douglas-Home were
caricatured as elderly and old-fashioned. Wilson also brought about Britain's first
reform of the coinage for many centuries, introducing a decimal system. In 1968,
the 5p coin, of the same value as the old shilling, was introduced, along with a
10p coin. The 50p coin appeared in 1969.

On 20 July 1969, an American astronaut of Scottish descent, Neil Armstrong,
became the first man to walk on the moon. As he did so, coins showing the head
of the great imperialist Queen Victoria, who came to the throne in 1837, still
jingled in British pockets. Full decimalisation arrived on 15 February 1971. By
that time, Wilson's government had fallen to the Conservatives, led by Edward
Heath, at the 19 June 1970 election.

In the 1960s, several new universities were approved for Scotland. Strathclyde
(1964) and Heriot Watt (1965) were previously excellent technical institutions.
Dundee was created in 1967 from a nineteenth-century satellite college of the
ancient St Andrews University. Demographically, a university was needed to
serve northern central Scotland. Controversially, the Labour government chose
Stirling as the location, rather than Perth.

The case for a university in Perth had been argued as long before as the
fifteenth century, but the county town always lacked the political clout to make
it happen. Perthshire's other Royal Burgh, Auchterarder, looked not to national
but to international politics to make its mark in the next decade.

42

The End of the Second Millennium

In which we see racism internationally outlawed in sport while Scottish local government becomes less local, and meet a hardworking bear

To the world in 1970, the adjective 'Scotch' meant whisky. The rest of Scotland's manufacturing and industrial reputation had fallen away. Sensitive to its alcoholic connotations, many Scots had stopped using the word 'Scotch' and replaced it with 'Scottish' to describe domestic culture and products. The global perception of Scotland was still the romantic heather and tartan image created by Sir Walter Scott in the early nineteenth century.

In the Auchterarder area, tourism and leisure became the most important industries. The town gained a good Heritage Centre, located conveniently for visitors in the same building as the Tourist Information Centre opposite the Aytoun Hall. High-quality hotels and restaurants thrived. The area was well promoted as a historic royal burgh with excellent leisure facilities.

Gleneagles Hotel was shrewdly marketed as a venue for major international events, rather than just a classy golfing hotel. In 1971, it hosted the Chief Executives Forum of the USA, a gathering of the super-rich.

In 1977, the British Government chose Gleneagles Hotel as the venue for the Commonwealth Heads of Government Conference. It had a global impact, producing the Gleneagles Agreement, the first international consensus on outlawing racism in sport.

In 1981, Gleneagles Hotel staged the NATO conference. It was becoming a major venue on the international political circuit. However, there was one big obstacle to expansion. For its first sixty years, Gleneagles Hotel closed for the winter.

New corporate ownership brought much-needed investment. In 1982, a major refurbishment and a newly built country club enabled the hotel to open without a five-month winter break. For the Auchterarder area, this offered much more all-year-round employment, both for hotel workers and for tradesmen and suppliers.

The final decades of the second millennium saw perhaps the greatest restructuring of Strathearn's place in the world since the ancient kingdom of Fortriu had evolved into a united Scotland near the end of the previous millennium. The restructuring took place at three levels of government. First, on 1 January 1973, after two decades of British ambivalence and French opposition, Conservative Prime Minister Edward Heath led Britain into the European Community. The agreement opened up new trading opportunities in Europe, but made the Westminster Parliament subservient to the European Parliament in Brussels in most aspects of policy. One of the first changes was that a new tax VAT (Value Added Tax) increased the price of goods. The other EC countries moved towards a single currency, the euro. Britain chose to keep the pound sterling.

Edward Heath resigned as Prime Minster in 1974. A Labour government, led by Harold Wilson, restructured the two levels of Scottish local government in 1975. Scotland's many town and county councils were swept away and replaced by a structure comprising only ten giant regional councils, each superior to a few new district councils. The remaining powers of the Royal Burghs were taken away. Auchterarder became part of Perth & Kinross District Council within Tayside Region. The new regional and district councils were soon in acrimonious conflict over planning and finance.

One of the last acts of the Royal Burgh of Auchterarder was to grant the freedom of the Royal Burgh to the Black Watch Regiment on 4 May 1974. Queen Elizabeth, the Queen Mother, Colonel in Chief of the Regiment, recorded the 'long and happy relationship between the Burgh and the Regiment'. At family level, the area continued its old tradition as a major recruiting ground for its local regiment.

The British Army was deployed in Northern Ireland in 1969 to deal with violence between Protestants and Catholics. An uncomfortable military peace-keeping presence remained as tensions escalated. The elusive and fragmented nature of armed political activist groups in Northern Ireland was hard for Scottish troops, many of whom had relatives in the Province.

Harold Wilson resigned as Prime Minister in March 1976. His amiable Labour colleague James Callaghan replaced him for three years, but was unable to cope with mounting economic problems and union disputes in the nationalised industries. In 1978, when the BBC was allowed to broadcast House of Commons debates live for the first time, listeners were shocked at the boorishness and low calibre of many MPs.

The Auchterarder economy had depended on agriculture and the textile mills. After Britain joined the European Community in 1973, agricultural priorities changed. Farmers could profit from 'Set-Aside', paid to allow good arable land to remain without crops for extended periods to balance production elsewhere in Europe. The policy caused offence to charities and politicians trying to tackle starvation in what became known as 'The Third World', a term used to describe impoverished countries that did not belong to either the Capitalist West or the Communist blocs. Mechanised farming continued to increase. In Strathearn, agriculture was now a tiny part of the job market, while the mills continued to decline in the face of foreign imports.

The Auchterarder Market finally closed in 1970. By the end of the century, its site was covered in houses, with no visible remaining trace of what had been the centre of the town's agricultural industry for nearly a thousand years. Close by, the Aytoun Hall, which previous local government administrations had regularly refurbished to provide good services for the community, was allowed to slide into decay, until its upper floor became unusable.

Political changes meant that 'grant-aiding' was withdrawn from private schools in the early 1970s. Able local children could no longer go free to Morrison's Academy in Crieff. However, the state school in Auchterarder was greatly improved. Instead of catering only for those who wanted to leave the moment they reached the recently introduced minimum school-leaving age of sixteen, it offered a more complete secondary education, enabling children to qualify for university places.

Ochil Tower School, geared to helping children with special needs, opened in 1972, in Belvidere, the splendid former home of the Youngs, the Auchterarder lawyer family. The school, a Rudolf Steiner School, is part of the Camphill movement, a respected and compassionate group started in Aberdeen, in 1940, by refugees from Nazi Austria.

Entry into the EC and the restructuring of local government were policies that applied throughout Britain. In 1970, however, Scottish independence became a serious talking point when BP (British Petroleum) discovered the Forties Oil Field in the North Sea. Three years earlier, North Sea gas had begun being pumped onshore near Durham in the north of England. Now Scottish nationalists demanded that the revenues from North Sea oil should belong exclusively to Scotland. Other political parties pointed out that Scotland was part of the United Kingdom, benefiting from economic activity elsewhere notably in the south-east of England, and should therefore be expected to share oil revenues while they lasted. When the first North Sea oil pipeline opened in 1975, the political arguments grew louder.

As revenues from North Sea oil grew, the Scottish National Party gained popularity by insisting that the oil 'belonged to the people of Scotland' and that Scotland would be better off as an independent nation. To thwart the SNP but appeal to Scottish voters' desire for more self-determination, the Labour government held a referendum on 1 March 1979, asking Scottish voters if they wanted a Scottish Parliament with powers to administer funds allocated by the British Parliament in Westminster. In effect it was a further local government restructuring, replacing the ten recently formed giant regional councils with an even bigger and more centralised body based in Edinburgh.

To bring this new body into being, the approval of 40 per cent of the Scottish electorate was needed. Despite vociferous promotion by the SNP and by the public sector, which saw an opportunity for thousands of new bureaucratic jobs, less than a third of the electorate voted in favour in 1979. The Scottish Parliament, abolished in 1707, remained extinct.

On 4 May 1979, Margaret Thatcher became Britain's first woman Prime Minister when the Conservatives defeated a demoralised and irresolute Labour government in a general election. Mrs Thatcher gained the nickname 'The Iron Lady' for confronting union leaders, especially the miners, and privatising the nationalised industries, forcing them to adopt modern technology and working practices. Unemployment rose to over three million but in 1983 she was re-elected in a landslide general election. The mandate allowed her to survive a miners' strike that lasted nearly a year.

No British politician in the twentieth century polarised public opinion as much as Margaret Thatcher did. The financial sector admired her support of free enterprise and small businesses. Socialists hated her sweeping public sector reforms and her destruction of the union 'jobs for life' culture. Nobody disputed her courage and sense of duty. When Argentina invaded the Falkland Islands on 2 April 1982, Mrs Thatcher dispatched a military task force to the South Atlantic that routed the Argentineans within three weeks. Northern Ireland proved much more intractable. Neither diplomacy nor military presence quelled the Troubles.

Strathearn voted Conservative during the Thatcher era, as it had done for generations. There was, however, one local resident who eclipsed Margaret Thatcher in popularity. Hercules the Bear began as a grizzly cub bought in 1974 by the professional wrestler Andy Robin and his wife Maggie. At first he lived at their Sheriffmuir Inn, near the site of the 1715 battle whose aftermath changed the face of Strathearn. Hercules rose from being a show-wrestling bear to starring in films and TV commercials. In 1981, the Scottish Tourist Board made him the Scottish Personality of the Year, something that Margaret Thatcher was never likely to achieve although she, like Hercules, was very popular when she toured the USA, the key Scottish tourist market. In the early 1980s Hercules moved to the Robins' new ranch in Glendevon, acting as a star guest at local events until he died in February 2000.

The landscape of Auchterarder and Aberuthven changed dramatically with the arrival of the A9 Auchterarder Bypass in 1983. To the south of Auchterarder, on the fertile ground much prized by the Abbey of Inchaffray in the Middle Ages, the Ruthven Water and Lochy Burn were re-routed with a fish-ladder constructed under the Bypass. At Loaninghead, the Bypass slip road cut into the earthworks of an ancient Celtic fort, which commanded the entrance to Gleneagles.

Unfortunately, a plan for a safe, grade-separated junction over the A9 Bypass, with a link to Gleneagles Station, was scrapped on grounds of cost. Just as with the building of Auchterarder Station in 1848, and Crieff Junction (now Gleneagles Station) in 1856, Auchterarder failed yet again to take advantage of new transport development, and connect the railway more closely to the town. Few trains stop at Gleneagles Station now. Happily, most of the Auchterarder area is well served by buses, particularly since April 2006, when people over sixty became entitled to Scotland-wide free bus travel.

The A9 Auchterarder Bypass transformed Auchterarder High Street, from a congested through-route for heavy goods vehicles to the north of Scotland, into an attractive town full of small shops, now more quickly accessible from main urban centres. The improved A9 also made Auchterarder desirable as a commuter town. In theory, Glasgow, Edinburgh and Dundee were only an hour's drive away. In practice, city rush-hour traffic created a new breed of Auchterarder residents who saw the town in daylight only in summer and at weekends.

A much larger engineering enterprise was completed on 12 March 1993, when a French train passed through the new Channel Tunnel and arrived at Folkestone in Kent. Sixteen thousand years before, at the end of the most recent Ice Age, melting ice created the North Sea and turned Britain into an island. Now there was a fast link, reconnecting Britain to the mainland of Europe. The concept of a Channel Tunnel was not new. Excavation work had begun in 1881 but for a hundred years no government had the will to complete the project. Mrs Thatcher was not lacking in will power. She and French President François Mitterand forced the scheme through, despite public alarm at escalating costs. The new physical link symbolised Britain's future as a partner in Europe.

Mrs Thatcher did not survive politically long enough to see the Channel Tunnel open. In 1989, she replaced the old domestic rates tax in Scotland with a 'Community Charge'. The public recognised the new tax as a flat-rate poll tax and resented the abolition of the old sliding-rate scale in which owners of high-value properties paid more tax than the poor. Mrs Thatcher, who had a primitive grasp of history, did not understand that poll taxes usually provoke riots. By the time the Community Charge was introduced in England in 1990, she had become so personally unpopular that her Conservative Party persuaded her to resign in favour of the genial, cricket-loving John Major who abolished the Community Charge in 1992 and won a general election.

The introduction of the divisive poll tax in Scotland coincided with the demolition of Europe's most hated barrier, the Berlin Wall, an 87-mile-long concrete and barbed wire structure, built in 1961 by communist East Germany to prevent its citizens escaping to the capitalist West. A new generation of Russian politicians, most notably the able statesman Mikhail Gorbachev and the flamboyant Boris Yeltsin, opened up Eastern Europe to private enterprise. On 9 November 1989, some young people attacked the Berlin Wall with sledgehammers. The authorities did not try to stop them. Within days, thousands of others joined in, demolishing the wall and allowing free passage between East and West. It heralded a new united Germany. The Cold War was finally over.

As one war zone ended, another opened up. On 2 August 1990, the Iraqi dictator Saddam Hussein invaded neighbouring Kuwait and took control of its oil fields. Britain and the USA, fearing a destabilisation of world oil prices, quickly sent troops in Operation Desert Shield to prevent Saddam from progressing further. On 17 January 1991, in Operation Desert Storm, Britain, the USA and Saudi Arabia drove the Iraqis from Kuwait by heavy bombing and ground assault. Families in the traditional military recruiting grounds of Strathearn saw soldier relatives redeployed from the grim, slogan-daubed streets of Belfast in Northern Ireland to the burning deserts of the Middle East.

After the Gulf War, the West withdrew its troops, allowing Saddam Hussein to remain in power in Iraq and redevelop his military resources. British policy in Northern Ireland was more successful. In 1994, the IRA (Irish Republican Army) and Protestant Loyalists agreed a cease-fire as John Major tried to broker a diplomatic peace deal, bringing the Republican, predominantly Catholic, Sinn Fein into the mainstream political process.

On 13 March 1996, a burst of gunfire destroyed the peace of Auchterarder's neighbouring town, Dunblane. Thomas Hamilton, whom the police had allowed to keep firearms despite behaviour that had caused concern, burst into Dunblane Primary School, shooting dead sixteen children and their teacher and wounding many others before turning one of his guns on himself. In response, local people asked their MP Michael Forsyth, as Secretary of State for Scotland, to lead a campaign for comprehensive effective gun control in Britain. He failed to do so. The government only approved a rushed ban on handguns.

Bizarrely, instead of tackling the gun problem about which people cared, Michael Forsyth devoted his energies to a symbolic gesture, which he hoped would endear Scottish voters to the Conservative Party. The Stone of Destiny, which King Edward I had removed from Scone in 1296 and placed under the coronation chair in Westminster Abbey to show his authority over Scotland, was carted back north after eight hundred years. Dressed in a kilt, Michael Forsyth led a procession over the border. The stone was then allocated no Scottish ceremonial function whatsoever, but placed as an historic curiosity in Edinburgh Castle far from its original politically important site in Perthshire. Voters were unimpressed. On 1 May 1997, a general election swept the Conservatives from power. Michael Forsyth lost his seat. The Conservative Party has subsequently failed to be a significant force in Scottish politics again.

Tony Blair, the most elusive and pragmatic politician of his generation, became Prime Minister of a Labour government with a huge majority. He was a formidable parliamentary debater and a much more shrewd image manipulator than Michael Forsyth. Blair appointed the new Secretary of State for Scotland Donald Dewar to revive the idea of a Scottish Parliament and consolidate Labour as the party of choice for Scottish voters. He moved fast. A carefully co-ordinated campaign sold the Scottish Parliament, not as yet another layer of local government, but as the way for Scotland to achieve self-determination while remaining within the United Kingdom of Great Britain and Northern Ireland.

The date for a new referendum on the Scottish Parliament was set for 11 September 1997. Just as the campaign reached its peak, the nation was distracted by the death of Diana, the divorced wife of Prince Charles, heir to the British throne. She had been the glamorous darling of the media, but had become a figure of fun after a series of revelations about her sex life. Diana's death in Paris, in a car crashed by the drunken chauffeur of her latest boyfriend, Dodi, son of the owner of Harrods Department Store in London, made the media veer back to idolising her. Newspapers and TV whipped up a storm of hysterical grief and tributes to a woman who had done genuine good, particularly for charities helping children, landmine victims and Aids sufferers. She had never been comfortable with the ways of the royal court and political establishment.

The Scottish Parliament referendum took place when people were looking for something positive to ease the sense of loss that came from Diana's death. Forty-five per cent of the electorate approved the Parliament. The optimism was soon dispelled. The former Royal High School on Calton Hill in Edinburgh had been the projected site for the new Parliament. It already had a debating chamber, created at considerable public expense as a meeting place for the old Convention of Scottish Local Authorities. The cost of further conversion was estimated at $40 million. Instead, Donald Dewar commissioned a lavish new Scottish Parliament building on the site of the old Holyrood Brewery. Amid charges of corruption and incompetence, the cost of the new building escalated from an estimated £109 million to £431 million. The Spanish architect Enric Miralles designed the debating chamber in the form of an upturned boat, condemning Scottish politicians to inhabit jokes about shipwrecks.

The Scottish Parliament building suffered many delays in construction. The Parliament opened, with Donald Dewar in the newly created job of First Minister, on 1 July 1999. It met, not on the Holyrood site, but in the Church of Scotland Assembly Rooms, high on the Edinburgh Castle Mound, in the gloomy shadow of Pittendrigh MacGillivray's statue of the Puritan John Knox. The new building was not ready until 2004.

The new Scottish Parliament began in 1999 as ignominiously as the old one had ended in 1707. Politically, it was not what Labour had hoped. The SNP saw it as a step towards full independence and campaigned accordingly. In the 1999 election, Strathearn was part of a new constituency, which included part of the city of Perth and elected the SNP candidate Roseanna Cunningham. She quickly established herself as an accessible and hard-working constituency MSP and retained her seat in the 2005 and 2011 Scottish Parliamentary elections.

In 1997, the same year as the decision to create a Scottish Parliament, another part of the old British Empire went a stage further and separated completely. Hong Kong, off the south coast of China, had been leased to Britain in 1898 for 99 years. It had grown in importance from a strategic harbour and trading base to become a major international financial centre. During the twentieth century, relations between Britain and China fluctuated from friendly to chilly.

By the time the lease ran out, communist China had re-entered the global market. Hong Kong, now known as Xianggang, became a special administrative region of the People's Republic of China, with an amicable handover from the British government. The last British forces to leave Hong Kong were the Black Watch. Though the military presence has gone, the Auchterarder area retains many commercial links with China and the rest of Asia.

The Labour government created a Scottish Parliament and a Welsh Assembly. Prime Minister Tony Blair's zeal for constitutional change led to a restructuring of the House of Lords. When he took office in 1997, it had 769 hereditary peers and 403 life peers. Hereditary peers have always been a nuisance to Commons-led governments, whose legislative programmes are aimed at current crises. Hereditary peers tend to evaluate proposed legislation by its likely impact on future generations and vote against populist stop-gap measures. Blair's government cut the number of hereditary peers in the House of Lords to only 90, but created a host of new life peers amenable to his way of thinking. There are currently nearly 700 life peers. The new composition of the House of Lords, always doomed to a preponderance of recent government placemen, is so unsatisfactory in both the short and long term that there is constant debate about revising it again.

43

The New Millennium and the Gleneagles G8 Summit

In which old ideologies clash again, as we watch the biggest invasion of Auchterarder since Roman times and see Prince William become Earl of Strathearn

Wars are fought to establish territorial and economic control, but justified by ideologies. By the end of the twentieth century, the conflict between doctrinaire capitalism and communism had dissolved as Russia and China opened up to a global economy, dependent on oil for powering industry and transport. The huge oil resources of the Middle Eastern and Gulf states were largely in the hands of Islamic governments. North American and British oil was controlled by governments in the Judeo-Christian tradition. Despite perennial Arab-Israeli hostilities, other conflicts and alliances were not consistent.

In the Gulf War of 1990–1991, the Christian Western coalition had come to the aid of Islamic Kuwait and Saudi Arabia. A Saudi dissident, Osama bin Laden, then established himself as leader of al-Qaeda, a stateless Islamic fundamentalist organisation, consisting of scattered cells, aimed at destabilising the global economy by acts of terrorism. The West believed that Osama bin Laden's objective was to foment sufficient Islamic discontent for him to seize control of Saudi oil. In practice, he based himself on the traditionally lawless border between Afghanistan and Pakistan, and initiated attacks on internationally symbolic targets.

On 11 September 2001, an al-Qaeda attack destroyed the World Trade Center in New York, when two hijacked airliners were crashed into the Twin Towers. Almost three thousand people were killed. British Prime Minister Tony Blair and other Western leaders condemned the attack. The American President George W. Bush demanded that the Afghan government, controlled by the Islamic fundamentalist Taliban, hand over Osama bin Laden. It did not. The 9/11 attacks prompted a show of retaliation.

On 7 October 2001, the USA and Britain launched air strikes and sent ground troops to overthrow the Taliban. On 22 December 2001, an astute moderate Hamid Karzai was appointed head of an Afghan coalition government and kept in power by the presence of Western troops. Across the world, Islamic and Christian moderates found themselves caught in a morass of suspicion and hysteria.

Britain had fought wars in Afghanistan in the nineteenth century. Soviet Russia had occupied Afghanistan from 1979 to 1989. No foreign power had ever been able to sustain long-term control of Afghanistan's mountainous terrain. After ten years, British and American troops are still there. The Black Watch Battalion is based in the dangerous Helmand Province. The West knows that to pull military resources out of Afghanistan would result in civil war and enemy victory, just as it did in Vietnam in the 1970s. The stalemate is currently unresolved.

Strathearn families have seen their soldier relatives serve in Afghanistan, and as peacekeepers in the civil war in Kosovo, part of the former communist Republic of Yugoslavia, which had been broken up by local nationalist movements. In 2003, another war zone opened up again. The West suspected Iraqi dictator Saddam Hussein of stockpiling 'weapons of mass destruction'. United Nations inspectors found no proof but in March 2003 the USA and Britain hit Baghdad and other Iraqi targets with saturation bombing, then seized control with a ground attack. Saddam Hussein was captured in December 2003 and handed over to his political enemies to be executed. The West withdrew, leaving Iraq with a wrecked infrastructure, looted museums and burning resentment within the population. Neighbouring Islamic Iran soon adopted a more hostile posture towards the West.

The financial cost of foreign wars was enormous. British Prime Minister Tony Blair and his Chancellor Gordon Brown borrowed heavily from international money markets. In December 2004, Labour began the most far-reaching reorganisation of Scotland's professional military forces since the early eighteenth century. The Black Watch and five other Scottish regiments were combined into the Royal Regiment of Scotland, with their old names subordinated. It was a further example of government centralisation and loss of local identity. Paradoxically, Auchterarder, which had granted freedom of the Royal Burgh to the Black Watch in 1974, was about to hit the international headlines.

In July 2005, the G8 Summit Conference was held at Gleneagles Hotel. It was the largest invasion of Auchterarder since the Romans had marched into the area two thousand years before. Hundreds of civil servants were bussed into the area each day to serve a horde of UK politicians and foreign delegations. Attending the summit were the eight heads of government from the most powerful industrialised nations in the world: the USA, Canada, Britain, France, Germany, Italy, Russia and Japan. Significantly, China and India, rapidly developing industrialised nations but not members of the G8, sent substantial delegations to the Gleneagles Summit.

Thousands of police personnel, hand-picked from every force in mainland Britain, provided maximum visible security. An army of protestors, passionate but rarely violent, camped and marched in the area. Thousands more of the world's journalists sent their stories from a specially built state-of-the-art media centre. Entertainment was lavish. Journalists were served three Gleneagles meals per day, plus all the snacks they could eat. The writer of this book, attending the G8 for research on another book, felt embarrassed eating these splendid meals at a conference whose main agenda was 1. Global Poverty and 2. Climate Change. Was the Gleneagles G8 merely an expensive public-relations exercise? No.

Like the Peace of Auchterarder in 1559, the Auchterarder Creed of 1716 and the Gleneagles Agreement of 1977, there was a genuine recognition of problems and a clear statement of intent. Nobody expected instant solutions.

There were two significant outcomes of the Gleneagles G8. Until that date, it had been the official position of the USA to deny that industrial pollution and climate change might be significantly related. In July 2005, at Gleneagles, the USA, the world's largest polluter, conceded that the problem required serious attention, and combined with the other G8 nations to draw up a plan of action. The second outcome was that the G8 drew up a policy for tackling poverty in Africa, focussing mainly on health and cancelling debt.

Resolutions on paper and practical results are two different things, but there is no doubt that the Gleneagles G8 achieved a greater international consensus on humanitarian intervention in Africa, and tackling the problems of climate change, than had ever been reached before.

The people of Auchterarder took the G8 Summit in their stride. The area had maintained widespread trade links for over two thousand years and was not disconcerted by the presence of foreign visitors, even in large numbers. By 2005, the global interconnections were corporate. For example, Gleneagles Hotel is owned by the multinational giant Diageo, which also owns both Johnnie Walker Whisky and the Shui Jin Fang brand of the Chinese alcoholic drink baijiu.

On 7 July 2005, while national security was focussed on protecting world leaders at Gleneagles Hotel, Islamic militant suicide bombers attacked London, killing passengers on a bus and in the Underground. The 7/7 assaults merely persuaded the world leaders, assembled round the Gleneagles conference table, to redouble their efforts against global terrorism.

During the G8, Auchterarder was filled with the sound of foreign languages. This was nothing new. Two thousand years ago, the Romans came. Five hundred years later, Irish Christians and Dál Riata brought Gaelic to Pictish Strathearn. A thousand years ago, the Normans transformed the language of business and law. Ever since, there have been many different waves of immigrants. Today, on the streets and buses, you can hear many Eastern European and Asian languages spoken by the latest generation of workers new to the area.

The physical environment of the Auchterarder area is going through a phase of rapid change. During the years of rationing in the Second World War and after, households generated tiny amounts of rubbish, much of it ashes from coal fires. By the twenty-first century, unprecedented levels of general wealth created a buying frenzy, and a gigantic environmental problem of discarded consumer goods and their bulky packaging. Instead of anxiety over postwar malnutrition, child and adult obesity began to loom large on Auchterarder High Street.

A huge new Community School was begun in 2000 and completed in autumn 2004. It had been intended to provide facilities for adults as well as children. As a gesture to a new unrealistic fashion for security, adults were not admitted during school hours, defeating the original purpose of the building.

Auchterarder has a long history of having unexpected impacts on the international scene. In 2007, when English cricket was in disarray, the English Cricket Board commissioned an Auchterarder man, Ken Schofield, to sort out their national game. Ken Schofield had already grown from a sports-mad boy to become Director of the European Golf Tour. Though the Auchterarder cricket pitch vanished under housing development in the 1960s, the Schofield Report's recommendations reshaped the administrative and professional support structure of English cricket and had a global influence on the game. By 2009, England had rebuilt sufficiently to defeat the mighty Australians and win The Ashes, the game's most famous trophy. By 2011, England had risen to be the most successful test cricket nation in the world.

Auchterarder has long been known as 'the lang toun', because visitors driving along the old A9 knew it as one long street, extending from the Strathearn Home and Cemetery at the western end all the way down through the Feus to Garth Terrace. There were many narrow wynds alongside the 'pendicles' of land, containing weaving sheds, byres, hen houses and vegetable gardens. Compared to other towns, however, Auchterarder had few crossroads or major side streets.

The housing boom, beginning in the 1990s, made the town expand sideways in both directions, mainly with detached three-bedroom homes. There was also a demand for much bigger new houses, particularly to the more prestigious west of the town, where medium-sized houses in large gardens were flattened and giant homes constructed instead.

Land values rocketed. A building plot at the Muirton cost £40 in 1962. A smaller plot nearby cost about £300,000 in 2007. The boom was fuelled by older people selling expensive houses in cities and moving to the Auchterarder area with its world-class leisure facilities. Young people found they could not afford to buy homes in their own town. Although the town now sprawls over much more land, there are many fewer people per house compared to fifty years ago.

Tourism in the Auchterarder area thrived in the twentieth century. For the twenty-first century, however, the creation of a Scottish Parliament brought a reorganisation of public services. When a new government body, Visit Scotland, replaced the old Scottish Tourist Board, it closed the Tourist Information Centre in Auchterarder as soon as the international publicity for the G8 was over. Perth and Kinross Council then closed the Heritage Centre, the area's main cultural attraction for visitors and the only resource for local history. These decisions cut Auchterarder off from Britain's annual £20 billion heritage tourism industry.

Most of the town's hotels have closed in the first decade of the twenty-first century. The upmarket Auchterarder House and Collearn have reverted to private houses. The Queen's Hotel was replaced by a block of flats. The Craigrossie (formerly The Railway Hotel) is empty and the Crown Hotel site has been redeveloped with only the Niblick Bar remaining as a pub. There is some bed and breakfast and holiday accommodation, but today's visitors tend to come for day trips, rather than longer holidays.

Immediately after the Gleneagles G8 in 2005, impressed by the relaxed, cosmopolitan attitudes of the Auchterarder community, which defused the likelihood of serious clashes with protestors, the Scottish Government awarded £500,000 to refurbish the Aytoun Hall and Girnal House. These buildings represented Auchterarder's Victorian civic pride and enterprise. By 2005, with the upper storey unusable and the rest suffering from generations of local authority neglect, they were desperately in need of refurbishment to meet community needs. Perth and Kinross Council, the current owners of the buildings, voted further funds but work did not begin until 2009 and still continues. Full re-opening will not take place until the Council prepares a business plan.

At the same time as the Aytoun Hall was undergoing refurbishment, Auchterarder Parish Church, formerly the Barony Church, was redeveloped, adding a substantial new community centre, designed by Edinburgh architects Hurd Rolland and built by J.B. Bennett of Kilsyth.

In his speech at the opening of the Auchterarder A9 Bypass in 1983, Provost James Fordyce said, 'It is essential that we have adequate information on our signs.' Nearly thirty years later, nothing has been done. There is no sign on the A9 to tell visitors they are close to a historic Royal Burgh with excellent shopping and recreational facilities. In the town itself, unlike in all the surrounding towns, there is a lack of wall plaques to make historic events of international importance come alive for today's visitors and young people.

The population in the Auchterarder area in 1881 was 3,600. Then, with the decline of weaving and agriculture, young people had to go elsewhere for jobs. By 1931, the town's population had declined to 2,300. The population in Aberuthven and the area's farms declined to about five hundred. After the Second World War, population numbers remained steady till the expansion of the 1960s. By 1972, the town had 2,765 residents.

The population of Auchterarder in 2006 was 3,945, of whom 47 per cent were male and 53 per cent female. Eighteen per cent of the population was under sixteen years old, about average for Scotland. However, 27 per cent were of pensionable age, compared to an average of 21 per cent for Scotland, showing that the numbers of working age were substantially lower than the national average, because of lack of jobs and affordable housing in the area.

Gleneagles Hotel remains by far the largest local employer. Many Auchterarder people drive to work in other towns, particularly Perth, Dundee, Stirling and Glasgow, despite the rapidly increasing cost of petrol. Agriculture has long since ceased to be a significant employer. With the end of the European set-aside scheme in 2007, farmers could no longer make money from leaving their land unworked. Instead, agricultural land and farm steadings have increasingly been used for housing development.

Gleneagles West, the biggest single development in the history of the area, is being developed while this book is written. Comprising another golf course and many large houses, possibly with a new upmarket hotel, it means that Auchterarder will soon reach as far as Blackford. The development is on land owned by His Excellency Madhi Mohammed Al Tajir from the United Arab Emirates, who also owns Highland Spring, the popular local mineral water which is exported round the world.

There is a plan for an even bigger development. This would increase the size of Auchterarder by building between 800 and 1,200 houses in the Castleton and the Kirkton on the north side of the town and at the Townhead on the south. There is fierce debate about the benefits this development might bring and the damage it might cause.

For the 5 May 2005 British general election, following the creation of the Scottish Parliament, the number of Scottish seats in Westminster was reduced from 72 to 59. Auchterarder became part of a new constituency, Ochil and Perthshire South, combining rural Strathearn to the north of the Ochils with industrial Alloa to the south. It was a political linkage not seen since the early fourteenth century, when Sir Malcolm de Innerpeffray was Sheriff of both Auchterarder and Clackmannan. Sir Malcolm owed his appointment to King Edward I, who had quartered his troops at Auchterarder Castle before removing the Stone of Destiny from Scone and placing it under the coronation chair in Westminster Abbey. Sir Malcolm later switched to supporting Robert Bruce.

Labour's intention in 2005 was to create a winnable seat. The boundary change worked for them. For the first time Strathearn gained a Labour MP when Gordon Banks narrowly beat Annabel Ewing from a leading SNP family. Gordon Banks developed a reputation as a middle-of-the-road, hard-working constituency MP and was re-elected with an increased majority in the 6 May 2010 general election, despite his party's heavy defeat nationwide.

Labour's collapse in 2010 was in part a personal failure for Prime Minster Gordon Brown, a dour Scot from Fife, who had taken over when the adroit Tony Blair stepped down on 27 June 2007. First as Chancellor, then as Prime Minister, Gordon Brown led a programme of government borrowing on an unprecedented scale, partly to finance new infrastructure, but more to pay for Britain's involvement in costly wars and a huge expansion in public sector jobs. The government and the banks encouraged a general culture of heavy borrowing. In 2008, it became obvious that levels of national and personal debt were unsustainable. Wild lending by American banks resulted in widespread defaults and triggered a global collapse of confidence.

Over the centuries, Scottish invasions of England have always led to disaster. The early twenty-first century saw another invasion, not a military but a financial one. The Bank of Scotland and The Royal Bank of Scotland charged recklessly into English and overseas money markets, only to suffer heavy losses in 2008, humiliating defeat and takeover, just as their political predecessors had done. Just as in the Wars of Independence and the Jacobite era, Auchterarder people preferred economic stability to flag-waving personal ambition and had little sympathy for power-hungry bankers.

Auchterarder's opinion of greedy financiers is consistent. In 1890, in his poem *Auchterarder Past and Present*, local poet George Oswald wrote:

The folk were better in oor day,
Nae rogues wi' sic a plot
As yon City Bank directors
Who ruined sic a lot.

It is no literary masterpiece, but his heart and his boot are in the right place.

The financial mess caused by the failure of the absurdly optimistic and badly planned Darien Scheme in 1700 led to the Union of the Scottish and English Parliaments in 1707 to bail out Scottish debt. The resurrection of the Scottish Parliament after the 1997 general election happened at a time of economic stability.

If the 2008 financial collapse had happened eleven years earlier, it is unlikely that the Scottish people would have voted to add an extra layer of politicians to their existing burdens. The Scottish National Party's demand for Scottish independence fell quiet when Scots realised that the British Government's £20 billion bail out of the Royal Bank of Scotland spread the cost over the entire population of nearly 60 million people. Had Scotland been independent, each Scot's personal liability would have been increased tenfold, plunging Scottish voters into poverty.

The SNP, however, remains strong in Scotland, largely because the other political parties are currently so ineffectual, while the SNP has a leader who has grown to become one of Britain's most adept politicians. Scottish First Minister Alex Salmond is a formidable debater with a shrewd sense of political timing, combining charm and ruthlessness in the manner of Tony Blair. He has also a genius for manipulating Scottish symbols.

In 2007, Alex Salmond made St Andrew's Day, November 30, a public holiday for Scottish Executive staff, endearing himself to the officials who deliver his policies and cleverly linking his Scottish National Party to Scotland's patron saint. When his party won the Scottish parliamentary election in 2011, he celebrated by wrapping himself and his deputy Nicola Sturgeon in the Scottish Saltire flag. The subliminal identification of the patriotic Saltire with the SNP is something that other Scottish political parties have allowed to happen by default.

The SNP encourages the press to refer to the Scottish Parliament as the Holyrood Parliament to distinguish it from the Westminster Parliament. In fact, the new building is equidistant from Holyrood and Dumbiedykes, locally pronounced 'Dummydykes'. Just as Sir Walter Scott renamed his new home 'Abbotsford', rather than retain its old name 'Clarty Hole', so the name 'Holyrood' confers a dignity on the Scottish Parliament. To call it the 'Dumbiedykes Parliament' would give a different impression.

For 2009, Alex Salmond's government devised the Year of the Homecoming to attract foreigners with Scottish ancestry to return as tourists. The scheme incurred huge administrative expenses and lost money. Alex Salmond's contribution to the Year of the Homecoming in the Auchterarder area was to be photographed at Gleneagles Hotel, clutching a giant pink inflatable Coca-Cola bottle printed with the image of Robert Burns. The opposition remained inarticulate.

Just as Auchterarder's most famous son, the seventeenth-century James Graham, 1st Marquis of Montrose, was a student at St Andrews University at the same time as his deadly rival Archibald Campbell, 1st Marquis of Argyll, so Alex Salmond was a St Andrews contemporary of the former Scottish Conservative Secretary of State Michael Forsyth. In 1997 Forsyth discovered too late that a party may rise to power by using symbols, but needs substance rather than symbols to keep it in office. Alex Salmond has yet to be seriously tested in this respect.

At present, Britain has a coalition government, something that has rarely happened, except in wartime. After the general election on 6 May 2010, the Conservative leader David Cameron became Prime Minister. He has a workable majority in the Commons only because of a pact with Nick Clegg the Liberal leader, who was made Deputy Prime Minister. Their main strategy is to reduce the huge national debt created by the previous Labour government. This requires massive cuts in the public sector and increases in taxation. Cameron's Conservative forbear Margaret Thatcher had the force of personality to maintain these policies in the face of rising unemployment and angry protest. It remains to be seen whether the present coalition government can survive a similar scenario.

The Boundary Commission published plans in October 2011 to further reduce the number of Scottish MPs in Westminster to 52. It is proposed that, for the first time, Strathearn will be split in half. Crieff will be joined with Stirling in a new constituency. Auchterarder will be part of a Perth and Kinross-shire constituency, detached from Labour-voting Alloa. Both of these new constituencies may be winnable by the Conservative Party. Or not.

The face of international politics changed on 2 May 2011 when the al-Qaeda leader Osama bin Laden was assassinated in an American attack on his compound in Pakistan. Al-Qaeda continues to have activist cells around the world, but more of their leaders have been killed. The Christian West is still fearful of attacks by Islamic suicide bombers. Osama bin Laden's entourage admires the 1995 film *Braveheart*, in which the mediaeval Scottish warlord William Wallace is celebrated as a freedom fighter. The popularity of xenophobia as entertainment is not to be underestimated. Mel Gibson, who played Wallace, won American Academy Awards as both actor and director.

Until Osama bin Laden's assassination, newspapers were preoccupied with the wedding of Prince William, second in line to the throne after his father Prince Charles. Prince William and his wife Catherine were married on 29 April 2011 and given the title Earl and Countess of Strathearn along with other titles in England, Northern Ireland and Wales. The Earldom of Strathearn, with its ancient connections to the Grahams and the Stewarts, is again a royal family title.

Auchterarder, where King Malcolm Canmore a thousand years ago built a royal castle to enjoy hunting in the surrounding woods and pasture, is again seen as a playground for the rich. Close to Gleneagles Hotel, which will host golf's Ryder Cup in 2014, international businessmen are investing in homes. In 2010, Indian steel billionaire Lakshmi Mittal spent a reputed £15 million, making his the most expensive house in Scotland.

The development of the Internet in 1991, by Tim Berners-Lee, allowed business, public sector and individual communication to become global with unprecedented speeds. Today, most adults and many children carry mobile phones, exchanging conversation, texts and images. The new technology makes it increasingly practical for senior businessmen to live in a pleasant, prestigious location like Auchterarder rather than in cities.

New social media networks, like YouTube, Facebook and Twitter, enable individuals to film and report news events without the regulation of government and press barons. In the 'Arab Spring' of 2011, Tunisia, Egypt and other North African and Middle Eastern nations saw uprisings filmed and relayed across the world from mobile phones. Most spectacularly, Colonel Muammer Gaddafi, the Libyan leader who had a love-hate relationship with the West since he seized power in 1969, was overthrown, following NATO military intervention. Like King James I of Scotland, Gaddafi tried to hide in a drain, but was dragged out and murdered. Unlike James's assassination in Perth in 1437, Gadafi's 20 October 2011 assassination in Libya was flashed round the world within minutes.

This book began by looking at how the climate and landscape of the Auchterarder area evolved before the first historical evidence of man. Today, in the course of looking out of my study window while writing this book, I have seen animals in my garden, ranging from roe deer, red squirrels, rabbits and hedgehogs to field mice and shrews. In farms nearby, there are sheep, cattle and pigs. Locally, horses are used only for recreation, not farm work. There are birds, resident and seasonally migrant, ranging from herons, red kite, geese, buzzards, owls, pheasants, crows and woodpeckers, to wrens, tree-creepers and goldcrests.

Many fields are yellow in spring with oilseed rape. Others are yellow in summer with barley, oats and wheat. Potatoes and turnips are widely grown. Two-metre-tall polytunnels, full of strawberries and other soft fruit, glisten like giant ploughed furrows. Apple trees flourish, though not on a commercial scale. On the Ochils, conifer plantations have blurred the eastern slopes of Craigrossie. There has been a dramatic decline in the bee population in recent years, causing anxiety over future crop pollination. Earthworms have also disappeared from much of the soil, creating potential ecological problems.

The water table has risen in recent years, creating difficulties for drainage in Auchterarder, the town whose name means 'a well-irrigated superior community' or 'that place up on the boggy ridge'. The twenty-first century began with a series of hotter summers and milder, wetter winters followed by long, bitter winters in 2008–2009 and 2009–10. In the 2010–2011 winter, snow lay in this writer's garden every week from 26 November to 24 March. Snowfalls were so great that the A9 was closed several times, cutting Auchterarder off from transport and food deliveries. Many houses in the Aberuthven area were without electricity for days. Forecasters say the long-term outlook is stormier. The winds of 2011–12 bear out that forecast.

To harness energy from natural turbulence, a wind farm was built at Greenknowes in 2008. Its huge white vanes whirl above the profile of the Ochils. The new wind farm lies in a direct line between this writer's study window and that greater wind farm which is the Scottish Parliament in Edinburgh. It is a counterpart to 'the gasworks', R.B. Cunninghame Graham MP's name for the Westminster Parliament. I leave it to future writers to say which source of power works better for the community.

Index

People and places recurring frequently in the text are listed *et passim*.